VIRTUE

NOMOS

XXXIV

NOMOS

Harvard University Press
I   *Authority* 1958, reissued in 1982 by Greenwood
         Press

The Liberal Arts Press
II   *Community* 1959
III   *Responsibility* 1960

Atherton Press
IV   *Liberty* 1962
V   *The Public Interest* 1962
VI   *Justice* 1963, reissued in 1974
VII   *Rational Decision* 1964
VIII   *Revolution* 1966
IX   *Equality* 1967
X   *Representation* 1968
XI   *Voluntary Associations* 1969
XII   *Political and Legal Obligation* 1970
XIII   *Privacy* 1971

Aldine-Atherton Press
XIV   *Coercion* 1972

Lieber-Atherton Press
XV   *The Limits of Law* 1974
XVI   *Participation in Politics* 1975

New York University Press
XVII   *Human Nature in Politics* 1977
XVIII   *Due Process* 1977
XIX   *Anarchism* 1978
XX   *Constitutionalism* 1979
XXI   *Compromise in Ethics, Law, and Politics* 1979
XXII   *Property* 1980

NOMOS XXXIV

Yearbook of The American Society for Political and Legal Philosophy

VIRTUE

Edited by

John W. Chapman, *University of Pittsburgh*

and

William A. Galston, *University of Maryland*

New York and London: New York University Press • 1992

NEW YORK UNIVERSITY PRESS
New York and London

Virtue: NOMOS XXXIV
edited by John W. Chapman and William A. Galston
Copyright © 1992 by New York University
Manufactured in the United States of America

Library of Congress Cataloging-in-Publication Data
Virtue / edited by John W. Chapman and William A. Galston.
        p.   cm. – (Nomos ; 34)
    Includes bibliographical references (p.   ) and index.
    ISBN 0-8147-1484-6
    1. Virtue. 2. Virtues.   I. Chapman, John William, 1923–
II. Galston, William A., 1947–   .   III. Series.
BJ1521.V56   1992
170–dc20   92-17749
                                                CIP

c 10 9 8 7 6 5 4 3 2 1

CONTENTS

PREFACE

This thirty-fourth volume of NOMOS began with presentations and commentaries at the meeting of The American Society for Political and Legal Philosophy held in conjunction with the annual meeting of the American Political Science Association in Atlanta, September 1989. We are grateful to Associate Editor William A. Galston for having organized the program for our meeting.

We are pleased to notice that VIRTUE: NOMOS XXXIV has an international flavor thanks to chapters by Jean Baechler of the Sorbonne, Annette C. Baier, resident alien of the University of Pittsburgh; Ronald Beiner of the University of Toronto; and Christopher J. Berry of The University, Glasgow. We welcome their presence in our pages and hope that it marks the beginning of an important intellectual trend.

J.W.C.

CONTRIBUTORS

JEAN BAECHLER
Philosophy, University of Paris-Sorbonne (Paris IV)

ANNETTE C. BAIER
Philosophy, University of Pittsburgh

RONALD BEINER
Political Science, University of Toronto

CHRISTOPHER J. BERRY
Political Science, University of Glasgow

J. BUDZISZEWSKI
Political Science, University of Texas, Austin

CHARLES LARMORE
Philosophy, Columbia University

DAVID LUBAN
Law, University of Maryland

STEPHEN MACEDO
Political Science, Harvard University

MICHAEL J. PERRY
Law, Northwestern University

TERRY PINKARD
Philosophy, Georgetown University

JONATHAN RILEY
Political Science, Tulane University

GEORGE SHER
Philosophy, University of Vermont

JUDITH N. SHKLAR
Political Science, Harvard University

ROGERS M. SMITH
Political Science, Yale University

DAVID A. STRAUSS
Law, University of Chicago

JOAN C. WILLIAMS
Law, American University

INTRODUCTION

WILLIAM A. GALSTON

THE REVIVAL OF THE VIRTUES

The past two decades have witnessed a multidisciplinary revival of scholarly interest in the virtues. Many philosophers have expressed mounting dissatisfaction with moral discussions bounded by debates between utilitarianism and deontology. To the dissenters, each of these standard approaches seems excessively focused on acts as opposed to character, and neither seems fine grained enough to capture the subtle diversity of our moral experience.[1]

Historians inspired by J. G. A. Pocock have reconstructed a "civic republican" tradition with roots in classical antiquity, a second flowering in the Renaissance, and important residua in early America. This tradition, which understands virtue as involvement in self-rule guided by devotion to the public good, has had a marked impact on contemporary legal scholarship as well as on historiography.[2]

As for political science: the current (as of this writing) president of the American Political Science Association has just published a collection of essays entitled *On Character,* which argues that the success of public policy depends on the existence (that is, the successful development) of individual virtue.[3] Within political theory, defenders of liberal democracy have advanced accounts that emphasize its reliance on virtuous citizens and not just on institutions that artfully arrange competing interests.[4]

1

Meanwhile, critics of liberalism—including communitarians and certain kinds of feminists—have offered arguments against theories that begin with fully formed adult agents and end in abstract rules, emphasizing instead two classic elements of virtue theories: social processes whereby human beings are formed and the capacity for responding appropriately to particular situations.[5]

These scholarly developments are in part driven, one may suggest, by powerful practical experiences. In the United States, anyway, there are growing qualms about the predominance of self-interest in both public and private life, spreading fears about the fragmentation and privatization of American society, mounting concerns about the effects of institutions—ranging from families to schools to the media—on the character of young people, and a renewed disposition to believe that without certain traditional virtues neither public leaders nor public policies are likely to succeed.

To take virtue seriously is to accept certain theoretical and practical imperatives. Within any type of moral theory, it is always possible to find a subordinate place for virtue understood as the enduring and effective disposition to do whatever that theory requires. So, for example, there are subsidiary conceptions of virtue associated with following deontological rules or utilitarian precepts. To give virtue pride of place, however, is to reverse this relation: within a particular situation, the right thing to do is defined relative, not to a rule, but rather to what a person with a virtuous disposition would do if he or she were in possession of the pertinent facts. This emphasis on particulars implies the need for cognitive virtues, such as attention, focus, imagination, and judgment, that enable the moral agent to size up ethically demanding situations accurately in order to act appropriately.[6]

However virtue is to be theoretically understood, it leads irresistibly to a practical concern with the social, legal, and political structures that help shape individuals. It is possible to believe (with Kant in one of his moods) that respect for the moral law is innate, consciencelike, a "fact" of practical reason. It is possible to believe that utilitarian results can be achieved through the adroit arrangement of institutions even when utilitarian motivations are lacking. It is not possible to believe that the virtues can be achieved, or be effective, without attention to the broader contexts within which they must be developed and exercised. In this respect, among many others, Aristotle has proved decisive for contemporary arguments; it is hardly accidental that so much of the recent revival of virtue theory has taken the form of reinterpretations (some would say selective reappropriations) of Aristotle's pioneering discussion in the *Nicomachean Ethics.*

Thus far I have spoken of "virtue" and "the virtues" as though they formed a homogeneous and uncontested tradition. But of course they do not. In the first place, it is bound to make an enormous difference whether one's point of departure is theological or secular. As J. Budziszewski reminds us in his chapter for this volume, Machiavellians and Augustinians will understand (and judge) civic concerns in very different ways. Thomas Aquinas's monumental effort to draw Aristotle into the Christian tradition required him to modify Aristotle's account of the virtues at critical junctures.[7] If liberalism originates in the urgent attempt to detach politics (so far as possible) from theological controversies, then the characteristically liberal understanding of public virtue is bound in some measure to leave theologically committed individuals unsatisfied.

Even if we set aside this controversy and focus on nontheological accounts of virtue, deep differences remain. To be sure, most secular virtue theorists unite in rejecting Kant's demand for a moral understanding that is detached from propositions about "the nature of man or . . . the circumstances in which he is placed."[8] While it is easy to sympathize with the considerations that moved Kant in this direction, his conclusion seems unsustainable to virtue theorists. If the human species had basic characteristics very different from the ones it now possesses, or had to deal with challenges very different from the ones it now confronts, the character of our virtues would surely shift as well. As Aristotle suggests, our ethics reflects our emotions, our bodily constitution, and our sociality—not just our rational capacities; the human virtues are the virtues of our "composite nature," which stands between the beasts and the gods.[9]

The human virtues, then, are doubly situated, and this duality is reflected in different ways of understanding them. If we look to human *nature,* we are led to view the virtues as intrinsic goods—that is, as dispositions that constitute our excellence or flourishing qua human beings. If we look to human *circumstances,* we tend to see the virtues as instrumental goods—that is, as dispositions that enable us to perform well the specific tasks presented by our situation. Within differentiated societies, the instrumental conception leads to an understanding of virtues attached to specific social roles. Within political communities, the instrumental conception leads to an understanding of the good citizen as possessing the virtues appropriate to specific regimes. These instrumental understandings come together in Aristotle's distinction between the good citizen, the content of whose virtue may differ within and between political communities, and the good human being, whose virtue is everywhere the same.[10]

As avenues for philosophical exploration, each possibility seems promising. For example, Martha Nussbaum has recently offered a reconstruction of the thesis that many virtues can be understood as intrinsically good for human beings, hence universal, even as they come to some extent under the gravitational influence of local particularity.[11] She offers her thesis in explicit opposition to contemporary virtue theorists (Alasdair MacIntyre, Bernard Williams, Philippa Foot) who oppose the "localism" of virtues embedded in the traditions and practices of specific communities to what they take to be the false universality (or dangerous abstraction) of deontological and utilitarian theories. Nussbaum implies (though she does not quite say) that if we want nonrelative virtues we must look for intrinsic virtues, the constitutive dimensions of human flourishing—and conversely, that if we focus on instrumental virtues we are necessarily led toward relativism.

In one sense, of course, this is true by definition: instrumental virtues are inherently relative to tasks or roles that are themselves situated within social contexts. But in another sense the suggestion I am imputing to Nussbaum is not necessarily true. If some social contexts enjoy normative superiority to others, then the virtues that sustain these preferred contexts themselves have a plausible claim to superiority. If not all contexts are created equal, then not all instrumental virtues are relative in the second, nontrivial sense of the term.

It may be contended that this argument displaces, without resolving, the problem of virtue relativism. Suppose that the normative worth of a political context rests ultimately (as many have taken Aristotle to hold) on its propensity to foster individuals who develop and exercise the intrinsic virtues. If this were the case, the instrumental thesis just sketched would turn out to be circular: the nonrelative instrumental virtues would after all depend on a rationally preferred account of the intrinsic virtues.

But what if this is not the case? What if it is possible to offer arguments for the normative superiority of a political context that rests on grounds other than the cultivation of intrinsic virtue? Many defenses of constitutional government and of liberal democracy have this character. Indeed, Aristotle himself partially lays the basis for it when he notes that the political community comes into being for the sake of life (as distinguished from the good life) and never sheds its founding concern for safety, stability, and a minimum level of material decency.[12]

It is not possible to pursue further, let alone resolve, the intricate debate between the proponents of intrinsic and instrumental approaches to the virtues. I conclude this portion of the discussion with two reflections. First, to the extent that philosophical liberalism is committed to diversity—that is, to the rejection of any unitary account of human flourishing—it must be (and historically has been) drawn to instrumental accounts of the virtues anchored in nonvirtue goods, such as life itself, that are taken to be less contested and less demanding than are classic depictions of the good life.

Second, efforts to develop persuasive accounts of the virtues as intrinsic have given rise to important but as yet unresolved lines of inquiry. Nussbaum catalogues, and tries to refute, three types of arguments against human flourishing as the basis of intrinsic virtue: the anthropological argument that even if certain spheres of experience are shared by many (perhaps all) cultures, they nonetheless will give rise to competing accounts of the virtues; the Foucauldian argument that even basic experiences are culturally determined; and the Marxist argument that certain spheres of experience (and therefore the virtues associated with them) represent social deformations to be overcome rather than accepted. Sarah Conly offers three additional arguments against the ethics of virtue: a narrow or unitary conception of flourishing seems implausible, at least to us today; a pluralist conception runs the risk of circularity—that is, of simply recapitulating in other terms the intuitions about the virtues we want to justify; and a broad conception of flourishing that invokes categories such as MacIntyre's "narrative unity" or Williams's "integrity" ends by including highly questionable conduct among the virtues.[13]

Suppose these difficulties to be overcome through some account of human good or flourishing capacious enough to encompass desirable diversity but determinate enough to shape a usable canon of the virtues. Other problems then come into view, of which I will mention just two. First, if the virtues are multiple, there is no guarantee they will fit together into a harmonious human life, and the efficacy of the obvious strategies for harmonizing them seems questionable at best.[14]

Second, links between individual flourishing and the social virtues are not altogether easy to forge. To be sure, if human nature is significantly social, then some virtues of social relations will be part of our individual perfection. If many of the goods we individually cherish can only be pursued through common projects with others, then the virtues corresponding to those projects are themselves desirable for individual agents who understand the circumstances of their agency.[15] And if (as Plato suggested) social vices, including injustice, stem from deformations of character harmful to vicious individuals and not just their victims, then individual flourishing will produce actions corresponding to the social virtues, though perhaps not the inner concern for others that these virtues are frequently taken to require.

Still, the suspicion of a motivational gap between individual self-perfection and social virtue remains. It is intensified by the fact that the material conditions of individual flourishing are typically in short supply and that the principles regulating their distribution cannot be developed from a conception of individual flourishing alone. It is further intensified by the reflection that the public expression of competing but legitimate (within-the-pale) understandings will typically give rise to the demand for rule-law or lawlike procedures of adjudication. Perhaps this is to say that while the virtues understood as self-perfection form a crucial part of the guidance we need as individual and social agents, they are *only* a part. But this limitation, while surely significant, is hardly a reason for disregarding them altogether.

THE VIRTUES: SUMMARIES AND DISPUTATIONS

The contributors to this volume of NOMOS are united in their belief that the virtues deserve sustained attention. They nonetheless manage to disagree vigorously about the nature, content, and source of the virtues; they disagree as well about the extent to which contemporary advanced industrial societies foster the virtues and provide arenas for their exercise.

Part 1 presents three powerful, historically rooted understandings of the virtues. Jean Baechler's account is broadly Aristotelian in spirit, if not in every detail. In the face of what he sees as the powerful forces of contemporary relativism, he dares to speak of "basic" or "primary" truths that are "always plain and simple." Among these truths are the universal and constant virtues, which Baechler juxtaposes to local and variable customs. With Aristotle (supplemented by Aquinas), he defines virtue as a permanent and deliberated disposition, based on reason, serving as a standard, and conducive to the good. The human need for virtue, so conceived, can be understood as both broadly utilitarian and as connected with human flourishing. Human beings are not born equal in their capacity for virtue: while some have unfortunate natures and others find the practice of virtue easy, most will be oriented toward virtue or vice by their specific upbringing. For the most part, virtue is acquired rather than innate, and we must therefore attend carefully to the circumstances within which it is formed. Ordinary experience often suffices for the acquisition of role-specific virtues, but deliberated virtue requires instruction through habituation guided by distant heroes (as presented in history or literature) and actually present moral exemplars, such as parents and teachers. It is not clear that contemporary circumstances are well suited to foster virtue: excessively rapid economic change obscures benchmarks and corrodes habits, and modern cultural demystifies heroes while exalting passions, instincts, and self-interest.

Baechler is aware that his argument is "only a sketch" and that to become persuasive rather than expository it would require a full-blown philosophical analysis of both human nature and human ends. He is also aware, indeed insists, that utilitarian arguments cannot get us all the way to virtue and that much weight must be placed on arguments from flourishing, toward which he has at best gestured. Nonetheless, Baechler does succeed in providing a good framework within which the enduring appeal of Aristotelian ethics can be understood and its philosophical requisites (and difficulties) specified.

With J. Budziszewski's chapter we enter a very different world. The quiet but firm intention of his argument is to remind us of the differences between secular interpretations of virtue (of which Aristotle's is an important instance) and their religious counterparts. These differences do not correspond to the customary dichotomy between reason and faith, he insists, because reason also involves faith. The issue is not whether to have faith, but what to have faith in. Faith in humanity (or in political power) leads in one direction; faith in the Christian God, in another. The life of public-spirited patriotism celebrated by civic republicans looks very different, and far less praiseworthy, when seen through authentically Christian eyes. The "civil religion" praised by many contemporary communitarians is a perversion from the religious standpoint: as an ultimate commitment, true faith is never to be used for other ends.

Yet Budziszewski is not content with mapping the gulf between religious and secular orientations; he also indicates how bridges may be thrown across it. He argues that both the Jewish and Christian traditions provide firmer foundations for tolerance than do purely pragmatic arguments, and he shows how the clash between rule orientations and virtue orientations in contemporary moral and political philosophy was explored millenia ago in prophetic utterances and theological disputations.

Like Baechler, Budziszewski sees the orientation toward virtue as entailing a concern for its development. The stakes are high. Because the state (he argues) cannot be morally neutral, neither can its civic education, and its content is bound to be contested: "the teaching of this common ground cannot be regarded with indifference by creeds whose ultimate concerns do not permit them to occupy it." In the past, there was considerable common ground between secular and religious orientations in the liberal state; their converging embrace of toleration is a core example of what John Rawls has called "overlapping consensus." This common ground may now be shrinking, and liberal civic education may now be seen as less inclusive and more partisan than heretofore. At any rate, it is bound to exclude and to affront at least some groups in an increasingly diverse society for, once fully understood, ultimate commitments cannot become subjects of bargaining and compromise.

Christopher J. Berry's chapter on Adam Smith brings us to the threshold of the modern age. Berry observes that while much of the contemporary turn toward virtue is animated by a critique of liberalism, the early-modern turn toward liberalism was animated by a critique of classical virtue. Conjoined, these two theses set up a double problematic: Can contemporary supporters of neo-Aristotelian approaches sidestep the early-modern critique of teleological and aristocratic ethics? And does the liberal rejection of the classical virtues entail the rejection of virtue *tout court,* or rather commitment to a revised postclassical conception of the virtues?

Adam Smith is sometimes taken (by enthusiastic free-marketeers) to have abandoned virtue in favor of the unfettered play of individual interests. And to be sure, Berry shows, Smith did reject the classical philosophical anthropology of limited needs in favor of an understanding of human desires as restless and boundless. For the classics, self-restraint was linked to a positive conception of civic freedom—a life of active public involvement available to the few; Smith's endorsement of liberated desire is linked to a negative (or at least less demanding) conception of private liberty available to the many.

It does not follow that Smith was indifferent to virtue. On the contrary, Berry shows, he advocated a revised canon of the virtues (honesty and justice, among others) appropriate to a commercial society, and he argued that the normal operations of such a society will tend to develop the virtues it needs. Not only the rigors of economic exchange, but also the pressures of social opinion, will foster the modern virtues. (In a striking passage,

Berry goes so far as to suggest that Smith's conception of society closely resembles the Hegelian conception of *Sittlichkeit* so often invoked by communitarians *against* liberalism.)

While confident of its superiority to classical and feudal orders, Smith was hardly blind to the moral costs of a commercial society. The narrowing and stultifying effects of economic specialization were to be countered through an ambitious system of public education. And although commercialism is not hospitable to the martial spirit, Smith boldly argued that commercial progress would enhance national military capacities and transform warfare in ways that would render individual heroism less important.

Overall, Berry concludes, Smith democratizes virtue while largely relegating it to the private realm. Many contemporary antiliberals seek to preserve the egalitarian inclusiveness of Smithian virtue while republicizing it. The question is whether this communitarian desire to have the best of both worlds can be requited.

With part 2 of this volume we return to Baechler's point of departure: the "primary" or "basic" truths about virtue. George Sher asks a deceptively simple question: how do we know? And he immediately links this epistemological issue to a political controversy: many liberals deny that we can acquire knowledge of virtue that is secure and objective enough to warrant state action to inculcate or enforce it. Without directly engaging this controversy, Sher suggests that at the very least, our knowledge of virtue is no less secure than are the other kinds of normative knowledge on which political partisans (including partisan liberals) typically rely.

Sher sketches three broad ways of understanding the virtues: the Aristotelian, as contributing to human flourishing; the deontological, as contributing to the performance of duty; and the perfectionist, as intrinsically valuable. He defends coherentism as a mode of objective moral argument that avoids the pitfalls of foundationalism, and he suggests that when applied to the three ways of understanding virtue, coherentism finds much truth in each of them. This is not to say that coherentism simply leaves our original intuitions or theories untouched. For example, while broadly accepting flourishing, it does not yield an endorsement of classic Aristotelian theses such as the primacy of politics in practical life or the ultimate superiority of the contemplative life.

Michael Perry raises two objections to Sher's analysis. The internal objection is that Sher's distinction between Aristotelian and perfectionist approaches does not hold up. Value or worth is always value or worth to somebody (self or others); there is no value that is just intrinsic and self-contained, unconnected to human interest or improvement. We are left with a dyadic choice—flourishing or deontology—and the former is to be preferred.

Perry's second, external objection is that Sher's inquiry is not radical enough. The Aristotelian account of human flourishing is a kind of universalism: some ways of life are conducive to the good of human beings qua human beings. This thesis is compatible with substantial pluralism across time, space, and culture. The real challenge is not pluralism but rather "nihilism"—the denial of any human commonalities. This denial rests on the currently fashionable claim that there is nothing outside of socialization or history that defines what it means to be human, that (as Richard Rorty suggests) we must replace universalist inquiries into the nature of human existence with localist interpretations of the meaning of particular cultures. In Perry's view, this move subverts most contemporary moral discourse, including the invocation of universal human rights against oppressive regimes. This is a serious cost, and unnecessary to boot: the nihilists conflate healthy skepticism with dogmatic anti-essentialism.

Approaching the argument from another angle, Rogers Smith also wonders whether Sher has been radical enough. Sher's epistemological discourse, Smith suggests, operates at too great a remove from the practical political controversy to which it is allegedly connected and is therefore of little use in resolving the dispute. The proponents of state moral intervention frequently embrace a form of moral objectivism much stronger than coherentism. Sher's modest moral realism, even his semiobjectivist account of moral value, will hardly satisfy those who believe that morality is cosmologically or theologically inscribed. For their part, the opponents of government moral intervention typically rest their case on sociological, not epistemological, grounds: the sheer diversity of conceptions of virtue that develop under modern conditions of social freedom means that intersubjective political agreement on moral matters is not to be expected. "Neutralist" liberals believe that in these circumstances, polities are far more likely to reach agreement on rules and procedures that allow individuals to pursue their own lives with a minimum of conflict and maximum of needed cooperation.

As Smith insists, this is an empirical claim for which neutralists give little evidence. But, he says, Sher does not engage the empirical issue either: metaethicists are at one with armchair sociologists in their studied distance from real-world politics. Rather than engaging in either of these forms of abstraction, Smith concludes, it is better to proceed with first-order substantive discussions of the matter at hand and see what turns up.

If part 2 addressed the challenge posed by Baechler's argument, part 3 picks up the gauntlets thrown by J. Budziszewski and Christopher Berry. The issue is the relation between liberalism and the virtues. Ronald Beiner exemplifies Berry's dictum that contemporary virtue talk tends to be connected with reservations against liberalism, and he tries to work out in some detail the implications of Budziszewski's assertion that no political community, whether liberal or nonliberal, can adopt a neutral stance on a wide range of disputed moral questions.

Beiner begins by (in effect) accepting Berry's contention that the real moral choice reduces to human flourishing versus moral duty—Aristotle or Kant—and he unhesitatingly makes that choice. We should shift, he insists, from the Kantian-liberal discourse of values, rights, and autonomy to the Aristotelian discourse of virtues and character formation. "Values" are inherently subjectivizing; "rights" are inherently adversarial; "autonomy" is inherently mystifying in societies in which the range of choices is much narrower than commonly supposed and the opportunity to develop the capacity for rational deliberation, much rarer.

The alternative is a neo-Aristotelian vocabulary of character formation oriented toward the human good. Liberals contend that this amounts to a monism that excludes diversity. Beiner works at length to refute this charge: Aristotelian moral philosophy recognizes and accommodates human differences, and the liberal dismissal of Aristotle as a monist is "grotesque." Aristotle, he insists, does not insist on the contemplative ideal, does not exceed the bounds of common sense in his advocacy of political involvement, and certainly does not rest his practical philosophy on a (discredited) cosmological teleology. (These contentions, he subsequently states, represent a strategy of disentangling the structure of Aristotelian thought from the historically contingent context of Aristotle's experience.)

Having defended neo-Aristotelianism, Beiner goes on the offensive. Liberal defenders of state moral neutrality (Beiner singles out Charles Larmore) say that this stance is needed to cope with the fact of diversity. But Beiner wonders, How much actual diversity is there in liberal societies? Are there really no moral ordering principles in liberal polities? Is liberalism really neutral? Is it valid to infer the desirability of moral neutrality from the necessity of religious toleration? And why should we feel bound to accord "equal respect" to manifestly unequal ways of life? We need a neo-Aristotelian vocabulary to express the answers our commonsense experience gives to these questions. This alternative vocabulary may not give us a concrete alternative to liberalism, but it will at least help us reflect critically on what life in liberal societies really means.

Charles Larmore vigorously dissents. While he agrees with Beiner about the desirability of pluralism, he insists that Aristotle was no pluralist. Aristotle meant what he said about the ultimate superiority of the contemplative life; he argued for full political participation as the peak of practical life, not Beiner's watery political awareness; and he was aristocratically unaware of the moral possibilities inherent in ordinary life. To be sure, Aristotle can be "loosened up" along the lines Beiner suggests, but he then becomes platitudinous and ceases to be instructive.

But whether or not Aristotle was really a pluralist is not really the point, Larmore continues. What is decisive for and about modern liberalism is not moral pluralism but rather the fact of reasonable disagreement about the good life, which generates the need for a way of living together without resorting to force to restrict or obliterate our differences. We can achieve this through a "minimal moral conception" (*not* just a pragmatic modus vivendi) that rests on rational dialogue and equal respect for persons and, so far as possible, refrains from taking sides in the conflict over the good life—including the conflict between proponents of individualism or autonomy and their Romantic critics. And thus, concludes Larmore, if neo-Aristotelian virtue means an ideal of self-realization and not just the one virtue of mutual respect, then the cultivation of virtue cannot be our common political bond and must not become the object of interventionist state policy.

In effect, David Strauss steps into the fray as a peacemaker. With Larmore, he says no to Aristotle. With Beiner, he says yes to the virtues, and therefore to a nonneutral understanding of politics. Liberalism, says Strauss, "presupposes a certain conception of the virtues—that is, a certain controversial view about what attributes are good in human beings." But in agreement with Adam Smith as presented by Berry, he distinguishes between classical and modern virtues: "The liberal virtues are not Aristotle's virtues, and importing a full Aristotelian vocabulary is not only unnecessary but incompatible with liberal premises."

There are, Strauss suggests, two ways in which liberal virtues are related to liberal theory. The first is what he calls "logical"— the role of these virtues in justifying the theory. Liberalism rests on two key virtues: tolerance of differences among individuals and groups; and openness to making choices, which Strauss characterizes as moral courage in the face of individual lives underdetermined by either nature or society. It is the latter virtue that separates Strauss from Larmore: tolerance is not enough, because there is an enormous difference between grudgingly accepting pluralism and affirmatively embracing the impermissibility of intervening to limit individual options.

The virtues also stand in what Strauss calls a "psychological" relation to liberalism; they are needed not only for the justification of liberal orders but also for their functional success. The liberal virtues help strengthen what would otherwise be the inadequate motivations of the more powerful to make sacrifices on behalf of the less powerful members of the community, and they provide guidance for the educative apparatus of the liberal state, which doctrines of neutrality cannot. Indeed, from his perspective as a legal scholar, Strauss concludes that neutralist interpretations of liberalism have contributed to the incoherence of constitutional law in this hotly contested arena.

Stephen Macedo's approach is broadly congruent with

Strauss's. He offer another, fuller account of the distinctively liberal virtues, and he ends by endorsing Adam Smith's version of liberal civic education.

Macedo's strategy is to disarm the communitarian critics of liberalism by undermining the neutralist interpretation of liberalism against which they contend. Thus, like Strauss, Macedo can accept many of Beiner's premises which rejecting his conclusion. Liberalism embraces not just pluralism, but an important measure of public agreement as well. Liberalism is not as neutral as it tries to appear, or as its Larmorean defenders try to portray it. Liberalism is not simply confined to public life, but shapes even intimate relations such as the family; even if not fully constitutive of liberal societies, it pervades them. Because liberalism is a form of community, it tends toward a kind of sameness as well as diversity (here Macedo concurs with Beiner); some valuable ways of life will come under pressure in liberal societies, while others may disappear altogether. But (and here Macedo echoes Larmore's riposte to Beiner) it is far from clear what in practice the communitarian alternative to liberalism amounts to.

Having thus cleared the deck, Macedo proceeds to spell out his canon of the liberal virtues: the disposition to respect the rights of those with whom we disagree; the ability to understand, even sympathize with ways of life that diverge widely from our own; the willingness to entertain criticism of, and even alter, one's own way of life; the capacity to accept ambiguity and uncertainty as the basis for reflective deliberation about personal and public life; the ability to maintain some critical and emotional distance from one's personal choices and community of origin; conversely, the ability to interpret and understand the traditions of one's society; and the capacity for autonomy, a kind of umbrella virtue that comprises a host of critical, deliberative, and self-directive competencies.

These virtues are numerous and not undemanding. Fortunately, Macedo claims, we do not have to rely simply on formal civic education to develop them. The same virtues that contribute to individual flourishing also contribute to the performance of liberal civic duties. Conversely, the practice of liberal politics (e.g., acceptance of the rule of law, involvement in evaluation of official decisions, engagement in public arguments) reinforces the liberal virtues, as does the almost imperceptible tutelage of liberal social life.

All these are general virtues, required of all members of liberal communities. To them Macedo adds certain role-specific virtues corresponding to the three branches of constitutional government. The executive virtues, he suggests, include initiative, independence, resolve, perseverance, diligence, and patience. Virtuous liberal legislators must display broad sympathy for individual and group differences, respect for the rights of all, and the disposition to cooperate and compromise whenever possible. And finally, virtuous judges must be capable of impartiality, the willingness to honor and protect individual rights, and the unswerving commitment to those basic principles that cannot be compromised.

It is around the question of judicial virtue that part 4 revolves. David Luban pursues this issue by examining a classic American legal doctrine, judicial restraint—the strong presumption that appellate courts and judges should defer whenever possible to legislative determinations rather than substituting their judgment for that of elected representatives. This doctrine, Luban notes, does not name a personal virtue, but rather a structural relation between the judiciary and other branches of government. But we can still ask what traits of character judges must possess in order to practice self-restraint. Of course, on this account these traits are virtues only if judicial self-restraint is itself a good thing. (This is an instance of a general strategy of argument discussed earlier in this introduction: some virtues can be identified, and justified, as needed for the pursuit of some nonvirtue good.)

Luban explores a number of classic defenses of judicial restraint: Alexander Bickel's famous discussion of the "countermajoritarian difficulty," separation of powers, fidelity to law, promotion of political deliberation, and democracy itself. In Luban's view, each of these arguments conspicuously fails, perhaps most surprisingly, the democratic argument: "Democracy means self-rule; it need not mean majority rule. Genuine self-rule requires widespread political deliberation; voting as such requires none."

Luban then turns to Justice Holmes's much more exotic defense of judicial restraint. From modern science, says Holmes, we learn that the universe is indifferent to human ideals, which are cosmologically arbitrary and gain meaning only by being affirmed. From an internal standpoint, however, they are deeply meaningful: their unattainability generates an Emersonian vital force that overcomes the inertia of everyday life, and their arbitrariness lends pathos to our obedience. The soldier's energizing faith, his virtue, is the blind, unswerving acceptance of duty; this is the virtue underlying judicial restraint. Why should the judge defer to legislative majorities? Because the majority represents the dominant force in the community. And why should we give normative authority to dominant force? Because it provides a vitality that is our salvation from despair, and because it represents an acceptance of the actual, not bootless hankering after the merely possible.

Luban flatly rejects Holmes's Nietzschean argument for judicial restraint. It cannot be a satisfactory public justification because it cannot pass the test of publicity. It cannot be a stable private view because it cannot be maintained without self-deception. And it cannot be a suitable basis for interpreting law, because civilian life is distorted if viewed through the lens of military extremity.

While Terry Pinkard accepts most of Luban's arguments against judicial self-restraint and against Holmes's Nietzscheanism, he is inclined to take the underlying problematic of self-restraint somewhat more seriously. Pinkard situates the issue in a philosophical history: an account of nineteenth- and early twentieth-century developments featuring a mounting tension between liberal republicanism on the one hand and democracy on the other, between the *Rechtsstaat* and the democratic rule of law. Within the framework of the *Rechtsstaat,* judicial restraint makes no sense, but within a democratic conception of the rule of law there is a case for it. It was because Holmes rejected both technocratic theories of expertise and the discovery-of-law ("oracular") model of judging that he concluded that nonrestrained judges were merely imposing their own views on the community, and he saw no reason why they should. The key Holmesian argument for restraint, Pinkard suggests, was not cosmological vitalism but rather a contextual faute de mieux choice among a short list of real possibilities.

This is not to say that Holmes's case is a sound one. It is to say that the problem with which he grappled was real, and is with us still. As long as we have powerful judges functioning within a tense balance between democratic and liberal-republican imperatives, Pinkard concludes, we will be challenged to determine when, and on what basis, judges may intervene against institutional expressions of the popular will.

Judith Shklar is far less comfortable than Pinkard with Luban's framework. She suggests that appellate courts, including the U.S. Supreme Court, are far too atypical to tell us much about judicial virtue. We should look rather at state trial judges, who exercise far greater discretion and policy-making authority and whose activities are the focal point of the discussion of these matters within the philosophical tradition. When we thus refocus the inquiry, we see that the issue is the familiar one of role morality, an instance of the familiar but troubled relation between the good human being and the good citizen.

For Plato, the good or rational person could not be a judge. For Augustine, the judicial virtue was not rationality but rather humility. For Aristotle (followed in a way by Hobbes), rationality was the key judicial virtue; but while for Aristotle the content of rational judging could only be as good as the (possibly defective) laws and ethos of the city would allow, Hobbesian judicial rationality amounted to rule following, the more mechanical the better. Our conception of judicial vices, Shklar suggests, is derived from this Aristotelian/Hobbesian model. Judges must not be capricious, arbitrary, dilatory, inconsistent, or dishonest; they must never show favoritism and must never take bribes.

So far, so good. But in seeking to exercise their discretion wisely, today's trial judges find little solace either in the formal rules of law or in the ethos of increasingly diverse and fragmented communities. In these circumstances, their virtues are these: the ability to cooperate with lawyers within the adversarial system to reach the most broadly acceptable decisions; the ability to exercise prudence as best they can within the framework of rules, precedents, and local understandings; the ability to preserve their good reputation; and the ability to describe their judgments with enough clarity and persuasiveness so their fellow citizens can believe in their fairness and honesty.

Part 5, the concluding section of this volume, is diverse but not miscellaneous, for each of its chapters develops into a meditation on some feature of liberalism and its virtues. Annette Baier writes as a resident alien about the virtues of resident alienage. To begin, she notes that there are more and less admirable reasons for choosing a host country. Once one is there, one can behave more or less well. Resident aliens can develop the capacity for offering their hosts semidetached evaluations of domestic practices based upon cross-national experiences. But this must be done tactfully; the role of Socratic gadfly is best played by citizens. There is, moreover, a special kind of courage corresponding to the special insecurities aliens are bound to face.

So far, this could be a characterization of virtuous resident alienage anytime and any place. But Baier offers a distinction that shifts the remainder of her argument into a distinctively modern and liberal mode: while resident aliens have no standing vis-à-vis the constitutional rights of particular citizenship, they do have standing vis-à-vis universal human rights. Not only will virtuous resident aliens defend their own human rights; they will go to the assistance of victims whatever their civil status (as, for example, some non-Chinese tried to do at Tienanmen).

This is but one aspect of the "cosmopolitanism" Baier sees both as the natural outgrowth of the resident alien experience and as perhaps its greatest virtue. While this orientation implies the devotion to peace and friendship across national borders, it is not incompatible with special attachments. It is, however, incompatible with ethnocentrism. Baier therefore concludes her paper with a critique of thinkers such as Michael Walzer, Alasdair MacIntyre, and Richard Rorty, whom she takes to be both recommending ethnocentrism and denying the possibility of genuine cosmopolitanism as she understands it.

Joan Williams is far more sympathetic to theorists of this stripe. Her concern is with the dominance of self-interest in contemporary liberal America; her hope is to revive the language of virtue as a counterweight to self-interest; her project is to link virtue with nonfoundationalism, and in particular pragmatism, through cultural criticism that mines the largely buried resources of our own tradition.

Williams explores four understandings of virtue found in

our history, and to some extent still operative today: the civic republicanism or humanism of J. G. A. Pocock; religion, understood as social fact though not (necessarily) as theological truth; domesticity—the family and feminine virtues defined in opposition to the self-interest of money and power; and the virtues of liberalism itself. Each has something important to contribute but, Williams argues, all run the same risk: the rhetoric of virtue that challenges self-interest can also sanction, even generate, oppression. Classic republicanism was linked to elitism, patriarchy, and militarism; religion can give rise to the contemporary radical Right; and the virtues of domesticity can perpetuate the marginalization of women, even when these virtues move out of the family into the public sphere as traditionally defined.

This is the problem Williams finds at the heart of the contemporary pro-choice movement. The defense of abortion in the language of rights—freedom, autonomy, choice—leaves the movement vulnerable to moral criticism from the standpoint of domesticity. "Career women" are allowed to be selfish, but mothers (expectant as well as actual) are expected to be selfless. Opting for abortion is thus condemned as expressing the vice of selfishness. If the language of domestic virtue is to foster liberation rather than oppression, Williams concludes, it must be employed by supporters of abortion rights and not just their foes; abortion must be redescribed as the expression of love or as the exercise of virtue under pressure.

Jonathan Riley also explores virtue as restraint on self-interest, developing further the idea of liberal virtues mentioned by Williams and discussed earlier in this volume by Strauss and Macedo. Liberal orders need their own sustaining virtues. In particular, they need not only justice but philanthropy as well—"liberal institutions designed to encourage, under threat of public humiliation or stigma but not of legal coercion, positive assistance for the projects of other members of the community." This virtue, Riley insists, is authentically liberal rather than preliberal; liberalism must not be reduced to its caricature as atomistic individualism. Indeed, there is a sharp distinction between liberal philanthropy and its antecedents: while preliberal philanthropy rests on devotion to some authority and emphasizes purity of motivation, liberal philanthropy includes the virtue of self-reliance and accepts responsibility for consequences as well. Liberal philanthropy as Riley understands it represents a middle way betwene crude individualism on the one hand and coercive socialism on the other; it is a distinctive moral virtue that constrains both markets and public authorities.

After exploring the justification of this virtue in the writings of Andrew Carnegie and, through him, of nineteenth-century British liberals, Riley moves the discussion forward to the present day. Empirical studies show that the wealthy in contemporary America fall far short of complying with Carnegie's precepts, pursuing instead both self-indulgence and the hereditary transmission of property Carnegie condemned. What is to be done? Riley recommends a series of legal changes, but in the end he returns (as do so many of the other authors in this volume) to the need for civic education that fosters the virtues undergirding healthy communities.

NOTES

1. This debate is well represented in Peter A. French, Theodore E. Uehling, Jr., and Howard K. Wettstein (eds.), *Midwest Studies in Philosophy.* Vol. 13, *Ethical Theory: Character and Virtue* (Notre Dame: University of Notre Dame Press, 1988).

2. For an accessible programmatic statement, see J. G. A. Pocock, "Virtues, Rights, and Manners: A Model for Historians of Political Thought," *Political Theory* 9, 3 (August 1981): 353–68. For evidence of the impact on legal scholarship, see "Symposium: The Republican Civic Tradition," *Yale Law Journal* 97, 8 (July 1988): 1493–1723, and Linda R. Hirshman (ed.), "Symposium on Classical Philosophy and the American Constitutional Order," *Chicago-Kent Law Review* 66, 1 (1990): 1–242.

3. James Q. Wilson, *On Character* (Washington, D.C.: American Enterprise Institute, 1991).

4. For a summary and some proposals, see William A. Galston, "Liberal Virtues," *American Political Science Review* 82 (December 1988): 1277–90.

5. See, for example, Michael Sandel, *Liberalism and the Limits of Justice* (Cambridge: Cambridge University Press, 1982); Charles Taylor,

Philosophy and the Human Sciences: Philosophical Papers, 2 (Cambridge: Cambridge University Press, 1985); Carol Gilligan, *In a Different Voice* (Cambridge, Mass.: Harvard University Press, 1982).

6. On this last point, see Amelie O. Rorty, "Virtues and Their Vicissitudes" and Joel Kupperman, "Character and Ethical Theory," both in French, Uehling, and Wettstein, *Midwest Studies in Philosophy.* Vol. 13; Martha C. Nussbaum, "The Discernment of Perception," *Proceedings of the Boston Area Colloquium in Ancient Philosophy* 1 (1985): 151–201; and "Finely Aware and Richly Responsible: Moral Awareness and the Moral Task of Literature," *Journal of Philosophy* 82 (1985): 516–29.

7. See Alasdair MacIntyre, *Whose Justice? Which Rationality?* (Notre Dame: University of Notre Dame Press, 1988), chapters 10–11; Harry Jaffa, *Thomism and Aristotelianism* (Chicago: University of Chicago Press, 1952).

8. Immanuel Kant, *Foundations of the Metaphysics of Morals,* Robert Paul Wolf (ed.), (Indianapolis: Bobbs-Merrill, 1969), pp. 5–6.

9. *Nicomachean Ethics* 1178a 8–21.

10. See Aristotle, *Politics,* book 3, chapter 4.

11. Martha Nussbaum, "Non-Relative Virtues," in French, Uehling, and Wettstein, *Midwest Studies in Philosophy.* Vol. 13.

12. The preceding six paragraphs are based on my "Toughness as a Political Virtue," *Social Theory and Practice* 17, 2 (Summer 1991): 175–97.

13. Sarah Conly, "Flourishing and the Failure of the Ethics of Virtue," in French, Uehling, and Wettstein, *Midwest Studies in Philosophy.* Vol. 13.

14. Rorty, "The Virtues and Their Vicissitudes," in French, Uehling, and Wettstein, *Midwest Studies in Philosophy.* Vol. 13.

15. On these points see David B. Wong, "On Flourishing and Finding One's Identity in Community" and Robert Merrihew Adams, "Common Projects and Moral Virtue," both in French, Uehling, and Wettstein, *Midwest Studies in Philosophy.* Vol. 13.

1

ANALYTICAL AND HISTORICAL PERSPECTIVES

1

VIRTUE: ITS NATURE, EXIGENCY, AND ACQUISITION

JEAN BAECHLER

TRANSLATED BY JOHN W. CHAPMAN

Could it be a sign of the times? For some ten or twenty years now the Académie Francaise has ceased to perform one of its annual rituals, imposition on one of its members the task of delivering a public lecture on virtue. It put an end to this, I suppose, because speaking in favor of virtue had something ridiculous about it. Ethics and virtue have become fashionable again, at least in talk if not in practice, however much one may doubt, aside from periods of sharp crisis, that the general level of vice and virtue varies greatly, in one sense or another, as between societies or epochs.

The intellectual discredit that struck virtue in the sixties and the years following is easily explained. The social sciences had known a triumph. But their success in discovering the "truth" lacked merit. Rather, we saw vulgarization that pushed to the limit their natural bent toward sociologism and historicism—in short, toward absolute relativism. Good and evil lack objectivity. They are merely categories that are "relative to" a civilization, religion, race, class, or climate of opinion. Consequently virtue is just a prejudice that an enlightened age can and should shed or, still worse, an illusion created by people who profit from it, namely, those who support and benefit from the going state of affairs. Another assault, perhaps even more powerful, came from the Freudians. Since all the evils that afflict mankind arise from impeded impulses and inhibitions, and because the virtues make for "civilization and its discontents," an urgent measure of personal and social hygiene demands that everyone quit prohibiting. Hence we have good reasons, with the blessing of "Science," to let loose the natural passions, which is always pleasant, at least in the beginning.

An intellectual reaction may be under way, either because life is given to fashion and fashion moves in a dialectical manner, or because what is clearly false comes to be recognized as such. For moral relativism, like permissiveness, is false on the face of it. Relativism confuses custom and morality. If, in fact, customs, which pertain to a given society, are relative and variable, morality, insofar as it defines good and evil and recommends choice of the former rather than the latter, is manifestly universal, and not only by way of an abstract distinction between the good and the bad. No civilization exists, nor any group or person, without mental deformation that places it outside humanity, that does not grasp the difference between good and evil. Evil in its concrete manifestations—robbery, murder, lying, incest, and sacrilege—is nowhere approved nor even considered a matter of indifference. Officials for whom a theft is a theft and a murder a murder may be variously titled, but they are always in attendance. As for permissiveness, inspired by a psychological pseudoscience, to carry it to its logical conclusion suffices to underline its absurdity and monstrosity. If human impulses are inherently good and attempts at control can only pervert them, then Auschwitz and the jungle are exemplary displays of human flourishing.

As always, when mistakes poison the climate of opinion, they are not so much intellectual errors as heresies, in the sense of taking one aspect of the truth to the point where others are neglected. This leads to an even more pernicious falsehood because it has the appearance of truth. For it remains the case that eighteenth-century philosophy was mistaken in basing virtue on either various forms of rationalism, or one brand or another of utilitarianism, or on "Nature" or "Society." Also entirely correct is that repression of instincts, passions, and feelings can hamper personal flourishing and so hinder happiness as well as virtuousness. Otherwise put, if historicism, sociologism, psychologism, and naturalism are false, they are so as heretical "isms," and not because vice and virtue have nothing to do with nature, the psyche, society, or history. In so intricate a matter the reasonable thing to do is to take one's bearings from the "primary truths." These may be found at the roots of reflection and have always been recognized, which does not preclude our seeking new formulations. A search will enable us to identify some of these by way of an examination in succession of the nature of virtue, its exigency, and its acquisition.

I. The Nature of Virtue

The most simple and efficacious way to proceed is to begin with the definition offered by Aristotle in the *Nicomachean Ethics* (II, 6, 15). Then we may comment as our purpose requires. "A virtue is a deliberated and permanent disposition, based on a standard applied to ourselves and defined by the reason displayed by the man of good sense." To clarify "good sense," perhaps it will not be unhelpful to attend also to St. Thomas Aquinas's definition: "Virtue is that which makes good he who has it and renders good his work." From these two remarkably dense assertions one can isolate and extract four decisive marks of virtue: virtue as a permanent and deliberated disposition, as a standard, as based on reason, and as conducive to good.

1. Virtue as a Permanent and Deliberated Disposition

Let us take an example. If not everyone, certainly the great majority thinks that courage is a virtue and cowardice a vice. Recalling the difficulties raised by Plato in the *Laches*, we risk calling courage the ability of people to assume a role despite the dangers they know they will face. A soldier shows courage in standing firm under an artillery barrage, the believer in confronting persecution, the scholar in disregarding the climate of opinion, resisting ideological pressure, and so on. No station in life is without more or less disagreeable features.

The general pattern or structure in which we can talk about virtue may be described as follows. First we have an actor who presents a sort of double face, on one of which he or she is engaged in an activity that dictates mobilization of his or her energy in its service; the other face inclines to resist this demand for it imposes diverse costs. Secondly, a role is put forward that also has two sides. On the one hand, it imposes specific behavior to gain the end from which it derives existence and meaning. For example, the soldier should act to guarantee the security of his state. On the other hand, the role may arouse opposition or disagreeable reactions on the part of the person who assumes it, or it may conflict with other and more pleasant activity. A soldier may well prefer to enjoy his wife over going under fire.

By combining these two elements of the virtuous disposition and their two sides, one obtains a more precise initial definition of virtue. It consists in the discharge of duty despite the attraction of alternatives. To be courageous does not mean having no fear of danger. Rather, it means to stick to one's post in fear and suppress the temptation to desert. But immediately objections appear. If this is the correct understanding, it follows that one who has no fear is not virtuous; the more fear one has, without fleeing, the more one is courageous; the more one is frightened by imaginary dangers, the more one is courageous; and so on. All these implications clash with common sense, as would defining as chaste a sexually obsessed person who does not go on to the act. Kleptomaniacs in control of themselves are not paragons of virtue. An elegant way of resolving the difficulty would be to recognize that the dichotomy of virtue and vice does not suffice to distinguish among the possible forms of conduct. A ladder with six rungs proves to be far more illuminating.

At the top we find virtue, defined as the capacity deliberately to seek the good for itself. Down a rung from the top comes "nonvice," understood as adherence to goodness not for itself nor from disgust of evil, but rather for various reasons to which we shall return, all of which rest upon a calculation, implicit or explicit, that it is better to abstain from than succumb to evil. Then one comes upon vice properly understood, which consists in an inclination to evil though knowing the evil full well and knowing that the good is preferable. On the next rung down we meet "nonvirtue," where the person does badly without knowing it and indeed thinks he does good. With corruption one reaches the rung on which a person submits to evil and chooses it deliberately. At the bottom of the ladder is perversion, where values undergo an inversion, and evil is substituted for good and vice versa. Here cowardice, egoism, servility, and injustice are defined as virtuous, and courage, self-sacrifice, honor, and justice as vices.

If one accepts this way of seeing things, one appreciates why virtue has to be a matter of deliberation. To practice virtue by natural disposition, from lack of occasion to be vicious or from debility of passion and feeling is to be "nonvicious," not virtuous. We understand also why virtue has to be a permanent and established disposition. If we put aside perversion, which presupposes an ideological taint, virtue appears as a conquest, so to speak, over the other four rungs, the better the more spontaneous, as we shall see. If virtue had to conquer again each time an occasion was present for its exercise, the risk of its being found lacking would be great. That virtuousness be firmly established is highly advisable, indeed, that one *be* courageous, prudent, just, and so on. Hence disposition to be virtuous should be spontaneous in those favored by God or Nature. Those failing grace must acquire it more or less painfully.

2. Objectivity of Virtue

A relativist attitude toward the good entirely ruins understanding of virtue. And ethical relativism leads to perversion. Ideology of various kinds perverts the nature of things. When Leon Trotsky wrote *Their Morality and Ours* and asserted that no absolute moral principles exist, that Stalin's crimes are not crimes as such but rather because they betray the "Revolution" and the "Working Class," he pushes almost to caricature the substance of relativism. Moreover, the situation is not much ameliorated by reducing the objectivity of values to the subjective and abstract universality of "Practical Reason" that endorses "you ought" and refuses to say "why."

We approach a vast and tangled question, and to expect to unravel it in a few sentences is perhaps unreasonable. However, since we have decided to retrieve basic truths, which are always plain and simple, perhaps we will be pardoned that we raise the stakes again.

Let us begin by putting aside the distinction between statements of fact and value judgments as too simple and misleading, a relic of logical positivism. Such is the proposition "to be courageous is necessary." To follow the precept of Aristotle and deal with the matter in a rational manner we should distinguish three separate propositions here as opposed to just one: (1) courage has a definite essence; (2) courage is preferable to cowardice; and (3) you ought to choose courage over cowardice.

Let us reserve consideration of the third proposition until we deal with acquisition of virtue. In spite of everything, let us emphasize that, if the second proposition is true, possible uncertainty about the third rests exclusively on "you" and not on "ought to choose courage over cowardice." It may be difficult or even impossible to demonstrate that one ought, logically, to accept a moral duty. But no reason of principle dictates that the difficulty or impossibility should appear again in the enunciation of duty. It is evident that the first proposition is true and factual. It could be the case that our definition of courage is mistaken. That all concepts are difficult to grasp adequately is certain. And it could even be that our understanding or our languages are inapt for conceiving courage veridically. Nevertheless, it does not rest any the less certain that courage and, by implication, cowardice have each a definite essence.

The second proposition is more delicate and at the heart of the controversy. To avoid complicating matters, let us work with a ladder of two rather than six rungs and so deal with courage and its opposite, cowardice. Two conclusions can be derived from the first proposition about essences. The first is that courage and cowardice are distinct and contradictory in reality. Courage is not cowardice; indeed, it excludes it, and vice versa. The second conclusion is that virtue like vice being an established disposition (whether spontaneous or acquired makes little difference), a person cannot be virtuous and vicious simultaneously, in an identical action. This is obvious, since the two are contradictory. But as ways of being and behaving the choice is not between vice and virtue, but rather between being virtuous and being vicious. That is not a moral obligation, but an empirical necessity. No third possibility is available. Either the soldier is courageous and does his duty or he is cowardly and fails to. He cannot choose to be neither the one nor the other. This is a matter of fact. Necessarily cowardice and courage are categorized with reference to one another. This imperative is clearly not hypothetical. For one discerns no hypothesis to which it could serve as a conclusion. Nor is it a categorical imperative since it does not impose a moral obligation. It is simply the incontestable conclusion of a line of reasoning conducted in a logical manner.

The problem is to discover and demonstrate the rank ordering: to choose courage in preference to cowardice is necessary. To contend that this is the ranking universally adopted does not suffice. Nor does the fact that one would be hard pressed to find a tradition—I do not say an "intellectual"—that reverses the order. We have no reason to ignore unanimity. At the very least it indicates the direction in which people naturally tend. Still we need to ground agreement in reason. What can it be that makes people prefer courage to cowardice and not the other way round? Two great lines of argument and analysis are possible. One is utilitarian, the other has to do with the natural ends of humankind. We shall deal with them at greater length in the second paragraph of the section on the exigency of virtue.

3. Virtue and the Good

We separate consideraton of virtue and the good from the preceding analysis more for expositional reasons than because matters demand it. Objectivity of virtue and of goodness are clearly connected. If courage and justice are aspects of the good, then to be courageous and just is simultaneously to be good and to strive well. Here a new problem appears. To what do good and evil apply? This question arises because many activities are neither good nor bad, except in a metaphorical sense or through pure abuse of language. A mathematical problem gets a true or false solution, a machine is useful or not, a painting succeeds or fails. In none of these examples can the categories of good or bad be introduced. Let us try to generalize these observations. Human activity, according to classical philosophy, can be divided into three great realms: knowing, making, and acting. To know is to serve the faculties of the human spirit, to respond to questions about reality. The questions are well or poorly put, the answers true or false. But neither the putting nor the responding has anything to do with good or evil. Good and evil can certainly be problematic. But the enterprise of knowing is neither good nor bad; it has to do with truth and falsehood. To make is to impose form on matter: sounds, colors, lines, volumes. Making is giving something an objective existence apart from its mental design. A creation of genius is useful or useless, efficacious or not, adequate or inadequate, a success or a failure—in itself, neither good nor bad.

Finally, to act or to strive is to pursue a goal in the face of obstacles and uncertainties. Now we are in the realm where the distinction between good and evil is applicable. For an end is good or bad. Indirectly we meet again the basic conception of virtue as a sentiment that disposes to the steady and deliberate aspiration to good ends. Knowing and making, of which acting has need to reach its goals, do not raise issues of goodness nor do they necessitate virtue in as much as they have to be only true or useful. This affirmation has nothing to do with the maxim that the end justifies the means. That is a kind of intellectual swindling or sophistry trading on the ambiguity of the term "means." On the one hand, "means" refers to knowledge and artefacts indispensable for action. As such, these must be valid or useful and efficacious. On the other hand, one understands by "means" simply putting to work knowledge and things that is the very nature of action itself. Since action is appropriate with reference to ends and since ends ought to be good, going into action, so to speak, ought to be good as well—good in the ethical sense— because the end is actualized in the very striving toward it. To specify an end by itself and then to consider means to bring it about is to confuse—the confusion is typically modern—acting and making. An end is not a mental entitity that must be realized. Rather, it is a reality that is already given as a virtuality and that must be actualized.

Is this to say that only men of action have to be virtuous? Obviously not. Acting, knowing, and making are the three modalities of human activity. They are found in varying proportions depending on the field of activity. The economy has to do above all with making, but it incorporates knowing in order to make and acting to confront the market successfully. In the last analysis, economic agents ought to be virtuous also, if only so they do not cheat in the market. Similarly science principally involves knowing, but it makes use also of making—to create the plans and procedures of experiments the purpose of which is to test hypotheses—and acting. For the scientist ought to respect a certain hygiene with regard to himself and display attitudes of honesty, tolerance, and justice towards his colleagues. That is, the scientist ought to practice certain virtues insofar as he is a scientist. Politics is the domain of action par excellence. It imposes on both politicians and citizens numerous and demanding virtues. It includes also knowing and making and is not indifferent to the true and the useful. To summarize, everybody has to be virtuous as they strive for and conform to the ends they pursue in acting. For the rest, they ought to know in both senses: knowing that and knowing how.

4. The Mean

The mean has two dimensions. One has to do with virtue itself, the other relates to us. The first does not teach that to be moderately virtuous is necessary, but rather that virtue is a tension between deficiency and excess. Two of the Chinese classics present pretty much the same doctrine, namely, the Great Learning and the Doctrine of the Mean. Why virtue is a victory over a deficiency is not difficult to explain. According to our previous analyses, virtue firmly anchors the virtuous in his duty against the contrary solicitations of instinct, passion, and feeling. Courage is victorious over fear, prudence over impetuosity, temperance over appetite, and so on. To take account of the danger posed by excess is a more subtle matter. Virtue signals the triumph of the spirit over the flesh or the human over the animal in man. That victory can be understood in two ways. Either animality is contained and controlled to the point of atrophy, and spirit no longer has at its disposal the psychic energy indispensable for action, so that an excess of prudence leads to indecision and defeat; or psychic energy is rightly directed but retains an impetuosity such that it overshoots the mark, so that courage becomes temerity, goodness weakness, and pride smugness.

With respect to ourselves the mean is important and imposes

itself in two principal ways. For whoever has an indecisive temperament a weaker dose of prudence is called for than for the person who throws himself or herself into action without thinking. Whoever fears nothing has less need of courage than the coward. Clearly these sorts of considerations should have important implications for acquisition of virtues. The second way has to do with the role a person occupies. Everyone needs courage to lead his life, but the soldier needs more than the grocer. Prudence is required of all political actors, but the head of state needs more than the citizen. Temperance is always a good thing, but one should exact it more from an airline pilot than from the passenger.

II. The Exigency of Virtue

Why is it necessary to be virtuous? We have already met this question, without treating it adequately or dealing with all of its ramifications. The question has three references: one's self, the others, and the group—that is to say, I, you, us. The answers, as we have seen, can follow two lines of justification. The first is utilitarian: to be virtuous pays, and to be vicious is costly. What shall we call the second? Let us call it "humanistic": virtue promotes the flowering of the humanity of mankind.

1. Exigency Addressed to One's Self

The utilitarian line of argument, as its name indicates, seeks always to justify an action in terms of its utility. I mean action, not knowledge or creativity. In the domain of making, by definition we have to do with utility. To ask that a machine or a pair of shoes be useful is not to be utilitarian; rather simply to recognize the nature of things. As for knowing, to be utilitarian is to incline to give priority to knowledge that advances efficiency. But reason and experience teach that, to be useful, knowledge must begin by being valid. Both reason and experience also dictate that in the quest for the true it is impossible to decide in advance which truths will prove useful. Hence utilitarianism applied to knowledge remains without durable consequences.

In the domain of acting the situation is more complex. Let us take an example. In business prudence is a virtue. To recommend imprudence would be unreasonable, for that would drive the entrepreneur into bankruptcy. One sees no field of action in which the outcome could be meaningful. Utilitarian reasoning endorses prudence to avoid bankruptcy and because economic success is a good thing. But why is it a good thing? Utilitarianism has a tendency either to hold that success is better than failure, or to transform the success into means toward a further objective. Success enriches, and with money one can do something else. If one presses a little further, it will probably be recognized that the ultimate goal is happiness. We can admit, despite this vague formula, that the proper destination of the human animal is happiness here and now or beatitude in the hereafter. The difficulty is to render precise the meaning of happiness so conceived. One does not see how utilitarianism could make for beatitude. The religious person does not respect divine imperatives because, in refraining from transgression, he expects to be repaid with eternal salvation, but rather because they express the will of God. Religious people are virtuous because, by being so, they actualize in themselves attributes that are the dim reflection of the nature of their creator, and not because they will be recompensed or, still worse, to escape the punishment they would incur by not cultivating their virtues. In a word, an ethic crowned with a theodicy cannot contemplate the merely nonvicious. Virtue is demanded, pursuit of the good for itself. Utilitarianism is by its very nature negative in the sense that its advice can always be framed in negative terms: if you do not do this, defeat will follow. If the soldiers are not courageous, the war is lost, and that is unwelcome. If entrepreneurs are imprudent, they are ruined, and that is vexing. If the politicians are unjust, the citizens revolt, which is disagreeable, and so on. Now to evade detestable outcomes nonviciousness suffices. Virtue, properly understood, is perhaps more beautiful and even more efficacious. But it is not indispensable. It could even be either a waste of energy or an act of naivete.

Utilitarianism surely fails in the quest for transcendent beatitude. That it does not do any better with respect to happiness here and now is probable. Like pleasure, happiness is not an end, but rather a reward that is dispensed spontaneously through accomplishment of ends according to their nature. Directly to seek happiness, like a treasure within reach, reminds one of Talleyrand's remark about Napoleon's court: "The Emperor attends to the amusing." If this experience is recognized as a basic truth, then the humanistic is decisively superior to the utilitarian analysis. To be virtuous is necessary, not because failing to be so does one's self a disservice, but rather because virtue is a positive ingredient in all human activities so far as they pertain to action. One becomes fully human, one actualizes a humanity maintained in virtuality by liberty, by seeking the truth, creating the useful, and striving for good. These three ends assigned to human activity are found mixed in the more circumscribed domains of life: the political, economic, religious, educational, and artistic. In each of these domains, which can conveniently be referred to as "orders" of life, we find understandings that should be valid, installations that should be useful, strategies that should be sound, and in consequence, people who ought to be enlightened, efficacious, and good, each with respect to the task he faces. In the classical age the French referred to these virtues as "devoirs d'état." Indeed, ethics can be defined as the "order" of life that administers the various "devoirs d'état." And these duties are positive. They are not content to spell out what must not be done. They prescribe what must be done. Consequently ethics cannot contemplate the merely nonvicious. Ethics aims at virtue, not for itself, not as an abstract categorical imperative, but simply because one is human only in conducting one's life as a person faithful to the ultimate purposes of humankind. And that is possible only through exercise of the virtues. As for happiness, that comes as a supplement to those gifted to get it and to the lucky.

2. Exigency in Relation to Others

As we know, all the particular virtues that render good our actions toward others are amalgamated and arranged in one unique virtue, namely, justice. As man is the "related" animal above all others—we stand in relation to the others, dead, living, and not yet born; with the living kingdom; with nature, the gods, God, the absolute, the infinite, and so on—one appreciates why classical philosophy considered justice the virtue par excellence.

Since I do not propose to analyze the virtues in particular, but rather virtue in general, it will suffice to define justice as that which enjoins each to render to each his due or own: *suum unicuique tribuere*. From this principle derive the principal prohibitions imposed by justice: robbery, murder, sacrilege, incest, lying, and so on.

Our immediate problem is more modest: what requires that people behave justly? The utilitarian answer is direct and appears compelling: to lack justice is to risk damaging reactions from the others. Consider a small virtue, amiability, and notice how important it is for social relations. Amiability is a virtue that consists in maintaining an agreeable commerce with others— that is to say, producing in people salutary impressions derived from the commerce itself. It cannot be indirect or impersonal. One is not amiable toward the public by providing it with the amenity of a good book or film. One is personally amiable towards specific persons. This virtue clearly reposes on a mean. One can lack amiability by being brusque, disagreeable, harsh, surly, and so on. But one can fail to be amiable also by way of excess, in being obsequious, soft, or unnatural.

The utilitarian sponsors amiability by the negative argument that its absence would be damaging. A shopkeeper cannot be disagreeable to customers, for he would lose them to competitors. One can affirm that civility is a social practice developed to mitigate the unhappy consequences for others of direct and undisguised expression of instincts, passions, and feelings—developed not to be agreeable or disagreeable, but to deflect retaliation. Civility is an ensemble of conventions that takes the edge off the harshness of social relations and rests on the self-interest of each, well understood. Amiability, according to the utilitarian, is a form of civility that facilitates daily life and so serves whoever practices it. The utilitarian always falls back on the same position: absence of vice, by way of excess or deficiency, is enough. Social life requires only that one be neither disagreeable nor soft.

Not in doubt is that civility does function according to rules and principles as outlined, and it makes up a good part of human sociability. But civility is not a virtue, rather an ensemble of social conventions that have to do with manners, not ethics. That is why civility stands open to an infinity of variations, more or less arbitrary, specific to different civilizations, social classes, and human groupings in general. By way of contrast, amiability towards one's fellows is a virtue, a matter of universal precept. This is so even if the circle of mutual beneficiaries be more or less grand, and even though concrete manifestations of what is thought amiable vary with manners. Amiability is a virtue because it is a modality of justice. It defines the share of the agreeable and the disagreeable that each ought to inject or suppress in his or her relations with others, as such.

The utilitarian analysis can be refuted by the reasoning presented earlier. It cannot offer an ultimate or final justification of the precept, be amiable. The utilitarian case does not depend upon having an end in view. It is necessary to be amiable in order not to lose one's clientele. It is necessary not to lose them to prevent ruin. It is necessary to avoid ruin in order not to be thrown into poverty, and so on. At no step in the analysis does one encounter a positive proposition. Here also humanistic analysis takes a different path in giving rise to a duty that pertains to the human condition, namely, a duty to be sociable. In this way of thinking, to be amiable is desirable not because it pays or because not being so injures. The point is to embellish the daily life of the other by being pleasant to him. That is why each ought to draw around himself concentric circles defined by the intensity, increasing or decreasing as one approaches or moves away from the center, of social relations entered into, and act more amiable the closer the circle is to him. As this circle is also that of contacts more constant and intimate, exercise of the virtue should be steady and vigilant, which is difficult. One is more easily amiable in chance encounters than in relations with the near.

I have used the example of a rather minor application of the virtue of justice, however great the importance of that virtue may be. The same reasoning can be applied to all the particular forms of justice. One ought not to steal, not because the law prescribes sanctions or to render one's own goods more safe. This is a duty of the human condition insofar as that is social. By generalizing our two examples we may obtain a justification of justice as the virtue that displays and expresses the duty intrinsic to the human social condition. From now on virtue is called for in its positive mode.

Nonviciousness is not enough, nor is abstention from injustice. We must strive to be just in our social relations.

3. Exigency towards Groups

The principal handicap and interest of the human and social sciences is the impossibility of constructing entities so circumscribed that they can be studied systematically by themselves. With man everything hangs together so tightly that if a problem is attacked all the others, or almost all, present themselves immediately. And if one presumes to ignore them, they take revenge by bringing the inquiry to grief. Here is an example. We wish to evoke the existence of a social duty that devolves on man as a social being. "Social" and also "society" are words too vague to be of any scientific use whatsoever. For scientific purposes we would have to explicate the modalities of the "social" and show that it as well as "society" in fact make up three distinct sets. We can use "sociability" for the networks that place individuals into relations with one another. "Sodality" refers to the groups formed by individuals and that are able to behave as active unities. "Sociality" refers to the cement that holds everything together. Émile Durkheim called it "solidarity."

The preceding point bears on "sociability" and justice. That pertains to "sodality" and the duty appropriate to that estate, which we can label "devotion." The groupings with which we are concerned are various: couples, families, enterprises, clubs, churches, schools, and so on. Before generalizing, and to facilitate analysis, let us take a specific example. This is the polity, by which I understand a group that is pacific internally and warlike externally. Let us neglect as unimportant for our purpose the fact that the configuration and structure of polities vary with "sociality," as one has do with tribes, nations, empires, feudalities, and castes. How and why does a polity elicit sacrifice and why should individuals and lesser groupings develop the corresponding virtue of devotion? Again we touch upon matters that demand lengthy exposition. Nevertheless one has hope to grasp the essentials in a few words. The polity is a group—that is, a unity of collective action. It is not merely a collection of individuals and lesser groupings. It is itself a group because it is constrained to act as a "unity of action" towards other polities in a transpolitical setting. As a group the polity pursues one or more common goods that are specified by its essence. Towards the exterior, the common good is called "security." Towards its interior, a polity combines a statement of the rules of the game or law—Aristotle's "general justice"—that should permit relations between citizens to be dealt with peacefully and permit penal or criminal justice, that is, punishment of cheaters who do not abide by the rules of the game. Now this common good is common not only in the sense that it concerns individually each of the nationals or citizens. It is also and in addition a "public good," as understood by economists. Once produced, this kind of a common good benefits all equally, whatever the part played by each in its production. If we assume that people are nonvirtuous, governed exclusively by their instincts, passions, and feelings, we postulate intelligent egoists—in other words, calculators. Now obviously a calculator will calculate that from the moment a good benefits everybody, his interest is to let the others produce it. If everybody makes the same calculation, obviously the good will not come into existence. That is why our calculator resorts to a more subtle calculus and thereby wins approval from the utilitarian. He estimates that he has an interest in sacrificing for the common good, taking the chance that a majority will follow the same line of reasoning, a majority large enough to constrain the less subtle calculators. Otherwise put, the citizens pay up in a negative way upon consideration of the unhappy consequences of failing to do so. They are nonvicious, not virtuous.

I think that, in fact, human groupings in general and polities in particular essentially rest on a mixture of interests well understood and sanctions aimed at people who do not know their real interests. But I would vigorously contest the notion that a combination of interest and fear is sufficient. Interest and fear do suffice, in normal conditions, to assure a certain level of security, prosperity, and justice. Beyond that, a new calculation becomes possible. Individuals can say to themselves that they would gain still more if they cheat, and even more so long as the number of cheaters remains small and the chance of getting away with it increases. Two strategies now come into play. The first consists in using all powerful positions to cheat, to prevent others from cheating, and to shelter one's self from sanctions. The outcome is either the anarchy of piracy, banditry, and organized crime, or tyranny, which can be defined as takeover by cheaters. The second strategy is to cheat legally, to extract from the authorities privileges, exemptions, and subventions in exchange for resources to get elected and reelected. The outcome is obvious. Contrary to the illusions of utilitarians and some liberal economists, who confound spontaneous harmonization of particular interests through markets with the procedures requisite to the satisfaction of common interests, "sodality" in general and political "sodality" in particular are not viable without a minimum of positive virtue. In this way emerge a new duty and a new virtue, namely, devotion or commitment. This new virtue joins others without dissolving them all into indistinction. At war the soldier should be courageous; that is his duty as a soldier. He should also be devoted to his country; that is his duty as a citizen. Likewise the duty of an engineer as engineer is to do his job as well as possible. In addition, as a member of an enterprise he has a duty to work for its success and perpetuity.

III. Acquisition of Virtue

In its greatest generality, the virtuous disposition presents itself as the aspiration to goodness of psychic energy guided by the will. We need to begin by grasping more precisely the composition of this disposition, if we wish to discern the respective roles of nature, interest, and deliberation in the acquisition of virtue.

1. The Virtuous Disposition

We have alluded to "the virtuous disposition" here and there in our analysis. Here the conception may be summarized as follows. On the one hand, we have a good that has an objective reality. On the other, we have man who ought to seek the good for itself. If the human species were genetically programmed spontaneously to apply itself to that search, there would be no place to speak of virtue. Virtue is required and can exist under three conditions: that man be fit for virtue, can be turned away from it, and yet can still return to it. The first condition raises no difficulty so long as we recognize that virtue is an ideal, and hence to be completely virtuous is impossible. Like all ideals, virtue indicates the direction in which to go, not a goal to be attained. Or better still, if one wishes to put it this way, virtue is a goal that recedes with the degree to which one approaches it. So, strictly speaking, no one is virtuous, only more or less virtuous, more or less vicious.

In its turn the second condition presupposes that there exist, alongside objective goods, other ends that are also objective, but neither good nor bad, only neutral. In turning away from the good man is susceptible to pursuing these. To locate in man that which corresponds to this idea is easy. To avoid spewing forth banalities or getting involved in a study of human nature that would be beyond our purpose, it will be enough to emphasize that man is the site of instincts and passions. One can regard these as psychic energy, specified in terms of instincts—sexual, nutritional, metaphysical, and so on—and in terms of passions such as ambition, avarice, hate, and so on. This psychic energy demands release and orients the person toward determinate objectives, at least so long as it does not vent itself in dreams and reveries.

The third condition stipulates that in addition man is endowed with certain faculties—perception, memory, intelligence, symbolic capacity, will, reflection—that enable us to perceive the good and recall it; to appreciate that our instincts and passions tend to turn us away from it; to wish to change direction and return to the good; and to have the power to do so. That final presupposition raises a problem. Consider ambition, the passion that drives people to want to occupy positions of power, to satiate their will to power. The nonvirtuous and the vicious, in the grip of this passion, will develop the most clever strategies and tactics that their faculties can supply the more surely to obtain the powerful positions offered by a given social milieu. What should the virtuous do? One cannot simply advise them to abandon ambition. That would open competition for power to the benefit of only the vicious. Furthermore, this would be impossible, for a passion cannot be commanded. The ideal solution—impossible to attain, but possible to envisage—would orient ambitions toward legitimate positions of authority, those that permit putting genuine competence in the service of the common good. Even a passion as despicable as envy can be reoriented to goodness, if it can be consecrated to denouncing and repairing injustices.

To summarize, acquisition of virtue would consist in using one's faculties to place the energy of instincts and passions at the service of the good.

2. Natural Virtue

If our analysis so far offers a plausible picture of reality and if we attempt rough generalizations, several configurations are possible: strong instincts and passions overwhelm the faculties; weak instincts and passions have slight influence on them; strong instincts and passions are governed by efficacious faculties.

I take it for granted that we would have to multiply configurations to distinguish the respective contributions of different faculties. The will can be strong and intelligence weak, and vice versa. Will can be strong and intelligence keen, but deficiency of reflection lets one stray down a vicious path. In this manner systematic analysis could generate a typology of "ethical temperaments," comparable to physiological, psychical, and intellectual typologies. That some people are easily virtuous, in the sense that they do not have to struggle very hard moderately to abide by ethical precepts, is common knowledge. By way of contrast, others are ethical heroes, not because they are noisy and ardent defenders of virtue, but because they have to overcome strong passions and constantly guard against deviation from the good.

In a modest way we shall derive from these reflections a commonsense conclusion. All of humanity arranges itself into three ethical subgroups. A vicious minority is inevitable, composed of those handicapped by excessive instincts and passions, by weak faculties, or by both at once. That minority can be taken as genetically established, since it is more than probable that instincts, passions, and faculties have a genetic component. I well understand that we need not conceive this component as a program destined to unfold implacably, but above all as an ensemble of oriented and convergent potentialities that are actualized by experience in the early years of life.

At the opposite extreme one finds a minority that is virtuous from birth, people who have natural affinity for goodness, who are endowed with faculties requisite to pursue and achieve it, and whose appetites are strong enough to supply the energy for good action. Everywhere one meets the temperate, the prudent, the just, and wise, who are naturally so, without effort. An indication of the sound working of a society is its capacity to establish institutions that give these, so to speak, "well born" easy access to roles in which they can provide good service to the others. Take care not to be misled by the typically Christian inclination to value virtue less than vice defeated. A certain style of salvationist evangelism puts the emphasis on repentance and its saving grace. It could be that this attitude is justified in the eyes of eternity. Other traditions, in particular the Chinese, are not aware of this accounting. From a strictly ethical perspective— which has an objective reality, independent of all religion—we have no reason to prefer a bloody tyrant who becomes enlightened towards the end of his life to the statesman whose wisdom has procured steady benefits for his fellow citizens.

Finally, there must be a majority of people who are neither vicious nor virtuous by nature, but who are apt to become one or the other or, more likely, one and the other, depending on domains, contexts, age, and other criteria, and according to the different virtues. One can be courageous and intemperate, just and imprudent, not in the same domain of activity, but rather virtuous in private affairs, vicious elsewhere, and vice versa. To say that the majority is both vicious and virtuous is perhaps to say too much; the majority is rather nonvirtuous and nonvicious. If ever nonvice prevails on average over nonvirtue, one should obtain human material nearly apt to sustain, in normal times, a society nearly morally liveable.

3. Acquired Nonviciousness

Let us agree to call a constraint a given that bears on a human activity, in the sense that people should take it into account as something that they cannot choose to ignore, nor do they have ability to modify it in the course of their activity. It is easy to show that the human condition is so structured that the constraints pressing on men force them to be nonvicious or moderately vicious, if not virtuous. Everything is scarce, including psychic energy. Few spend much in the business of knowing. But many spend a lot in the activities of making, since we need to live, and that means work. Since the Neolithic era a good part of the time and energy of humankind has gone into work. This uses up much of the time and above all the energy that could have been spent on vice. Slaves, farmers, and workers are not known for regularly giving over to sexual debauchery. But we may be sure that vices of the flesh affected above all the leisured elites.

Without doubt, one can do one's work badly. But to keep this up is never possible; the constraints are just too powerful. A farmer, in a premodern economy, who did not put his heart into the task, would not only risk reprisal from his proprietor if he does not own the land, but quite simply his own and his children's survival. Virtue demands that one work as well as possible, not to secure a benefit or avert an ill, but rather for the perfection of the work itself. In aiming at perfection, man perfects himself. This would be asking too much of a serf, even if the possibility that some serfs may have been virtuous cannot be excluded. More likely nonviciousness suffices the serf to produce what is necessary to pay his taxes and sustain himself.

One can generalize from this case. It illustrates a general conclusion that derives from our analysis of the nature of virtue. If virtue is the capacity to discharge the duty imposed by one's station in life, one may also affirm that each imposes constraints strong enough to impel the majority to nonviciousness. The chief executive officer of a company cannot let himself be imprudent in investments or commercial strategy, because more prudent competitors will eject him from the market and into bankruptcy. No doubt if the plays of the game were single or unique, the imprudent would have no occasion to correct themselves. And so it goes in certain activities, in particular war. An imprudent general loses the war, and that loss can be irreversible. But most of the time plays are multiple and it is possible to derive from them successive lessons. I mean to reach a thoroughly unoriginal affirmation: the multifarious constraints at work in all human activities force the great majority to serve their progressive apprenticeship if not in virtue, at leaast in nonvice. Acquisition of nonviciousness is above all a matter of the lived experience of the person in interaction with others and the human condition.

In this context the utilitarian thesis is vindicated: men are nonvicious because they have a stake, either positive or negative, in being so. The interest is negative if vicious conduct brings a penalty more heavy than the effort required to be nonvicious. In European peasant societies a young girl had an interest in remaining chaste if she did not wish to face the ferocity of public opinion against "fallen women." It would take an irrepressibly ardent temperament or mental retardation to consent to pestering by the boys. The interest is positive if the vicious conduct has a balance more negative or less positive than nonviciousness. In the local community acts of mutual aid are both spontaneous and numerous because they function as assurance of reciprocity. I come to your assistance today so you will help me tomorrow, if I need it. Hence the virtue properly called "altruism" may not be superfluous, but neither is it indispensable. Enlightened self-interest leads primitive peoples to share.

Usually this is how things go. In abnormal times everything inverts and the nonvirtuous and vicious take over. The sources of abnormality are not hard to identify: war, anarchy, political tyranny that corrupts because it is corrupt itself. Also probable is that too rapid change—accelerated industrialization, for example—raises the risk of vice by altering the constraints that operate on people and, in consequence, their benchmarks and orientation.

4. Deliberated Virtue

If nonviciousness is assimilated in the course of experience, virtue properly so-called will be the aim of instruction. This conclusion is inscribed in the very definition of virtue as a deliberated and enduring disposition. The naturally virtuous are not completely so, since they are not always striving to be more virtuous. Because virtue is an ideal, to go further down the road of virtue is always possible. This reflection allows resolution of a minor difficulty: is it virtuous to think of one's self as virtuous? For a virtuous person to think of himself as vicious would be either hypocritical or to display a defect of judgment. This would render one's virtuousness dubious, at least if one is not looking at oneself in a transcendental perspective. For man as creature and sinner is always infinitely distant from divine perfection. But the religious is not the ethical point of view. In the ethical perspective one can feel virtuous, but never virtuous enough, for to do better is always possible.

Virtuous deliberation does not pertain to knowledge, or only secondarily so. Well understood is that we need to know the good as thoroughly as possible and the virtues that enable aspiration to it, if not achievement of it. This is a hard task, after all, for the understanding: who would dare to declare with total certainty that he or she knows the political good, not in general, which is not all that difficult, but here and now, in a given polity, facing a problem at a definite moment in its history? Who would with assurance define with the utmost rigor justice in general, let alone the just thing to do in a specific social context? But to know is not good enough. Even given full knowledge, it remains to act virtuously. As with the good, virtue has to do with action. The deliberation involved applies to the will, not to knowledge of ends or means. To be virtuous is to will the good for its own sake, to will to discharge the duties of one's station as well as possible. At the same time instruction in virtue would not consist in transmission of knowledge in the way that mathematical or scientific knowledge is transmitted. Even if the courses on morality that the Third Republic imposed on primary school children were not injurious—and if it is highly probable that never to talk about ethics with children is harmful—they certainly did not suffice to raise the moral level of the French. Moral instruction can be only indirect, that is, by way of imitation. By doing as the virtuous do eventually a person becomes virtuous.

In all known societies that apprenticeship in virtue by the best, who are probably the minority favored by nature, is performed conjointly according to two methods. The first puts up for admiration by the coming generations exemplary heroes, whether they be mythical, legendary, historical, or a little of each all at once. The *Iliad* and the *Odyssey* have served as collections of exemplars for young Greeks down the centuries. The Bible and the saints have offered models to Christians. Secularization since the eighteenth century has substituted for religious heroes either literary heroes like the Cid or real people somewhat canonized, like Louis Pasteur in France. To do a comparative study of heroes would be possible and not at all difficult, and to show how they are destined by their exemplariness to illustrate the virtues to be inculcated in the young. Also possible and more difficult would be to appraise the modern situation, in which we find a strong tendency to multiply heroes, to place on the same level the good and the bad, to enhance the value of instinct and passion, and to emphasize interests. In short, we see an array of developments that would appear to blur clear perception of virtues by our children.

The other method involves contact with virtuous adults, beginning with parents. By observing virtues being practiced one gets a chance of practicing them in turn. This poses the eternal question: who should educate the educators? To attempt an answer would take us away from our purpose. For one could not hope to begin a response without appealing to history and sociology.

IV. Conclusion

You will understand that this study is only a sketch. A sketch can and should be a step toward a more thorough work. Personally I see two possible lines of advance. The first would excavate, consolidate, and complete our fragments into a theory of ethics and virtue. It appears clear that this theory would rest, on the one hand, on a theory of human nature, and on the other, on a conception of human ends. The theory and the conception are, of course, to a high degree complementary. A second line of advance, much more ambitious and probably beyond the abilities of a single person, would take the theory of human nature and ends as an hypothesis and test it in the laboratory of experience that human history offers us. We would search in what measure mythologies, religions, and explicitly codified ethics (in India, China, Greece, Rome, and Europe) display interpretations convergent or divergent with the hypothesis. On a matter that directly and immediately interests human beings, likely the different intellectual traditions have long since hit upon essentials, but have presented them in their own idioms.

In addition, it would be necessary to try to estimate the actual, operational practice of the virtues in differing cultural, historical, and social contexts. But I doubt that documentation, at least for the past, would be abundant enough to get beyond indeterminate calculations and generalities.

2

RELIGION AND CIVIC VIRTUE

J. BUDZISZEWSKI

Introduction

This chapter considers four successive virtues, then two successive problems. The first virtue, faith, is not civic in character, but must be put in perspective if religious outlooks on civic virtue are to be understood at all. Each of the next three virtues is thoroughly civic: patriotism, tolerance, and justice.

Both problems afford an opportunity to consider religious views of governmental efforts to promote civic virtue. One of these is civil religion; the other is civic education.

I will move swiftly. Rather than attempting a comprehensive survey of the topic, I simply sample its difficulties and possibilities. When illustration is necessary I choose from among Western religions, especially Christianity.

No writer can discuss these matters without a point of view. I have tried to make my own perfectly transparent, while avoiding tendentiousness.

Virtue 1: Faith

A widespread prejudice is that secular political creeds depend on reason, while religions depend on faith. Is faith a virtue at all? It seems so reasonable to depend on reason alone that one often muses on how much finer our *civic* virtue would be if only faith could be kept out of politics altogether. This is the basis of a variety of attitudes ranging from militant civic atheism to the milder theological "neutralism" popular today.

But the dichotomy of faith and reason is misconceived. I refer not merely to the fact that many of the creeds conventionally called "religions" give a high place to reason, and that many of the creeds conventionally called "secular" expect blind acceptance of dogma; these may be no more than instances of mislabeling. What goes to the root of the matter is that the exercise of reason itself depends on faith.

In the first place, the very act of reasoning to learn about the world depends on several presuppositions. Perhaps it does not depend on as many presuppositions as we once thought. We need not assume that perception is altogether prior to interpretation; that only one way of perceiving the world does it justice; that perception is wholly reliable; that everything in the universe can be fathomed by finite reason; that everything that takes place is causally determined; or that between every pattern of thought and language, and some ontological structure, there is a precise match. We can probably jettison many other presuppositions as well. However, we cannot do without presuppositions entirely. We must assume, to put matters in the mildest of terms, that perception is not *wholly* an illusion, and that the consequence relation—"if this, then that"—does correspond to something in reality. If someone were to claim to have a way of reasoning that did not depend on these presuppositions, we would have to conclude that he or she did not understand what is meant by "reasoning."

The point of this is that the truth of the two presuppositions cannot be established by reason itself. Its own foundations are dark to it. It has to accept them without proof before it can prove anything else. This is an act of faith, not an act of reason, and it is no light matter. The option of refusing it is available to anyone at any time. Nietzsche held that reason is merely a form of thinking we cannot escape; likewise, deconstructionists hold that rational discourse has no greater claim to validity than any other form of discourse.

In the second place, just as reason in general depends on faith in one way, particular acts of reasoning depend on faith in another. No argument for any conclusion at all in any field—and that includes politics and ethics as well as the axiomatic disciplines like mathematics—can be so completely drawn as to eliminate its dependence, conscious or unconscious, on undemonstrable first premises, over and above the presuppositions of reasoning as such. True, the premises of one argument may be the conclusions of a prior argument rather than ultimate starting points. However, this regress cannot be infinite because human reason is not infinite. At some point one must say, "Here I stand, I can do no other." Like accepting the presuppositions of reason as such, accepting first premises in any argument is an act of faith. Among their first premises, various secular creeds might hold that progress is inevitable, that pleasure is the sole good, or that life is will to power. To get to any of these takes just as great a leap as to get to a doctrine like the Trinity.

To sum up what we have found so far, the issue between secularists and believers is not whether to have faith; it is whether to have faith in this or that.

A further point is this. Every religion proposes some ultimate concern,[1] some ultimate viewpoint from which all lesser concerns are to be judged. In Christianity the ultimate concern is God, in Buddhism escape from suffering, in Voodoo the acquisition of power, and so forth. Whatever the ultimate concern may be, this is the religion's "god" (small g). In its view, all other gods, from Moloch to mammon, are idols: more or less defective images of the ultimate concern that are ceded ultimacy but do not deserve it, and that can be served only at the risk of utter ruin. If a theorist too may be said to recognize as his or her "god" whatever it is to which he or she makes all else subordinate, then secular creeds reek not only with faith, but with "theology." The god of classical utilitarianism is the community, understood as a suprapersonal organism whose sole good is pleasure. Likewise the god of Naziism is the race, and the god of Leninism is the dictatorship of the proletariat.

I do not claim that every secular creed gets all the way to professing an ultimate concern. By contrast with classical utilitarianism, for instance, Millian utilitarianism posits a plurality of concerns that are not further ranked: "the permanent interests of man as a progressive being." But even an incomplete ranking of concerns carries implications for what *could or could not* be professed as ultimate. This is sufficient for the conclusion stated above, though if another reason were needed, another could be offered. Choice, by its nature, is never neutral. In the long run, the necessity of choice in moral quandaries drives every incomplete ranking, willy-nilly, toward completion.

Therefore, the conclusion stands. The issue between secularists and believers is not even whether to have faith in a god, or faith in something other than a god; it is whether to have faith in this or that kind of god. It is, in other words, strictly analogous to the issue between believers in different religions.

VIRTUE 2: PATRIOTISM

Patriotism is the paradigmatic civic virtue. Not even justice can claim this title. Justice presupposes only a social relation. Patriotism presupposes the *civitas* itself—the City.

But to say that patriotism is the paradigmatic civic virtue tells us nothing about whether it is a true virtue. Perhaps the City is irrelevant to virtue. Perhaps the City is inimical to virtue. Perhaps it is relevant to virtue in some ways, but problematic in others. To know whether patriotism ought to be practiced, and if so, in what shape, one would have to know the place the City holds in a greater system of concerns. Religion is obviously relevant here because it proposes an ultimate concern. Because different religions propose different ultimate concerns, in each of them the status of patriotism is different too. Let us use Christianity as an example.

Jesus, approached by tax collectors on certain occasions and Roman soldiers on others, did not command them to resign their posts, but did expect them not to use their posts for theft. Asked point-blank whether the Roman tribute tax should be paid, he asked whose head was stamped on the coin, then said to pay to Caesar what was due to Caesar and to God what was due to God.[2] Roman Catholic tradition sees this as establishing the legitimacy of government, subordinate to God; Protestants often view it as more ambiguous, perhaps even as deliberately ambiguous. The apostle Paul was more direct. He wrote in a letter that was later incorporated into the New Testament that political authorities ought to be obeyed. However, his treatment clearly presupposes a government that "serves God" by working within the bounds of morality and for the common good.[3] This leaves open the possibility that government may be disobeyed when it commands what is wrong. Indeed, when the apostles were commanded to stop speaking of Jesus they always refused; to the Sanhedrin they declared that "obedience to God comes before obedience to men."[4] These statements establish the limits within which all Christian thinking about patriotism is to contain itself.

It has often enough transgressed these limits. When persecution became state policy, Christian apologists pleaded for toleration in terms of concerns to which they thought their persecutors would respond. Among other things, certain writers pointed out that the *pax Augusta* and the birth of the Christian faith had coincided, and suggested that this was not merely an accident—that God's hand was in it. Thus Melito, bishop of Sardis, writing to the emperor Marcus Aurelius around A.D. 176:

> The wisdom of the faith which we profess, once flourished in the midst of barbarians; but later, when it spread among the inhabitants of your imperial provinces, after the memorable reign of Augustus, one of your ancestors, it brought untold blessings upon the Roman Empire. For it was from that time that the majesty and prestige of the Roman Empire expanded so rapidly. You are now its popular heir, and so you will be together with your son, provided you preserve the religion that was born with the Empire and grew with Augustus and was respected by your ancestors side by side with other religions. What makes it so certain that our faith grew and developed for the common benefit together with the Empire is that, after a promising start, since Augustus no calamity has occurred, but, on the contrary, everything has gained in splendor and prosperity, in the opinion and according to the wishes of all.[5]

From its beginnings as a plea for tolerance this idea grew and took on a life of its own. Despite Jesus's statement to Pilate that his kingdom was "not of this world"[6] and Paul's assertion that in Christian unity, national divisions no longer exist,[7] after the outward conversion of the Empire most Christians found it difficult to distinguish the emperor's realm from God's. It was left to Augustine to rebuke this attitude, drawing attention to the shortcomings of the Empire in his great work, *The City of God,* and explaining that the two Cities draw to different destinies.

Augustine's rebuke has not been entirely successful. To this day Christians are often confused about the status of patriotism in their faith. In our own country they are easily taken in by flags in church, prayers in Congress, and the notion that America is a Christian nation. Nevertheless, the rebuke has had more impact, on secular as well as Christian political thinking, than many secularists would wish. Even the jingo slogan "My country, right or wrong" is not what it appears to be. It betrays a guilty awareness that *my country* and *what is right* are not, by definition, the same; that the City is not the ultimate concern. For this reason, a pagan serving in the emperor's armies might well have found the slogan demoralizing. That is why Machiavelli is only the best known of a multitude who have blamed Christianity for the decline of patriotic valor.

VIRTUE 3: TOLERANCE

Pragmatic tolerance—that is, tolerance for the peace and unity of the City—is nothing special. For instance, though Rome expected all nations to show their gratitude to the emperor by worshipping his *genius* alongside their national gods, they made an exception for the Jews when they discovered how troublesome it would be to make these stubborn monotheists conform. The Ottomans too allowed the practice of a variety of faiths even though Islam taught holy war.

What is unusual is tolerance for the sake of concerns that *transcend* the City: tolerance that might be granted even when the City would forbid it, or withheld even when the City would demand it. Nietzsche recognized only the second branch of this disjunction. He thought that if Christians still cared about saving souls, they would still be burning bodies at the stake. This was naive, in that it made no attempt to penetrate the Christians' understanding of their ultimate concern. God might be of such a nature as to abhor such "service"; souls might be of such a nature that they cannot be saved in this way.

Some basis for tolerance in the name of God can be found in the Jewish Bible, called by Christians the Old Testament. Al-

though the Law was hard on ethnic Jews who deviated from the
Jewish faith,[8] it warned in at least seven places not to oppress the
"stranger."[9] When Solomon built altars for resident aliens who
did not worship Jahweh, this was seen as problematic not because non-Jews were to be suppressed, but because Jews themselves were not to go "whoring"[10] after strange gods.

In Christianity the ethnic distinction disappeared, and the
theme of fair dealing with strangers was generalized. Now it
explicitly included tolerance of religious diversity, so long as the
religions in question did not demand acts, for example child
sacrifice, which were themselves abhorrent to natural or divine
law. This is not to deny that Christians have often preached and
practiced religious intolerance. The horrors of the Inquisition
are too well known to be rehearsed here. My claim is more modest: that the Christians' own tradition originated the standard by
which their intolerance could be condemned.

Christian arguments against intolerance began before, but
continued after the outward conversion of the empire. In the
earlier period they were addressed to the persecutors of Christianity. In the later period they were addressed to the persecutors of Christian heresies. A sampling may be instructive. "God
does not want unwilling worship, nor does He require a forced
repentance," says Hilary of Poitiers.[11] Says Lactantius, "If you
wish, indeed, to defend religion by blood, if by torments, if by
evil, then it will not be defended, but it will be polluted and
violated. There is nothing so voluntary as religion."[12] Tertullian
suggests that "it is the law of mankind and the natural right of
each individual to worship what he thinks proper, nor does the
religion of one man either harm or help another."[13] He adds,
"No one, not even a man, will be willing to receive the worship of
an unwilling client."[14] According to Isidore of Pelusium, "it
seems not good forcibly to draw over to the faith those who are
gifted with a free will"; in fact, "human salvation is procured not
by force but by persuasion and gentleness."[15] Gregory of Nazianzus asserts that in Old Testament passages that prescribe stoning
as the penalty for religious offenses, stones should be interpreted "mystically," not as physical rocks, but as "true and sound
discourses."[16] John Chrysostom warns that under the supposed
"protection" of Christian emperors, Christianity actually deterio-

rates.[17] Likewise Athanasius warns that state power can be used
to defend heresy as easily as truth, and suggests that the use of
force is an argument *against* the godliness of one's doctrine.[18]

The first of the passages from Tertullian is particularly interesting because according to contemporary prejudice, no one expressed a natural-law basis for tolerance until Locke's *Second
Letter,* about fifteen centuries later, and no one expressed the
thought that one person's religion neither helps nor harms another until Jefferson's *Notes on the State of Virginia,* later still.[19]

Both Locke and Jefferson, of course, are commonly considered secularists. Actually, Locke was a heterodox Christian and
Jefferson a Deist. Moreover, their rationale for natural rights
presupposes that human beings were made for God's purposes
rather than for those of one another.[20]

This section opened with a quite different rationale for
tolerance—the pragmatic rationale that takes the City itself as
the ultimate concern. Before leaving the subject, worth stressing
is that the pragmatic argument can go against tolerance as easily
as for. Thus the classical utilitarian James Fitzjames Stephen,
arguing against John Stuart Mill, asserted that the Romans were
right to persecute the Christians on behalf of the ancient religion, but that once the Christians came to power it would have
been desirable that they turn the tables. For though classical
utilitarians do not state categorically that all must believe in the
same god as they, they do require that, whether knowingly or
unknowingly, all act as it demands. That is, they require that
others' beliefs promote social order and otherwise lead them to
act in ways that maintain the aggregate happiness of the community at the highest feasible level. One consideration classical utilitarians must take into account is that some belief systems have
this effect to a greater degree than others. But another is that
sheer change in belief systems, not to mention competition between them, may be disruptive to social order and therefore to
social happiness.[21]

VIRTUE 4: JUSTICE

Ethical life requires both rules and virtues. This provokes the
chicken-and-egg question: which comes first? A point of view

that is especially prominent in discussions of law and justice is that rules come first, and virtues are derivative. John Rawls, for instance, defines virtues as dispositions regulated by a desire to act from the corresponding moral principles;[22] the virtue of *justice* becomes a disposition regulated by a desire to act from the principles of justice. One of the most striking features of the recent revival of virtue ethics is its challenge to this view. Two criticisms are offered. One is that rules can never be specified in such exhaustive detail as to do away with the need for judgment that is informed by something beyond the rules themselves. The other, more radical but not as fully developed, is that even when they are adequate guides to conduct, the rules are merely the *form* of morality, not its *point*.[23]

The virtue ethicists seem to be winning. Secular ethical and political theory are beginning to witness a growth from a rule-*based* to a rule-*basing* understanding of virtue in general, and the virtue of justice in particular. What has *not* been noticed in these debates is that they largely recapitulate a development that began in Jewish ethics no later than the seventh century B.C.E. with the prophet Isaiah, reached maturity with Micah, and was carried forward in Christian ethics by Jesus and Paul. Indeed, the earlier change is articulated most thoroughly just where the contemporary shift is weak. That is, it concentrates on the second, the more radical of the two criticisms mentioned above, the one that distinguishes the form of morality from its point.

The place to begin is the attitude of the prophets toward the Law. The unfolding of their actual attitude may be easier to characterize if I distinguish between four possible attitudes: *ritual scrupulosity, ethical scrupulosity, conscientious ardor,* and a *right heart.* By "ritual scrupulosity" I mean punctilious observance of the ceremonial requirements of the Law, concerning such things as sacrifices, holy days, and ritual cleanliness. By "ethical scrupulosity" I mean equally punctilious observance of the ethical requirements of the Law, concerning such things as fair dealing and provision for the helpless. Conscientious ardor is a transitional stage in which the motive for obeying these requirements deepens, from fear and consciousness of duty to *love* of the Law. Beyond this transition lies awareness that the Law itself is merely the form of obedience—that its substance lies in love of God and neighbor.

A scrupulosity that begins and ends with ritual requirements is nowhere expressed in the prophets, but must have been widespread because it is often criticized by them. In one of the historical books, the prophet Samuel is represented as asking, "Is the pleasure of Yahweh in holocausts and sacrifices or in obedience to the voice of Yahweh? Yes, obedience is better than sacrifice, submissiveness better than the fat of rams."[24] Jeremiah carries the theme further where he has God declare, "Hear, earth! I am bringing a disaster on this people: it is the fruit of their apostasy, since they have not listened to my words and, as for my Law, they have rejected that. What do I care about incense imported from Sheba, or fragrant cane from a distant country? Your holocausts are not acceptable, your sacrifices do not please me."[25] Obedience to God is here explicitly linked to the Law, but it is equally clear that the heart of the Law is not found in its ritual requirements. Where, then? Isaiah had already made this clear where God asks, "When you come to present yourselves before me, who asked you to trample over my courts? Bring me your worthless offerings no more, the smoke of them fills me with disgust. . . . Your hands are covered with blood, wash, make yourselves clean. Take your wrong-doing out of my sight. Cease to do evil. Learn to do good, search for justice, help the oppressed, be just to the orphan, plead for the widow."[26] Likewise Amos: "Let me have no more of the din of your chanting, no more of your strumming on harps. But let justice flow like water, and integrity like an unfailing stream."[27]

These passages, of course, are still ambiguous between ethical scrupulosity, conscientious ardor, and a right heart. Justice, doing good, and integrity may mean no more than dutiful observance of the ethical letter of the law, and the motives for this observance are not completely clear. Other passages, though, are clearer on these points. The later Psalms rise lyrically to the stage of conscientious ardor; Psalm 40, for instance, declares, "You, who wanted no sacrifice or oblation, opened my ear, you asked no holocaust or sacrifice for sin; then I said, 'Here I am! I am coming!' In the scroll of the book am I not commanded to obey your will? My God, I have always loved your Law from the depths of my being."[28] Psalm 119 carries this theme to a crescendo: "Your commandments fill me with delight, I love them deeply. I stretch out my hands to your beloved commandments, I meditate on your statutes."[29] The editors of the Jerusalem Bible point out that every verse but one of the psalm's 176 verses contains a synonym for the Law: decree, precept, statute, commandment, promise, word, judgment, way.[30]

Conscientious ardor rises in turn to right heart in the prophets Hosea and Micah. Hosea has God ask, "What am I to do with you, Ephraim? What am I to do with you, Judah? This love of yours is like a morning cloud, like the dew that quickly disappears. . . . What I want is love [or mercy], not sacrifice; knowledge of God, not holocausts."[31] Micah, asking what sacrifice would be acceptable to Yahweh, mentions for dramatic effect both commanded and forbidden gifts: "Shall I come with holocausts, with calves one year old? Will he be pleased with rams by the thousand, with libations of oil in torrents? Must I give my first-born for what I have done wrong, the fruit of my body for my own sin?" His reply follows immediately: "What is good has been explained to you, man; this is what Yahweh asks of you: only this, to act justly, to love tenderly and to walk humbly with your God."[32] To read "tender love" in this passage as meaning no more than devotion to God's ethical rules is patently impossible. By extension, the same must be true of justice and humility. In right heart, the Law has been *transcended:* not in the sense of being abrogated, but in the sense of being fulfilled. Virtue is no longer viewed as derivative of Law, but as its very source.

The centuries immediately before the Common Era were in some ways a Golden Age for Judaism. To be sure, Jewish national aspirations were stifled under the Romans. On the other hand, the worship of God was transformed. Although the temple was still the center of national religious life and the only place where sacrifices were offered, the Law and the prophets were eagerly studied in synagogues all across the land. Jesus, however, seemed to believe that this carried risks as well as promise. Obsession with the Law without understanding of the prophets could lead to regression in the ethical life of the people—fixation at the levels of ethical or even ritual scrupulosity without anything resembling a right heart. Hence his use of Hosea and Micah is no light decision.

Twice Jesus rebukes the punctilious Pharisees with the words of Hosea, "what I want is mercy, not sacrifice": once when they ask why he eats with sinners and tax collectors, again when they reproach the disciples for violating sabbath requirements by picking and eating corn when they are hungry.[33] On another occasion he reproaches them with an allusion to Micah—"You pay your tithe of dill and mint and cummin and have neglected the weightier matters of the Law—justice, mercy, good faith!"—adding that they are like "whitewashed tombs that look handsome on the outside, but inside are full of dead men's bones and every kind of corruption."[34] To the experts in the Law he declaims in the same vein: "Alas for you lawyers who have taken away the key of knowledge! You have not gone in yourselves, and have prevented others going in who wanted to."[35]

Put by his enemies on the spot to declare which is the greatest commandment, Jesus finds the heart of the prophets in the Law itself, quoting first from the book of Deuteronomy—"You must love the Lord your God with all your heart, with all your soul, and with all your mind"—and second from the book of Leviticus—"You must love your neighbor as yourself."[36] This teaching was continued by the apostles. The difference between the form and substance of the virtues, as between the possession and right use of God's gifts, is particularly clear where Paul writes as follows to the young church at Corinth: "If I have all the eloquence of men or of angels, but speak without love, I am simply a gong booming or a cymbal clashing. If I have the gift of prophecy, understanding all the mysteries there are, and knowing everything, and if I have faith in its fullness, to move mountains, but without love, then I am nothing at all. If I give away all that I possess, piece by piece, and if I even let them take my body to burn it, but as without love, it will do me no good whatsoever."[37] More on Paul's view of the relation between love on the one hand, and Law or justice on the other, can be gleaned from numerous passages in his other letters.[38]

Without pronouncing on the obvious disagreements between Jews and Christians on the mission, authority, and identity of Jesus, we can at least say this: part of the significance of the apostles' work is that it carried the mature teaching of the prophets beyond the Jews to the gentiles. Perhaps it does not go too far to say that recent work on the form and substance of justice by secular theorists of the virtues merely digs up parts of a cultural treasure that an earlier generation of secularists had buried.[39]

PROBLEM 1: CIVIL RELIGION

A widespread desire is that politics learn to domesticate the wild beast of faith, put it in harness with the commonweal, and set it to treading out the grain of the *civitas*. This may mean a civil use of the available religion, a civil reform of the available religion, or a civil religion de novo; it may be brought about by nobly intended lies, ignobly intended lies, or sheer physical coercion. It has been proposed by figures as diverse as Plato, Aristotle, and nominally Islamic proponents of the *falasifa* of the Middle Ages, Machiavelli, Rousseau, Comte, and the contemporary sociologist Robert N. Bellah;[40] it has been implemented in regimes as diverse as ancient Rome, revolutionary France, and the Union of Soviet Socialist Republics.

Add that it has often been attempted in the United States. Thus Thomas M. Cooley, eminent nineteenth-century scholar of American constitutionalism, as approvingly quoted by Chief Justice Rehnquist of the U.S. Supreme Court: "public recognition of religious worship . . . is not based entirely, *perhaps not even mainly,* upon a sense of what is due to the Supreme Being himself as the author of all good and of all law; but the same reasons of state policy which induce the government to aid institutions of charity and seminaries of instruction will incline it also to foster religious worship and religious institutions, as conservators of the public morals and valuable, if not indispensable, assistants to the preservation of the public order."[41] Likewise Justice Brennan, in so many other respects poles apart from the Chief Justice: "I would suggest that such practices as the designation of 'In God We Trust' as our national motto, or the references to God contained in the Pledge of Allegiance can best be understood, in Dean Rostow's apt phrase, as a form of 'ceremonial deism,' protected from Establishment Clause scrutiny chiefly because they have lost through rote repetition any significant religious content. Moreover, these references are uniquely suited to serve such wholly secular purposes as solemnizing public occasions, or inspiring commitment to meet some national challenge in a manner that simply could not be fully served if government were limited to purely nonreligious phrases."[42] We may put these points less wordily. What Cooley suggests, in a tradition going back to Washington's *Farewell Address,* is that religion is interesting to government more for its usefulness in forming citizens than for any possibility of its truth. What Brennan suggests is that God talk that the government does not take seriously be used to make citizens, who *do* take it seriously, do things to which they would not otherwise consent.

What needs to be said here is little more than an inference from what was said in the earlier analysis of patriotism. How should one judge the civic use of religion? That depends on one's ultimate concern—one's god. If one's god is power, then using religion is always good policy. If one's ultimate concern is civic virtue itself, the answer is more complicated. Here a distinction must be made between idealistic and cynical uses of religion, noble and ignoble lies; the former are good, but the latter are bad. If, on the other hand, one's god is God, the answer becomes simple again. Religion is not to be *used*. If it does command civic virtue, it must do so at His bidding, not the City's; He and the City may have different ideas about what the City needs.

PROBLEM 2: CIVIC EDUCATION

Civic education is an especially difficult problem, in no small part because adherents of various secular and religious creeds so often talk past each other about it. Take, for instance, the approach to ethical teaching in the secondary schools called "values clarification," which is urged by many secular people and criticized by many religious people. One of the reasons some of those in the former group like it is that they consider it ethically neutral and nonauthoritarian. The teacher takes no position in class discussion, instead encouraging the students to come to a clearer understanding of the values they already hold. These advocates take their opponents to be mirror images of themselves. That is, opponents are viewed as agreeing about what values clarification achieves, but rejecting instead of affirming it. The opponents are supposed to want teachers to be *authoritarian* and *non*neutral. But is this so? Some of the opponents are indeed authoritarian.

But many of them oppose values clarification for quite different reasons. They hold that values clarification itself is nonneutral: that the particular methods it uses to help children understand their own values really inculcate the notion that "anything goes." This *undermines* the values the students already hold, but *not* the secularist values, which, being covertly built into the technique itself, are thereby rendered immune to its corrosive. These opponents further hold that inculcation that pretends not to be inculcation is ipso facto all the more effective; that it is, in fact, a kind of bad-faith authoritarianism.

Whether values clarification inculcates what these opponents say it inculcates is an empirical question. At least in one respect, however, they are surely on solid ground: it must inculcate something. Nothing is neutral. Asked to justify this allegedly value-neutral technique, even its advocates express a hope of building certain virtues, notably "responsibility" and "tolerance." Moreover, their interpretations of these virtues manifestly differ from the interpretations religious people give them.

The real question, then, is not whether a neutral approach to civic education can be devised, but what values it will teach. The techniques, presumably, would be modeled after the values themselves, though if bad-faith authoritarianism is a genuine possibility, even this is not certain. Religious people have just as good reason to fear civic education falling into the hands of secularists as secularists have to fear civic education falling into the hands of the religious. For that matter, adherents to different religious creeds and different secular creeds have just as good reason for anxiety about each other. What we take to be "neutral" is usually either a reflection of the ultimate concern of those in power, or a queasy common ground among different ultimate concerns, *not* a "compromise": true compromise is possible only between lower goods for the sake of another that is conceded to be higher than both. By very reason of its ultimacy, an ultimate concern cannot submit to true compromise.

This is not necessarily as Machiavellian as it sounds, though, depending on one's ultimate concern, it might be. For instance, as we saw in a previous section, the uncompromising character of one's ultimate concern does not necessarily militate against tolerance. One's ultimate concern might be of such a nature as to *demand* tolerance. Then again, it might not. All depends on the particular ultimate concern to which one has pledged. Or, if one has not yet finished ranking one's concerns, all depends on which ones are still in the running.

Rough consensus on what virtue is and how virtue should be taught has been possible in the past only because there *has been* some common ground among the limited number of ultimate concerns to which people in our culture have adhered. As our culture becomes more diverse—as ultimate concerns that only a few have followed previously are followed by ever larger numbers, and as followers are drawn to new and previously unheard of ultimate concerns—this common ground may shrink. There are, of course, two kinds of diversity. To use acoustical metaphors, one kind is cacophony, the other symphony. The former is a thousand jarring sounds in competition. The latter is a thousand blending sounds in harmony. But the latter presupposes agreement about rhythm, theme, and the laws of harmony. I mean the former.

Needless to say, what one thinks about this depends on where one stands. I, for instance, probably like most of the readers of this chapter, stand within a tradition that goes back to about 1688 and that some political theorists call "liberal": a tradition constituted by an agreement about the qualified goodness, for whatever reasons, of representation, constitutionally limited government, and rather more extensive personal liberties than most cultures have enjoyed. This tradition is a *common ground* in the sense explained above: it is inhabited by adherents of various creeds that profess various ultimate concerns. The ultimate concerns of Christians, such as myself, as well as Jews, Deist contractarians, Millian utilitarians, and adherents to several other secular and religious creeds, permit, while not necessarily requiring, political residence somewhere in this tradition. Moreover, each of these concerns is consistent with at least limited tolerance toward each of the others: sufficient tolerance to agree (1) that the schools will teach only what lies on the common ground, only what all the creeds in question can agree about; (2) that for the rest, parents may teach their children as they see fit; and (3) that adherents to any of these creeds may try to persuade adherents of any of the others to change allegiance so long as no force or fraud is used.

The teaching of this common ground obviously cannot be regarded with indifference by creeds whose ultimate concerns do not permit them to occupy it. However, this is irrelevant to the *justice* of teaching this common ground, because neutrality among ultimate concerns is impossible. Even tolerance is non-neutral. One must simply be willing to say *I believe, by faith and reason, that the ultimate ground whereon I stand, and which allows me to occupy the common ground, is true.* If one's ultimate concern does not even require truth, that is no objection either, for in that case there can be no discourse between us.

NOTES

1. The phrase "ultimate concern" belongs to the theologian Paul Tillich. See his *Systematic Theology* (Chicago: University of Chicago Press, 1951), Vol. 1, Pt. 2, Chap. 2.A.1, and *Dynamics of Faith* (New York: Harper and Row, 1957), Chap. 1.

2. Matthew 22:15–22.

3. Romans 13:1–7, emphasis added: "You must obey the governing authorities. Since all government comes from God, the civil authorities were appointed by God, and so anyone who resists authority is rebelling against God's decision, and such an act is bound to be punished. Good behavior is not afraid of magistrates; only criminals have anything to fear. If you want to live without being afraid of authority, you must live honestly and authority may even honor you. *The state is there to serve God for your benefit.* If you break the law, however, you may well have to fear: the bearing of the sword has its significance. The authorities are there to serve God: they carry out God's revenge by punishing wrongdoers. You must obey, therefore, not only because you are afraid of being punished, but also for conscience' sake. This is also the reason why you must pay taxes, since all government officials are God's officers. They serve God by collecting taxes. Pay every government official *what he has a right to ask*—whether it be direct tax or indirect, fear or honor." This translation, and all other scripture translations in this essay, are from Alexander Jones, gen. ed., *The Jerusalem Bible* (Garden City: Doubleday, 1966).

4. Acts 5:29.

5. Quoted in Francis Dvornik, *Early Christian and Byzantine Political Philosophy: Origins and Background,* Vol. 2 (Washington, D.C.: Dumbarton Oaks Center for Byzantine Studies and Trustees for Harvard University, 1966), at 584.

6. John 18:36.

7. Galatians 3:27–28: "All are baptized in Christ, you have all clothed yourselves in Christ, and there are no more distinctions between Jew and Greek, slave and free, male and female, but all of you are one in Christ Jesus." Colossians 3:9–11: "You have stripped off your old behavior with your old self, and you have put on a new self which will progress towards true knowledge the more it is renewed in the image of its creator, and in that image there is no room for distinction between Greek and Jew, between the circumcised or the uncircumcised, or between barbarian and Scythian, slave and free man. There is only Christ; he is everything and he is in everything."

8. Deuteronomy 13:6–11 instructs that those who entice others to serve strange gods should be put to death by stoning; the next five verses go on to instruct that should an entire city be found to have gone over to idolatry, its inhabitants should be exterminated—the city and all its spoils burned, to lie in ruins forever, never to be rebuilt.

9. Thus Exodus 23:9: "You must not oppress the stranger; you know how the stranger feels, for you were strangers in the land of Egypt." Compare Exodus 22:21, Leviticus 20:33–34, and Deuteronomy 1:16, 10:18, 23:7–8, and 24:14. The theme is also repeated in the prophets; see Malachi 3:5.

10. This metaphor for religious infidelity was characteristic of prophetic writing; see for instance Ezekiel 16, 23, Jeremiah 3, and Hosea 1–2.

11. Hilary, *To Constantius,* quoted in Lord Acton, "Political Thoughts on the Church," in J. Rufus Fears, ed., *Selected Writings of Lord Acton,* Vol. 3 (Indianapolis: Liberty Classics, 1988), at 24.

12. Lactantius, *Divine Institutes,* Bk. 5, Chap. 19, in Mary Francis McDonald, trans., *Lactantius: The Divine Institutes* (Washington, D.C.: Catholic University of America Press, 1964), at 379–80.

13. Tertullian, *To Scapula,* Chap. 2, in Rudolph Arbesmann, Emily Joseph Daly, and Edwin A. Quain, trans., *Tertullian: Apologetical Works, and Municius Felix: Octavius* (New York: Fathers of the Church, 1950), at 152.

14. Tertullian, *Apology,* Chap. 24, in *ibid.,* at 76.

15. Isidore of Pelusium, *Epistles* 3.363 and 2.129, both quotations as found in Margaret A. Schatkin and Paul W. Harkins, trans., *Saint John*

Chrystostom, Apologist (Washington, D.C.: Catholic University of America Press, 1983), at 83, note 30. I have changed "seemeth" to "seems."

16. Gregory of Nazianzus, *Second Theological Oration—On God* (also known as *Oration 28*), in Edward Rochie Hardy and Cyril C. Richardson, trans., *Christology of the Later Fathers*, Vol. 3 of the *Library of Christian Classics* (Philadelphia: Westminster Press, 1954), at 137.

17. John Chrystostom, *Discourse on Blessed Babylas and against the Greeks*, Sec. 42, in Schatkin and Harkins, *ibid.*, at 99.

18. Athanasius, *History of the Arians*, Secs. 33 and 67, in John Henry Parker, trans., *Historical Tracts of S. Athanasius* (London: Oxford, 1843), at 245–46 and 278–70, respectively.

19. Thomas Jefferson's famous remark is found in Query 17: "It does me no injury for my neighbor to say that there are twenty gods, or no god. It neither picks my pocket nor breaks my leg."

20. See Locke, *Two Treatises of Government*, Peter Laslett, ed. (New York: New American Library, 1965), Second Treatise, Chap. 2, Sec. 6, p. 311: "Men all being the workmanship of one omnipotent and infinitely wise Maker—all the servants of one sovereign master, sent into the world by his order, and about his business—they are his property whose workmanship they are, made to last during his, not one another's pleasure; and being furnished with the like faculties, sharing all in one community of nature, there cannot be supposed any such subordination among us that may authorize us to destroy one another, as if we were made for one another's uses as the inferior ranks of creatures are for ours."

21. James Fitzjames Stephen, *Liberty, Equality, Fraternity*, ed. R. J. White (Cambridge: Cambridge University Press, 1967).

22. John Rawls, *A Theory of Justice* (Cambridge: Harvard University Press, 1971), at 192. The same general view of virtue is expressed by other authors, for instance Lester Hunt, "Character and Thought," *American Philosophical Quarterly* 15 (1978), Sec. 10, at 183.

23. Compare Edmund Pincoffs, *Quandaries and Virtues: Against Reductivism in Ethics* (Lawrence: University Press of Kansas, 1986), Alasdair MacIntyre, *After Virtue: A Study in Moral Theory* (Notre Dame: Notre Dame University Press, 1981), and my *The Resurrection of Nature: Political Theory and the Human Character* (Ithaca: Cornell University Press, 1986), esp. 81–94.

24. 1 Samuel 15:22.

25. Jeremiah 6:19–20.

26. Isaiah 1:12–13, 15–17.

27. Amos 5:23–24.

28. Psalm 40:6–8.

29. Psalm 119:47–48.

30. *The Jerusalem Bible,* at 903, note 119.a.

31. Hosea 6:4, 6.

32. Micah 6:6–8.

33. The incidents are recorded in Matthew 9:10–13 and 12:1–8.

34. Matthew 23:23, 27. Compare 23:23–28 with the parallel account at Luke 11:39–44.

35. Luke 11:52.

36. The incident is recorded in Matthew 22:34–40. Compare parallel accounts at Mark 12:28–34 and Luke 10:25–28. Jesus's two quotations of the Law are from Deuteronomy 6:4–5 and Leviticus 19:18.

37. 1 Corinthians 13:1–3.

38. On the insufficiency of Law *as such,* for instance, see Galatians 3:21–22. The passage speaks of faith; Galatians 5:6 goes on to explain that this faith "makes its power felt through love." Galatians 5:13 indicates that Law *as such* is bondage, but that love is liberty. It further contrasts this liberty with licentiousness and gives another echo of Leviticus 19:18. 1 Timothy 1:9 explains, "We know, of course, that the Law is good, but only provided it is treated like any law, in the understanding that laws are not framed for people who are good"; rather, they are framed for restraining those who have no love from evil deeds.

39. Compare MacIntyre, *ibid.*

40. For Bellah, see his *Beyond Belief: Essays on Religion in a Post-Traditionalist Age* (New York: Harper and Row, 1970); *The Broken Covenant: American Civil Religion in a Time of Trial* (New York: Seabury, 1975); and, with Richard Madsen, William M. Sullivan, Ann Swidler, and Steven M. Tipton, *Habits of the Heart: Individualism and Commitment in American Life* (Berkeley: University of California Press, 1985).

41. Cooley, *A Treatise on the Constitutional Limitations Which Rest upon the Legislative Power of the States of the American Union,* 6th ed. (Boston: Little, Brown, 1890) at 578–79; emphasis mine. The term "seminaries" should be read "schools." The case in which this passage is cited is *Wallace v. Jaffree,* 105 S.Ct. 2479 (1985), at 2515–16 (Justice, now Chief Justice, Rehnquist, dissenting).

42. *Lynch v. Donnelly,* 104 S.Ct. 1355 (1984), at 1381 (Justice Brennan, dissenting). The internal reference is to Eugene V. Rostow, "The Enforcement of Morals," in *The Sovereign Prerogative: The Supreme Court and the Quest for Law* (New Haven: Yale University Press, 1962). This, in turn, was written in defense of Lord Patrick Devlin, *The Enforcement of Morals* (London: Oxford University Press, 1965).

3

ADAM SMITH AND THE VIRTUES OF COMMERCE

CHRISTOPHER J. BERRY

It is, I think, plausible to say that much of the contemporary interest in "virtue," especially its relation to conceptions of community, is animated by a critique of liberalism.[1] In its formative period liberalism in its turn engaged in a critique of classical virtue. When thus juxtaposed liberalism can be identified as the middle term in a dialectic. To identify liberalism in this way has the advantage of highlighting the problem that these contemporary critics face: they must preserve while transcending. Furthermore, given this perspective, it is no surprise to discover that many liberal countercriticisms of communitarian virtue take the form of pointing out that the transcendence is only achieved at the cost of preservation, for example, that communal concord undercuts individual rights.[2]

In this chapter I examine the "negative moment" in this dialectic in the form of a necessarily selective and, as a consequence, inescapably partial, interpretation of the thought of Adam Smith. Smith is a suitable subject for this exercise for two general reasons. Firstly he is, of course, assured of a place in the liberal pantheon but, secondly, his particular preoccupation with the character and "inner logic" of commercial society provides a clear contrast to the classical view of virtue and, in addition, throws into relief what it is that contemporary critics of liberalism both object to and seek to overcome.

In the light of this agenda my examination of Smith will focus on two issues. The first is the place and role he allots to human desire; the second is his account of the moral coherence, or virtues, of commercial society. The first issue represents a rejection of the philosophical anthropology that underpins the assessment of virtue in classical thought; the second represents a reappraisal of the virtues in modern society.

PHILOSOPHICAL ANTHROPOLOGY

I open with a grand and sweeping generalization. It is the hallmark of modern thought to reject the teleological world view and to deal with efficient rather than final causation so that the nature of a thing becomes not its end but its matter. Regarding human nature this becomes a depiction of how humanity is materially, that is to say, a creature of desire. The material facts of human nature are such that, as Bentham put it, humankind is "under the governance of two sovereign masters, pain and pleasure."[3] Pleasure and pain as sensations are bodily attributes. They are "sovereign" because it is impossible for humans to be impervious to their senses. Since humans react to what pleases or pains, it follows that they are always "on the move"; as sensory input keeps changing so what is desired is transient.

Smith is in perfect accord with this generalization when he remarks that "desire of bettering our condition [is] a desire . . . which comes with us from the womb and never leaves us till we go into the grave." Nor is this a mere background condition for, still in accord with the generalization, Smith also declares, "there is scarce perhaps a single instant in which any man is so perfectly and completely satisfied with his situation as to be without any wish of alteration or improvement of any kind." The positive consequence that Smith immediately draws is that this restless desire creates opulence because "an augmentation of fortune is the means by which the greater part of men propose and wish to better their condition" (*WN*, 341).

That Smith here draws a positive consequence places his assessment of "desire" fundamentally at odds with the philosophical anthropology that supports the classical account of virtue. It is important that the fundamental nature of this opposition be appreciated. To bring this out I now turn to the classical view. Two related perspectives in this view are of relevance: the "philosophical" perspective, where virtue is a state of tranquility, and the "civic" perspective, where virtue consists in activity in the political world. These are related in that both take an explicit stand against the corruption that they see emanating from bodily desire and both see this corruption embodied in a life given over to luxury.

LUXURY AND DESIRE

Livy conveniently sets the scene when, writing at the very start of his *History,* he remarks of Rome that

> no state [*res publica*] was ever greater, none more pious or richer in good examples, none into which avarice and luxury entered so late, or where poverty and frugality were so honoured. For it is true that the less wealth there was, the less desire [*cupiditatis*] there was. More recently riches have imported avarice and excessive pleasures [*voluptates*] with the craving for luxury and wantonness to the ruin of oneself and everything.[4]

For Livy luxury and avarice signal a decline into corruption. This constitutes a loss of virtue. This loss can be understood from both the civic and the philosophical perspectives.

The philosophical perspective is best exemplified in Stoicism. To the Stoic a life of luxury lacked virtue because it was life given over to the pursuit of bodily pleasures. Such a life was, in effect, no better than an animalistic, slavish life, because—in Stoic thought—the body was included among those things that are naturally slavish. According to Seneca, for example, the refusal to be influenced by one's body "assures one's freedom."[5] In similar vein Epictetus opened his *Manual* by contrasting things that are in our power and things that are not. The former are "by nature free, not subject to restraint or hindrance"; the latter, which include "the body," are "weak, slavish, subject to restraint, in the power of others."[6] To fail to understand this contrast, to think in particular that things that are naturally slavish *(phusei doula)* are really "free," is to suffer grief and inner turmoil. Generically these sufferings are regarded as perturbations *(pathe)* of the soul. Since the natural life is the rational life, then these perturbations are irrational impulses or "pathological disturbances of the personality" in Rist's felicitous definition.[7] The rational life is an "apathetic" or tranquil life and to live *kata phusin* is to live a life of virtue.[8]

Nevertheless the fact that the soul is embodied demands appropriate acknowledgment and this takes the form of living according to Nature. There is, however, a proper limit to meeting the body's requirements, because fulfilment of these requirements is itself naturally limited.

We can discern two crucial assumptions at work here. The first is a functional or teleological perspective: why is food, say, needed? To which question the answer is, to keep the organism alive. The corollary is that this need can be met with a definite quantum of sustenance because "naturally" the stomach can only hold so much. The second assumption is that qualitative factors are nonfunctional or contrary to the natural telos: all that Nature demands is that the belly be filled, not flattered. This enables *luxuria* to be identified as "excess." While it was common for guests to vomit in the course of a Roman banquet, so that they might continue to gorge, this "excess" is better understood qualitatively rather than quantitatively. For the Romans, luxury signified fine, or qualitative, distinctions where in Nature none exist.[9]

Luxurious excess is contrasted with the "natural life." Since "it is self-evident" that Nature's requirements are few, small, and inexpensive then the "natural life" is also the simple life.[10] The simple or frugal life is not, however, a life of poverty. For Seneca poverty consists not in having too little but in desiring more.[11] The element of desire is decisive. The definitive characteristic of desires that focus on the body is that they are infinite or boundless; a criterion of the "unnatural" is that it has no terminus.[12] Accordingly, should the natural bounds be exceeded or become relaxed, then these desires will be "set free" and in order to live virtuously, to live an appropriately human life, the passions and desires of human nature must be controlled. The "philosopher," or sage, is the truly virtuous man, who has achieved this control by removing "all desire from himself."[13]

The sage will fill his stomach when hungry and his hunger will make stale bread seem soft and wheaty. To insist always on fresh bread, and to refuse to eat stale, is to allow the stomach, that is bodily desire, to hold sway; as Seneca put it, "a stomach firmly under control . . . marks a considerable step towards independence."[14] Once that independence is lost then objects of bodily desire such as life or riches will be valued and, viewed from that perspective, human life will always appear too short. Those who see matters in this way have "become soft through a life of luxury."[15] They have lost the rational control constitutive of virtue, because, in their desire to prolong life, they become afraid of death.

Those who place a high value on life are falling away from virtue and into error for, as Seneca puts it, there is "nothing very great about living." He supports that judgment immediately by remarking that "all your slaves and all the animals do it."[16] Cicero spells out the significance of this remark. Since brutes can only enjoy bodily pleasures then a person who becomes addicted to sensual pleasure is transformed into a "mere brute." To seek pleasure is an inappropriate activity for man, who should, rather, simply preserve his health and strength. In accord with that injunction it follows that to wallow in luxury, softness, and effeminacy (quam sit turpe diffluere luxuria et delicate ac molliter) is unworthy and base and that to lead a frugal life of temperance, strictness, and sobriety is proper and becoming (honestum).[17]

CIVIC VIRTUE

We now approach the civic dimension in Roman discussions of virtue. The crux is Cicero's association between luxury, softness, and effeminacy—an association that is already present in Plato.[18] The underlying assumption is that proper manly activity is exhibited in warfare and that easy, soft living emasculates. The implicit causality is that devotion of luxury makes for military weakness; it produces bad, cowardly soldiers.[19]

The frugal life, on the contrary, produces, or at least sustains, a militarily effective state. This is the "message" of Livy's judgment quoted above. That Roman virtue is now corrupt is a convention exploited in the ideological battles of the late Republic. Sallust, perhaps, provides the most revealing analysis of this convention since it is given succintly as part of a deliberately heightened depiction of Roman corruption as manifested in the Catilinean Conspiracy.

Sallust says Catiline himself was incited by the corruption of a society plagued by the "disastrous vices—love of luxury and love of money *(avaritia)*."[20] In line with the convention, this condition is contrasted with the past age of virtue—that is, when Rome was frugal, when harmony was at a maximum and avarice at minimum.[21] But thanks to conquests "abroad," another standard ingredient in the story of Rome's decline, and the availability of riches, avarice emerged to destroy "honour, integrity and every other virtue *(fidem, probitatem ceterasque artis bonis)*."[22] Ambition, too, is let loose. *Ambitio* is the desire to attain distinction *(gloria)* and power by deceit. Fellow citizens, as a consequence, are treated not according to their merits but according to personal advantage. While Sallust says ambition made most headway initially, because it is a perversion of the search for glory, which is a virtue, avarice is more serious; it acts as a poison to weaken both body and spirit. Indeed, in language that we have already met, he declares that avarice emasculates *(virilem effeminat)*.[23] Like all vices that center on the body it is insatiable. Furthermore, once wealth itself becomes established as the norm then poverty and frugality, the concomitants of virtue, become a disgrace. The cumulative effect of this upon the next generation is that they become prey to "luxury, avarice and pride."[24]

A life of luxury, given over to bodily desires, is a corrupt life. From the civic or republican perspective the most obviously serious expression of this corruption is its emasculation of *virtus*. Once men find satisfaction in bodily pleasures they become effeminate and unable and unwilling to act for the public good when that might involve risk or even death. Less dramatic but just as serious is the corruption more generally of the ideal of public service. In the past, when the Republic was virtuous, which is also to say when its citizens were frugal, any "surplus" was spent, as Cicero remarked, on public splendor.[25] But once

wealth and riches are desired for private consumption then the
bases of virtuous citizenship are destroyed. Once bodily desires
have been stimulated, then, according to the operative philosophical anthropology, they will feed upon themselves and place
a premium upon self-gratification. The more "selfish" pleasures
are indulged, the less commitment to the public good will be
exhibited, and without that commitment virtue and manly freedom will be lost.

Opulence and Freedom

In his lectures at the University of Glasgow Smith professed that
"opulence and freedom" are "the two greatest blessings men can
possess" (*LJ*, 185). Against the backcloth of the Roman perspectives, this can be seen as a vindication of the modern over the
ancient world.[26] Smith's association of opulence, or luxury, with
freedom yokes together what were to the ancients two mutually
incompatible "forces," selfishness and the public good. Yet in
Smith's eyes, this "selfishness," properly understood, is everyone's natural desire to better his or her condition. This desire,
this incessant activity, renders Stoic tranquility "unnatural"; it
teaches a perfection "beyond the reach of human nature" (*TMS*,
60; cf. 292). But, and here is his rejection of the civic view of
virtue, the arena for this activity is not the public or civic life,
with its goals of honor and glory, but the private, self-interested
"economic" life. Meeting household (*oikos*) needs or procuring
the basic wherewithal for life, that, as Seneca had observed, was
the inferior, subhuman/submasculine concern of animals and
slaves, has become, in Smith, the natural business of humanity.

Though Smith in this way devalues the classical understanding of politics as the vehicle for the expression of virtue he does
not, of course, omit consideration of either politics or virtue.
According to Smith's own philosophical anthropology, humans
possess "the desire" to better their condition. However, to enable
that desire to generate opulence efficiently, individuals should
enjoy the *private* liberty to decide for themselves how to deploy
their resources (*WN*, 454). This is the "obvious and simple, system of natural liberty" where every man "is left perfectly free to
pursue his own interest his own way" (*WN*, 687). This private

liberty will promote the public good, without any deliberate positive intention to that effect. Individuals are led to this goal of classical civic virtue not by overt public commitment but by an "invisible hand" (*WN*, 456).

The opulence generated by private economic liberty reposes, significantly for our purposes, upon the confidence provided by a system of impersonal rules or the "justice of government" (*WN*, 910). Smith believes that a society based on a system of rules is superior to one that embodies the practice of virtue. This superiority is the superiority of liberty under law, or justice, to the "republican" realization of virtue in political activity.[27] For Smith, what is necessary for social existence is not beneficence, since a company of merchants can subsist without it (*TMS*, 86), but justice. Society cannot subsist at all among individuals who are ready to injure each other—that is, where injustice prevails. Justice, therefore, is "the main pillar that upholds the whole edifice. If it is removed, the great, the immense fabric of human society . . . must in a moment crumble into atoms" (*TMS*, 86). Justice is essentially negative because it requires abstention from injuring others so that indeed "we may often fulfil all the rules of justice by sitting still and doing nothing" (*TMS*, 82).

Hence, contrary to the classical republican tradition and its modern adherents who stress active participation,[28] we can fulfil our public/political duties without any direct engagement, by "doing nothing." In dealing with others it is sufficient to follow rules in order to practice the virtue of justice and so enjoy freedom under the law. Provided that society is peaceable then support of the established government is the "best expedient" to promote the interests of our fellows and to be, thereby, a "good citizen" (*TMS*, 231).

Implicit here is a difference of the utmost significance between Smith and the republicans. As initially articulated by Aristotle, the virtue of the citizen is only made possible because his ownership of a household gives him "leisure" and independence. This citizen is free to participate in the affairs of the *polis* (in public matters— *res publicae*) because he is free from the demands of daily life thanks to his slaves. But Smith's "negative" approach means that by making few demands in this way freedom and the just life can be in the reach of all and need not be reserved to those with the resources necessary to underpin an active political life. And, as part of his own account of modern freedom ("freedom in the present sense of the word" [*WN*, 400] Smith does not neglect to point out the dependence of the classical republics upon slave labor (*LJ*, 226). Indeed, Smith's declaration that opulence and freedom are humankind's greatest blessings occurs in the context of a discussion of slavery.

Slavery is not only morally objectionable but also unproductive (*WN*, 387; 684). Wealth is increased by the "liberal reward of labour," since where wages are high there "we shall always find the workmen more active, diligent and expeditious" (*WN*, 99). Given further that "servants, labourers and workmen" constitute a bulk of a society's population, then what improves their lot makes for a "flourishing" society (*WN*, 96). By "flourishing" Smith means enjoyment of *material* comforts and satisfaction of bodily desires. Nothing is virtuous or ennobling about poverty. Smith points out that those who are "miserably poor" frequently resort to "directly destroying, and sometimes . . . abandoning their infants, their old people, and those afflicted with lingering diseases, to perish with hunger, or to be devoured by wild beasts" (*WN*, 10). Only in a developed market society is material happiness enjoyed; in that society there is a "universal opulence which extends itself to the lowest ranks of the people" (*WN*, 22). The presence of universal opulence means that, for example, a "common day labourer in Britain has more luxury in his way of living then an Indian sovereign" (*LJ*, 429) and that the accommodation of even the lowest "exceeds that of many an African king, the absolute master of the lives and liberties of 10,000 naked savages" (*WN*, 24). Although the abodes of the lowest rank in commercial society are far inferior to those of the rich, nevertheless, despite this inequality, this society enjoys the second great human blessing of liberty under law, liberty from an *absolute* master.

SYMPATHY AND SOCIALIZATION

In the modern world everyone "becomes in some measure a merchant" (*WN*, 37) and this necessitates a new assessment of the relations between individuals. In a market society the individual "stands at all times in need of the cooperation and assistance of

great multitudes, while his whole life is scarce sufficient to gain
the friendship of a few persons" (*WN*, 26). The individual deals
mostly with others who are strangers to him or her. In that
circumstance individuals must, as Rousseau laments, appeal to
advantage. Hence,

> It is not from the benevolence of the butcher, the brewer, or the
> baker, that we expect our dinner, but from their regard to their
> own interest. We address ourselves, not to their humanity but to
> their self-love, and never talk to them of our own necessities but
> of their advantages. Nobody but a beggar chuses to depend
> chiefly upon the benevolence of his fellow-citizens. (*WN*, 26–27)

This reinforces the point that Smith does not look to benevolence to establish social cohesiveness. Of course, he does not
deny the virtuousness of benevolence but society can subsist without it, though it will indeed, he concedes, be as a consequence
"less happy and agreeable" (*TMS*, 86). What is required for cohe-
sion is justice[29] but, as we have seen, in modern society the just
life is in the reach of all.

What sustains the superiority of commercial society in this
regard is Smith's sociological account of moral sentiments. In the
light of the subsequent communitarian critique of liberalism,
especially of its individualism as manifest in the primacy ac-
corded to justice or rights, it is noteworthy that Smith's account is
based upon *social* interaction. A significant instance of this is
when at the conclusion of his explicit discussion of virtue in the
Moral Sentiments he remarks that "the *sentiments of other people* is
the *sole* principle which, upon most occasions, overawes all those
mutinous and turbulent passions" (*TMS*, 263: my emphases).
The sage in his independence from all worldly attachments
would be incapable of a life of Smithian virtue.

Justice consists in rule following and Smith likens the rules of
justice to the rules of grammar. The basis of this similarity is that
the rules in each case are distinguished by their precision, accu-
racy, and indispensability (*TMS*, 175). This means that they are
susceptible to instruction; we "may be taught to act justly." This is
of far-reaching importance. Because the bulk of mankind is
made of the "coarse clay," then the ideal conduct enjoined by the
Stoics is not to be expected; but

> there is scarce any man, however, who by discipline, education, and example, may not be so impressed with a regard to general rules, as to act upon almost every occasion with tolerable decency, and through the whole of his life to avoid any considerable degree of blame. (*TMS*, 163)

Once again the exclusivity of classical virtue is contrasted with the inclusivity of modern justice.

Nonetheless, Smith has to explain how the general rules of justice will be adhered to in a society where self-love is prevalent. This explanation lies at the heart of his moral psychology, because it is devoted to showing how social interaction humbles the arrogance of self-love (*TMS*, 83). The linchpin of Smith's moral psychology is his analysis of the principle of sympathy. Sympathy, in Smith's technical sense, is the human faculty of compassion or fellow-feeling. By use of imagination one person sympathizes with another and feels what the other feels (or should feel) (*TMS*, 10). Hence upon hearing that someone's father has died one is able to sympathize. This process operates even though the bereaved is a complete stranger, a significant point as we shall see. The greatest consolation for the bereaved is to see others sympathize with him—"to see the emotions of their hearts, in every respect, beat time to his own" (*TMS*, 22). However, an inevitable shortfall appears between the two since no compassion can ever match up exactly with the original. In consequence (to continue this example) the bereaved learns to lower the pitch of his or her grief so that spectators can the more easily sympathize.

That this is a learning exercise is important. People learn from experience of life, through "discipline, education and example," what is proper. In this way, and despite its different epistemological roots, Smithian morality is comparable to Hegel's *Sittlichkeit*, not *Moralität*, which is the inspiration for modern communitarians like Charles Taylor and Michael Sandel. Morality is a social phenomenon to be explained in correspondingly social terms. In a key passage Smith remarks,

> were it possible that a human creature could grow up to manhood in some solitary place, without any communication with his own species, he could no more think of his own character, of the propriety or demerit of his own sentiments and conduct, of the

> beauty and deformity of his own mind, than of the beauty or
> deformity of his own face. Bring him into society and he is imme-
> diately provided with the mirror which he wanted before . . . and
> it is here that he first views the propriety and impropriety of his
> own passions. (*TMS*, 110–11)

Morality is a matter of socialization, of "insensible habit and experience" (*TMS*, 135). Social intercourse teaches individuals what behavior is acceptable and, in due course, these social judgments are internalized as conscience as they come to view their actions and motives as an "impartial well-informed spectator" would (*TMS*, 130). Through the dynamics of social interaction the agent's and the spectators' emotions can harmonize. Although it is impossible that their emotions will ever be as one, yet there will be concord and, significantly, this concord is sufficient for "the harmony of society" (*TMS*, 22).

The extent to which emotions will harmonize differs with circumstances and Smith claims, though this is implicit rather explicit, that the circumstances of commercial society are well suited to maintain harmony. This fit, so to speak, explains Smith's confidence that the general rules of justice will be adhered to in a society where everyone is a merchant.

COMMERCIAL VIRTUES

Commercial society will develop its own appropriate virtues. In that society most interactions involve strangers. On Smith's rendering of the dynamics of sympathy an agent can expect less sympathy from a stranger than from a friend. The ubiquity of strangers in a commercial society will have the effect of strengthening the character by making habitual the need to moderate one's emotions (cf. *TMS*, 147). A stranger is more like the impartial spectator (cf. *TMS*, 153–54). This spectator corrects "the natural misrepresentations of self-love" and "shows us the propriety of generosity and the deformity of injustice" (*TMS*, 137). Indeed "the real man of virtue" is solely he who governs his conduct in line with the spectator (*TMS*, 245). The upshot is that in a commercial society, where most mingle increasingly with those who are strangers to them, agents will moderate their emotions so that tranquility is called forth (*TMS*, 23).

In the light of the Stoic view, Smith can be interpreted as associating the ideal of tranquility with the modern world of commercial interdependence and not with the miserably impoverished world of self-sufficiency. Furthermore this socially induced ability on the part of agents to tone down their emotions is the source for Smith of that central Stoic virtue of self-command, the virtue from which, Smith allows, "all the other virtues seem to derive their principal lustre" (*TMS*, 242). Because of this Alasdair MacIntyre claims that Smith is to be accounted a Stoic.[30] But this amounts to little.[31] The thrust of Smith's analysis—as MacIntyre himself perhaps concedes when he notes Smith's link between virtuousness and rule following—is to undermine both the philosophical and civic assumptions of the Stoics.

Self-command, like all the virtues, is a product of social learning or socialization. Moreover, commercial society need not go to the extremes of "savages and barbarians," where self-denial is cultivated at the cost of humanity (*TMS*, 205). Indeed, when self-denial expresses itself in suffering torture without any complaint whatsoever, then the whole merit of self-command is taken away (*TMS*, 245). A wide difference exists between the degrees of self-command required in "civilized and barbarous nations." The latter, as the case of the passive victim of torture exemplifies, "necessarily acquire the habits of falsehood and dissimulation" and when they give way to anger their vengeance is "always sanguinary and dreadful" (*TMS*, 208).

The former, by contrast, become "frank, open and sincere." This gives rise to characteristically commercial virtues. In the world of commerce honesty is the norm. This point is made explicitly in the *Lectures:* "when the greater part of the people are merchants they always bring probity and punctuality into fashion, and these therefore are the principal virtues of a commercial nation" (*LJ*, 539). The very interdependence of that world contributes to the maintenance of these virtues. Commercial societies are characterized by a preponderance of individuals "in the middling and inferior stations of life," none of whom can ever be great enough to be above the law but are, rather, overawed into respect for "the more important rules of justice" (*TMS*, 63).

Justice, moreover, is self-supporting in commercial society. This is borne out in practice (Smith affirms) by "that equal and

impartial administration of justice which renders the rights of
the meanest British subject respectable to the greatest, and
which by securing to every man the fruits of his own industry,
gives the greatest and most effectual encouragement to every
sort of industry" (*WN*, 610). It is also borne out in theory because
the "reward" for acting justly, for keeping to the rules, is "the
confidence, the esteem and love of those we live with . . . it is not
in being rich that truth and justice would rejoice but in being
trusted and believed" (*TMS*, 166). To act justly, therefore, brings
forth trust and confidence and they, in their turn, make it rational and feasible to specialize, to increase the extent of the
division of labor and the market, and so create opulence.

MARTIAL VIRTUE AND COURAGE

Despite Smith's commitment to the superiority of commercial
society he is not blind to its drawbacks. Hence while specialization enhances dexterity, this is at the expense of the "intellectual,
social and martial virtues" of the great body of the people (*WN*,
782). Smith sees it as a legitimate task of government, one of its
public works, in commercial society to "prevent" this occurrence,
chiefly through provision of elementary education.

In the light of the classical view of virtue it is noteworthy that
Smith lays some stress here on the enervation of "martial virtue"
and the deleterious consequences of cowardice. These consequences affect both the individual and his or her society. Regarding the former, cowardice necessarily involves "mental mutila-
tion, deformity and wretchedness" while, regarding the latter,
the "security of every society depends, more or less" upon the
martial virtues (*WN*, 787). Though these remarks do indeed
indicate Smith's appreciation of the classical conception of virtue,[32] he is not to be placed in the camp of the civic humanists.

The compulsory military exercises, with attendant prizes for
those who excel, of the Greeks and Romans are cited as a more
effective means of sustaining the "martial spirit" than modern
militias. But Smith has already demonstrated that the division of
labor in modern societies, together with advances in military
technology, have made professional standing armies, *not* the citizen militias favored by the civic humanists, the superior force

(*WN*, 700). He even argues that so long as the civil and military authorities are complementary, then, contrary to "men of republican principles," a standing army is favorable, not dangerous, to liberty (*WN*, 706–7). The admitted advantage of martial virtue is that it would enhance that process and also help to reduce the size of a professional army (*WN*, 787). Smith does allow that commercial society threatens this advantage and that, in consequence, some governmental action should seek to offset it as part of its general educational responsibilities.

When all allowances have been made, what remains decisive is the superiority of "opulent and civilized" over "poor and barbarous" nations (*WN*, 708). The *historical* fact of artillery is crucial. This bears directly on the general assessment of virtue and its intimate connection with martial pursuits. In the classical picture, as the etymological links between *aner/andra* and *andreia* and *vir* and *virtus* bear out, virtuous action is identified as that which is characteristic of manliness, and courage on the battlefield is paradigmatic. Smith, however, is far less impressed by courage and here he again exhibits a sentiment common to the "modernity."[33] Not only have modern conditions of battle reduced the "skill factor" but more significantly the very individualism, the heroism, of the virtuous/courageous individual is rendered suspect. He points out that "the most intrepid valour may be employed in the cause of the greatest injustice." Courage, while sometimes useful, is "equally liable to be excessively pernicious" and will be called upon when law and justice are "in a great measure impotent,"— that is, "in times of great public disorder" (*TMS*, 241; cf. 264).[34]

Again the contrast is with "the gentler" exertions of temperance and modesty, of chastity and industry, that "can seldom be directed to any bad end." Indeed, the conduct of those who "are contented to walk in the humbler paths of private and peaceable life" is no less pleasing than that which accompanies the more "dazzling" actions of "the hero, statesman, or the legislator" (*TMS*, 241–42).

MODERN VIRTUE AND LIBERALISM

The age of heroes or of sages suffused with *virtus* is past. Yet this age is presupposed by the civic humanists and Stoic philosophers in their critique of luxury and commerce. To this critique Smith rejoins that it is not only anachronistic but also based on an unsound view of human nature. Both republicans and sages suffer from an overdemanding, superhuman understanding of virtue. Whereas the premodern view sees a threat to virtue and liberty in the boundless uncontrollability of human bodily desires, modern, Smithian, liberalism accommodates these desires. Virtue is largely domesticated or privatized and concordantly liberty is to be found in individuals pursuing their own ends. Understood in this manner neither virtue nor liberty calls for superhuman qualities but are tasks in which every human partakes and for which every human is qualified. Modern virtue and liberty, as found in Smith, are in accord with a realistic conception of human nature and, in that sense, they are less exclusive than the classical versions, which are, in comparison, elitist and sexist.

Modern critics have to preserve this inclusivity along with their dialectical transcendence of liberalism. This also entails that any sustainable conception of virtue must be "democratized." It is, accordingly, no surprise that virtues of citizenship are reinvoked by a number of these modern writers; MacIntyre, for example, refers to "a moral community of citizens."[35] This virtuous community is to be sustained by more than a passive framework of legal and political rights; it will actively engage all citizens in "shared understandings."[36] In this way citizens will not be strangers. As we have seen Smith's general argument, by contrast, is that the postclassical world is irretrievably a world of strangers and that in this world we must look to the public realm for rules to govern us and to the private for virtue. In this way Smith's arguments, as well as remaining a challenge to those who attempt to find virtue in community, also provide the resources for a response to these critics.[37]

NOTES

The following abbreviations of Smith's works are cited in parentheses in the text and notes.

WN: An Inquiry into the Nature and Causes of the Wealth of Nations, eds. R. H. Campbell and A. S. Skinner [Glasgow Edition of the works and correspondence of Adam Smith] (Indianapolis: Liberty Classics, 1981).

LJ: Lectures on Jurisprudence, eds. R. L. Meek, D. D. Raphael, and P. G. Stein [Glasgow Edition] (Indianapolis: Liberty Classics, 1982).

TMS: The Theory of Moral Sentiments, eds. A. L. Macfie and D. D. Raphael [Glasgow Edition] (Indianapolis: Liberty Classics, 1982).

1. Cf. inter alia A. MacIntyre, *After Virtue,* 2nd edit. (London: Duckworth, 1985); M. Sandel, *Liberalism and the Limits of Justice* (Cambridge: Cambridge University Press, 1982); M. Walzer, *Spheres of Justice* (Oxford: Blackwell, 1983); C. Taylor, "Atomism" in A. Kontos (ed.) *Powers, Possessions, and Freedom* (Toronto: University of Toronto Press, 1979); A. Gilbert, "Democracy and Individuality" in E. Paul (ed) *Marxism and Liberalism* (Oxford: Blackwell, 1986); P. Selznick, "The Idea of a Communitarian Morality" *California Law Review,* 75 (1987) 315–30; C. Cochran, "The Thin Theory of Community" *Political Studies,* 37 (1989) 422–35.

2. Cf. inter alia A. Gutmann, "Communitarian Critics of Liberalism" *Philosophy and Public Affairs,* 14 (1985) 308–22; H. Hirsch, "The Threnody of Liberalism" *Political Theory,* 14 (1986) 423–39; A. Buchanan, "Assessing the Communitarian Critique of Liberalism" *Ethics,* 99 (1989) 852–82; S. Benn, *A Theory of Freedom* ch. 12 (Cambridge: Cambridge University Press, 1988); C. J. Berry, *The Idea of a Democratic Community* (Hemel Hempstead: Wheatsheaf, 1989).

3. J. Bentham, *An Introduction to the Principles of Morals and Legislation* ed. W. Harrison (Oxford: Blackwell, 1948) p. 125. Cf. Smith, "Pleasure and pain are the great objects of desire and aversion: but these are distinguished not by reason, but by immediate sense and feeling" (*TMS,* 320).

4. Livy, *The History of Rome.* Preface, 10. Translation based on D. Spillan (London: Bohn, 1854) and E. Sage (London: Loeb Library, 1934).

5. Seneca, *Epistle* 65. Translations are based on R. Campbell in *Letters from a Stoic* (Harmondsworth: Penguin, 1969), R. Gummere (London: Loeb Library, 1934), and E. P. Barker (Oxford: Clarendon, 1932).

6. Epictetus, *The Manual,* tr. G. Long in *Essential Works of Stoicism* ed. M. Hadas (New York: Bantam, 1961) p. 85.

7. J. Rist, *Stoic Philosophy* Cambridge: Cambridge University Press, 1969) p. 27.

8. Cf. D. Laertius, "Life of Zeno" in *Essential Works of Stoicism* op. cit. p. 25.

9. I have developed this in my "Luxury and the Politics of Need

and Desire: The Roman Case" *History of Political Thought*, 10 (1989) 597–613.

10. Cicero, *Discussions at Tusculum*, tr. M. Grant in *Cicero on the Good Life* (Harmondsworth: Penguin, 1971) 5, 35 (p. 106).

11. Seneca, *Epistle* 2.

12. Seneca, *Epistle* 16.

13. Epictetus, *Manual*, p. 99.

14. Seneca, *Epistle* 119. The bread example is Seneca's.

15. Seneca, *Epistle* 78.

16. Seneca, *Epistle* 72.

17. Cicero, *The Offices*. Translations are based on W. Miller (London: Loeb Library, 1913) and T. Cockman (London: Routledge, 1894) bk. 1 ch. 30.

18. Cf. C. J. Berry, "Of Pigs and Men: Luxury in Plato's *Republic*" *Polis*, 8 (1989) 2–22.

19. The historian Florus provides a revealing example of this causality in operation. He records that King Antiochus of Syria, having seized the Greek islands, then spent his time in *otia et luxus*. But, the historian continues, as a direct consequence of this indulgence, when the Romans took the field against him he succumbed easily. The explanation Florus supplies for his defeat was that he had already been defeated by his own luxury. *Epitome of Roman History*, tr. E. Foster (London: Loeb Library, 1934) bk. 1 ch. 24.

20. Sallust, *The Conspiracy of Catiline*, tr. S. Handford, (Harmondsworth: Penguin, 1963) p. 178. *De Coniuratione Catilinae* ed. W. Summers (Cambridge: Cambridge University Press, 1930) par. 5.

21. Sallust, par. 9.

22. Sallust, p. 181 par. 10.

23. Sallust, par. 11.

24. Sallust, p. 183 par. 12.

25. Cicero, *Pro Flacco* 28 (London: Loeb Library, 1977). For the mundane reality whereby such "splendor" was an integral part of "politicking" see P. Veyne, *Le Pain et le Cirque: Sociologie Historique d'un Pluralisme Politique* (Paris: Editions du Seuil, 1976) and Berry, *History of Political Thought* op. cit.

26. I have pursued this line more systematically in my essay on Smith in *The Philosophers of the Enlightenment* ed. P. Gilmour (Edinburgh: Edinburgh University Press, 1989). Cf. R. Teichgraeber, III, *"Free Trade" and Moral Philosophy* (Durham, N.C.: Duke University Press, 1986).

27. MacIntyre op. cit. p. 236 says Smith was a life-long republican. His unacknowledged source for this would appear to be J. Rae's *Life of Smith* (New York: Kelley Reprints of Economic Classics, 1965) p. 174.

Rae himself quotes Smith's pupil the Earl of Buchan as evidence. For wise words on the limited weight that such "republicanism" can bear see D. Forbes, "Sceptical Whiggism, Commerce, and Liberty" in *Essays on Adam Smith* eds. A. Skinner & T. Wilson (Oxford: Clarendon, 1975) p. 195.

28. The now classic account of civic humanism/republicanism is J. Pocock, *The Machiavellian Moment* (Princeton: Princeton University Press, 1975). A more recent essay that bears most directly on the Scottish Enlightenment is "Cambridge Paradigms and Scotch Philosophers: A Study of the Relations between the Civic Humanist and the Civic Jurisprudential Interpretation of Eighteenth-Century Social Thought" in *Wealth and Virtue: The Shaping of Political Economy in the Scottish Enlightenment* eds. I. Hont and M. Ignatieff (Cambridge: Cambridge University Press, 1983) pp. 235–52. For comment on Pocock's account of the Scottish Enlightenment, and the debate in which his essay engages, see C. J. Berry, "The Nature of Wealth and the Origins of Virtue" *History of European Ideas*, 7 (1986) 85–99.

29. It is true that Smith thinks bare observance of rules without more positive acts of virtue lacks certain feelings of humanity (*TMS*, 82). But justice and benevolence are not inversely related; one who acts justly will also exhibit humanity and benevolence (*TMS*, 218).

30. MacIntyre op. cit. p. 234.

31. It is true that Smith does not regard the possession of riches as a sufficient condition for happiness. He even says at one point that "real happiness," namely, "ease of body and peace of mind," is as enjoyable by the beggar as by the king (*TMS*, 185). Though this does echo the Stoic position it does I think remain moot whether Smith holds this to be true *historically*. I believe that the most plausible interpretation of this passage is that it presupposes *modern* freedom—that is, the beggar enjoys liberty under the law. That Smith's "theory of morals" is "redundant outside the context of a commercial society with a complex division of labour" is maintained by N. Phillipson, "Adam Smith as a Civic Moralist" in *Wealth and Virtue* op. cit. 181–182.

32. Cf. inter alia A. Hirschman, *The Passions and the Interests* (Princeton: Princeton University Press, 1977) esp. pp. 155–56; J. Robertson, "Scottish Political Economy beyond the Civic Tradition" *History of Political Thought*, 4 (1983) 451–82; D. Winch, *Adam Smith's Politics* (Cambridge: Cambridge University Press, 1978) ch. 5. Elsewhere Winch makes clear the limitations of viewing Smith as a civic humanist; see "Adam Smith's 'enduring particular result' " in *Wealth and Virtue* op. cit. pp. 253–69.

33. Cf., for example, Hume, who thinks that development in weap-

onry has "rendered battles less bloody and has given greater stability to civil societies" (*History of England* [London: Routledge, 1894] v. 1 p. 498). Hegel similarly remarks, "the principle of the modern world . . . has given courage a higher form" as the invention of the gun has made bravery less personal and more abstract (*Philosophy of Right,* tr. T. Knox [Oxford: Clarendon Press, 1952] par. 328 Remark, p. 212).

34. Hegel thinks that virtue proper is commoner in uncivilized communities where ethical conditions are more a matter of private choice; in the modern state virtue is to be found in adherence to a rational system of laws (op. cit. p. 108; cf. p. 260). Hume, too, associates the predominance of courage with "uncultivated nations" (*An Inquiry concerning the Principles of Morals* ed. C. Hendel [Indianapolis: Bobbs-Merrill, 1957] p. 79).

35. MacIntyre op. cit. p. 254.

36. Walzer op. cit. p. 313. Cf. Taylor op. cit. p. 60; Sandel op. cit. p. 161. For comment see C. J. Berry, *Idea of Democratic Community* ch. 5.

37. This paper draws on some work that was undertaken while I was the recipient of an ESRC Personal Grant (no.E 00242057).

2

EPISTEMOLOGY
OF THE VIRTUES

4

KNOWING ABOUT VIRTUE

GEORGE SHER

When we say that traits such as courage, wisdom, generosity, and justice are virtues, are we merely applying a conventional classificatory scheme, or are we making an objective normative claim? If we are making an objective claim, what sort of claim is it? And how, if at all, can we know it to be true?

Taken together, these questions define a topic that we may call *the epistemology of virtue.* We have various reasons to study it, not the least of which is that its questions arise naturally when we think reflectively about the sorts of persons we ought to be. But the questions also have a more political significance, and it is best to bring this out immediately. In recent years, many, though not all, liberal theorists have endorsed the thesis that the state should not favor any particular conception of the good, but should merely provide a neutral and just framework within which each person can pursue the good as he or she conceives it.[1] Clearly part of what they mean is that governments have no business trying to make their citizens virtuous.[2] Equally clearly, one important argument for such neutrality is that claims about virtue and the good cannot be objectively grounded, but are mere reflections of ignorance, prejudice, ideology, or self- or class-interest.[3] Against this, thinkers of various persuasions, including some communitarians and many on both the political Right and Left, maintain that we can know that certain traits are objectively desirable and that governments sometimes should promote these.

In this chapter, I shall take up some of the epistemological issues that the virtues raise. I shall argue that while beliefs about virtue may be vulnerable to challenge, they are no more vulnerable than any other normative claims. To show this, I shall make a number of positive, though highly programmatic, suggestions about the ways in which they can be known.

What Virtue Is: Rival Conceptions

Before we can decide whether knowledge about virtue is possible, we must have some idea of what virtue is. Unfortunately, despite the resurgence of interest in virtue, no single analysis has won general acceptance. Hence, the obvious way to begin is by reviewing the main competitors.

1. Perhaps the most familiar way of understanding the virtues is to see them as traits that are conducive to their possessors' flourishing, or to a person's living a life that is in his or her best interest. I shall call all accounts of this general form *Aristotelian*.[4] The Aristotelian tradition is itself not uniform, since its proponents disagree both about where a person's true interest lies and about how the virtues are connected to it. According to some, traits such as courage, wisdom, generosity, and justice are virtues because they issue in actions whose effects will probably benefit their possessors; according to others, these traits are virtues because possessing them, and being disposed to act in the corresponding ways, just *is* a part of living the sort of life that is best for humans. But whether an Aristotelian takes the relation between virtue and one's interest to be instrumental, constitutive, or a mixture of the two, he or she will say that virtues are traits that are conducive to their possessors' flourishing. A closely related view, which seeks to defend the link between virtue and flourishing against the objection that even unjust persons can flourish, is that virtues are traits conducive to the flourishing of their possessors *or others*.[5]

2. But not all philosophers have sought to understand the virtues in terms of flourishing. An important rival tradition seeks instead to understand them as traits conducive to right conduct. Within this tradition, the crucial question is not whether a trait contributes to anyone's well-being, but whether it leads its pos-

sessor to fulfill his or her moral duties. I shall call this second way of understanding virtue *deontological.*[6] Of course, like its Aristotelian competitor, the deontological approach can be worked out in different ways. Its proponents disagree not only about the contents of our duties but also about the degree to which they can be codified in rules or principles. In addition, just as traits can contribute in more than one way to flourishing, so too can they contribute in more than one way to dutiful action. For example, because there are duties of charity and justice, these traits may contribute simply by inclining their possessors to act as they should. However, because there is no duty to be wise, the trait of wisdom must make the less direct contribution of enabling its possessor to discern where his or her duties lie and how best to fulfill them.

3. At first glance, the Aristotelian and deontological approaches may seem to exhaust the field. However, on closer inspection, a third alternative appears. If courage, wisdom, and the rest are virtues, the reason may be neither that they lead to dutiful acts nor that they are conducive to or constitutive of any further good, but more simply that their *own* existence is a good. It can be maintained, in other words, that a trait is a virtue whenever it, or its possession, has intrinsic value or worth. Like the Aristotelian approach, this proposal construes virtue in terms of good rather than right; but unlike the Aristotelian approach, it equates the virtues not with character traits that are good *for their possessors,* but rather with traits that are good *in themselves.* To mark the difference, I shall call this third approach *perfectionist.*[7]

Given the deep differences among the three approaches, it is tempting to suppose that one or another must be true across the board. This, indeed, is a working assumption of many virtue theorists. Thus, one recent writer flatly asserts that appeals to flourishing "cannot be successful in providing a criterion of virtue and vice,"[8] while another deplores a preoccupation with duty that "blinds us not only to the treasures that this classical literature contains, but to the worthlessness of much modern ethics."[9] But while such turf wars may be unavoidable, the assumption that virtue has a single essence is neither obviously warranted nor, for our purposes, necessary. Insofar as our concern is to discover what sorts of persons we should strive to be and which traits, if any, the state should promote, the crucial question is not what is meant by the term "virtue," but rather which character traits, if any, can be known to be objectively valuable. To answer that question, we have no obvious need for any analysis of virtue beyond the unilluminating formula "character trait that is for some important reason desirable or worth having."[10]

But although we need not adjudicate among the competing accounts, they remain useful in another way. Even if none of them captures the essence of virtue, the Aristotelian, deontological, and perfectionist analyses can still help us by suggesting nonexclusive alternative ways of establishing that traits have value. For example, the Aristotelian approach suggests that we might establish a trait's value by demonstrating its contribution to human flourishing. Clearly, to mount this sort of argument is not to rule out the possibility of mounting others.

The harder question, though, is whether any such argument can really advance our inquiry. Before we can judge a trait to be valuable on the grounds that it promotes human flourishing, we must know what is to count as human flourishing and why *it* is valuable. Before we can judge a trait to be valuable because it leads to dutiful action, we must know what duty requires and why conforming to it is important. Before we can judge a trait to have intrinsic value, we must know what determines this. In each case, what needs to be established seems as problematic as the question it is introduced to answer. Even taking the proposed arguments into account, our prospects for achieving knowledge may not seem bright.

COHERENTISM AS MORAL EPISTEMOLOGY

But pessimism is premature. It is true that beliefs about duty, flourishing, and intrinsic value are neither themselves self-evident nor deducible from other self-evident principles or intuitions; but if anything about moral epistemology has become clear, it is precisely that this foundationalist model of justification cannot be taken for granted. In morals as elsewhere, a belief's justification may reside not in its probability or certainty relative to some epistemically privileged beliefs, but instead in its overall coherence with everything else the subject believes.[11] In Rawls's influential terminology, a belief may be justified when, and because, it would survive if the subject were to bring all of his or her beliefs into "reflective equilibrium."[12]

In what follows, I shall ask what we can know about the virtues if some version of coherentism is true. While I cannot of course defend coherentism here, it is surely plausible enough, and widely enough accepted, to warrant the proposed investigation. It is accepted both by many internalists, who hold that a belief's justification must be accessible to the person who holds it, and by many who reject this internalist requirement. It is also common ground to many naturalists, who see no discontinuity between philosophy and the natural and social sciences, and many others who are more *a prioristically* inclined.[13] Moreover, it draws philosophical support both from the unavoidable fact that all inquiries must be initiated and pursued against a background of already-formed beliefs and from the many technical difficulties that beset the idea of a class of self-justifying beliefs.[14] Given all this, the bearing of coherentism upon the proposed ways of justifying virtue claims is clearly of considerable interest.

To ascertain that bearing, let us first look more closely at the coherentist position. As I have suggested, its basic insight is that no belief is epistemically privileged. Whatever a belief's content, it is justified when and only when it would survive (or, in some versions of the theory, has survived) a process in which the believer evaluates each of his or her beliefs in light of all the others, and makes whatever additions and deletions are needed to render the whole set as coherent as possible. In this context, coherence involves considerably more than simple logical consistency. In addition, it encompasses a belief-set's scope, simplicity, and explanatory power.[15] Thus, other things being equal, a more comprehensive belief-set is more coherent than a less comprehensive one; and a belief-set's coherence is further increased if it contains general beliefs that unify and explain disparate particular ones, and if it contains causal principles that license second-order beliefs that various first-order beliefs are likely to be true.[16] Because each person is constantly acquiring new beliefs, each belief's justificatory status is always subject to revision in light of new information. Hence, even beliefs whose rejection is now unimaginable may later have to be abandoned if they fail to cohere with other beliefs.

How, exactly, does this model apply to normative claims? Because many ethical arguments consist mainly of attempts to square moral principles with moral intuitions, we may be tempted to suppose that justifying a normative belief consists exclusively of showing it to cohere with other normative beliefs. But on closer inspection, this cannot be correct. The problem is not merely that without appealing to nonnormative premises, we could not know which actions satisfy whatever criteria of rightness or goodness we accept. It is, more deeply, that without appealing to folk and theoretical psychology, we would have no basis for discounting moral beliefs that were formed under conditions unconducive to rational thought; that without appealing to the full range of political, economic, and scientific theories, we could not know which social and political arrangements were feasible; and that without marshaling philosophical arguments, we could not decide which sorts of evidence are relevant to normative claims. Because we obviously must invoke these and various other considerations, it seems best to set no *a priori* limits on the kinds of beliefs that can contribute to the justification of normative claims. Reverting again to Rawls's terminology, it seems best to opt for wide rather than narrow reflective equilibrium.[17]

What light does moral coherentism shed on our ability to know which character traits are objectively valuable? If the question were whether the theory can defeat general or moral skepticism, its answer would be unclear. A general skeptic asks what reason we have to accept *any* of our beliefs. Instead of supposing that those beliefs correspond to reality, why not suppose that they have been produced en masse by a Cartesian demon, or by a mad scientist stimulating a brain floating in a vat? Confronted with these questions, coherentists often appeal to background theories that imply that our having various beliefs is best explained by the very facts that would make those beliefs true.[18] However, because the background theories are themselves part of what the skeptic doubts, it is unclear whether this maneuver can avoid begging the question.

Moreover, even if coherentists could answer the general skeptic, their answer would not necessarily work against *moral* skepticism. Here the problem is to provide a theoretical account of how our moral beliefs could be shaped by moral facts, or, alternatively, of why it does not matter if they are not. Despite the strenuous efforts of naturalists to show that the moral supervenes on the nonmoral as (say) the psychological supervenes on the physical, it is far from clear that moral facts are part of the best explanation of the existence of our moral beliefs in the same way that nonmoral facts are part of the best explanation of the existence of our nonmoral beliefs.[19] Nor, despite the equally strenuous efforts of constructivists to explain how moral belief can have objective content without aspiring to truth, is it clear that any nonrealist notion of moral objectivity can be both intelligible and intellectually satisfying.[20] Of course, a plausible account along one or both lines may still emerge. There may also be room for a nonvacuous Platonism that combines the naturalist's aspiration to moral truth with the constructivist's insistence that ethics, unlike science, is not in the business of providing causal explanations of anything, including beliefs.[21] However, at present, the only thing that is certain is that the metaphysics of morals is very much in flux.

But even if it is not clear that a coherentist can justify any moral beliefs at this deepest of levels—and a foundationalist can certainly do no better—we can still ask what form our moral thought should take at less deep levels. Indeed, it is precisely in the context of daily life and politics that reflection on morality is most urgently needed. Moreover, at this level, moral skepticism is not a live option; for if taken seriously, it would undermine our ability to defend *any* action or set of political arrangements. To cite just one example, a consistent moral skeptic could not argue that because no one can defend any conception of virtue or the good, the state should provide a neutral and just framework within which each citizen can pursue his or her own conception. The reason, of course, is that neutralism is itself a normative stance, and so itself requires precisely the sort of defense that, according to the skeptic, can never be applied.

We may, then, set aside our skeptical worries. For us, the question is not whether we can tell a plausible story about moral objectivity and how we make contact with it, but is instead how to integrate our preexisting beliefs about what is good and right with each other and with what we believe most firmly about the world. More specifically, the question is whether the resulting normative theory will attach significant value to any particular traits, and if so, which and why. In the remainder of this chapter, I shall contend, first, that each competing conception of virtue does give us reason to regard various traits as valuable, and, second, that the resulting insights are not undermined by any general disqualifying considerations.

WHY VIRTUES ARE VALUABLE

Consider first the idea that virtues are traits that contribute to human flourishing. For Aristotle, an entity flourishes when it performs its natural function properly or well. Because most contemporary philosophers reject Aristotle's teleological metaphysics, many are also suspicious of appeals to flourishing. However, I think their suspicions are not well founded. The core idea of flourishing is simply well-being; and attempts to specify the conditions under which persons fare well are surely intelligible. Moreover, from a coherentist perspective, these attempts pose no special justificatory problems; for claims about well-being can be tested against a broad range of moral and nonmoral facts.

Perhaps most obviously, such claims are evidentially linked to many facts of biology and psychology. It is, for example, surely pertinent that human beings need food, clothing, and shelter and crave sex; that they have various physical and mental capacities; and that up to a certain point, but not beyond it, exercising a capacity serves to develop it. Assertions about flourishing are also evidentially linked to what we know about what people enjoy—about those ways of living that tend to bring satisfaction and happiness, and those others that tend to bring frustration and dissatisfaction. In a more normative vein, conceptions of flourishing can be tested against both our own intuitive judgments about where people's interests lie and our beliefs about what others believe about these matters. While no one sort of belief decisively establishes any specific conception of well-being, each coheres better with some conceptions than with others. Hence, if many of them converge on a particular conception—if a given way of life is at once within most people's capacities, satisfying to most people, and endorsed by our own and others' firm intuitive judgments—then it will, on the coherence account, be decidedly superior to its alternatives.

How likely *are* our background beliefs to converge on any determinate conception of flourishing? They are, we may concede, unlikely to yield any conception as unified as Aristotle's. Aristotle located each person's good in the same combination of intellectual and political activities.[22] However, as Charles Larmore observes,

> even if the image of the polis has not lost its charm for all modern moral thinkers . . . most have found no reason to attribute to politics, in contrast to other areas of the social world, any greater capacity for realizing our humanity.[23]

Nor, we may add, does the full realization of every person's humanity require the pure contemplative activity that Aristotle also favored. There is no reason to regard any single kind of activity as a prerequisite for human thriving.

But even if no specific way of life is best for everyone, our background beliefs may still identify various dimensions along which people's lives can be more or less successful. They will, for example, almost certainly imply that, other things being equal, lives containing rich and varied human relations are better than lives without them. Similarly, they are very likely to imply that people tend to be better off when they develop and exercise some subset of their intellectual and physical powers, and when they pursue with some success an integrated, realistic, and moderately complex plan of life. Of course, some people are happy without attachments or complicated plans, and some plans actually preclude close personal ties. But because both generalizations contain ceteris paribus clauses, and because happiness is in any case only one index of flourishing, such facts do not undermine what has been said. By collating and integrating these and related observations, we can piece together a loose-jointed and imprecise, but still contentful, characterization of the conditions in which humans tend to thrive.

And this is all we need; for if we can know even this much about flourishing, we must be warranted in attaching value to whatever character traits generally contribute to it. In this way, we can expect to vindicate many of the traditional virtues. While Alasdair MacIntyre takes a very different approach to flourishing—he maintains at one point that "the good life for man is the life spent in seeking the good life for man"[24]—his remarks about the value of justice, courage, and honesty are instructive. These traits, he writes, not only "sustain practices and enable us to achieve the goods internal to practices" but also "[enable] us to overcome the harms, dangers, temptations, and distractions which we encounter" in the search for the good life.[25] More specifically, justice, courage, and honesty are crucial to our ability to participate in practices as diverse as painting, football, and the study of physics, for to engage in any of those practices,

> We have to learn to recognize what is due to whom; we have to be prepared to take whatever self-endangering risks are demanded along the way; and we have to listen carefully to what we are told about our own inadequacies and to reply with the same carefulness for the facts.[26]

Because justice, courage, and honesty sustain the practices that in turn sustain the quest for the good life, they themselves share in the good life's value.

This important suggestion is easily detached from MacIntyre's notion of flourishing. Just as those who lack the justice to acknowledge "what is due to whom" are to that extent less likely to succeed at football or the study of physics, they are also less likely to succeed at maintaining close human relations, or at cultivating their powers or pursuing and accomplishing complex goals. Even more obviously, one has little chance of sustaining a close relations, etc., if one is not ready "to take whatever self-endangering risks are demanded," or if one is unwilling "to listen carefully to what [one is] told about [one's] own inadequacies and to reply with the same carefulness for the facts." In these and related ways, justice, courage, and truthfulness do seem to protect us from the harms, dangers, temptations, and distractions that threaten the elements of a flourishing life. And, though I lack the space to make the argument, I believe the same can be said of a variety of other traits—for example, integrity, perseverance, self-control, and loyalty.

Hence, if we accept the coherentist approach, we may indeed hope to demonstrate a trait's value by tying it to a defensible conception of flourishing. But so, next, can we argue for a trait's value by tying it to a defensible conception of *duty*. This, indeed, appears much the easier task; for while flourishing is a contested notion, we find far less disagreement about either the content of our moral duties or the importance of heeding them.

The amount of agreement about the content of our moral duties is partially obscured by the lack of consensus about their grounding. At the deepest normative levels, utilitarians, Kantians, contractarians, and pluralists offer very different justificatory accounts. But what is most striking about their differences is precisely that they have so few practical implications. Virtually all normative theorists agree that wanton killing and cruelty are morally forbidden, that lying and breaking promises are generally wrong, and that acts that would greatly help others at little cost or risk to the agent are sometimes required. There is, I would argue, also surprisingly little disagreement about what duty requires on many particular occasions. Because so many common beliefs about the content of our duties are supported by all normative theories, the case for accepting them is surely strong.

Moreover, if justification is a matter of coherence, then so too is the case for believing it important to *do* one's moral duty; for this belief, too, is either presupposed or implied by many central elements of our belief system. It is supported, inter alia, by the value of the interests that moral duties protect; by the prominent role of moral evaluation in public and private discourse; and by the felt urgency of the need to justify our conduct to others. These considerations do not necessarily establish that doing one's moral duty is *overridingly* important—this remains a disputed question—but they leave little doubt that it is *among* the things that are important.[27] And because our aim is to show that the traits that contribute to dutiful action are themselves valuable, this may seem to be quite enough.

Unfortunately, the issue is not quite this straightforward. As Kant stressed, acts that are merely *in accordance with* duty differ greatly from acts that are done *from* duty. Moreover, many would agree with Kant that what has moral worth is not just doing the right thing, but doing it for the right reasons. Hence, to show that honesty, justice, and similar traits do have moral value, we may have to show that the acts to which they lead *are* done for the right reasons. But are they? These acts, it seems, are motivated by settled desires to act honestly and justly; and being motivated by such a desire is not obviously the same as being motivated by a reason supplied by duty. Hence, it is also unclear that honesty and justice can acquire moral value merely by *leading* people to act honestly and justly.

This objection raises several new issues. Fully to explore it, we would have to examine both the case for believing that only actions done from duty have moral worth and the possibility that acts that lack moral worth but conform to duty might still have, and thus confer, value of some other sort. We would also have to ask whether the objection extends to acts motivated by conscientiousness, which just *is* a settled desire to do one's duty. But rather than pursue these issues, I want to proceed directly to the main question: are acts generated by traits like honesty and justice really too unconnected to duty to satisfy the Kantian requirements for moral worth?

This is, I think, unlikely; for while the desires that constitute these traits are no doubt distinct from an awareness of duty, they may still be intimately linked to it. Indeed, this link can take no fewer than four (nonexclusive) forms. First, a given duty may be implicated in a desire's object, so that what, say, an honest person wants is precisely to act as the duty to be honest requires. Second, the duty to be honest, or an agent's awareness of it, may be what originally leads him or her to want to act honestly. Third, the duty to be honest, or an agent's awareness of it, may be what sustains his or her desire to act honestly. And, fourth, even if one's desire to act honestly is not at first connected to any awareness of duty, the honest acts that it motivates may themselves produce a connection. As Aristotle noted, it is precisely by becoming accustomed to acting in certain ways that we often become responsive to the reasons for acting in those ways.

Once again, each link raises issues that cannot be pursued here. But even without further analysis, we can see that if any of them holds, the trait of honesty will indeed have moral value. For if honesty is tied to duty in any of the first three ways, then all the acts that arise from it are, at least mediately, motivated by duty; while if honesty is linked to duty in the fourth way, then it is causally efficacious in leading agents to be motivated by duty. Because we may reasonably expect one or more of the links to hold, we may also reasonably expect the trait of honesty to have moral value. Moreover, by the same reasoning, we may draw similar conclusions about such other traits as justice, charity, kindness, tact, generosity, and sensitivity to suffering.

COHERENTISM AND THE VALUE OF VIRTUE

Both the Aristotelian and the deontological analyses offer promising ways of justifying virtue claims. But what, finally, of our third approach to virtue? Does coherentism also allow us to argue that certain character traits have value just in themselves?

That depends on how well perfectionism fits together with all our other beliefs. It is therefore significant that many prereflective beliefs do, at least on the surface, appear perfectionist. For example, most people probably would agree that even if lives spent in pursuit of trivial or mindless gratification are successful on their own terms, they are less worthwhile than lives of intellectual, personal, political, or artistic engagement. Moreover, unlike Mill, most of us seem willing to say this whether or not we believe that anyone who is competently acquainted with both sorts of life would choose the latter. Along similar lines, most of us believe that many forms of excellence are in themselves worth achieving, and that outstanding intellectual, athletic, and aesthetic accomplishments are great goods. We also attach value to various traits, such as dignity, grace, and humor, that do not obviously contribute to duty or remove impediments to flourishing. At the other end of the spectrum, we believe that servile, cringing behavior is unseemly and that indifference to filth in one's surroundings or person is degraded. It would of course beg the question to say that any one of these beliefs is justified merely because it is held. However, it does *not* beg the question to say that we hold so many of these beliefs that rejecting perfectionism would require a wholesale revision of our belief system.

But while this argument is not question begging, it is also not decisive; for despite initial appearances, the claim that these beliefs are perfectionist is not self-evident. Even if introspection supports a perfectionist reading—and that itself is unclear—introspection is not infallible and other interpretations remain possible. One alternative is that our apparently perfectionist beliefs are really about flourishing, and that we only value excellence, dignity, and the rest because we regard them as good *for persons*. Another possibility, elaborated by Hume, is that we only value those pursuits, achievements, and traits that we take to be useful or pleasing to their possessors or others.[28] Because we must value utility, pleasure, and, I have argued, flourishing anyhow, both alternatives presuppose a simpler value scheme than does perfectionism.

However, in other respects, each alternative introduces new complications. The first suggestion—that we only value excellence, decency, and the rest because we take them to be good for persons—is problematic because it raises, but does not answer, the question of *why* we take just these pursuits, accomplishments, and traits to be good for persons. Because trivial, unambitious, and even degraded lives can be pleasant enough, the reason is unlikely to lie solely in our beliefs about what makes people happy. The obvious alternative is that we believe that persons benefit from having traits, engaging in pursuits, and achieving goals that are inherently worthwhile. It is natural, in other words, to see our conception of human flourishing as itself rooted in perfectionism. But if so, then we cannot without circularity say that all apparently perfectionist beliefs are really beliefs about flourishing.

This point may be made in another way. Recently several philosophers have made a plausible case for the view that practical deliberation aims at establishing not what will best satisfy our desires, but rather what we ought to desire.[29] If this is so, then we cannot, from the deliberative perspective, regard desire satisfaction as the only thing with value. Nor, for similar reasons, can we regard our own well-being as the only thing with value; for, as Joseph Raz says, it is neither tautological nor true that we pursue our well-being. That is, it is false that we pursue our goals, which define our well-being, because they are our goals. We pursue them because they are, as we believe, worth pursuing.[30]

Of course, in trying to decide whether a goal is worth pursuing, we may indeed consider its probable effects on our lives. However, even when we do, any expectation of enhanced well-being is arguably a consequence rather than the basis of our assessment of its value.

Therefore, it seems unlikely that all beliefs that seem perfectionist are really about what is conducive to well-being or flourishing. But what, next, of the related view that our apparently perfectionist beliefs are really about what is generally useful or pleasing to the agent *or others?* Because the judgment that utility and pleasure have value does not seem parasitic on other beliefs about value, this suggestion does not obviously reintroduce perfectionism at any deeper level. Moreover, the suggestion may well account for a subset of our apparently perfectionist beliefs. For example, when we attribute value to intellectual accomplishments, or to traits like grace and wit, our judgments may well be grounded in our awareness that intellectual accomplishments often yield useful knowledge and that grace and wit ease social friction.

But in many other cases, the Humean move is far less plausible. It is, in particular, quite implausible when used to explain the value that we attach to pursuits, accomplishments, and traits that have no discernible utility beyond the fact that their existence pleases us. If we were to say that we value these pursuits, accomplishments, and traits merely *because* they please us, we would be unable to answer the question of *why* they please us. Why, for instance, are we delighted by the agility and toughness that a wide receiver displays in making a hard catch, or the sheer brilliance of a writer's use of language? And why are we impressed by displays of dignity and poise but appalled by self-abasement and degradation? If these reactions are not to be brute, inexplicable facts, they must themselves be grounded in evaluative beliefs; and here again, the obvious candidates are perfectionist. When we are pleased by excellence, dignity, and the rest, the reason appears to be precisely that we do regard them as valuable; and the same holds, mutatis mutandis, of our displeasure at self-abasement and degradation. But if what pleases us does thus reflect prior perfectionist commitments, it will again be circular to dismiss those commitments as mere manifestations of what pleases us.

We have, then, powerful independent grounds for regarding our ordinary belief system as perfectionist. When these grounds are taken into account, the case for perfectionism rests not merely on our prereflective beliefs but also in a meta-argument for a particular way of interpreting them. Of course, fully to make that case, we would no doubt have to draw on many other elements of our belief system. Also, fully to defend any specific perfectionist claim, we would have to show that it is a part of the most coherent overall reconstruction of our belief system, and not a mere product of bias or accident of our cultural history. Because these tasks, too, are beyond our scope, I shall again simply register my confidence that they can be accomplished. If they can, we may hope to vindicate yet a further group of familiar virtue claims.

CONCLUSION: THREE DIFFICULTIES

In the preceding sections, I presented a number of complementary answers to the question, "How can we know which traits are objectively worth having?" While I provided few details, the thrust of my argument is that virtue poses no special epistemological problems. But precisely because it makes the epistemology of virtue so unproblematical, my way of framing the issue is sure to invite suspicion. To end, I wish to consider three possible sources of difficulty.

1. *Conflict.* Perhaps the most obvious worry is that the proposed account proves too much. As long as virtue is understood exclusively in terms of either flourishing or duty, we may have some hope of limiting the virtues to a set of mutually compatible traits. Even if we abandon the Platonic idea that anyone who has one virtue *must* have all the rest, we may hope to retain the weaker view that anyone who has one virtue *may* have all the rest. This is important because unless the virtues are at least compati-

ble, an inquiry into their value will not show us why we should strive to be one sort of person rather than another. However, if the epistemology of virtue is as pluralistic and eclectic as I suggest—if virtue claims can be justified through appeals to either flourishing *or* duty *or* inherent value—then the virtues are probably *not* compatible. For, to cite just one well-known example, the dedication and single-mindedness that are required to achieve, say, artistic excellence seem positively inimical to the concern for others that is required by duty.

While there is clearly something to this, the amount of conflict among the traits that acquire value from different sources should not be overstated. Even if some of those traits do conflict, many more do not. For instance, gentleness and tact, which are valuable because they are elements of moral goodness, seem fully compatible with the single-mindedness and dedication that are required by artistic excellence. Conversely, intellectual curiosity, which is essential for certain forms of achievement, seems fully compatible with the conscientiousness that is conducive to dutiful action. And, as we saw, many other traits, such as honesty, justice, and courage (and, we may add, self-discipline, patience, and good judgment) seem valuable both because they make possible various elements of a flourishing life and because they help agents to do the right thing.

Given these and many similar considerations, the degree of conflict among the traits that our approach counts as virtues is likely to be small. But even so, the fact that the account shows *any* virtues to be incompatible may seem disquieting. For if it does not paint a unified picture of the virtuous person, it may seem to preclude any full answer to the question, "What sorts of persons should we be?"

It is not clear how much, if at all, a theory's inability to answer this question fully should be held against it. But even if nothing less than a full answer will do, nothing yet said shows that our account cannot provide one. To establish that, one would have to show not merely that the account classifies incompatible traits as virtues, but also that the values that make these traits worth having are themselves incommensurable. If instead the underlying values *are* commensurable—if, say, the value of achieving (a certain degree of) artistic excellence can be compared to the value of having (a certain amount of) moral goodness—then the conflict between the single-mindedness that is necessary for artistic excellence and the concern for others that is required by moral goodness will not show that we cannot know whether to cultivate the single-mindedness or the concern. Instead, it will show only that to find out which trait, or which mixture of the traits, to cultivate, we must ask whether artistic excellence or moral goodness is more valuable.

The deeper question, then, is whether distinct values are always commensurable. That is yet another large issue that cannot be resolved here. However, one argument for incommensurability warrants special attention, both because of the popularity of its guiding premise and because of its larger resonance. This is the appeal to what Raz calls "the dependence of value on social forms."[31]

2. *Social Forms.* As Raz and numerous others have noted, many if not all significant activities derive their specific nature from the social setting in which they are performed. That setting includes a background of "shared beliefs, folklore, high culture, collectively shared metaphors and imagination, and so on."[32] Taken together, these beliefs and understandings confer meaning on what are otherwise gross physical events. For example,

> in principle one may be born into a society with no medical practice or knowledge endowed with an innate knowledge of medicine. One could then cure many diseases, but one could not be a medical doctor, of the kind we have in our society. It takes more than medical knowledge or curing powers to do that. A doctor participates in a complex social form, involving general recognition of a medical practice, its social organization, its status in society, its conventions about which matters are addressed to doctors and which are not . . . and its conventions about the suitable relations between doctors and their patients.[33]

Generalized, these remarks suggest that virtually all valuable activities depend for their content and meaning on a social and intellectual climate that could easily have been otherwise and is constantly evolving. And from this, Raz concludes that "the existence of certain social forms is a contingent matter likely to frustrate any attempt at comprehensive ranking [of values] from any point of view."[34]

But for our purposes, this argument is doubly inconclusive. First, even if it did establish the incommensurability of the value of practicing medicine in our society as compared to other societies, or the incommensurability of the value of practicing medicine and, say, law in our society, the argument would not establish the incommensurability of the broader values of well-being, moral goodness, and excellence. While it is true that persons cannot achieve these values without participating in various activities that are constituted by social forms, it is also true that achieving well-being, etc., does not require participation in any particular activities. Hence, as Raz himself insists, neither well-being nor moral goodness nor excellence presupposes any particular set of social forms. So, even if the contingency of social forms did show various specific activities to be incommensurable in value, it would not show this about the broader values to which we have appealed.

But neither, secondly, does the contingency of social forms show that even specific activities are incommensurable in value. Indeed, strictly speaking, nothing yet said shows value to depend on social forms at all. What has been shown, instead, is only that the *nature* of many valuable activities depends on social forms. For example, what depends on the prevailing attitudes toward medicine is not the value of that practice, but only what it currently involves. And because of this, it seems perfectly consistent to say both that medicine in its current form is constituted by the prevailing attitudes and that the value of the practice as it now exists can be compared to the value of the practice as it would exist given different attitudes. Nor is it any less consistent to compare the value of the practice of medicine that is made possible by the prevailing attitudes toward doctors, health, etc., with the value of the practice of, say, architecture that is made possible by the prevailing attitudes toward nature, human needs, the environment, etc.

By holding firm to the insight that social forms determine the nature of the activities available to us but not the value of those activities, we can also disarm a related objection. I have tried to show that, and how, we can know that various traits are valuable. However, the objectivity of these conclusions would itself be threatened by the dependence of value on social forms. Because

social forms are accidents of history—because they involve many
beliefs, metaphors, and attitudes that lack roots in the nature of
things—the dependence of value on social forms would suggest
that value, too, is not objective, but is merely a matter of convention. But the threat of conventionalism will *not* arise if it is only
the *nature* of a valuable activity that depends on social forms. In
that case, it will indeed be a matter of convention that our activities have the nature they do; but it will not be a matter of convention that activities with this nature, when they exist, have or lack
value. Because of this, the contribution of social forms will not
preclude the possibility that values are objective.

3. *Knowing and Being.* At the outset, I offered some reasons
for taking the epistemology of virtue seriously. However, despite
what is said there, the tenor of my analysis may seem inappropri-
ately cognitive. What really matters, it may be said, is not how
much someone *knows* about virtue, but how virtuous he or she *is*.
What is important is not having justified true beliefs about which
traits are valuable, but actually having valuable traits. And because the real issue is character and not knowledge, my emphasis
on the latter may seem misplaced.

It is important to be clear about *why* an emphasis on knowledge can seem problematical. The problem cannot be merely
that knowing a trait to be worth having does not guarantee having it. If that were the difficulty, we could simply concede the
point but insist that knowing about virtue is important for other
reasons. Those reasons could include either the inherent value
of knowledge or the need for guidance in our efforts at moral
education and self-improvement. Alternatively, we could revert
to the controversy about whether any conception of virtue is
sufficiently well grounded to provide a sound basis for political
action.

But while any of these replies would disarm the objection
that knowledge about virtue does not guarantee its possession,
none would obviously meet the further objection that in order
to acquire such knowledge, a person must have attitudes that
are actually *incompatible* with virtue. The thought here is that
the detachment and open-mindedness that are prerequisites of
philosophical inquiry are not fully consistent with the engagement of the truly virtuous person. To the inquirer, it must be

genuinely possible that traits like honesty and justice might turn out not to have value, or even be disvaluable. But to the just and honest person, abandoning honesty and justice are not real possibilities. Although G. E. M. Anscombe does not reject all theorizing about virtue, she seems to have something like this in mind when she writes that

> if someone really thinks, *in advance* that it is open to question whether such an action as procuring the judicial execution of the innocent should be quite excluded from consideration—I do not want to argue with him; he shows a corrupt mind.[35]

While Anscombe's point is undermined by the extremity of her anticonsequentialism—it is surely not corrupt to entertain the possibility that *some* outcomes might be so disastrous that acting unjustly to prevent them is justified—a more moderate version of her claim seems sound. If someone were to think, in advance, that it is genuinely open to question whether justice or honesty provides any reason for doing *anything,* he or she *would* show a corrupt mind.

But is this sort of open-mindedness really needed to prevent inquiry from degenerating into apologetics? Doubts arise when we consider the partially parallel topic of open-mindedness about logic. To someone with good inferential habits, the validity of a rule like *modus ponens* is, in one sense, not genuinely open to question. If such a person is convinced of both "p" and "if p then q," he or she will automatically also accept "q." Yet his or her commitment to *modus ponens* clearly does not prevent him or her from investigating the foundations of deductive inference, or from regarding even *modus ponens* as theoretically open to revision. When we say that the validity of *modus ponens* is for this person not genuinely open to question, what we mean is only that before seriously considering rejecting it, this person would have to reject many other central elements of his or her belief system that, at the moment, he or she sees no reason *to* reject.

And precisely the same is true of the virtuous person. In this case, too, the importance of acting honestly and justly is, in one sense, not open to question. If he or she judges an act to be dishonest or unjust, he or she will automatically recoil from performing it. Yet having this sort of commitment to honesty and justice—having an uncorrupted mind—surely need not prevent the virtuous person either from investigating the foundations of morality or from regarding his or her beliefs about the importance of being honest and just as theoretically open to revision. Here again, the sense in which the truth of those beliefs is not an open question for the virtuous person is only that before seriously considering rejecting them, he or she would have to reject many other central elements of his or her belief system that, at the moment, he or she sees no reason *to* reject.

This concludes my survey of the objections to the proposed account. I see no reason to retract the conclusion that virtue is epistemically on par with other normative notions. Of course, to say this is not to solve many substantive problems. While I have considered some aspects of some virtues by way of illustration, I have not tried to produce either a full list of the virtues or an account of which of them are most important. I also have not asked whether moral theory should be organized around virtue and character or around duty and action; and still less have I addressed the controversy about whether governments should try to make their citizens virtuous. If the magnitude of these unresolved questions is daunting, it is heartening that we at least have the epistemic resources to address them.[36]

NOTES

1. See, for example, John Rawls, *A Theory of Justice* (Cambridge: Harvard University Press, 1971); Ronald Dworkin, *A Matter of Principle* (Cambridge: Harvard University Press, 1985), part 3; Bruce Ackerman, *Social Justice in the Liberal State* (New Haven: Yale University Press, 1980); Charles Larmore, *Patterns of Moral Complexity* (Cambridge: Harvard University Press, 1987); D. A. Lloyd Thomas, *In Defense of Liberalism* (Oxford: Blackwell, 1988); and Thomas Nagel, "Moral Conflict and Political Legitimacy," *Philosophy and Public Affairs* 16, 3 (Summer 1987), 215–40.

2. For explicit versions of this claim, see Dworkin, "Liberalism," in *A Matter of Principle,* pp. 181–204, and Ackerman, *Social Justice in the Liberal State,* pp. 139 ff.

3. Not all proponents of neutralism endorse skepticism about vir-

tue and the good, and Rawls and Dworkin explicitly disavow it. Still, I think these epistemological worries are very much in the air, and are often an important unacknowledged source of the neutral-framework view's appeal. For a skeptical defense of neutralism, see Ackerman, *Social Justice in the Liberal State,* pp. 368–69. For an epistemological defense that turns on the difficulty rather than the impossibility of knowing which traits and ways of life are best, see Lloyd Thomas, *In Defense of Liberalism.*

4. Aristotle discusses virtue in the *Nicomachean Ethics* and the *Eudemian Ethics.* For illuminating commentary, see John Cooper, *Reason and Human Good in Aristotle* (Cambridge: Harvard University Press, 1975). Two modern treatments of virtue that have close affinities to Aristotle's are Alasdair MacIntyre, *After Virtue,* 2d ed. (Notre Dame: University of Notre Dame Press, 1984) and Philippa Foot, *Virtues and Vices* (Berkeley: University of California Press, 1978).

5. See, for example, Richard N. Boyd, "How to Be a Moral Realist," in Geoffrey Sayre-McCord, ed., *Essays on Moral Realism* (Ithaca: Cornell University Press, 1988), pp. 181–255.

6. Rawls defines virtues in terms of duty in *A Theory of Justice;* see p. 192 and passim. For defense of the deontological approach, see Sarah Conly, "Flourishing and the Failure of the Ethics of Virtue," *Midwest Studies in Philosophy.* Vol. 13, *Ethical Theory: Character and Virtue,* eds. Peter A. French, Thomas E. Euhling, Jr., and Howard K. Wettstein (Notre Dame: University of Notre Dame Press, 1988), pp. 83–96.

7. The perfectionist approach has fewer explicit defenders than the others. However, many whose official position is Aristotelian devote most of their attention to the question of why some traits are superior to others, and very little to the question of why having superior traits is a benefit. Often these theorists either leave this connection unexplained or else simply stipulate that it holds. When they do, they in effect take the position I call perfectionist.

8. Conly, "Flourishing and the Failure of the Ethics of Virtue," p. 84.

9. Richard Taylor, "Ancient Wisdom and Modern Folly," *Midwest Studies in Philosophy.* Vol. 13. p. 55. See also G. E. M. Anscombe, "Modern Moral Philosophy" in her *Ethics, Religion, and Politics: Collected Philosophical Papers.* Vol. 3 (Minneapolis: University of Minnesota Press, 1981), pp. 26–42.

10. Given the heterogeneity of the traits that have been considered virtues and the many cross-cutting ways in which those traits have been classified, we cannot rule out the possibility that virtue *has* no essence beyond what this formula expresses. I am sympathetic to this idea, but

shall not defend it here. Compare Edmund L. Pincoffs's suggestion that we "understand virtues and vices as dispositional properties that provide grounds for preference or avoidance of persons" (Edmund L. Pincoffs, *Quandaries and Virtues: Against Reductivism in Ethics* [Lawrence: University of Kansas Press, 1986], p. 82).

11. Although it is hard to measure these things, it seems to me that acceptance of foundationalism has recently been on the decline. This judgment is shared by Bernard Williams, who writes that "the foundationalist enterprise, of resting the structure of knowledge on some favored class of statements, has now generally been displaced in favor of a holistic type of model, in which some beliefs can be questioned, justified, or adjusted while others are kept constant, but there is no process by which they can all be questioned at once, or all justified in terms of (almost) nothing" (Bernard Williams, *Ethics and the Limits of Philosophy* [Cambridge: Harvard University Press, 1985], p. 113).

12. Rawls, *A Theory of Justice*, sec. 9 and *passim*. See also John Rawls, "Outline of a Decision Procedure for Ethics," *The Philosophical Review* 60 (1951), 177–97, and "The Independence of Moral Theory," *Proceedings and Addresses of the American Philosophical Association* 47 (1974/75), 5–22.

13. Compare, for example, the versions of coherentism advanced by W. V. O. Quine and by Lawrence BonJour. Quine develops his naturalistic version in many places, among them "Two Dogmas of Empiricism" in *From a Logical Point of View* (New York: Harper and Row, 1953), pp. 20–46. BonJour's version appears in *The Structure of Empirical Knowledge* (Cambridge: Harvard University Press, 1985).

14. What one regards as the crucial problems will depend on one's views about other matters. To an internalist, one very important problem is that even if a belief is infallible or highly reliable, a person is not justified in holding it unless he or she has good reason to regard it *as* infallible or highly reliable. This means that he or she must rely on some further belief about what *makes* the original belief infallible or highly reliable. But if the original belief's justification does thus depend on a further belief, then it is not self-justifying after all.

15. For discussion, see BonJour, *The Structure of Empirical Knowledge*, pp. 93–101, and W. V. O. Quine and J. S. Ullian, *The Web of Beliefs* (New York: Random House, 1970), ch. 5.

16. See, for example, W. V. O. Quine, "The Nature of Natural Knowledge" in *Mind and Language: Wolfson College Lectures*, ed. Samuel Guttenplan (Oxford: Oxford University Press, 1975), pp. 67–81, and BonJour, *The Structure of Empirical Knowledge*, part 2. The role of second-order beliefs is emphasized by Michael Williams, "Coherence,

Justification, and Truth," *Review of Metaphysics* 34 (December 1980), 243–72.

17. See Rawls, "The Independence of Moral Theory" and Norman Daniels, "Wide Reflective Equilibrium and Theory Acceptance in Ethics," *Journal of Philosophy* 76, 5 (May 1979), 256–82.

18. For example, they cite physiological theories that allow us to infer, from the fact that we believe we are confronted by an object with characteristic C, that our sense organs are probably being stimulated by an object with C; psychological theories that give us reason to regard our inferential practices as, within limits, reliable; and biological theories that suggest mechanisms through which reliable inference patterns might have developed in creatures like us. If a belief's truth is suggested by a combination of such considerations, then—so these theorists argue—our background theories provide evidence that it probably *is* true.

19. The supervenience of the moral upon the nonmoral is defended by Boyd in "How to Be a Moral Realist." See also Nicholas Sturgeon, "Moral Explanations" in David Copp and David Zimmerman, eds., *Morality, Reason, and Truth* (Totowa, N.J.: Rowman and Allanheld, 1985), pp. 49–78; Peter Railton, "Moral Realism," *Philosophical Review* 95, 2 (April 1986), 163–209; and David O. Brink, *Moral Realism and the Foundations of Ethics* (Cambridge: Harvard University Press, 1989). For criticism of the view that postulating moral facts helps us explain the existence of moral beliefs, see Gilbert Harman, *The Nature of Morality* (New York: Oxford University Press, 1977), ch. 1.

20. The constructivist approach is defended by John Rawls in "Kantian Constructivism in Moral Theory: The Dewey Lectures 1980," *Journal of Philosophy* 77, 9 (September 1980), 515–72; see especially 554–72. Rawls's constructivism is criticized by Brink in *Moral Realism and the Foundations of Ethics,* appendix 4.

21. Platonism is often thought to be refuted by its inability to explain how Platonic forms, or nonnatural moral facts, could causally influence our beliefs (or how, if they cannot causally influence our beliefs, we could possibly come to know them); see Paul Benacerraf, "What Numbers Could Not Be," *Philosophical Review* 74 (1965), 47–73. However, on a coherentist view of justification, the claim that all entities or facts are part of a single causal network is itself something that must be accepted or rejected on the basis of its coherence with our other beliefs. Hence, our independent commitment to moral objectivity, and the inadequacy of other theories of objectivity, itself exerts pressure against that claim.

22. For discussion of Aristotle's views, see Cooper, *Reason and Human Good in Aristotle.*

23. Larmore, *Patterns of Moral Complexity,* p. 34.

24. MacIntyre, *After Virtue,* p. 219. MacIntyre complicates but does not retract this contention in the discussion that follows.

25. Ibid., p. 219.

26. Ibid., p. 191.

27. This conclusion may seem to ignore the difficulties posed by amoralism. There is, notoriously, an unresolved question about what price, if any, a person pays for ignoring his or her moral duties. But the amoralist could ask that question even if he or she *did* concede that conforming to duty is important—indeed, the question "Why should I care about what is important?" is merely a variant of "Why should I care about conforming to duty?"—so establishing the importance of acting dutifully will not improve our prospects of answering him or her. By contraposition, the difficulty of answering him or her cannot damage our ability to show that acting dutifully is important.

28. David Hume, *An Enquiry concerning the Principles of Morals,* in *Hume's Enquiries,* 2d ed., ed. L. A. Selby-Bigge (Oxford: Oxford University Press, 1902, 1955).

29. See, for example, G. R. Grice, *The Grounds of Moral Judgement* (Cambridge: Harvard University Press, 1967); E. J. Bond, *Reason and Value* (Cambridge: Harvard University Press, 1983); and Joseph Raz, *The Morality of Freedom* (Oxford: Oxford University Press, 1986).

30. Raz, *The Morality of Freedom,* p. 316.

31. Ibid., p. 398.

32. Ibid., p. 311.

33. Ibid., p. 310–11.

34. Ibid., p. 398.

35. Anscombe, "Modern Moral Philosophy," p. 40.

36. This chapter has been improved by the constructive suggestions of Hilary Kornblith, Arthur Kuflik, and Derk Pereboom.

5

VIRTUES AND RELATIVISM

MICHAEL J. PERRY

George Sher calls his topic "the epistemology of virtue."[1] By "virtue" Sher means simply a "character trait that is for some important reason desirable or worth having."[2] At one point Sher identifies his central question as, "what can we know about the virtues if some version of coherentism is true"?[3] At another point he asks, "How can we know which traits are objectively worth having?"[4] He concludes that "while beliefs about virtues may be vulnerable to skeptical challenge, they are no more vulnerable than any other normative claims."[5] According to Sher, "virtue is epistemologically on a par with other normative notions."[6]

Sher sketches three approaches to the question of how, if at all, we can know what virtues there are—that is, what character traits are "desirable or worth having": the Aristotelian approach, the deontological approach, and the perfectionist approach.[7] The bulk of his argument is devoted to showing, "first, that each competing approach to virtue does give us reason to regard various traits as valuable, and, second, that the resulting insights are not undermined by any general disqualifying considerations."[8]

In this chapter I do two things. First, I comment briefly on a peripheral but not unimportant aspect of Sher's chapter. Second, I comment on the problem of relativism about virtue, one part of which—the pluralism part—Sher addresses, another, more fundamental part of which—the nihilism part—he does not.

ARISTOTELIANISM AND PERFECTIONISM

My brief comment concerns Sher's effort to distinguish between Aristotelianism and what he calls perfectionism. Sher writes,

> [I]f courage, wisdom, and the rest are virtues, the reason may be . . . [not] that they are conducive to or constitutive of any further good, but more simply that their *own* existence is a good. It can be maintained, in other words, that a trait is a virtue whenever it, or its possession, has intrinsic value or worth. Like the Aristotelian approach, this suggestion construes virtue in terms of good rather than right; but unlike the Aristotelian approach, it equates virtues not with character traits that are good *for their possessors,* but rather with character traits that are good *in themselves.* To mark this difference, I shall call this . . . [latter] approach *perfectionist.*[9]

This passage seems to me confused. It doesn't make sense to distinguish character traits that are good "for their possessors" from character traits that are good "in themselves"—that is, intrinsically good. It would make sense to distinguish, for example, traits that are good merely for their possessors from those that are good for others as well as their possessors. It would also make sense to distinguish traits that are intrinsically good from those that are merely instrumentally good. But value or worth—whether intrinsic or instrumental—is *always* value or worth *to someone(s),* or *to something.* A character trait that is intrinsically good must be so *for someone,* whether its possessor or someone else. To say that a character trait is intrinsically good for its possessor is simply to say that the trait is at least partly constitutive of, not merely instrumentally related to, its possessor's well-being. The notion of something being intrinsically good or "inherently worthwhile"[10] independently of its relation to anyone, whether a human being, a nonhuman sentient creature, or a suprapersonal God, is perfectly opaque. Putting aside things that are values either for nonhuman sentient creatures or for God, we may say that "the category of values is anthropocentric, in that it corresponds to interests which can only take root in creatures with something approaching our own affective make-up. . . . [V]alues are only ascribable from points of view constituted by human patterns of affective response. A wholly dispassionate eye would be as blind to them as a black-and-white camera to chromatic colors."[11]

I would therefore omit from the catalogue of "competing approaches to the epistemology of virtue" the position Sher calls perfectionism. Any plausible Aristotelian approach, that is, any plausible conception of human good, will include elements that are perfectionist in this sense, not to be confused with Sher's sense: It will include, inter alia, claims that some things are good for some or all human beings, whether or not they are desired. It will also include claims that some things are good for human beings if and only if desired. (Like many others, I am skeptical of deontological claims of morality—that is, of the possibility of justifying claims about what one morally ought to do, including claims about moral duty or obligation, except on the basis, ultimately, of claims about the requirements of authentic human well-being.)[12]

Relativism, Nihilism, and Aristotelian Virtue

My longer comment concerns the problem of relativism—or, more precisely, as I shall explain, the problem of nihilism—that challenges the Aristotelian approach to virtue.

My own conception of morality is Aristotelian.[13] I agree with Sher about the Aristotelian approach to the question, How we can know what character traits are valuable? As Sher seems to acknowledge, for the Aristotelian that question is secondary. A character trait is valuable for a person or persons, in the Aristotelian view, if its possession by the person is conducive to her living a good or fitting life (good/fitting for her, given the particular human being she is), if its possession is, in that sense, conducive to her well-being. So, to know what character traits are valuable for a person is simply to know the character traits the possession of which is conducive to living a good life, to well-being. The primary question, therefore, is, How can we know what way or ways of life are good for a person—that is, how can we know what a person's well-being consists in?

Is there reason to think that there are any nonrelative or universal virtues: character traits valuable not just for some, at

least one, person(s), but for all persons? Sher's answer, quite
plausible in my view, is affirmative.[14] Note, however, what an
affirmative answer implies: that some ways of choosing, for example, courageously, wisely, generously, justly[15]—and, in that
sense, some ways of living—are good, not just for some persons,
but for all. An affirmative answer implies, in that sense, that
some ways of living are conducive to *human* good or well-being:
to the good or well-being of all human beings.

But is there reason to think that there are ways of living good,
not just for this person or that, or for this group or that, but *for
human beings generally?*[16] That is, is there reason to think, with
Aristotle, that there are ways of life that are good in a nonrelative/
universal sense and, therefore, that some traits are virtues in a
nonrelative sense? As Martha Nussbaum has recently reminded
us, Aristotle himself was a nonrelativist, a universalist, about the
human good and, therefore, about virtue."[17]

I wish to distinguish pluralism from nihilism about the human
good. The more fundamental challenge to the Aristotelian-
universalist approach is not pluralism but nihilism.

The universalist position is not inconsistent with the pluralist
view that human beings are different from one another in many
significant respects, that human beings have many different
needs and wants. The universalist position is that whatever the
significant differences among them, human beings have many of
the same needs, that some needs are common to all human
beings, that, therefore, some things are of value to every human
being, that what satisfies some needs, common human needs, is,
at least in normal circumstances, good for every human being,[18]
and that there are some things all human beings must have or do
if they are to live fulfilling lives, or at least lives as fulfilling as any
of which they are capable.[19] To accept the universalist position
that there are common human needs is not to deny that particular conceptions of needs are "culturally constructed and discur-
sively interpreted."[20] At the same time, however, to accept that
particular conceptions of needs, including particular conceptions of common human needs, are socially constructed[21] "is not
to say that any need interpretation is as good as any other."[22]

Any plausible conception of human good must be pluralist.[23]
Human beings differ from one another across time, of course.

But they also differ from one another across space. They differ from one another interculturally. They even differ from one another intraculturally. Indeed, the differences are sometimes greater intraculturally than interculturally.[24]

Sher's position on human good is, sensibly, pluralist. He acknowledges that different ways of life can be good for different persons. Indeed, different ways of life can be good, albeit in different ways, for the same person. But Sher suggests, quite plausibly, that there are nonetheless at least some features that any life good for some human beings has in common with any other life good for other human beings—that at least some ways of living/choosing, and so some character traits, are valuable across the different ways of life that are good for different persons. He suggests, that is, that pluralism about human good is not incompatible with universalism about human good.[25]

A view of human good or well-being can be universalist as well as pluralist: it can acknowledge sameness as well as difference, commonality as well as variety.[26] Inevitably differences exist as to how universalist and how pluralist a view of human good should be.[27] Such differences, different and competing conceptions or interpretations of common human needs, are often reasonable, given the inconclusive state of moral anthropology. But is a radically anti-universalist position reasonable? Is it plausible to insist that human beings do not have significant needs in common— that is, significant *social* needs beyond the merely biological needs all human beings obviously share? Is it plausible to deny that there are needs common to all human beings, such that what satisfies them is good for every human being? Such a view, which Richard Rorty, among others, seems to advance,[28] is not pluralist ("although some things are good for all humans, other things are good only for some humans"), but nihilist ("nothing is good for all humans").

Why would anyone doubt that there are significant needs common to all human beings? Some significant appetites and senses, social appetites and senses no less than biological, certainly seem to be shared across the human species. Of course, shared appetites and senses can be and often are shaped in different ways by different cultures *and* by different individual histories within a culture. Not all differences are due merely to

differences in how common appetites and senses have been
shaped: Some significant appetites and senses are not shared
across the human species. Nevertheless, some appetites and
senses are shared. This means, of course, that some significant
social needs are shared across the human species: the needs that
are the correlates of the shared appetites and senses. Some needs
are universal and not merely local in character. It is silly to suppose that this fact does not have implications for morality, including the morality of virtue. Philippa Foot has put these points
succinctly and eloquently:

> Granted that it is wrong to asssume an identity of aim between
> peoples of different cultures; nevertheless there is a great deal
> that all men have in common. All need affection, the cooperation
> of others, a place in a community, and help in trouble. It isn't true
> to suppose that human beings can flourish without these things—
> being isolated, despised or embattled, or without courage or
> hope. We are not, therefore, simply expressing values that we
> happen to have if we think of some moral systems as good moral
> systems and others as bad. Communities as well as individuals can
> live wisely or unwisely.[29]

Given the seeming obviousness of these allied premises—that
there are significant needs common to all human beings, that
therefore some things (whatever satisfies a common human
need) are of value to every human being, that there is, in that
sense, a good common to every human being, a *human* good—
what might lead one to doubt or even deny all this? Why would
anyone deny what according to Rorty "historicist thinkers [ever
since Hegel] have denied[:] that there is such a thing as 'human
nature' or the 'deepest level of the self.' Their strategy has been
to insist that socialization, and thus historical circumstance, goes
all the way down—that there is nothing 'beneath' socialization or
prior to history which is definatory of the human. Such writers
tell us that the question 'What is it to be a human being?' should
be replaced by questions like 'What is it to inhabit a rich
twentieth-century democratic society?' "[30]

This "historicist" or "postmodern" insistence that it's socialization all the way down is not merely some innocuous if silly position in a far corner of academic philosophy. The denial of *human*

good or well-being, of *human* needs—the denial, in that sense, of "the human," of "human nature," in the sense of the social as distinct from merely biological dimension of human being[31]—is quite common among contemporary thinkers.[32] More importantly, the denial is clearly subversive of discourse about human rights, a discourse many of us, I assume, take very seriously.[33] The question is all the more urgent, therefore: What might lead to, what might explain, a denial of the human? What might lead to or explain nihilism, as distinct from pluralism, about human good?

I don't have a confident answer. Perhaps a partial explanation is that some such denials confuse conceptions of human nature with human nature itself. It is one thing to insist that conceptions of human nature are irreducibly contingent, that they—like the languages, the vocabularies, that infuse the conceptions—bear the traces (and nothing but the traces?) of particular times and places, of particular histories and cultures. To insist that there is no such thing as human nature is another thing altogether. It is one thing to insist that conceptions of human nature are socially constructed and that there are good reasons to be wary about any such conception. It is another thing altogether to insist that we can get along quite nicely, thank you, without any conception of human nature—or to insist that putative human nature itself is socially constructed ("there's no there there, it's socialization all the way down").[34] A recent comment by Robin West, though directed specifically to feminist theorists, is relevant here: "Surely we can have this both ways. A skepticism toward particular claims of objective truth, a particular account of the self, and any particular account of gender, sexuality, biology or what is or is not natural, is absolutely necessary to a healthy and modern feminism. But that skepticism need not require an unwillingness to entertain descriptions of subjective and intersubjective authenticity."[35]

As Philippa Foot, Martha Nussbaum, and Robin West understand, but Richard Rorty and other "historicists" apparently do not, questions about *human* good, about what is good for human beings generally, including questions about *human* rights, are not misconceived. Contra Rorty, the question, "What is it to be a human being?" should not be replaced by other questions. This is not to deny that there are other important, and sometimes complementary, questions, such as, "What is it to inhabit a rich twentieth-century democratic society?" Nor is it to deny "the very poignant sense in which we may be unable to choose between cultures" or between ways of life within a single culture: "We may indeed be able to understand the transition [from one culture or way of life to another] in terms of gain or loss, but there may be some of both, and an overall judgement may be hard to make."[36] It bears emphasis, however, that this inability to adjudicate between or among cultures or ways of life, as Charles Taylor has recently explained,

> presupposes that we can, in principle, understand and recognize the goods of another society [or of another way of life] as goods-for-everyone (and hence for ourselves). That these are not combinable with out own home-grown goods-for-everyone may indeed be tragic but is no different in principle for any of the other dilemmas we may be in through facing incombinable goods, even within our own way of life. There is no guarantee that universally valid goods should be perfectly combinable, and certainly not in all situations. . . . It may be that our contact with certain cultures will force us to recognize incommensurability, as against simply a balance of goods-and-bads-for-everyone that we cannot definitively weigh up. But we certainly shouldn't assume that this is so a priori.[37]

NOTES

1. George Sher, "Knowing about Virtue," this volume, p. 91.
2. Id., p. 94.
3. Id., p. 95.
4. Id., p. 106. It is not clear what work Sher wants "objectively" to do here or elsewhere in his paper (e.g., at p. 91: "[A]re we making an objective normative claim?"). Why not ask simply, How can we know which traits are worth having? Is Sher's "objectively" the "objectively" of the epistemological foundationalist? Surely not, given his embrace of epistemological coherentism. See id., pp. 94–98. Is it then the "objectively" of the anthropological universalist? See note 17 (Martha Nussbaum on the sense in which Aristotle's account of the human good is "objective").
5. Sher, "Knowing about Virtue," p. 92.

6. Id., p. 112.

7. Id., pp. 92–94.

8. Id., pp. 98–112.

9. Id., p. 93.

10. Id., p. 104.

11. A. W. Price, "Varieties of Objectivity and Values," *Proceedings of the Aristotelian Society* 83 (1983): 103, 106. See also David Hume, *A Treatise of Human Nature*, L. Selby-Bigge, ed. (Oxford: Oxford University Press, 1973), p. 469: "Virtue and vice, therefore, may be compar'd to sounds, colours, heat and cold, which, according to modern philosophy, are not qualities in objects, but perceptions in the mind: And this discovery in morals, like that other in physics, is to be regarded as a considerable advancement of the speculative sciences; tho', like that, too, it has little or no influence on practice"; Anthony Kronman, "A Comment on Dean Clark," *Columbia Law Review* 89 (1989): 1748, 1755: "[The view] that there are goods which are not the goods of any human beings at all, is likely to appear . . . wholly unintelligible, for it conflicts with what is perhaps the deepest and most widely shared orthodoxy of modern moral thought—the assumption that only the goods of human beings (or perhaps sentient beings) count in assessing different practices and institutions." Cf. Robin Lovin, "Empiricism and Christian Social Thought," *Annual of Society of Christian Ethics* (1982): 25, 41: "Ethics will never be like physics, chemistry, or certain types of sociology, because it understands the moral reality to be about an interaction between persons and the world which can only be known from the reports of those who experience that interaction."

12. See Ronald Beiner, *Political Judgment* (Chicago: University of Chicago Press, 1984), pp. 144 and 186 n. 18 [quoting John McDowell, "Virtue and Reason," *Monist* 62 (1979): 331, 347–48]:

> The study of ethics, according to the classical conception, does not tell one what to do or furnish maxims for conduct; rather, it forms the kind of person one is— making one, for instance, more reflective, more discriminating, more attentive— and it is only in this indirect way that it has an influence upon practice. . . . It is sometimes complained that Aristotle does not attempt to outline a decision procedure for questions about how to behave. But we have good reason to be suspicious of the assumption that there must be something to be found along the route he does not follow.

See also Bernard Williams, *Ethics and the Limits of Philosophy* (Cambridge, Mass.: Harvard University Press, 1985), pp. 4–5:

> [Socrates' question, "How should one live?"] is not immediate; it is not about what I should do now, or next. It is about a manner of life. The Greeks them-

selves were much impressed by the idea that such a question must, consequently, be about a whole life and that a good way of living had to issue in what, at its end, would be seen to have been a good life. . . . The idea that one must think, at this very general level, about *a whole life* may seem less compelling to some of us than it did to Socrates. But his question still does press a demand for reflection on one's life *as a whole,* from every aspect and all the way down, even if we do not place as much weight as the Greeks did on how it may end.

For a recent essay on "the primacy of ethical decisionmaking, which takes character or the process of character formation as crucial," see Joel Kupperman, "Character and Ethical Theory," in Peter A. French, Theodore E. Uehling, Jr., and Howard K. Wettstein (eds.), *Midwest Studies in Philosophy.* Vol. 13, *Ethical Theory: Character and Virtue* (Notre Dame: University of Notre Dame, 1988); the quotation is from p. 115.

For an extended discussion of the "Why be moral?" problem from a neo-Aristotelian perspective, see Rüdiger Bittner, *What Reason Demands* (Cambridge: Harvard University Press, 1989). See also Stephen Scott, "Motive and Justification," *Journal of Philosophy* 85 (1988): 479, 499: "When he was deliberating about how to live, St. Augustine asked, 'What does anything matter, if it does not have to do with happiness?' His question requires explanation, because he is not advising selfishness nor the reduction of other people to utilities, and even qualification, because other things can have some weight. All the same, the answer he expects is obviously right: only a happy life matters conclusively. If I had a clear view of it, I could have no motive to decline it, I could regret nothing by accepting it, I would have nothing about which to deliberate further." Cf. Richard Taylor, "Ancient Wisdom and Modern Folly," in French et al., *Midwest Studies in Philosophy.* Vol. 13, pp. 54, 57, 58: "The Greek *eudaimonia* is always translated 'happiness,' which is unfortunate, for the meaning we attach to the word happiness is thin indeed compared to what the Greeks meant by *eudaimonia. Fulfillment* might be a better term, though this, too, fails to capture the richness of the original term. . . . The concept of happiness in modern philosophy, as well as in popular thinking, is superficial indeed in comparison."

13. See Michael J. Perry, *Morality, Politics, and Law* (New York: Oxford University Press, 1988), chs. 1 and 2. See also note 12.

14. Sher, "Knowing about Virtue," pp. 99–100.

15. See id., p. 91.

16. See Martha Nussbaum, "Non-Relative Virtues: An Aristotelian Approach," in French et al., *Midwest Studies in Philosophy.* Vol. 13, p. 33: "To many current defenders of an ethical approach based on the virtues, the return to the virtues is connected with a turn toward relativism—toward, that is, the view that the only appropriate criteria of

ethical goodness are local ones, internal to the traditions and practices of each local society or group that asks itself questions about the good. . . . [These writers] all connect virtue ethics with a relativist denial that ethics, correctly understood, offers any transcultural norms, justifiable with reference to reasons of universal human validity, with reference to which we may appropriately criticize different local conceptions of the good."

17. See id., p. 33: "[Aristotle] was not only the defender of an ethical theory based on the virtues, but also the defender of a single objective account of the human good, or human flourishing. [Aristotle's] account is supposed to be objective in the sense that it is justifiable with reference to reasons that do not derive merely from local traditions and practices, but rather from features of humanness that lie beneath all local traditions and are there to be seen whether or not they are in fact recognized in local traditions."

18. Though not necessarily congenial to the actual preferences of every human being, of course.

19. To claim that there are common human needs is not to deny that it might be possible to satisfy such a need in various ways. See note 26.

20. Nancy Fraser, *Unruly Practices: Power, Discourse, and Gender in Contemporary Social Theory* (Minneapolis: University of Minnesota Press, 1989), p. 181.

21. For a brief, commonsense discussion of "social constructionism," "essentialism," etc., see John Boswell, "Gay History," *Atlantic*, February 1989, p. 74 [review of David F. Greenberg, *The Construction of Homosexuality* (Chicago: University of Chicago Press, 1988)].

22. Fraser, *Unruly Practices*, p. 181; see also pp. 181–82. Cf. note 34 (commenting on Fraser).

23. See Hilary Putnam, *Reason, Truth, and History* (Cambridge: Harvard University Press, 1981), p. 148:

If today we differ with Aristotle it is in being much more pluralistic than Aristotle was. Aristotle recognized that different ideas of Eudaemonia, different conceptions of human flourishing, might be appropriate for different individuals on account of the difference in their constitution. But he seemed to think that ideally there was some sort of constitution that every one ought to have; that in an ideal world (overlooking the mundane question of who would grow the crops and who would bake the bread) everyone would be a philosopher. We agree with Aristotle that different ideas of human flourishing are appropriate for individuals with different constitutions, but we go further and believe that even in the ideal world there would be different constitutions, that diversity is part of the ideal. And we see some degree of tragic tension between ideals, that the fulfillment of some ideals always excludes the fulfillment of some others.

As Putnam goes on to emphasize, however, "[B]elief in a pluralistic ideal is not the same thing as belief that every ideal of human flourishing is as good as every other. We reject ideals of human flourishing as wrong, as infantile, as sick, as one-sided." Referring to a "sick standard of rationality" and "sick conception(s) of human flourishing," he adds that "we have just as much right to regard some 'evaluational' casts of mind as sick (and we all do) as we do to regard some 'cognitional' casts of mind as sick" [id., pp. 140, 147]. See also Bernard Williams, *Ethics and the Limits of Philosophy*, p. 153: "There are many and various forms of human excellence which will not all fit together into one harmonious whole, so any determinate ethical outlook is going to represent some kind of specialization of human possibilities. That idea is deeply entrenched in any naturalistic . . . or historical conception of human nature—that is, in any adequate conception of it—and I find it hard to believe that it will be overcome by an objective inquiry, or that human beings could turn out to have a much more determinate nature than is suggested by what we already know, one that timelessly demanded a life of a particular kind."

24. See Amelie Rorty, "Relativism, Persons, and Practices," in Michael Krausz (ed.), *Relativism: Interpretation and Confrontation* (Notre Dame: University of Notre Dame Press, 1989), pp. 418, 419: "Sometimes there is unexpectedly subtle and refined communication across radically different cultures; sometimes there is insurmountable bafflement and systematic misunderstanding between relatively close cultures. For the most part, however, we live in the interesting grey area of partial success and partial failure of interpretation and communication. The grey area is to be found at home among neighbors as well as abroad among strangers."

25. Sher, "Knowing about Virtue," pp. 108–10.

26. Cf. Stuart Hampshire, *Two Theories of Morality* (Oxford: Oxford University Press, 1977), pp. 48–49:

That there should be an abstract ethical ideal, the good for men in general, is not inconsistent with there being great diversity in preferred ways of life, even among men living at the same place at the same time. The good for man, as the common starting-point, marks an area within which arguments leading to divergent conclusions about moral priorities can be conducted. The conclusions are widely divergent, because they are determined by different subsidiary premises. Practical and theoretical reason, cleverness, intelligence and wisdom, justice, friendship, temperance in relation to passions, courage, a repugnance in the face of squalid or mean sentiments and actions; these are Aristotle's general and abstract terms, which do not by themselves distinguish a particular way of life, realizable in a particular historical situation. The forms that intelligence and friendship and love between persons, and that nobility of sentiment and motive, can take are at least as various as human cultures; and they are more various still, because within any one culture there will be varieties of individual temperament, providing distinct motives and priorities of interest, and also varieties of social groupings, restricting the choice of ways of life open to individuals.

27. Inevitably, too, there are differences as to which universalist position is most credible. Some differences have figured prominently in international debates about human rights, for example, between proponents of liberal-democratic rights of the sort advanced in the First World and proponents of socialist human rights of the sort advanced in the Second World. See David Hollenbach, *Claims in Conflict: Retrieving and Renewing the Catholic Human Rigths Tradition* (Mahwah, NJ: Paulist Press, 1979), esp. ch. 1; Max Stackhouse, *Creeds, Society, and Human Rights: A Study in Three Cultures* (Grand Rapids, MI: Eerdmans, 1984). Moreover, some Third World participants, in debates about human rights, argue that First World universalist rhetoric is sometimes just another strategy for imposing Western values on non-Western cultures. See James Nickel, *Making Sense of Human Rights: Philosophical Reflections on the Universal Declaration of Human Rights* (Berkeley: University of California Press, 1987), pp. 65–68. For a recent discussion of the problem in the context of traditional African cultures, see Ronald Nhlapo, "International Protection of Human Rights and the Family: African Variations on a Common Theme," *International Journal of Law and the Family* 1 (1989): 1.

28. See, e.g., Richard Rorty, *Contingency, Irony, and Solidarity* (Cambridge: Harvard University Press, 1989), esp. introduction and ch. 9. See also Bernard Williams, "Auto-da-Fé," *New York Review of Books*, April 28, 1983, p. 33: "Rorty is so insistent that we cannot, in philosophy, simply be talking about human beings, as opposed to human beings at a given time. . . . Rorty . . . contrasts the approach of taking some philosophical problem and asking . . . 'What does it show us about *being human?*' and asking, on the other hand, 'What does the persistence of such problems show us about *being twentieth-century Europeans?*' " (emphasis in original). Rorty's position is reminiscent of Joseph de Maistre's well-known statement two centuries ago, commenting on then-recent developments in revolutionary France: "I have seen in my time Frenchmen, Italians, and Russians. I even know, thanks to Montesquieu, that one may be a Persian, but as for Man, I declare that I have never met him in my life; if he exists it is without my knowledge." For a critical discussion of Rorty's position, see Perry, *Morality, Politics, and Law,* pp. 44–48.

29. Foot, "Moral Relativism," in Jack W. Meiland and Michael Krausz (eds.), *Relativism: Cognitive and Moral* (Notre Dame: University of Notre Dame Press, 1982), pp. 152, 164, For an excellent defense of a non-

relativist position on human good, see Martha Nussbaum, "Non-Relative Virtues," p. 32. See also Jonathan Jacobs, "Practical Wisdom, Objectivity, and Relativism," *American Philosophical Quarterly* 26 (1989): 199; John Kekes, "Human Nature and Moral Theories," *Inquiry* 28 (1985): 231; Bimal Matilal, "Ethical Relativism and Confrontation of Cultures," in Krausz (ed.), *Relativism: Interpretation and Confrontation,* pp. 339, 357: "The common dispositions, constitutive of the concept of 'the naked man,' may be recognized as numerous simple facts about needs, wants, and desires, for example, removal of suffering, love of justice, courage in the face of injustice, pride, shame, love of children, delight, laughter, happiness"; Amelie Rorty, "Relativism, Persons, and Practices" (a relevant portion of this essay in quoted in note 34).

30. Richard Rorty, *Contingency, Irony, and Solidarity,* p. xiii. Rorty writes approvingly of "this historicist turn," which, he says, "has helped free us, gradually but steadily, from theology and metaphysics—from the temptation to look for an escape from time and chance. It has helped us substitute Freedom for Truth as the goal of thinking and of social progress" (id.). For an excellent critique of this and related aspects of Rorty's views, see Thomas Jackson, "The Theory and Practice of Discomfort: Richard Rorty and Pragmatism," *Thomist* 51 (1987): 270.

31. See note 30 and accompanying text. Cf. Martha Nussbaum, "Aristotle on Human Nature and the Foundations of Ethics," typescript draft, p. 27: "To find out what our nature is seems to be one and the same thing as to find out what we deeply believe to be most important and indispensable [in a human life, as distinct from, at one extreme, a beast-ly life or, at another, a god-ly life]."

32. For a discussion of one group of such thinkers, see Robin West, "Feminism, Critical Social Theory, and the Law," *University of Chicago Legal Forum* (1989): 59.

33. As Noam Chomsky has written, "A vision of social order is . . . based on a concept of human nature. If in fact man is an indefinitely malleable, completely plastic being, with no innate structures of mind and no intrinsic needs of a cultural or social character, then he is a fit subject for the 'shaping behavior' by the state authority, the corporate manager, the technocrat, or the central committee. Those with some confidence in the human species . . . will try to determine the intrinsic human characteristics that provide the framework for intellectual development, the growth of moral consciousness, cultural achievement, and participation in a free community." *For Reasons of State* (New York: Random House, 1973), p. 404.

34. See Amelie Rorty, "Relativism, Persons, and Practices," pp. 418–19 (emphasis added):

[R]elativists are quite right to insist that even such dramatically basic activities as birth, copulation, and death, such basic processes as eating and sleeping, physical growth and physical decay, are intentionally described in ways that affect phenomenological experience. Events and processes are encompassed and bounded, articulated and differentiated, within the web of a culture's conceptual and linguistic categories; their meaning is formed by its primary practices and social books, songs, and rituals. Even the conceptions of social practices and meaning are sufficiently culturally specific so that it is tendentious to refer to conceptions *of* culture practices, as if *culture* or *practice* were Platonic forms, waiting to be conceptualized this way or that. Indeed the very practices of interpretation and evaluation are themselves culturally variable. But nothing follows from this about the impossibility of crosscultural interpretation, communication, or evaluation, particularly among cultures engaged in practical interactions with one another. The core truth of relativism—the intentionality of practice and experience—does not entail that successful communication and justified evaluation require strict identity of meaning. *There are, furthermore, basic culturally invariant psychophysical and biosocial salience markers that set the boundaries of attention, however variously these foci may be identified, interpreted, or evaluated.*

See also Martha Nussbaum, "Non-Relative Virtues," p. 33.

For an (apparent) example of the slide from "an appreciation of the historically and socially constructed character of such categories [as 'human nature']" to the "anti-essentialist" position that there is no human nature, see Nancy Fraser, *Unruly Practices,* p. 106. There seems to be in Fraser's work a tension between her position on human nature and her position on needs. See notes 20 and 22 and accompanying text.

35. West, "Feminism, Critical Social Theory, and the Law," pp. 96–97.

36. Charles Taylor, *Sources of the Self: The Making of the Modern Identity* (Cambridge, Mass.: Harvard University Press, 1989), p. 61. See also Perry, *Morality, Politics, and Law,* p. 49.

37. Taylor, *Sources of the Self,* pp. 61–62.

6

ON THE GOOD OF KNOWING VIRTUE

ROGERS M. SMITH

The "epistemology of virtue" is a somewhat rarefied topic. One of the virtues of George Sher's lucid chapter is that it helps out those of us who primarily study politics by pointing us to a political context out of which the topic arises. That context is the recurring debate over whether government should take actions to promote virtue in their citizens, or steer clear of the business. Those who advise government to steer clear, Sher indicates, argue among other things that claims about virtue and the good are inherently too subjective and biased to be the basis of governmental action, unlike perhaps, claims about justice or fair processes. Those who say government should promote the virtues claim instead that we can have objective knowledge of the virtues and their desirability.

Sher does not try to settle the debate about government's proper role, but he does try to make a start toward doing so. He addresses the epistemological aspect of the controversy and contends, along with many moral philosophers in recent years, that the virtues are indeed in a certain sense objectively knowable. Hence he appears to be striking a blow on the side of those who favor governmental action. A "coherentist" epistemology, he says, gives us reason to assign objective value to our familiar lists of the virtues, on various grounds. They contribute to or are constitutive of human flourishing; they help us fulfill what we take to be our duties; and they are in certain ways good in themselves.

I agree with much of Sher's epistemological argument, and he says it well, so I'm going to focus instead on its implications for the political quarrels to which he refers.[1] Regrettably, I do not think he gives us much of a start toward resolving the political controversies to which he links these epistemological debates. And I must add that I fear such failure is all too characteristic of the sorts of epistemological and meta-ethical inquiries that have dominated philosophers' discussions of these topics in recent years.[2]

To show why I think Sher's account is broadly right but not very helpful, let me consider what I take to be the typical epistemological claims of the rival factions in the political debates Sher invokes. In brief, I'll suggest that when political actors claim the virtues are objectively knowable, they are generally making claims that are much stronger and more specific than the claims for objectivity Sher considers and defends. His account will seem too weak, too vague, and too subjectivist to them. On the other hand, when people contend that claims about virtue are more subjective than claims about justice, they are generally not contending that knowledge of justice rests on a different epistemology than knowledge of virtue. I do not think they are disputing Sher's epistemology at all. They are simply contending that, in practice, members of complex, pluralistic modern societies can hope for more *intersubjective* agreement over principles of justice and fair process than over doctrines of virtue and the good. Sher's analysis is too nonempirical to give us much sense of whether or not this is so.

First, with reference to those who think we can have objective knowledge of the virtues: I believe that, outside the community of professional philosophers, most such advocates, from Moral Majoritarians to ardent human rights activists, would reject the "coherentist" epistemology that Sher defends and, I think, rightly defends. They believe something much stronger than the claim that various notions of the virtues' desirability seem likely to cohere relatively well with our other normative and empirical beliefs in reflective equilibrium. Advocates of governmentally fostered virtue are claiming that the virtues have some sort of objective existence "out there," independent of our minds and beliefs, written into nature or manifest in the being of God. And they claim that we can grasp this objective existence with virtual certainty, by some sort of direct intuition or moral sense, or by the authority of great texts like Aristotle or the Bible, or by a reason that does not merely range over the whole set of our beliefs but somehow pierces through them to clear perception of the great and real world beyond.[3]

In contrast, many of the philosophic advocates of moral realism wholeheartedly endorse Sher's position, that the best we can hope to do is come up with theories in which our various moral beliefs mesh with each other and with what we believe about the physical and social world. Most acknowledge that this perspective gives little ground for the kinds of claims of transcendental moral objectivity that older theological and natural law theories advanced. For example, in an influential philosophic defense of "Moral Realism," Peter Railton says;

> A teacher of mine once remarked that the question of moral realism seemed to him to be the question whether the universe cares what we do. Since we have long since given up believing that the cosmos pays us any mind, he thought we should long since have given up moral realism. I can only agree that if this were what moral realism involved, it should—with relief rather than sorrow—be let go. However, the account offered here gives us a way of understanding how moral values or imperatives might be objective without being cosmic. They need be grounded in nothing more transcendental than facts about man and his environment, facts about what sorts of things matter to us, and how the ways we live affect these things.[4]

Sensible as Railton's position may be, it nonetheless is clearly anathema to those who believe God cares what we do, and also to those who think moral values are things that simply and universally matter, not things that merely "matter to us." For them, philosophers like Railton and Sher leave knowledge of virtue too much a matter of reflective but still subjective judgment, as everyone equilibriates for himself or herself.

To be sure, I expect that many more traditional proponents of virtue would contend that, if the weighing of our various beliefs reflective equilibrium involves were performed properly, other sensible people would come to agree with them on what the substance of the virtues is and what their ontological status is.

But except as a rare, rhetorical concession, few are willing to accept that their views of virtue are only highly corrigible products of such reflection, legitimately disputable by others, likely to change in the future. They believe the external objectivity of virtue can be asserted more strongly, that their views of the virtues rest on more direct and certain apprehensions of them.

Like many contemporary philosophers, Sher does not really think these sorts of strong "foundationalist" claims for moral realism are much worth discussing. When he contrasts "realist" and "constructivist" accounts of virtue, he is only contrasting positions like Railton's which assert that our claims for moral principles are ultimately dependent on facts about our physical world, social practices, and concerns with accounts that say none of these factors can be assigned causal force in our ultimate moral judgments, which must be seen as more decisively matters of human decision and creation. Sher does not think his "coherentist" approach can as yet decide between such philosophic "realist" and "constructivist" accounts of virtue. He still thinks he can help realists, however, because he thinks that they can rely on a coherentist epistemology just as much as Rawlsian constructivists. But again, the political, as opposed to the philosophic, defenders of the objectivity of virtue are not likely to want to do so.

Thus I do not think Sher really helps to uphold the "objectivist" side actually present in contemporary political debates. Yet neither has he undertaken to be its critic, at least not here. To see if his "coherentism" really has important implications for their views, positive or negative, something more needs to be argued than his essay provides.

Sher does give one argument that puts him closer to this hardcore objectivist camp. He suggests that while the *nature* of various activities may depend on the particular social forms that prevail in a particular time and place, the intrinsic *value* of those activities does not. We are to judge value by a process of equilibriating reflection on all we believe, a process that is not confined to the particular social forms in which an activity is manifest. Hence our judgments can claim to be more transcendent, not rooted inextricably in those social forms.

I see two problems with this argument. First, its defense of the

transcendental character of our value judgments is still only relative, not the absolutist defense that I think defenders of objective
virtue want. While our reflections can range beyond the particular social forms in which an activity is manifest, they cannot
range beyond the large but still finite set of our beliefs, all of
which remain rooted in some social forms. On this coherentist
approach there is, at a minimum, no guarantee that we will ever
rise above the limitations in our partial perspectives that arise
from the particular array of social forms we have in some way
experienced. So while we can claim relative breadth of view, we
cannot, without more, claim to have fully transcended contingency and partiality in our moral outlooks and truly grasped
virtue.

Second, even if we find such breadth of view transcendental
enough, it comes at a cost. As Sher acknowledges, if we try to
compare many specific practices in terms of values that are attainable to some degree by all of them, we are inevitably led to rely on
rather "broad-gauged" values, like well-being or moral goodness.
This "broad-gauged" quality will usually mean that these values
are "concepts" in Ronald Dworkin's terms: general notions that
need specification to be operational and that can be specified as
any of a number of distinguishable "conceptions" of well-being,
moral goodness, etc.[5] I do not myself think their generality renders all such values meaningless or hopelessly indeterminate, but
it does militate against claims of certainty about what they require
in particular situations. There will unavoidably be room for deliberation, judgment, and reasonable disagreements. And again,
room for disagreement is sharply disagreeable to most of the
political advocates of propagating virtue. They usually want to
show that governmental institutions can discern rather specific
requirements of virtue fairly incontrovertibly and then promote
them effectively. Acknowledging uncertainties and ambiguities
undercuts both these claims. So even on this point I do not think
Sher really does much to strengthen the "objectivist" arguments
in contemporary political debates, although he also does not explicitly oppose them.

As for those who oppose using government to foster virtue—a
group that is much more confined to academia than the first—I
do not think Sher takes on their main point. He strives to show

that claims about the virtues rest on epistemological grounds no more vulnerable than those offered for other normative claims— specifically, I presume, claims about social justice. Virtue claims can rely on precisely the same vindication via reflective equilibrium that Rawls and others invoke for their principles of justice. So far I think Sher is quite correct. If there are deontological advocates of justice who really insist that claims for virtue *must* be made in different ways, I think Sher gives them a case they will have much trouble refuting.

I do not think, however, that the strongest arguments made against propagating virtues have really been epistemological at all. They are, rather, sociological. I believe Rawls or Bruce Ackerman would agree that if one wishes to decide what to regard as virtues, he or she should probably engage in reflective equilibrium and develop a coherentist view. As Sher is aware, Rawls in fact has advanced a theory of the virtues, derived from his principles of justice and so ultimately justified on coherentist grounds.[6] But Rawls believes, as does Ackerman, and many practicing politicians, that if in modern societies we consider conceptions of the virtues not deduced from theories of justice, persons will come up with so many different notions that intersubjective agreement on them, political agreement on the virtues, will prove unattainable. Rightly or wrongly, these writers are more optimistic that most members of such societies will be able to reach agreement on certain rules of the game, principles of justice and fair processes, that will allow most people to engage in their preferred pursuits with a minimum of conflict and a maximum of necessary kinds of cooperation. The very fact of extensive pluralism in persons' deepest values, which makes agreement on the virtues impossible, is in this view the strongest source of pressure for people to agree on allegedly more minimal moral standards of justice and fairness.[7]

Now, the advocates of justice over virtue do not give much empirical evidence for this claim. Rawls appears to think it fairly self-evident; he repeatedly simply cites the fact of modern moral pluralism and then asserts that the promotion of conceptions of virtue not derived from his principles of justice is impractical. We might well disagree. Perhaps convergences on meaningful conceptions of virtue are just as empirically and analytically likely as the convergence Rawls and Ackerman anticipate but have not achieved.

But Sher does not make this critique of Rawls, et al. Instead, he repeats a failing of theirs that helps to keep this whole question somewhat cloudy. It is often unclear in Rawls, Sher, and others, how far reflective equilibrium is thought to be a process simply inside the individual philosopher's mind, or whether we cannot rest until we've reached equilibrium via discourse with at least some others, perhaps fellow philosophers, perhaps even fellow citizens.

Usually the philosophers' language suggests a quite individualistic view. Sher, for example, says that a subject's task is to "bring all of *his* beliefs into 'reflective equilibrium' " (emphasis added), and he uses similar singular pronouns several other places. But clearly he is writing not simply to report to us the results of his own quest for reflective equilibrium. He also suggests that on reflection we will or should agree with him; and indeed he sometimes uses plural pronouns and speaks as if he is showing all of us, his readers, perhaps his fellow citizens, that all *our* background beliefs can converge on certain general views of human flourishing, duties, etc., and so on the virtues, just as much as on conceptions of justice.

Now, if Sher could indeed show that reflective equilibrium, understood as an intersubjective process of deliberation among multiple persons, ultimately the whole interested citizenry, is as likely to converge on conceptions of virtue as on justice, then he would have dealt a powerful blow to the philosophic critics of propagating virtue politically. But he does not clearly define, much less undertake, this admittedly arduous, partly empirical task. He shows at most that it is possible for one or a number of us to converge on certain general notions of virtue. But most of the arguments for converging on particular notions, much less on their applications in concrete contexts, and much less their acceptability to the actual public at large, are all left unaddressed. Such gaps, however understandable, leave Sher in my view without a strong case against those who claim that agreement will prove impossible to achieve.

So I do not think that, despite its other strengths, Sher's chapter gives much of a start to those of us concerned to address the political debates that are one important source of the epistemological issues he considers. And throwing caution to the winds, let me add that I do not think these failings are special weaknesses in Sher's able work. I believe contemporary moral philosophy too often tends to pursue meta-ethical inquiries as ends in themselves, probing the logical possibilities for making various sorts of claims with great insight and ingenuity, but in ways that often lose contact with the real-world controversies they are supposed to be addressing. I do not mean that this work is always useless. I recognize that, like mathematicians developing theorems to determine if a certain class of equations is in principle solvable or not, we benefit from learning in the abstract what types of moral arguments can hope to prove feasible and which cannot. But I'm afraid I think the much greater indeterminacy in all moral reasoning makes these inquiries on the whole less productive in moral philosophy than in mathematics or, perhaps, certain areas of formal logic. I think that more often, the best way we can determine what substantive arguments on a topic like the virtues are sustainable is to go ahead and try to argue them, with enough specificity and enough assessment of actual empirical conditions to make their implications for concrete problems reasonably clear.

NOTES

1. I have briefly addressed the epistemological issues, in ways largely consonant with Sher's "coherentism," in "The New Institutionalism: Reply to Professor Barber," 3 *Studies in American Political Development* 74–87 (1989). As I note there, many moral realists, such as the lawyer-philosopher Michael Moore, also explicitly embrace a "coherentist" foundation for their views, though not always plausibly. See Moore, "Moral Reality," 82 *Wisconsin Law Review* 1108, 1112–13, 1143 (1982); "A Natural Law Theory of Interpretation," 58 *Southern California Law Review* 312 (1985).

2. I refer particularly to the extensive debates over whether some version of "moral realism" is philosophically defensible. For a representative collection, see Geoffrey Sayre-McCord, ed., *Essays on Moral Real-*

ism (Ithaca: Cornell University Press, 1988). I should note that much of Sher's other work deals directly and usefully with contemporary policy controversies.

3. Few would dispute, I think, that advocates of public virtue like Jerry Falwell regard their moral standards as existing entirely externally to all human reflection and judgment, since the standards are thought to derive from God. Similarly, some natural law theorists like Sotirios Barber go beyond realists like Moore to speak of a "physical and moral reality" external to human minds about which we can, at least sometimes, claim to know more than simply what seems right in "reflective equilibrium" [Barber, "Normative Theory, the 'New Institutionalism,' and the Future of Public Law," 3 *Studies in American Political Development* 56–73 (1989)]. I take a similar sort of objective existence to be at least suggested by human rights advocates like Henry Shue, who insists that some standards apply globally and without reference to subjective human beliefs: "There are some things one does not do. Not many, perhaps, but some. And if the 'one' is a government, it doesn't matter. . . . Similarly, there are some things one must do." Shue, "Morality, Politics, and Humanitarian Assistance," in Gil Loescher and Bruce Nichols, eds., *The Moral Nation: Humanitarianism and U.S. Foreign Policy Today* (Notre Dame: University of Notre Dame Press, 1989), pp. 13–14.

4. Peter Railton, "Moral Realism," 95 *Philosophical Review* 200–201 (1986). Similarly, another recent defender of moral realism and objectivism, Susan Hurley, sharply distinguishes her view from "Platonism," the view "that values are prior to, independent of, and determining with respect to preferences. " Such Platonism, she says, "is not a live option." S. L. Hurley, *Natural Reasons: Personality and Polity* (New York: Oxford University Press, 1989), pp. 4–5.

A few realists like Moore do insist that there are moral "natural kinds," while agreeing that we can only theorize about them in reflective equilibrium and admitting that such means give us little idea about "what kind" of things these might be. Moore, "Moral Reality," pp. 1124–25, 1145–46, 1152–53.

5. Ronald Dworkin, *Taking Rights Seriously* (Cambridge: Harvard University Press, 1977), pp. 134–36.

6. John Rawls, *A Theory of Justice* (Cambridge: Harvard University Press, 1971), pp. 436, 440–46.

7. This theme of how only a focus on standards of justice and the right, not particular conceptions of the good, is necessary under the conditions of modern society has been central to Rawls's work from early on, and he has only emphasized it more heavily in his recent writings. The same is true of Ackerman. See, e.g., Rawls, *Theory,* pp. 30–

33, 502–4, 528; "A Kantian Conception of Equality," 76 *Cambridge Review* 93–99 (1975); "Justice as Fairness: Political Not Metaphysical," 14 *Philosophy and Public Affairs* 223–51 (1985); Bruce A. Ackerman, *Social Justice in the Liberal State* (New Haven: Yale University Press, 1980), pp. 359–71, 375; Bruce A. Ackerman, "Why Dialogue?" 86 *Journal of Philosophy* 5–22 (1989).

3

LIBERALISM, NEUTRALITY, AND LIBERAL VIRTUES

7

THE MORAL VOCABULARY
OF LIBERALISM

RONALD BEINER

The student of politics must obviously have some knowledge of
the workings of the soul, just as the man who is to heal eyes must
know something about the whole body. In fact, knowledge is all
the more important for the former, inasmuch as politics is better
and more valuable than medicine, and cultivated physicians devote much time and trouble to gain knowledge about the body.
Thus, the student of politics must study the soul.

Aristotle, Nicomachean Ethics

Talk of "virtue" immediately strikes the modern ear as somehow
illiberal, certainly antiquated, perhaps perverse. It must surely
be galling to liberal moralists that this old-fashioned language is
back in vogue to some extent; in any case, the liberal will inevitably see in all this Aristotelian talk something vaguely threatening
to the much more familiar liberal notions of rights, autonomy,
value pluralism, the privacy of moral conscience, and the protection of moral diversity. In what follows, I want to offer some
account of why this older moral language is in some measure
back in favor; to examine why liberals would be, with good reason, inclined to see it as subversive of the prevailing moral language; to consider some of the ways in which ancient moral
thought may perhaps be more coherent than the established

moral categories of modern liberalism; and finally, to argue that it truly matters, that something genuinely is at stake, in whether we opt for one mode of moral discourse or the other. My thesis, basically, is that the moral self-understanding of liberalism would be notably strengthened, both theoretically and practically, if it were to shift from a Kantian discourse of rights and individual autonomy to an Aristotelian discourse of virtues and character formation. In this regard I think that the organizer of this conference, William Galston, has performed a valuable service, in his recent work proposing a moral vocabulary more oriented towards the substantive virtues that legitimize, or at least recommend, a liberal way of life, although, I must add, I find myself less persuaded than he is of the moral soundness of existing practices in liberal society.

Before I can embark on a sketch of an alternative moral vocabulary, it will be necessary for me to state, at least briefly, a few standard objections to some main terms of liberal discourse with which I am dissatisfied. I will later consider typical liberal objections to my preferred moral vocabulary.

1. *Values.* One of the chief theoretical advantages of an Aristotelian moral language is that it allows one to speak of moral and political phenomena without ever having to resort to the reductive notion of "values," whether individual or collective. For some reason, liberals tend to have difficulty appreciating why avoidance of this unfortunate language constitutes a theoretical advantage, or indeed why the ubiquity of this language in liberal society is a pathological feature of modern moral experience. Whether the captives of this vocabulary are aware of it or not, what it suggests is that "value" originates not in what is admirable or worthy of being cherished *in the world,* but in the idiosyncrasies of our own inner lives. It is an intrinsically *subjectivizing* vocabulary.[1] It has the effect of canceling out the claims to real validity anchored in the world; it is a self-defeating moral language. Talk of values implies that we do not find goodness in the good things out there in the world, but *confer* value from out of our own subjectivity.

The language of value is inseparable from the notion of an exhaustive dichotomy between facts and values, where it is presumed that the world consists of evaluatively neutral facts that we then as it were "inject" with value on the basis of our own prejudices and proclivities. However, the dichotomous conception of a world of facts charged with value from without, at the initiative of value-dispensing subjects, is unfortunately entirely unequal to the way we actually experience the world commonsensically. We experience a world that is already a repository of good, not one that depends parasitically upon us for any "value" it can manage to borrow or scrounge. The Aristotelian language of virtue is incalculably superior to the modern language in retaining this truth of common sense experience.

Liberals assume that the language of values is a neutral vocabulary, but this is merely one among numerous instances of a spurious liberal neutralism. The discourse of values, intended to be neutral, is already predisposed towards a particular way of experiencing and thinking about moral and political phenomena.

2. *Rights*. According to Amy Gutmann, "most prominent political philosophers are now rights theorists."[2] This is certainly a striking pronouncement about the development of contemporary theory. It seems fairly clear that this development mirrors in some important way the reality of a liberal social order; whether it is expressive of the moral strength or moral weakness of liberal society is still an open question. Here I would merely mention the accusation, familiar by now, that part and parcel of rights discourse is a tendency towards forms of social life that are excessively adversarial, litigious, and geared towards modes of self-assertion, whether of individuals or collectivities. It is an interesting question whether the latter features of liberal public culture are the *outcome* of the prevailing moral language, or, perhaps more plausibly, whether the resort to the language of rights as the dominant moral and political vocabulary is merely a symptomatic *expression* of these features. As Alasdair MacIntyre says, "since in modern society the accommodation of one set of wills to the purpose of another continually requires the frustration of one group's purposes by those of another, it is unsurprising that the concept of rights, understood as claims against the inroads of marauding others in situations where shared allegiances to goods that are goods of the whole community have been attenuated or abandoned, should become a socially central concept."[3] To see at a glance why this might be so, consider an argument

between two individuals of differing political persuasions concerning whether it would be *good* (for the society as a whole) for the state to make available a certain social service (say, universal state-funded daycare). Now imagine how the tone of the debate would be altered if it suddenly turned into a contest between, on the one side, the *right* of one of the parties to receive the service in question and, on the other side, the *right* of the other party not to be burdened by the higher taxes necessary to supply the service. I will not pursue this argument in detail, but I cannot deny my sympathy for this general line of critique.

3. *Individual autonomy.* In *A Theory of Justice,* John Rawls makes much of the ideal of designing for oneself a "rational plan of life." It might indeed be possible for a few rare artists or intellectuals to contrive a plan of life of their own design. But the great majority of individuals in any society are simply socialized to given roles that may be fulfilling or banal depending upon the organized practices of the society in question. Activities and choices are *ranked* by any given society, and so the liberal model of unlimited individual choice with respect to "lifestyles" is disingenuous. The very term "lifestyle" betrays the fatuousness of this vision, for of course the lifestyles from which one makes one's selection are all already carefully prepackaged, or rather form a prepackaged set, which thus belies the appearance of a pluralism of self-designed options. This is the nub of truth in MacIntyre's statement, which might otherwise have the appearance of a gross simplification, that liberal society is in essence a society of aesthetes, managers, and therapists.[4] MacIntyre surely did not overlook that many individuals in liberal society have the opportunity, and avail themselves of the opportunity, to pursue vocations other than these. It should be sobering for contemporary liberals that one of the greatest of modern liberals, Max Weber, conceded to Nietzsche that modern society was evolving in the direction of a culture ruled by "specialists without spirit, sensualists without heart."[5]

Rawls's example of an individual who exercises rational autonomy by maximizing his or her resources for a life devoted to counting "blades of grass in various geometrically shaped areas"[6] undoubtedly expresses a ludicrously truncated understanding of practical reason. But even on a less absurd account of rationality, it is less than clear that the exercise of individual autonomy ought to loom as large as it does in the preoccupations of modern liberals. My suspicion is that the actual substance of autonomy and diversity in liberal society is in inverse ratio to the vigor and enthusiasm with which liberals celebrate it as the characteristic strength of a modern pluralistic society. It would indeed be excellent if liberalism made available the genuine pluralism it promises; as it is, much of what is so extravagantly advertised turns out to be hollow. What is worse, the *rhetoric* of pluralism serves to squelch a concrete examination of social practices that would validate or invalidate the claim of wondrous diversity.

But of course these challenges to liberal theory are all familiar, and should not be belabored. In any case, perhaps they apply more to the popular idiom of liberal culture than to the most refined statements of liberal philosophy. Yet the point is that it should be the task of theory as such to challenge and provoke the popular idiom, rather than to rationalize it and help it to feel content with itself. Relative to this standard, I do not think contemporary liberal social theory has been doing as good a job as it might of fulfilling its philosophical mandate.

Having run through some leading terms of liberal discourse, let us now proceed with the alternative vocabulary. What is neo-Aristotelianism? Its basic conception is that moral reason consists not in a set of moral principles, apprehended and defined through procedures of detached rationality, but in the concrete embodiment of certain human capacities in a moral subject that knows those capacities to be constitutive of a consummately desirable life. The characteristic Aristotelian themes are encapsulated in the Greek word *ethos,* which encompasses character formation and habituation to good character, as well as the kinds of social milieu that engender good character and proper habituation. Clearly, this whole conception of virtues understood as realized capacities that tend to the perfection or completion of the human organism rests upon the postulate of a human good that is simply there, not freely designed; it forms a rational standard for moral judgment. The content of this human good is not grasped by reason alone, but rises to self-consciousness in the embodied praxis of a moral agent who makes good choices and is pleased by activities that confer worthy pleasures. The stan-

dard liberal challenge to Aristotelian moral reflection is that the
very notion of an objective human telos evinces an ethical and
political "monism" that does violence to modern experiences of
pluralism, diversity of goals and aspirations, and moral conflict.
Much of what follows is intended as an attempt to respond in
various ways to this liberal challenge. Among the most controversial of neo-Aristotelian theses are the following: (1) the notion of
a summum bonum; (2) the unity of the virtues; (3) prudence as
the ruling virtue; and (4) politics as architectonic science. Some
brief observations on each of these may help us to clarify both
the liberal critique and the outline of an Aristotelian rejoinder.

1. *Summum bonum.* The central thought of Aristotelian ethical
theory is that human activities, for all their unquestioned diversity, are nonetheless governed from within; there is a center to
human action; there are patterns of coherence in human existence. The proper unit of moral analysis is "the happy life." It
should be clear that this entails no "monistic" principle in the
understanding of ethical life. An appropriate analogy might be
the variety of forms of artistic activity. All these activities, in some
fashion or other, strive after "the beautiful work." It would be
ludicrous to employ aesthetic theory to dictate a single binding
route to the creation of beauty. On the other hand, it would be
equally crazy to suggest that there are no standards whatever in
the evaluation of relative success or failure in the realization of
"the beautiful work." There are intelligible standards of judgment governing those works already belonging to the canon of
great art, and there are also intelligible standards of judgment
governing the enlargement or expansion of the canon by new
works of genius. The truth lies neither in some kind of monistic
algorithm nor in the concession to orderless diversity. Rather, it
is a matter of embodied judgment. The same is surely true of
ethical practice. We neither seek to impose a single pattern of
"the happy life" by the fiat of reason, nor can we deny the
existence of patterns of coherence, forms of ethical order that
are not of our own making. Furthermore, these practices are,
inescapably, situated within a social dimension that is *also* subject
to embodied judgment. There is nothing strange or farfetched
about these claims; they seem perfectly in accord with ordinary
everyday experience.

The starting point of Aristotle's analysis in the *Nicomachean Ethics* is not the affirmation of a latent or attainable moral consensus, but the *fact* of moral disagreement: different individuals conceive differently the nature of the good. But can one make sense of this disagreement if one jettisons the claim that there *is* a "nature of the good"? Can one really deny that all human beings seek to live well, and care about whether their judgments as practical agents are conducive to their living well? Moreover, is it not the case that they cannot help but care about whether the social context in which they live promotes or hinders the living of a complete and satisfying life? The fact that different agents disagree substantively in their actual judgments does not contradict these Aristotelian claims, but is perfectly compatible with them. If we all set off in pursuit of an elusive fox, we may disagree about how to hunt our quarry, what routes to take, what strategies to pursue. But out quarry is the same. Moreover, at the end of the day, our quarry may finally have eluded us; but this does not prove that we have not shared in a common quest. This is true also of ethics. That we are never in possession of a final moral certainty does not prove that we do not participate in a shared moral quest; nor does the variety and mutual opposition of our choices negate the existence of a shared human telos.

I have trouble seeing what it means to accuse Aristotelians of failing to perceive moral conflict. Of course there are conflicts in moral belief and moral perception. How could anyone fail to be aware of that? The point, however, is what moral conflict or differences in moral perception are *about*. If we disagree morally, what is the object of our disagreement? If our ends are simply different in an ultimate and absolute sense, are we really talking about "disagreement" or something more like the habitation of separate moral universes? The latter, it seems to me, is basically unintelligible. When Aristotle speaks of a single end, a singular telos, shared by all human beings, at the beginning of the *Ethics*,[7] what he is referring to is the fact that all human beings share an interest in living well, and cannot help being concerned with whether their judgments in this regard are suitable or unsuitable to their constitution as human beings. It seems nonsense to call this "monism." It may indeed be monism in the culpable sense to insist, as Aristotle does in book 10 of the *Ethics*, that any human beings who do not live the contemplative life are defective or fall short of being full human beings. But this does not apply to the very idea of a human telos, and, as Aristotle argued, it is not clear that one can think coherently about ethical life at all without the supposition of such a telos.

It is striking that even philosophers who are in deep sympathy with Aristotle find it difficult to embrace the doctrine of the summum bonum. In a searching analysis, William Galston concludes, in light of Aquinas's restatement of the Aristotelian argument, that the idea of a highest good "is fundamentally hypothetical," and depends on unproven assumptions about the essential unity of human nature.[8] And Stuart Hampshire, in the context of an essay *defending* Aristotelian ethics, writes, "We cannot suppose that there must be some one form of life, called 'the good for man,' identifiable a priori, merely because it is a condition of conclusiveness in practical reasoning that there should be such a norm."[9] An Aristotelian answer to these challenges might go something like this. We have no "theoretical" proof that human nature can find fulfillment, or can unify its diverse strivings, in a virtuous life. At best, we can locate moral *exemplars* who *embody* this (relative) unity and finality. To be sure, *eudaimonia* in the exhaustive sense implies the life of a god, and this is out of reach. Still, the relative success of the practical exemplar in shaping a life that is a full life and a happy life serves to reassure us that our strivings both for the satisfactions of praxis and for the satisfactions of *theoria* have a direction that is not merely contingent or arbitrary. Even this more modest achievement of contentment can supply a *standard* by which to judge critically the lesser achievements of individual lives and social ways of life.

Aristotelian intuitions of ethical order are supported by commonplace moral experiences. We know, as a matter of fact, that there are some individuals, like Christina Onassis (to cite an extreme instance), whose lives are nothing but a frustrating succession of desires, where the obtaining of desire X + 1 confers no more satisfaction than the obtaining of desire X. By Hobbes's account, in *Leviathan*, chapter 11, this is the inescapable fate of all human beings, however they choose to live their individual lives. But this is simply not the case. We know, as a matter of common experience, that there are individuals whose lives are not simply a futile succession of desires, where a new desire arises the instant that its predecessor desire has been satisfied. There *are* individuals whose desires and strivings have been organized into a stable order. But we also know that a distressingly high proportion of individuals in our society live lives that are a watered-down or less dramatic version of Christina Onassis's life. Therefore, the Aristotelian ideal of a life that is not mere restless striving furnishes a critical standard for appraisal of a society that tends to breed such individuals.

2. *Unity of the virtues.* This doctrine is less ambitious than it looks at first glance, especially if it is taken, as it must be, in conjunction with the thesis of the primacy of prudence as the ruling virtue. A virtue would not be a virtue, in the sense of an excellence productive of an excellent life, if it is seen in isolation, separate from the moral quality of a person's life as a whole. A virtue is defined as a moral attribute conducive to *eudaimonia,* and *eudaimonia* is a global property of a life viewed as a whole. It hardly makes sense to say that someone is courageous but lacks the moral insight to judge occasions suitable for the exercise of courage, or that someone is generous but lacks the moral insight to judge suitable occasions for the exercise of generosity. If we lack knowledge of how to concretize our experience of the virtues we cannot practice them, and if we cannot practice the virtues we do not have them. The virtues come into play as virtues within the organized conduct of a moral life whose center of gravity is prudence. Therefore it is entirely reasonable that Aristotle, in book 6, chapter 13 of the *Ethics,* rejects as mistaken the argument "that the virtues exist independently of one another."[10]

3. *Prudence.* As we have seen, what distinguishes Aristotelian moral theory is a preoccupation with virtues embodied in character. When one refers to character, what is intended is something abiding, so that the felicity or infelicity of the agent's choices and commitments is not fortuitous, but flows from an organized pattern of life, the lifelong sway of a rational principle. Therefore to speak in an Aristotelian way about the virtues requires that one make central reference to the capacity for making good judgments, and having the fortitude to put those good judgments into action, and doing so not merely episodically but

on the basis of enduring dispositions that are deeply entrenched in one's character. This is the virtue of prudence, *phronesis,* and as we saw in the preceding section, it is what lends intelligibility to the doctrine of the unity of the virtues. As Aristotle says (*Nicomachean Ethics,* book 6, chapter 13), "in the case of those virtues which entitle a man to be called good in an unqualified sense . . . as soon as he possesses this single virtue of practical wisdom, he will also possess all the rest."

The doctrine of the unity of the virtues does *not* imply that this unity finds its concrete realization always in an identical fashion, or that the ensemble of virtues is organized into a unity identically in every virtuous human being. Nor does the doctrine presuppose that the achievement of this unity in an exemplary life represents a seamless harmony. Indeed, why should it be assumed that Aristotle thinks, any more than any of us today thinks, or any more than Isaiah Berlin thinks, that even the happiest and most well-constituted individual will in every instance be able to reconcile each and every one of his or her leading goals and aspirations? Rather, the idea of the happy life is that over the course of a whole life one will be able to fit one's various purposes into a pattern that makes sense and achieves a reasonable coherence. If Aristotelian ethics were as harmony seeking and as blind to competing goals as the pluralists charge, prudence would not only be the central virtue; prudence would be *superfluous.* Prudence occupies the center of Aristotelian ethical thought precisely because the adjudication of alternative possibilities in a concrete situation requires an exemplary performance on the part of the moral agent. And Aristotle gives us no reason to doubt that each such performance will be a unique performance. Again, Aristotelian teleology does not imply that one individual who has achieved, or approximated to, *eudaimonia* will turn out identical to every other individual who has achieved, or approximated to, *eudaimonia* (virtue clones!). What *is* implied is that there is a distinction, and one not of our own invention, between a "well-turned-out" human being and a "poorly-turned-out" human being. And here the "pluralist" who renounces teleological categories is much more out of line with common sense than the Aristotelian.

Thrift is a virtue, and stinginess is a vice, but where is one to draw the line between thrift and stinginess? The whole thrust of

Aristotle's doctrine of prudence is to suggest that a merely theoretical drawing of the line would, in cases like this, be abstract to the point of uselessness; an answer of any meaningful substance would have to be determined at the level of context-bound judgment. A *theory* of the virtues simply tells us what we already know (for instance, that there *is* a distinction between one as a virtue and the other as a vice), but does little to guide conduct. The difficulty of judgment in practice does not impugn the reality of the analytical distinction, but on the other hand, being able to distinguish analytically between them does not make it any easier to resolve the problem of practical choice. And indeed, practical judgment is what really counts here, governed as it is by the contingencies of the situation, the distinctive moral dispositions of the agent, and the larger context of moral life that informs these particularities of character and circumstance. The privileged status of prudence among the virtues underlines the strictly limited practical helpfulness of a mere theory of the various virtues.

4. *The preeminence of politics.* The Aristotelian claim that full humanity presupposes a living awareness of politics, the exercise of political understanding, and beyond that, the cultivation of forms of practical competence required to uphold one's political concerns in the public realm sounds grossly arrogant—easy to dismiss.[11] But is this sort of claim as farfetched as the pluralist assumes? Recently, my sixteen-year-old stepdaughter, a high school student, was unable to name the president of the United States. (She, and her friends too, she assured me, thought that Ronald Reagan was still president.) Is it so implausible to say that a life lived in such ignorance of the larger forces shaping one's destiny is a less than properly human existence? And, that a society that abides such ignorance is failing in its responsibility to nurture properly human capacities?

One is alarmed to reflect just how widespread are ignorance or indifference concerning the shaping political forces of our world in modern societies, when the stakes of such oblivion are so much greater than they have ever been. The majority of citizens of the modern state simply have no idea of the dimensions of political responsibility being exercised on their behalf yet beyond their cognizance. For twenty-nine days in the autumn of 1969, for reasons that are somewhat obscure, the Strategic Air Command of the United States went on full alert. Nuclear-armed B-52s "were pulled off their routine training and surveillance duties and placed in take-off position on runways across the United States, fully armed, fueled, ready to fly attack missions anywhere in the world."[12] No public announcement was made of the orders to initiate the alert. No newspapers reported it. Only a handful of American citizens had any awareness that something out of the ordinary was occurring. "The alert amounted to a secret between the White House and [military and political leaders inside] the Soviet Union."[13] It is difficult to conceive of anything of more immediate and more urgent interest to ordinary citizens, both in the United States and throughout the world, than the possibility of one superpower readying itself for all-out nuclear war against its rival superpower, and doing so for no apparent reason! Yet no civilians anywhere were privy to this confidence between the White House and the Kremlin. Under the shadow of these possibilities, it does not seem to me unreasonable to speak of the generalized condition of apathy and apoliticism in terms of a pathological deformation of human nature.

To summarize: for the Aristotelian, moral life is ordered, not episodic or haphazard. The central purpose of a society, understood as a moral community, is not the maximization of autonomy, or protection of the broadest scope for design of self-elected plans of life, but the cultivation of virtue, interpreted as excellence or as a variety of excellences, moral and intellectual. The last of these theses is set in sharp relief in the following statement by Alasdair MacIntyre: "the good life for man is the life spent in seeking for the good life for man, and the virtues necessary for the seeking are those which will enable us to understand what more and what else the good life for man is."[14] This passage makes clear that it is not a question of a single commanding excellence that is prescribed, but a finite, and not indefinite, set of excellences by which one judges the moral and political achievement, or moral and political deficiency, of a given society. Clearly, none of the above discussions are anywhere near adequate to a full defense of Aristotle; at most, they suggest why an Aristotelian account, even with respect to its most controversial claims, is not obviously implausible, and merely gesture in the direction of a fuller argument as to its plausibility.

To probe a bit more deeply some of the most problematical aspects of Aristotelian ethical theory, let us examine in greater detail Galston's thorough interrogation of the argument of the *Nicomachean Ethics* in chapter 4 of his book on Kant. It should be noted that Galston's critique is of the devil's advocate variety, constructed as it were in the light of Kantian preoccupations. At the outset of his critique he says that he will let himself be "implicitly guided by . . . the major premises of Kantian morality,"[15] and at the conclusion of the critique he writes that his purpose has not been to demonstrate "the superiority of the Kantian ethics to those of Aristotle," since the former is no more free of difficulties than the latter.[16] What we shall try to explore in dialogue with Galston's critique is whether Aristotle's reflections on ethical life form, or are intended to form, a moral "system." The very notion of a summum bonum *seems* to suggest this. However, if Aristotle's ethics is seen as a strict "science of ends," governed by a strict, and readily discernible, ethical hierarchy, the Aristotelian will be drawn into a dual trap. On the one side, the liberal pluralist will protest that the very systematicness of Aristotelian ethics convicts it of monism or inattention to moral complexity. On the other side, critics will show how the system succumbs, as it inevitably will, to various tensions and antinomies. My strategy will be to defend Aristotle on both fronts by arguing that his intentions are misunderstood if viewed through the prism of the more "systematic" Aristotelianism of Aquinas.[17]

One of Galston's arguments is that there is a tension between happiness and morality in Aristotle that Kant alone succeeds in dissolving by liberating morality from its subordinate relation to happiness. The source of the tension may be glimpsed in the fact that Aristotle's theory of the virtues is set within, and as it were delimited at both ends by, a larger theory of the good—which suggests that moral reflection and moral action do not exhaust the broader question of the good, and forms a part, but only a part, of the more comprehensive inquiry.[18] It follows that the realization of any particular moral virtue stands in an uncertain relation to the realization of the highest good for humanity, which is not exhausted by the ensemble of moral virtues. For Kant, as for Aristotle, the conjunction of morality and happiness constitutes a summum bonum for humanity, but for Kant, in opposition to Aristotle, morality must not be pursued with a view to the achievement of this summum bonum, and the imperative-ness of morality is in no way affected by the prospects of its achievement. The Stoics also dissolved the tension, but only by means of a highly implausible identification of happiness and morality that even Aristotle would certainly have rejected.[19] (In the words of Marcus Aurelius, "every action in accord with na-ture should be regarded as a delight."[20]) As Galston points out, the tension is manifest in the very first virtue treated in Aris-totle's theory of the virtues, namely courage, for this Aristotelian virtue is typically exercised by human beings in situations of peril that threaten rather than promote our securing of the compre-hensive good.[21] From the Kantian point of view, Aristotelian ethics renders morality all too contingent upon a summum bonum that in turn may or may not be supported by a fickle, if not hostile, nature. Again from the Kantian perspective, the harmony of virtue and happiness can only be saved by the an-thropomorphic optimism of Aristotelian cosmology.[22]

What answer can the Aristotelian, or neo-Aristotelian, give to this modern critique? For one thing, the Kantian challenge to Aristotle, as Galston emphasizes, rests upon the antiteleological premises of modern science, which until recently have been gen-erally assumed to be more theoretically decisive than they per-haps are. (A modest resurrection of teleological categories was the object of Charles Taylor's book, *The Explanation of Behavior;*[23] a more ambitious resuscitation of teleology is attempted in Hans Jonas's book, *The Phenomenon of Life.*[24]) In any case, it is not clear that ethical teleology is as wedded to cosmological teleology as Galston, in common with many other readers of Aristotle, sup-poses.[25] Of course, one of the most familiar objections to Aristo-telian practical philosophy is that it depends upon a set of meta-physical and cosmological doctrines that are today highly implau-sible, or even unintelligible.[26] Stoic ethical theory is indeed so dependent, with frequent appeals to the rational structure of the universe, the moral intentions of the gods, and cosmic provi-dence. In Aristotle, by contrast, the whole stress is on the *inner structure* of the virtues, with only minimal reference to metaphysical or cosmological assumptions. (In this respect, it strikes me that Leo Strauss is correct to emphasize as he does the opposition between natural law, for example, the Stoics, and natural right, for example, Aristotle.[27]) What is striking is the autonomy of the ethical world in relation to cosmological doctrines. In fact, if anything the emphasis in Aristotle, for instance, in book 6, chapter 7 of the *Ethics*, is on the *contrasts* between the eternity of the cosmos and the transience and mutability of everything human, the transcendent order of the former and the relative contingency of the latter, and so on.

To return again to the issue of the tension between virtue and happiness, the problem is often merely one of perspective, with Aristotle's position being misconstrued by being viewed against the backdrop of more extreme alternatives. For instance, both the Stoics and Kant adopt the more radical Socratic position that the just person is the "happy" person, regardless of the fate he or she suffers in the external world; Aristotle rejects it. Aristotle does not embrace the position of Eudoxus, affirming pleasure as the good, but he *appears* to approximate to a Eudoxian position relative to the more radical position of Socrates and the orthodox Socratics. (Plato may or may not be counted among these orthodox Socratics.) Perhaps the tension would appear less intractable if *arete* were translated by "excellence" rather than by the rather misleading term "virtue." In fact, one would avoid multiple confusions in the reading of Aristotle if one were to avoid altogether the terms "virtue," which "sounds" Kantian, and "happiness," which "sounds" utilitarian.[28] The advantage of rendering *arete* and *aretai* as "excellence" and "excellences," and *eudaimonia* as "well-being" can be seen in the fact that it would be that much more difficult even to state the Kantian problem of virtue versus happiness; that it appears *as* a problem shows that we are already within a horizon of Kantian premises (though this would seem to have the curious consequence that the moral horizon of Socrates in book 2 of *The Republic* would have to be seen as closer to Kant's than to Aristotle's).

Another of Galston's critical arguments is that Aristotle's account of virtue is deficient or incomplete relative to Aquinas's because Aristotle presupposes a science governing the apprehen-

sion of the good (corresponding to the function of nous in theoretical science) that would supply ends for *phronesis* as a science
of means. Aquinas, with his concept of *synderesis,* supplies this
faculty for the apprehension of ends, and Aristotle *should* do
likewise, but fails to. He thereby implicitly concedes the missing
ground in his moral theory: the foundations are lacking a crucial
pillar.[29] But this misstates the character of *phronesis,* and fails to
convey the outstanding modesty of the theory as a whole.
Phronesis is not a science of means that waits upon a theoretical,
or quasitheoretical, apprehension of ends supplied by some
other faculty; it is itself the capacity for defining the ends *through*
the effort to embody them in the concrete exigencies of particular situations.[30] Hans-Georg Gadamer has given us a brilliant
explication of how the contribution of *phronesis* to articulating
the nature of the good is much more decisive than Aristotle
himself sometimes implies, and of how, correspondingly, the provision of a "science of ends," theoretically defined, is indeed
superfluous.[31] As Gadamer writes, "The idea of the good lies
beyond the scope of any science. . . . We cannot conceptualize
the idea of the good. . . . The theoretical man remains subordi-
nated to phronesis."[32] The core of Aristotle's thought is that we
can only test our notions of what our ends are through a living
engagement with choice of means—understanding of the end
(happiness or the good) as mediated by deliberation upon means
in a specific situation—and this can only be brought to pass in
the exemplary performances of a person of practical wisdom,
not in "theoretical" apprehension of any kind.

Let us address one further major challenge to Aristotelianism
to which Galston draws attention. Near the beginning of the
Ethics, Aristotle argues that human life would be a senseless anarchy unless it were ordered in the direction of a highest good. He
goes on to say that this highest good is easy to name *(eudaimonia),*
but that its content is highly controversial. Yet by book 10 it
appears that the controversy concerning the content of the highest good has been settled; it is the contemplative life: *theoria.*[33]
But what constitutes the highness of this highest good? Aristotle
lists several considerations, but the main one is the sublime object of *theoria,* which is infinitely more stable and worthy of contemplation than the paltry objects of prudence. Yet it would

seem that modern natural science has rendered highly implausible, to say the least, that inanimate planets possess an ontologically higher status than animate things on this planet, especially human beings. Does this not impugn the whole project of locating a highest good, as Hobbes, among others, suggests? However, a closer look at the account in book 10 raises questions about whether *theoria* is as straightforwardly privileged over praxis as it appears at first glance, and as it especially appears relative to Kant; and therefore, also, whether it is so easy to dismiss the idea of a moral hierarchy with the contemplative life at its summit. As Galston himself shows, *theoria* such as human beings experience it carries us no closer to *eudaimonia* in the pure sense than does the corresponding experience of striving for moral completeness in the domain of praxis.[34] *Gods* enjoy bliss, but human beings can merely grope in the direction of full contentment, and though *theoria* can offer us intimations of divine understanding, it can likewise offer us no more than intimations of divine happiness. If this is the case, then *theoria* and *arete* are actually closer in rank than the initial assertion of the superiority of *theoria* in book 10 suggests. When the practical virtues are judged relative to the standard of happiness conferred by *theoria*, the practical life is held up to a standard that even philosophy fails grossly to satisfy.

Theoria is privileged in relation to the life of politics (pursuit of honour) and the life of pleasure. But it is not so clear that *theoria* is absolutely privileged in relation to the moral life in general; more likely, *theoria*, as well as the moral life, stands in a relation of part to whole to the full human life. *Theoria* is *more* sufficient than pursuit of honor or pleasure. But is it fully self-sufficient? The virtuous person who is cut down in his or her prime is judged to fall short of happiness. But what about the contemplative person who theorizes or philosophizes very intensely in his or her twenties, and is also cut down in his or her prime, or suffers horrible misfortune? Does not the latter fall short of proper happiness in just the same way that the person of virtue does?[35] The fact that the summum bonum presents itself to us as an object of interminable aspiration confirms that it cannot be fully identified with either the contemplative or the practical life. The priority assigned to the contemplative life is itself a part of the practical life, and therefore itself subject to the comprehensive arbitration of *phronesis*. As we argued earlier, a quest is intelligible only in relation to a definite object. The highest good is our target, even if our arrow falls short, just as, in the life of theory, truth is our object, even if it continually eludes us. For otherwise how could we make sense of the very activity? This principle applies as much to the practical life as to the contemplative life, and as much to the contemplative life as to the practical life. All of these supposed tensions in Aristotle—between virtue and happiness, nobility and pleasure, moral praxis and *theoria*—have to be seen not as posing an either/or, but rather, as in a relation of part to whole. A life of virtue without contentment is incomplete, but so is a life of theoretical contemplation without moral excellence. It is impossible to offer a perfect theory that resolves all tensions and gaps in moral experience, and Aristotle had no hope or expectation of articulating a moral teaching that did so. On the contrary, the great strength of Aristotle's ethics is its wonderful sensitivity to the complexity and multidimensionality of human ethical experience. That is why the liberals' charge of "monism" against Aristotle is so grotesque.

Let us now proceed to some more directly political challenges to Aristotelianism. The liberal argument is that liberal political institutions are required in order to cope with inexorable moral diversity and otherwise intractable conflicts of moral aspiration. This argument has been ably articulated in various versions by, amother others, Rawls, Thomas Nagel, Richard Rorty, Stuart Hampshire, and, of course, Sir Isaiah Berlin. However, does this argument really stand up to rational scrutiny? How much moral diversity is there in liberal societies? Is there, perhaps, as much sharing in aspirations as divergence in aspirations in these societies? Does attention to the unity or identity at the core of liberal society's way of life perhaps bring us closer to real insight into liberal reality, as opposed to the promises of liberal theory? Aristotle's notion of an "architectonic ranking" of activities may strike us as bizarre, or at any rate historically outdated. But "ruling practices" there are in modern societies, and in liberal societies no less.

Critics of liberalism might argue that the liberal social and political order offers an ideology of pluralism, or a rhetoric of pluralism, to mask its organization of social life according to a distinct and overarching vision of communal life. Thus the profession of pluralism serves as a cover for the privileging of a singular understanding of the dominant human end, say, the maximization of individual autonomy and choice making.[36] Interestingly enough, some liberals have now begun to concede the force of this line of attack, and have sought to restate the grounds of their liberalism so as to defuse it. For instance, Charles Larmore has recently argued that the commitment to maximizing autonomy is still expressive of a controversial conception of what is good, which is true, and that therefore it cannot be the raison d'être of the liberal state conceived as a set of public institutions founded on the ideal of political neutrality towards controversial conceptions of the good.[37] From this point of view, the liberalism of Kant, J. S. Mill, and the pre-1980 John Rawls is still too metaphysically ambitious.[38] According to Larmore, the aim of political liberalism is not to foster any positive ideal of liberal personality, but simply the negative goal of averting conflict and moral stalemate. Larmore bases his ideal of liberal neutrality on a conception of "equal respect." Moreover, he insists that this conception depends on no classical liberal assumptions about the desirability of autonomy, which he rejects because they are ineliminably controversial, that is, nonneutral.[39] Yet why should I "respect" a view of life that is servile, conformist, and unreflective? How can we know that different forms of life are respectworthy in advance of examining their substance? If Larmore is right that classical liberal arguments violate the neutrality principle, would it not make more sense for the liberal to renounce the neutrality principle rather than to renounce the arguments on behalf of autonomy and voluntary agency?[40]

It is often suggested that the application of premodern moral categories to our modern situation amounts to an impotent moralism.[41] This accusation is central to Larmore's theory of liberalism. His book warrants further examination because it tries to offer a conceptualization of liberalism that is at the furthest extremity from Aristotelian ways of thinking about ethics and politics. If Larmore is right about what is theoretically attractive about the liberal state, then all the central Aristotelian categories that I am concerned to revive are beyond redemption. Larmore, along with a host of other liberals, endeavors to jettison the Kantian or Millian visions of autonomous personhood or romantic self-development, and to construe liberal society instead according to the unromantic image of a modus vivendi. Here individuals agree to disagree at the political level so they can localize their pursuit of individual and group purposes that are unshared. Pluralism, on this revised understanding, is no longer a noble moral aspiration, a shared moral commitment. Instead, it becomes merely the exigency of mutual political accommodation. Liberalism thus responds to its moralistic critics by becoming even less moralistic, more hard-headed.

Larmore subscribes to the standard pluralist critique of Aristotle as a "monist" that I have tried to rebut throughout this chapter.[42] But perhaps it is the case that while Aristotle himself is not a monist, contemporary theorists become Aristotelians because of their yearning for monism. This is, indeed, Larmore's understanding of MacIntyre.[43] Here we may recall the encapsulation of MacIntyre's Aristotelianism cited earlier: "the good life for man is the life spent in seeking the good life for man." Is this dogmatic monism? Yet Larmore has trouble making sense of how an antipluralist like MacIntyre can be committed to an open-ended teleology like this.[44] Perhaps the difficulty lies not in the coherence of MacIntyre's enterprise but, rather, in the monism/pluralism distinction adopted by Larmore. Perhaps these categories fail to capture the point of MacIntyre's critique of modern experience. Is there, after all, only one way to challenge modern pluralism, namely, by proposing a dogmatic moral hierarchy? Is it not the point of MacIntyre's challenge to direct attention at the *ways* in which we pursue moral conflict, and the *language* in which we articulate our nonidentical aspirations? Larmore is puzzled by MacIntyre's Aristotelianism because he simply imputes to MacIntyre a romantic yearning to *abolish* moral conflict that MacIntyre himself never for one moment embraces. Surely, there are possibilities of rational disagreement that transcend the "self-assertive shrillness" that characterizes much moral argument today.[45] And *that*, surely, is the point of MacIntyre's challenge to contemporary moral pluralism.

As we mentioned earlier, the leading accusation leveled by liberals against their critics is one of impotent moralism. Surely, though, it is a gross trivialization of the Aristotelian challenge to characterize it as the product of a hankering after imaginary experiences of community. Someone like MacIntyre is making claims about the historical properties of the liberal state (its capacities to socialize its members to humanly worthwhile practices, its vulnerability to social crises, its power to elicit sacrifices from citizens, and so on) that may or may not be empirically valid, and that deserve to be taken seriously as such. Conversely, the main puzzle in Larmore's defense of liberalism is the notion, verging on blind assumption, that it will be possible to sustain within the private domain character formation, constitutive attachments, socialization into substantial ways of life, *Sittlichkeit*, all of which he affirms, within the horizon of a public philosophy of neutrality or agnosticism concerning the relative superiority of different conceptions of the good life. How can we be habituated to social roles, forms of virtue, and enduring moral character within local sectors of social life when the official philosophy of the society is morally agnostic? Larmore is quick to dismiss the "organic model of society" as historically obsolete, but he fails to ask *why* Aristotelians might be anxious about the fostering of *Sittlichkeit* in a liberal social order, apart from the question-begging assertion that they are driven merely by sentimental romanticism. The confrontation here is not between idealistic longings on one side and undeluded realism on the other, but rather, between two competing *empirical* characterizations of liberal society. Empirically, the evidence is not sufficient either to validate the worst fears of the critics of liberalism or to rule out these fears entirely.

While Larmore will charge Aristotelians like MacIntyre with being blind to the advantages of modern pluralism over ancient monism, someone like MacIntyre can counter that liberals are blind to the monistic tendencies in liberal society itself. From an Aristotelian perspective, the most implausible feature of this liberal philosophy is its claim that there are no ordering principles that bind together and shape a liberal social and political community. In the words of John Rawls, social contract theory assumes "that society as a whole has no ends or ordering of ends in the sense that associations and individuals do."[46] The distinctive advantage of this theory, he says, is that it offers "a moral conception that can take appropriate account of social values without falling into organicism."[47] Larmore no doubt would say that it is *because* society as a whole has no ends or ordering of ends that the neutralist conception of a modus vivendi to reconcile conflicting ends is required. But liberal society itself is more "organic" and less "neutral" than liberals profess. One may apply to Larmore himself the dictum that he applies to utilitarianism, namely, that "a lack of neutrality, a commitment to some disputed view about the good life, may lie concealed in what appears to be a purely formal principle."[48] For instance, Larmore admits that modern liberal states cannot fail to interest themselves in the efficiency or inefficiency of their prevailing economic practices, but he, curiously, denies that this violates the neutrality stipulation.[49] Unfortunately, he nowhere explains how one can maintain full commitment to maximal economic growth, as all modern liberal states do, without foregoing the claim to neutrality between conflicting substantive ends. Surely the modern state has taken sides in a very clear way in what is one of the most considerable controversies concerning the good life for humanity.

It is not surprising that Larmore bases his modus vivendi theory of liberalism on the toleration doctrines of Bodin, Locke, and Bayle.[50] The question, however, is whether this model, geared to the avoidance of religious wars, is suitable for political disagreements that do not presuppose incompatible religious visions of personal salvation.[51] It is reasonably clear why Catholics and Protestants in Belfast, or Christians and Muslims in Beirut, must establish a modus vivendi; it is much less clear why, say, citizens supporting and opposing state controls on environmental pollution should, or could, revert to a neutral modus vivendi. What would it mean to say that the liberal state must aim to be "neutral" between those whose view of the good subordinates the pursuit of profit to concern for ecological well-being, and those whose view of the good subordinates ecological well-being to concern for profit? One way or the other, the state will inevitably be forced to establish a moral hierarchy, vindicating once again the commonsensicalness of the Aristotelian understanding of politics. Larmore's neutrality thesis is pitched at such an abstract level of generality that he is never obliged to specify how the neutrality doctrine can be rendered meaningful outside the classical liberal context of life-and-death religious combat.

At least it is intelligible why one would invoke the language of neutrality in reference to the claims of religious absolutism, although even in this case it is highly questionable whether the absence of a public theology in the liberal state constitutes political *neutrality*, for such a regime is hardly "neutral" towards theocratic politics. The notion of neutrality is all the more suspect when applied to the broader range of social and economic policy. For instance, it is difficult to know even what Larmore means when he suggests that state intervention in regulating the distribution of wealth "must be neutral with regard to the interests of rich and poor."[52] Who actually imagines that such neutrality is, even in principle, attainable? Can we have, say, a neutral political order that accommodates both a libertarian and a socialist? Surely, it is impossible to design institutions that will make both equally happy or equally unhappy (unless we opt for a dictatorship equally oppressive of liberty and equality). In general, the very enterprise of designing political institutions, or even conceiving what *constitutes* a "political" institution, will be weighted to one side or the other. Even in a case such as policy towards abortion, where there is, admittedly, the need for a modus vivendi, it is unclear what neutrality might signify. What would count as a neutral policy in a conflict where one side sees abortion as such as evil and the other side sees it as an inalienable prerogative of women?[53] In such a case, one could only approach a resolution by changing the moral fabric of the terms in which the issue is debated, not by pretending to a spurious "neutrality."

Another version of the neutrality thesis has recently been formulated by Will Kymlicka.[54] He, too, argues vigorously for the traditional liberal distinction between state and society: state neutrality versus social nonneutrality; the renunciation of "state perfectionism" versus the acceptance of individual perfectionism as this unfolds within civil society. But contrary to Kymlicka's argument, the fact is that the liberal state is part and parcel of liberal society. The liberal state is no more neutral towards moral ends and cultural aspirations than is liberal society. It is surely no coincidence that the liberal state is governed by the same principles of bureaucratic social organization, technocratic management, and pursuit of higher productivity that drive liberal society. In short, the liberal dichotomy of state and society raises more questions than it answers.[55]

The questioning of Larmore's philosophy of liberalism may be pressed on two distinct fronts. First, one may ask whether, as an empirical matter, the liberal state *is,* or could be, neutral. Second, one may ask whether, even if empirically the state falls short of neutrality, neutrality itself is a coherent political ideal, something to which we *should* aspire? Having posed some questions on the first front, let us now devote some attention to the second. In accordance with Larmore's neutrality principle, the liberal state ought to be uncompromisingly neutral between a conception of the good life centered on the principle of doing as little as one can get away with and endeavoring to get others to subsidize one's indolence, and on the other hand, a conception of the good life centered on notions of effort, conscientious work, and pride in what one does. It should be neutral between a conception of the good life geared towards the attainment of chemical euphoria at every possible opportunity and a conception of the good life focused on ideas of social responsibility. (I allow that the formulation of these examples is not neutral.) It should not require a very sophisticated moral reflection to see that this provides a recipe not for principled liberal statesmanship but for the moral self-destruction of the liberal state. To the extent that the state comes to understand itself in these terms, it brings down upon itself just this kind of self-vitiating calamity.

In one place Larmore suggests that the account of liberalism in the famous "race of devils" passage in Kant's *Perpetual Peace* is superior to the standard Kantian account of liberalism, based on the protection and promotion of autonomy, because the former account makes the least possible moral demands upon members of the state (and therefore does not prejudice the individual's choice of his or her own "personal ideal"—which may have nothing to do with the pursuit of autonomy).[56] Now it may be the case that citizens of the liberal state simply *are* devils, and that it would be a moralistic fantasy to hope to transform them into something other than devils. But surely it cannot be a matter of indifference to the state whether its citizens are or are not devils;

and it would be truly extraordinary to regard a state that was indifferent to whether they were devils or not as on principle morally superior to a state that was not indifferent to whether they were devils or not, on grounds of the imperative of liberal neutralism. On this minimalist rendering of liberalism, liberal statesmen would be left simply having to pray that citizens do not adopt those conceptions of the good life that would render the state morally uninhabitable.

In a revealing passage, one that is most remarkable in a treatise mainly devoted to the moral definition of political community, Larmore rules out as "next to impermissible" the violation of deontological duties involving, say, harm to the innocent "for the sake of some particularistic commitment."[57] But of course participation in a political community is a particularistic commitment that quite commonly entails the overriding of such duties, such as when citizens are enlisted in wars to defend the political community, and when this cannot be done short of conducting all-out war involving the killing of innocent civilians. That the example of citizenship as a particularistic commitment does not occur to Larmore in this context is a symptom of the poverty of his account of what is required to hold a political society together.[58] By his reckoning, the only alternative to the "neutral" state is the reactionary "organic" model of political society, which he assigns to all critics of liberalism, whether conservative or radical.[59] Larmore is disdainful of MacIntyre's challenge to the effect that "from an Aristotelian point of view a modern liberal political society can appear only as a collection of citizens of nowhere who have banded together for their common protection."[60] However, MacIntyre here is not simply giving expression to romanticist fancy; he is posing a problem that the neutralist conception of political community not only has not even begun to address but abstains in principle from addressing.

As we have seen, on Larmore's view, the liberal political order does not seek to foster institutions or practices expressive of a certain vision of human life, philosophical anthropology, or metaphysical conception of personality, but merely offers a neutral modus vivendi between individuals whose philosophies of life cannot be otherwise reconciled. And as we noted earlier, Rawls too has increasingly seen his enterprise in these terms. In fact, in

the latest statement of his views ("The Priority of Right and
Ideas of the Good"), Rawls's position fully converges with that of
Larmore. The function of political liberalism is not to promote
autonomy or individuality since this is merely another controversial moral-philosophical ideal to be avoided. Rather, the conception takes its point of departure from the historical circumstance
that pluralism is simply a fact—a sociological given. Notwith-
standing differences of terminology, it is clear that Rawls's vision
of liberalism is also a neutralist vision.[61]

Although Larmore is insistent throughout that the chief aim of
his neutralist political philosophy is the repudiation of any architectonic political morality, it should be fairly obvious that his political philosophy does contain a moral ranking, and must contain
one. It ranks the virtue of tolerance (or decency, or civility) above
other virtues, as all liberal political philosophies cannot help doing.[62] Even liberal philosophy, as anti-Aristotelian as it tries to be,
fits within an Aristotelian meta-ethic of ranking of excellences, or
hierarchies of virtue.[63] But why should it be imagined, as
Larmore clearly assumes, that the avoidance of a forthright moral
ranking (especially one with metaphysical sanction) actually
strengthens rather than weakens liberal philosophy?[64] Not the
least of the puzzles generated by recent developments in liberal
theory is the question of exactly why metaphysical economy
should be considered the outstanding criterion of philosophical
progress. The great classic liberals, like Kant, were more honest in
acknowledging that one could not pursue moral theory very far at
all without committing oneself to a fairly ambitious philosophical
anthropology (although Kant himself generally, though not always, concealed his philosophical anthropology by presenting his
theory as a theory of moral agency *for all rational agents*, not necessarily limited to the class of human beings).[65] Perhaps we can await
the return to a philosophically more inspiring phase of liberalism
when liberal philosophers at last lay aside Occam's razor.

What does the celebration of modern pluralism come to? Before we can render our ultimate verdict, we must try once again to
clarify the classical, antipluralist position that the pluralists repudi-
ate. Does it mean, as the pluralist suggests, that all differences in
the ends, projects, and aspirations of unique human beings are
considered aberrations from a fixed norm? (In Larmore's formu-

lation: "a wish to live life as a whole animated by a single dominant purpose, and a hope for an existence uncompromised by moral loss and unriven by unsettleable conflict.")[66] For instance, I choose to become a violinist, raise a family, and pursue the middle-class dream; my neighbor decides to devote his life to the priesthood, to forgo the cares of family life, and departs for Central America where all his energies will henceforth be dedicated to alleviating the hardships of the poor. Does the Aristotelian commitment to the idea of a human telos entail that at least one of these lives is misguided, and that the two cannot both be legitimate ways to live a life, since the human good is unitary, and the two human lives sketched here pursue incompatible paths of fulfillment? Aristotelianism would then display obliviousness to the brute fact of human diversity. Clearly, this would be absurd. From the fact that Aristotle expressly criticizes Plato for trying to reduce all "goods" to a singular "Good," one may gather that Aristotle too regards this as absurd.[67] What, then, is the Aristotelian after? Consider a second set of alternatives. Imagine a child raised in a loving environment, with supportive parents, ample educational facilities, and opportunities to develop his or her highest capacities (playing the violin, helping those in need, etc.). Now picture the same child raised in a ghetto, without adequate parental care, starved of cultural and intellectual nourishment to stimulate his or her curiosity, surrounded by dope pushers, and so on. Here the Aristotelian language of human flourishing commands great power. In fact, it seems to me that the liberal vocabulary of rights, liberties and autonomy-maximizing diversity can hardly begin to do justice to this situation. Far more apt are the naturalistic Aristotelian metaphors of the plant that thrives in favorable conditions and withers or atrophies or is stultified when it suffers certain definable kinds of deprivation. Admittedly, what constitutes proper care of a fern will kill a cactus, and vice versa. But Aristotle makes full allowance for differences of this kind. A healthy plant is a healthy plant, even if different plants require different conditions for maximal healthiness; so too for the notion of a flourishing human being.[68] By contrast, if diversity as such is what we desire, as liberalism suggests, then why should life in the ghetto be considered one of J. S. Mill's "experiments of living"?[69] Moreover, one need not choose such extreme examples for Aristotelian language to prove itself. If we compare the musically gifted child whose talents are encouraged with the one deprived of help or instruction, it is reasonable to speak of the frustration or consummation, stunting or flourishing, of aspects of the human telos. And the same applies, more generally, to possibilities of moral life as such. As I learn to behave decently, act generously, choose wisely, make good judgments, I build capacities, develop forms of human potential, help to realize human nature at its best, that once again warrant the naturalistic metaphors of a flourishing versus truncated existence.

Why does the pluralist oppose this particular way of talking about the human condition? What is objectionable about a teleological moral vocabulary? It strikes me that the pluralist's fears of "monism" or dogmatic naturalism are misplaced. Needless to say, it is not difficult to read Aristotle as advancing a neat hierarchy, with philosophers at the top, Athenian aristocrats next to the top, and everyone else judge as grossly inferior by this dual standard. But certainly neo-Aristotelians can avail themselves of the considerable strengths of a teleological moral language without incurring the least risk of such crude dogmatizing. A reasonable pluralism, it seems to me, maintains that there are a variety of possible ways of life, of which the way of life of modern liberal society is one, and confronted with this plurality one can compare and criticize various strengths and weaknesses of these different alternatives. An unreasonable pluralism maintains that the supreme advantage of liberalism is that it supplies a neutral political framework for the coexistence of opposing ways of life, as if it furnished a kind of "meta-" way of life, and were for that reason elevated above the standards of social criticism applicable to nonpluralistic societies.

I fear that what the celebration of pluralism comes to is complacency about the moral adequacy of existing liberal society. Furthermore, much is distressing in contemporary liberal societies that must be overlooked or forgotten in order to sustain this complacency. Every liberal society, even the most generous and just, accommodates large masses of human beings with capacities stunted, aptitudes truncated, possibilities of human nature unconsummated. The *question* of the human good, posed relentlessly by the Aristotelian, even if, as for MacIntyre, the answer is recognized to be elusive, renders ethical complacency impossible to maintain. This points to my final theme, which is that of conflicting conceptions of the place of theory, a problem that perhaps more than any other puts the Aristotelian and his critic at odds.

Clearly, a neo-Aristotelian strategy of theorizing must involve to some extent the disengagement of the Aristotelian meta-ethic from some of the historically contingent contents of Aristotle's own ethical thinking, for example, the compatibility of justice with the institution of slavery, historically specific features of the description of *megalopsychia*, the moral superiority of the philosopher, and so on.[70] But, it may be countered, if Aristotelianism is detachable from a set of specific ethical ideals to which Aristotle himself was in fact committed, what moral guidance can we hope to secure from this reversion to ancient ethics? My answer is that what Aristotle makes available to us above all is a certain moral vocabulary, a language in which to discuss and debate our ethical and political concerns, and that in the realm of morals and politics, *vocabulary matters*. It matters, for instance, that J. S. Mill appropriates Aristotle to the vocabulary of utility, rather than allowing his own thought to be subsumed within Aristotelian vocabulary.[71] It matters that we speak the language of rights, interests, and preferences rather than the language of virtues, character formation, and telos. Electing to speak in terms of ends rather than values, virtues rather than rights, judgments rather than preferences, would *make a difference,* and not just theoretically but also practically. It matters *politically* whether we are under the sway of a political discourse that privileges Kantian notions of the fortressing of individual rights, or conversely, one that privileges Aristotelian notions of the socialized building of character.[72]

Liberals often denounce theories deriving from alien philosophical traditions because they assume that antiliberal theorizing will immediately issue in antiliberal practice. This in turn presupposes that theory can have only one function, which is to direct practice. But the task of theory, as I see it, is not to tell us *what to do,* but to help us understand *how to reflect upon* what we do, and to conceive and reconceive the theoretical idiom (the partially theorized past idioms and incompletely theorized future idioms) in which we think about diverse possibilities of social and political life. Aristotle offers little direct guidance on the living of a complete life. There are intimations of a hierarchy, but no *prescriptions* (or at least none but the sketchiest) on how to realize this hierarchy in an actual life.[73] Again, what Plato and Aristotle make available to us is not so much a specific orientation prescribing the *content* of political choices as a distinctive *moral vocabulary* that may govern a range of political alternatives. (Plato and Aristotle, perhaps in common with most great theorists, stand in an immensely complex and—for us—almost infinitely elusive relation to the realm of concrete political alternatives.) One can affirm capitalism *or* socialism within a liberal vocabulary of rights and values, or one can affirm capitalism *or* socialism within a Platonic-Aristotelian vocabulary of virtues and fulfillment of a human telos. The leading question for the theorist is, on what basis does one choose between these alternative vocabularies?[74]

MacIntyre, in common with other critics of liberalism, seems to think that we need to get our philosophy right because social reality is a direct or nearly direct reflection of the adequacy or inadequacy of our philosophical beliefs. I certainly do not share this assumption. The moral language current in our society represents in such a bastardized fashion the most refined efforts of theorists that even an appreciably improved liberal philosophy offers no guarantee of reformed practices in the social reality of liberalism. What is needed is not Aristotelian theory but Aristotelian practice. (And this was Aristotle's own position, as I understand it from the *Nicomachean Ethics*.) Yet this does not mean that an Aristotelian can or should be indifferent to the liberal philosophies that supply moral categories for the liberal experience of the world. Even ideological bastardization preserves something of the moral character of·the doctrines that are bastardized. Reform of philosophy will not automatically induce reform of the world, but it might at least dry up some of the wells of respectable intellectual support for certain familiar kinds of nonsense (for instance, the liberal nonsense that antipornography statutes violate "freedom of expression," or the nonsense that individuals have the "right" not to be screened for AIDS, even if this right threatens the safety of others, and so on).

My major objection to Larmore's philosophy of liberalism, and kindred philosophies, is that it places intolerable constraints on the exercise of political judgment. It is not even clear what it means to say that neutrality concerning competing conceptions of the good life is strictly a *political* doctrine, limited to one specific sector of social life, the domain of state action, and should in no way inhibit judgment of the relative validity of extrapolitical goals and aspirations. Suppose I wish to render critical judgment on the phenomenon of endemic crack addiction in contemporary Western societies, and what it signifies with respect to global properties of these societies. Can this be anything other than a *political* judgment about the soundness of the way of life of entire societies? Presumably, Larmore would say that this is impermissible, that it turns legitimate judgments about personal ideals into illegitimate global judgments about society regarded holistically, or that it projects an historically antiquated model of social unity upon complex, differentiated social systems. But surely this is mistaken. All judgments that really count pertain to the unifying principles of whole societies. They cannot be localized to distinct subdivisions of social life, or reduced to judgments about personal life projects. A *political* judgment about crack addition is not reducible to judgments about commercial transactions in inner-city subcultures, or the complexities of legal enforcement, or the personal aspirations of addicts. Here we have, inescapably, a judgment about entire constellations of social life. It is difficult to imagine how critical judgment could even get off the ground if global or holistic judgments are excluded on a point of principle. For similar reasons, the slogan "pluralism of values," wielded by a wide phalanx of liberal theorists, represents, from my point of view, a tremendous flattening of possibilities of critical judgment.

It can hardly come as any news to anyone that a modern society is different from a premodern society, and that it would be both extremely difficult and extremely dangerous to try to transform a modern society into a premodern society. Twentieth-century experiments in this direction have certainly been sufficiently sobering to give pause to even the most naive enthusiast. I am convinced that even Rousseau, the arch-nostalgic according to the perspective of liberals from Constant onwards, was perfectly well aware of the inexorability of modernization, and the hazardousness of attempting to reverse it. But this is not the issue. The issue is, by what theoretical standards ought we to judge a modern society?

The problem with the liberal commitment to individuality, diversity, pluralism, and toleration is certainly not that these are bad things, or unworthy of concern, but that liberal individuality and pluralism are too often a phony individuality and phony pluralism. How can we know whether the individuality and diversity fostered by a society is genuine without looking at the substantive choices and forms of character cultivated by members of that society, which the liberal will regard as itself a kind of "moral intrusiveness" destructive of liberal autonomy.[75] Despite the processes of modernization and differentiation upon which the liberal insists so emphatically, every society, liberal society not excluded, has a center out of which it ranks the paradigmatic practices that define it as a society—perhaps not physically imposed from above by the state, but shaped less discernibly by the moral impulse of social life as a whole. This impalpable moral unity of liberal society, surely subject to ethical and political appraisal, the theoretical partisan of liberalism in large measure fails to acknowledge.[76] Here is something that we may still learn from book 1 of the *Nicomachean Ethics,* whose lessons turn out to be not yet obsolete after all.

NOTES

1. It is a common strategy of liberals to deny that their commitment to political liberalism in any way entails moral scepticism concerning the ranking of superior and inferior forms of life; the liberal commitment merely affirms the illegitimacy of the imposition of any ranking through the agency of the state. However, the subjectivizing tendency of liberal philosophy usually shows through nonetheless. For instance, John Rawls, in his discussion of "the principle of perfection" in *A Theory of Justice* (sect. 50), states that "the freedom and well-being of individuals, when measured by the excellence of their activities and works, is vastly different in value. . . . Comparisons of intrinsic value can obviously be made." Yet a few pages later he argues for the exclusion of perfectionist criteria as political principles—that is, the rejection of notions of excellence as applied to the determination of public policy—on grounds that this would

involve our being "influenced by subtle aesthetic preferences and personal feelings of propriety." Rawls, *A Theory of Justice* (Cambridge: Harvard University Press, 1971), pp. 328, 331. For a particularly ingenious attempt at reconciling liberalism and perfectionism, see Will Kymlicka, "Liberalism and Communitarianism," *Canadian Journal of Philosophy,* 18 (1988), 181–204.

2. Amy Gutmann, "The Central Role of Rawls's Theory," *Dissent,* Summer 1989, 338.

3. Alasdair MacIntyre, "Rights, Practices, and Marxism," *Analyse & Kritik,* 7 (1985), 239. Cf. George F. Will, *Statecraft as Soulcraft* (New York: Simon & Schuster, 1983), p. 160: the expression of all social issues in the language of individual rights "raises the general level of truculence in civic relations."

4. Alasdair MacIntyre, *After Virtue* (Notre Dame: University of Notre Dame Press, 1981), p. 29.

5. Max Weber, *The Protestant Ethic and the Spirit of Capitalism,* trans. Talcott Parsons (New York: Scribner's, 1958), p. 182.

6. Rawls, *A Theory of Justice,* pp. 432–33.

7. All references to the *Ethics* are to the *Nicomachean Ethics.*

8. William A. Galston, *Kant and the Problem of History* (Chicago: University of Chicago Press, 1975), p. 135.

9. Stuart Hampshire, "Ethics: A Defense of Aristotle," in *Freedom of Mind and Other Essays* (Oxford: Clarendon, 1972), p. 79. This essay offers a powerful statement of the surpassing strengths of the Aristotelian approach to moral theory, without neglecting its possible weaknesses.

10. MacIntyre, for one, rejects Aristotle's thesis of the unity of the virtues. At issue is whether, for instance, an otherwise immoral Nazi can possess, say, the virtue of courage (as MacIntyre holds), or whether (as argued by P. T. Geach), what we normally call "courage" is in this case "not really courage," or, if we insist on calling it "courage," that it is at any rate in this instance not a virtue. MacIntyre, *After Virtue,* pp. 167–68; Peter Geach, *The Virtues* (Cambridge: Cambridge University Press, 1977), pp. 159–62. See also Philippa Foot, *Virtues and Vices* (Oxford: Blackwell, 1978), pp. 14–17. To my mind, there is more to be said for Geach's view here than MacIntyre allows. But apart from this case of courage in its relations with the other virtues, Geach too, as it happens, denies the unity of the virtues. Geach, *The Virtues,* pp. 162–68. See also Bernard Williams, *Ethics and the Limits of Philosophy* (Cambridge: Harvard University Press, 1985), pp. 36–37, 43, 153. I would be inclined to say, in answer to MacIntyre *and* Geach, that Aristotle's ethical theory is not a theory of the separate human virtues, but a theory of general human flourishing, and is concerned with the virtues, and with their mutual relation, insofar as

they bear upon the possibility of general human flourishing. So while it is true that one may be an honest person and yet a coward, or a fearless person and yet a fool, one has to affirm some kind of unity of the virtues for the theory of the virtues to have the relevance for the problem of the possibility of *eudaimonia* that Aristotle intended it to have.

11. For a canonical statement of the liberal repudiation of Aristotelian "civic humanism," see Rawls, "The Priority of Right and Ideas of the Good," *Philosophy & Public Affairs,* 17 (1988), 272–73. Rawls, along with other liberals, assumes that politics represents merely one among many sectors of social life, and that it would be metaphysically extravagant to privilege one among many possible outlets of social interaction. I am not persuaded that Aristotle has in any way been refuted in his conception that the political relation encompasses and orders the multitude of lesser social relations, that the former denominates the whole in relation to which the latter stand as parts.

12. Seymour M. Hersh, *The Price of Power: Kissinger in the Nixon White House* (New York: Summit, 1983), p. 124.

13. Ibid. The mystery has perhaps now resolved itself. The Soviets have just now, twenty years later, admitted that the Soviet military was involved in combat activity in Egypt commencing in October 1969.

14. MacIntyre, *After Virtue,* p. 204.

15. Galson, *Kant and the Problem of History,* p. 133.

16. Ibid., pp. 188–89.

17. For instance, in his doctrine of prudence, Aquinas, precisely by resolving the ambiguity in Aristotle as to whether *phronesis* appoints ends or merely selects means, actually diminishes the status of prudence. In consequence, *phronesis cannot* loom as large in Aquinas's moral theory as it does in Aristotle's ethics, despite the fact that the doctrine of prudence is intended by Aquinas to be faithfully Aristotelian. The doctrine is more categorical but less Aristotelian. See St. Thomas Aquinas, *Summa Theologiae,* Volume 36: *Prudence,* ed. Thomas Gilby O.P. (London: Eyre & Spottiswoode, 1974), p. 23 (2a2ae, Question 47, article 6). (Chapter 5 of Geach's book *The Virtues* should offer a sufficient illustration of the difference between Thomist prudence and Aristotelian prudence.)

18. As I understand the structure of the *Ethics,* the "theory of the good," interspersed with various digressions, is composed of the following passages: 1094al–b12; 1095a14–a30; 1095b13–96a10; 1097a15–98a19; 1098b7–1102a4; 1176a30–79a33. The "theory of the virtues," strictly speaking, or, more strictly, the theory of excellences of character, runs from 1102a5 to 1176a29. Read like this, the theory of the virtues represents almost a kind of large "digression"!

19. Galston, *Kant and the Problem of History,* pp. 178, 183.

20. Marcus Aurelius, *Meditations*, book 10, sect. 33.

21. Galston, *Kant and the Problem of History*, pp. 157–58.

22. Ibid., pp. 189–90.

23. Charles Taylor, *The Explanation of Behavior* (New York: Humanities, 1964).

24. Hans Jonas, *The Phenomenon of Life: Toward a Philosophical Biology* (Chicago: University of Chicago Press, 1982).

25. Galston, *Kant and the Problem of History*, pp. 161–62, 168, 172.

26. This thesis of the dependence of Aristotelian ethics on Aristotelian cosmology is affirmed by, among many others, Leo Strauss. See Strauss, *Natural Right and History* (Chicago: University of Chicago Press, 1953), pp. 7–8; "Letter to Helmut Kuhn," *Independent Journal of Philosophy*, 2 (1978), 24; *The Rebirth of Classical Political Rationalism*, ed. Thomas L. Pangle (Chicago: University of Chicago Press, 1989), p. 34. Strauss avows that, much as he would wish to embrace Aristotelianism, he is debarred by the incredibility of Aristotelian cosmology. Although MacIntyre seems also to be committed to this thesis in *After Virtue*, p. 183, he adopts a radically different line in "Bernstein's Distorting Mirrors," *Soundings*, 67 (1984), 38–39. For further discussion of this question, see my presentation of Gadamer's Aristotelianism in "Do We Need a Philosophical Ethics?," *Philosophical Forum*, 20 (1989), 231–32; and Charles Taylor's account of his own Aristotelianism in relation to MacIntyre's, in "Justice after Virtue," in *Kritische Methode und Zukunft der Anthropologie*, ed. Michael Benedikt and Rudolf Burger (Vienna: Wilhelm Braunmuller, 1985), p. 24.

27. Leo Strauss, *Studies in Platonic Political Philosophy* (Chicago: University of Chicago Press, 1983), pp. 140–41.

28. Similar points are made by Martha Nussbaum in *The Fragility of Goodness* (Cambridge: Cambridge University Press, 1986), p. 6n. Inexplicably, though, she employs the very un-Aristotelian language of value (ibid., p. 7n.).

29. Galston, *Kant and the Problem of History*, pp. 153–57, 173, 186–87.

30. Cf. Hampshire, *Freedom of Mind and Other Essays*, p. 59.

31. Hans-Georg Gadamer, *Truth and Method* (New York: Seabury, 1975), p. 525, note 225. More generally, see *Truth and Method*, pp. 278–89, 489–90; Gadamer, *Reason in the Age of Science*, trans. F. G. Lawrence (Cambridge: MIT Press, 1981), pp. 133–34; and Gadamer, *The Idea of the Good in Platonic-Aristotelian Philosophy*, trans. P. C. Smith (New Haven: Yale University Press, 1986), chapter 6.

32. "Gadamer on Strauss: An Interview," *Interpretation*, 12 (1984), 12.

33. The problem of whether book 10, chapters 6–8 of the *Ethics* is consistent or inconsistent with the broader intent of Aristotle's ethical theory is posed sharply in Nussbaum, *The Fragility of Goodness*, pp. 373–77.

34. Galston, *Kant and the Problem of History*, pp. 137–38, 174.

35. Cf. *Nicomachean Ethics*, book 10, chapter 7: 1177b24–26.

36. See, for instance, Strauss, *Studies in Platonic Political Philosophy*, p. 149: "by virtue of being an -ism, pluralism is a monism."

37. Charles E. Larmore, *Patterns of Moral Complexity* (Cambridge: Cambridge University Press, 1987). In "The Priority of Right and Ideas of the Good," Rawls voices strong sympathy and support for Larmore's reformulation of political liberalism.

38. On Rawls, see Larmore, *Patterns of Moral Complexity*, pp. 125–26 and 174–75, notes 67 and 68. In "Justice as Fairness: Political not Metaphysical," *Philosophy & Public Affairs*, 14 (1985), 245–47, and again in "The Priority of Right and Ideas of the Good," pp. 267–68, Rawls states explicitly that his concern is not autonomy as such. But it would seem that here Rawls's drive for metaphysical parsimony, like Larmore's, has gotten the better of the inner impulses of his own liberalism.

39. Larmore, *Patterns of Moral Complexity*, p. 65.

40. The former alternative is the one opted for by William Galston in his defense of liberalism. See, especially, "Defending Liberalism," *American Political Science Review*, 76 (1982), 621–29.

41. For Larmore's critique of "Aristotle's whole/part model of society," see *Patterns of Moral Complexity*, pp. 39, 96–99, 103–4, 106–7, 168–69 (note 21), 170–71 (notes 33 and 34). For similar assertions as to the obsolescence of the classical Aristotelian framework of social theory on the part of Larmore's mentor, Niklas Luhmann, see *The Differentiation of Society*, trans. S. Holmes and C. Larmore (New York: Columbia University Press, 1982), pp. 223, 229, 251, 257, 343, 391 (note 7), 392 (note 10), and for commentary, xv–xvii, xx. For helpful filling in of the "Luhmannesque" background of Larmore's argument, see the introduction to *The Differentiation of Society*, coauthored by Larmore and Stephen Holmes.

42. Larmore, *Patterns of Moral Complexity*, pp. xii, 10, 34–35, 37–38.

43. Ibid., pp. 35–37.

44. Ibid., pp. 36–39. The curious thing about Larmore's quarrel with MacIntyre is that Larmore and MacIntyre actually *agree* that Aristotle is a monist, and that monism of this kind is to be avoided. Hampshire, another ambivalent Aristotelian, agrees too: see *Morality and Conflict* (Oxford: Blackwell, 1983), pp. 1, 140–41, 144, 148. So Larmore concludes that MacIntyre is, despite his using Aristotle as a club with

which to batter modernity, in fact "a pluralist *malgré lui*" (*Patterns of Moral Complexity*, p. 39). But the fact that certain Aristotelians and anti-Aristotelians can agree on this does not prove that they are right about Aristotle. Indeed, Larmore himself concedes ignorance "of any passage where Aristotle explicitly rules out the possibility of moral conflict"—with the exception of a single passage of dubious authorship (ibid., pp. 159–60, note 39). For a challenge to MacIntyre's account of Aristotle, see Hans-George Gadamer, "Gibt es auf Erden ein Maß," *Philosophische Rundschau*, 32 (1985), 1–7, esp. 4–5. A further paradox of Larmore's polemic against neo-Aristotelianism is that MacIntyre (at least in *After Virtue*) emphasizes the dependence of Aristotle's ethics upon cosmology, whereas Larmore, closer to my own reading of Aristotle, downplays it (*Patterns of Moral Complexity*, pp. 32–33, 159, notes 20 and 25). See note 26 above.

45. MacIntyre, *After Virtue*, p. 68.

46. John Rawls, "The Basic Structure as Subject," *American Philosophical Quarterly*, 14 (1977), 162.

47. Ibid., 165.

48. Larmore, *Patterns of Moral Complexity*, p. 48.

49. Ibid., pp. 45–46.

50. Ibid., pp. 76, 130.

51. It is certainly the case that on issues such as abortion, there are radically opposed points of view grounded in fundamentally different moral and religious commitments that will either be abated by an agreement to disagree (modus vivendi, mutual accommodation, liberal civility and tolerance), or proceed with unremitting hostility and anger. But why should this be posited as the appropriate model of all political disagreement? Or rather, does it not raise doubts about the political soundness of liberal society that this *does* suggest itself as an appropriate model of political disagreement in general? For an argument similar to Larmore's, to which I would raise a similar challenge, see Thomas Nagel, "Moral Conflict and Political Legitimacy," *Philosophy & Public Affairs*, 16 (1987), 215–40.

52. Larmore, *Patterns of Moral Complexity*, p. 129.

53. Cf. William A. Galston, "Pluralism and Social Unity," *Ethics*, 99 (1989), 720–21. Galston cites the same example to argue towards the same conclusion. Also: Michael J. Sandel, "Moral Argument and Liberal Toleration: Abortion and Homosexuality," *California Law Review*, 77 (1989), 531–33.

54. Will Kymlicka, "Liberal Individualism and Liberal Neutrality," *Ethics*, 99 (1989), 883–905, esp. 893–98.

55. For further probing of the liberal neutrality argument, see my

review of D. A. J. Richards, *Toleration and the Constitution* in *University of Toronto Law Journal*, 38 (1988), 109–14; and "What's the Matter with Liberalism?," in *Law and the Community: The End of Individualism?*, ed. Allan C. Hutchinson and Leslie Green (Toronto: Carswell, 1989), pp. 37–56.

56. Larmore, *Patterns of Moral Complexity*, p. 83. The passage from Kant is in *On History*, ed. Lewis White Beck (Indianapolis: Bobbs-Merrill, 1963), p. 112.

57. Larmore, *Patterns of Moral Complexity*, p. 114. Cf. p. 148.

58. Cf. John Dunn, *Western Political Theory in the Face of the Future* (Cambridge: Cambridge University Press, 1979), p. 71: "if nationalism as a political force is in some ways a reactionary and irrationalist sentiment in the modern world, its insistence on the moral claims of the community upon its members . . . is in many ways a less superstitious political vision than the intuitive political consciousness of most capitalist democracies today"; and Will, *Statecraft as Soulcraft*, p. 94: "Liberal, bourgeois, democratic—in a word, Lockean—societies have more complex prerequisites than they seem to think. . . . The aim is not to make society inhospitable to pluralism, but to make pluralism safe for society."

59. Larmore, *Patterns of Moral Complexity*, pp. 119, 126.

60. Ibid., p. 175, note 71. The quotation is from MacIntyre, *After Virtue*, p. 147.

61. Rawls states that he prefers to avoid the terminology of neutrality because of the tendency to confuse "neutrality of aim" (what the state intends) and "neutrality of effect" (what actually results) ("The Priority of Right and Ideas of the Good," p. 263). Likewise, Rawls says he is unhappy with a modus vivendi terminology because it tends to imply an instrumentalist relation to the political community, rather than "a moral conception affirmed on moral grounds" (ibid., p. 274). But despite these terminological preferences, Rawls's liberal doctrine is, no less than Larmore's, a neutralist doctrine. The heart of political liberalism, he says, is "the fact of pluralism" (ibid., pp. 259, 275).

62. For a more candid acknowledgment that liberalism involves a moral ranking, albeit a negative ranking of vices to be avoided rather than a positive ranking of virtues to be sought, see Judith N. Shklar's *Ordinary Vices* (Cambridge: Belknap, 1984). Of course, Shklar's orientation to the "table of vices" is compatible with the inverse ranking of vices yielding a corresponding ranking of virtues, with the virtue of tolerance at the summit.

63. Cf. Stuart Hampshire, *Morality and Conflict*, p. 19; and Hampshire, *Freedom of Mind and Other Essays*, p. 85.

64. Larmore, *Patterns of Moral Complexity*, pp. 66, 92.

65. Cf. Taylor, "Justice after Virtue," pp. 33–34.

66. Larmore, *Patterns of Moral Complexity*, p. 152. Cf. Hampshire, *Morality and Conflict*, p. 140: "as moral philosophers we must be looking for the perfect specimen of humanity, without defect, lacking nothing that contributes to the ideal whole person and the ideal whole life. The idea of the human good, presented in this framework, implies that any falling-away, any comparative failure in total achievement, will be a defect and a vice, a form of incompleteness."

67. For a contrary account, emphasizing Aristotle's underlying residual Platonism, see Hampshire, *Morality and Conflict*, pp. 151–53.

68. Conditions of botanical flourishing and conditions of human flourishing may stand in a less remote relation to each other than one might think. I recently came across a report describing an experiment involving the comparison of plants, otherwise similarly conditioned, placed in front of speakers playing classical music on the one hand, heavy metal and hard rock on the other. Results of the experiment showed consistently that "the plants listening to classical music grow at a 45-degree angle toward the speakers, and they develop very healthy root systems with many more branches and hairs than a normal plant," whereas "the plants listening to rock music either die or their growth is dramatically retarded. Those that survive end up with poor, sparse root systems." Examination of the "root systems" of regular human listeners to heavy metal music may, I suspect, yield similar conclusions ("A spoonful of music," *Toronto Star*, January 15, 1990, p. C1).

69. John Stuart Mill, *On Liberty*, ed. David Spitz (New York: Norton, 1975), p. 54.

70. These are examples brought up by Hampshire in *Morality and Conflict*, pp. 130, 149, 153.

71. Mill, *On Liberty*, p. 25.

72. There is also, of course, as Judith Shklar has especially emphasized, a Kantian discourse about habituation to virtue (*Ordinary Vices*, pp. 232–36). But as Larmore rightly points out, "What is wrong in Kant's ethics is not that it has nothing to say about character, but rather that it gives an inadequate account of it" (*Patterns of Moral Complexity*, p. 174, note 60). Indeed, it is hard to see how Kant *could* give a coherent account of character within the framework of his moral-philosophical premises. For Kant, morality is synonymous with freedom, and freedom means unconditioned spontaneity. This is theoretically incompatible with Aristotle's (correct) understanding of the intimate relation between ethics and ethos, virtue and habit. So the problem with a Kantian virtue discourse is that it gives either a deficient or an inconsistent account of the relation between moral excellence and habituation.

73. For an energetic defense of Aristotelian ethics along these lines, see D. S. Hutchinson, *The Virtues of Aristotle* (London: Routledge & Kegan Paul, 1986), pp. 51–52, 62. As Hutchinson points out on pp. 46–47, Plato's *ergon* argument in *Republic,* 353b–c, which Aristotle likely draws upon in *Nicomachean Ethics,* book 1, chapter 7 and book 2, chapter 6, is governed by a similar indeterminacy.

74. That the decisive issue is the choice of a paradigmatic moral vocabulary can be seen from the side of liberal philosophy as well. Rawls's difference principle can be used to justify just about any social-economic policy across the spectrum of alternatives, from the policies of Margaret Thatcher at one extreme to those of Mikhail Gorbachev at the other. (Thatcher, too, can perfectly well insist that her policies will eventually secure the long-term interests of the least advantaged.) Rawls himself offers very little help in selecting specific policies.

75. For a typical instance, see Nancy L. Rosenblum's critique of Michael Walzer in "Moral Membership in a Postliberal State," *World Politics,* 36 (1984), 581–96, esp. 592–593.

76. Will Kymlicka's response to my critique of liberal neutralism is based on a radical misunderstanding ("Liberal Individualism and Liberal Neutrality," *Ethics,* 99 [1989], 895–96, note 29). On Kymlicka's account, the nonneutrality of activities in liberal society is not incompatible with the liberal's commitment to state neutrality; indeed, far from refuting the neutralism of the liberal, it is the very ground of the liberal imperative that the *state* remain neutral. This presupposes that civil society instantiates a rich diversity of moral aspirations, which is precisely what the liberal celebrates, and that this social pluralism must be protected from the threatening monism of the state. However, what I meant in asserting the nonneutrality of liberal society is that this axiom of social pluralism is largely mythical, that the activity of civil society as a whole is tilted in a certain direction (the maximization of social productivity, the organization of social life so as to enhance efficiency and technological control, the privileging of scientific over other forms of knowledge, the favoring of ways of life consistent with maximal individual mobility, etc.), and therefore, that liberal society itself embodies a form of monism of which the monism of the liberal state is but one aspect. The liberal state is certainly in complicity with liberal society, even if it does not impose the liberal way of life in exactly the way that the Islamic theocracy in Iran imposes the Islamic way of life. If this claim is right, then the liberal assurance of *political* neutrality fails to be redeemed by the altogether different character of the social realm.

8

THE LIMITS OF ARISTOTELIAN ETHICS

CHARLES LARMORE

Ronald Beiner's central claim is that "the moral self-under-standing of liberalism would be notably strengthened, both theo-retically and practically, if it were to shift from a Kantian discourse of rights and individual autonomy to an Aristotelian discourse of virtues and character formation." This change of perspective, he feels, would lead liberals not just to understand better what they already believe but also to revise some of their most characteristic positions. In his neo-Aristotelian argument, my book *Patterns of Moral Complexity* figures as an object lesson, displaying the sort of implausibility and incoherence to which our thought is subject if we seek to occupy "the furthest extremity from Aristotelian ways of thinking about ethics and politics." I remain unrepentant. One reason is that he has misunderstood some key aspects of my ver-sion of liberalism. But a more important reason is that he has misidentified the point at which, to me and to many other liberal thinkers as well, Aristotle's ethics seems fundamentally inade-quate to the task of political philosophy in modern times.

PLURALISM AND ARISTOTELIANISM

Liberal thinkers have often charged that Aristotelian ethics is unacceptably "monistic": It leaves no room for the "pluralism" that has come to seem a distinctive element of modern experience. For Beiner, this is the chief liberal objection to Aristotelianism. His defense of Aristotle proceeds, not by rescuing monism, but rather by arguing that Aristotle, too, had a pluralist understanding of what is important in life.

Beiner is less clear about the meaning of "pluralism" than we might have wished. In this he is not alone. The first, and far from insignificant thing to note about pluralism is that it is a doctrine. It is an affirmation, opposed to monism, about the nature of value. (I find the term "value" to be more innocent than Beiner does. He claims that "value" is a loaded, because inherently subjectivist term, but this is not confirmed by ordinary usage: we can indeed "confer" value upon things, but we can also "see" that something is valuable. The ontological question whether value is part of the world or a project of our interests is one we can leave aside for present purposes.)[1]

The next thing to observe is that pluralism may be an affirmation about the nature of morality or an affirmation about the nature of human self-realization. Often it presents itself as both. The two affirmations are nonetheless logically independent. Morality is not the same thing as self-fulfillment or the good life. There are other things of value besides doing what we ought morally to do. Of course, it may not be possible to find, or wise to seek, a precise and permanent distinction between the two. But usually morality is understood to be one ingredient in the good life. It is also thought to consist of the constraints we should observe in our pursuit of the other dimensions of the good life. Conceivably, one might be a pluralist about morality, without being one about the other aspects of the good life, and vice versa.

What exactly does pluralism assert? In its general form it holds that the kinds of moral claims upon us and the forms of self-realization we acknowledge are in the end not one, but many. It is, in other words, a doctrine about the *sources* of value. Moral pluralism, in one plausible version, is the view that our moral commitments cannot all be understood in terms of the consequentialist principle of bringing about the most good overall. Some duties do fit this principle, but others are better understood as strict (deontological) demands that we must honor, whatever other people may do as a result of what we do; and still other duties seem to be ours only because we stand in particular bonds of affection to the people to whom we owe them.[2] Similarly, pluralism about the good life is the view that the value we find in different ways of life cannot be illuminatingly explained in terms of their all embodying a single good, such as the maximization of pleasure or the exercise of freedom. These different forms of the good life simply call on the different concerns and interests that make up our malleable and complex humanity.

Pluralism is often associated with an appreciation of the possible conflicts among our values and with the recognition that not all good things can exist together in life and society. Beiner makes this point a central part of his understanding of pluralism. Yet it can be a misleading view of pluralism. Monism, too, has room for value conflict and regret, as utilitarians are happy to admit.[3] If instead we view pluralism as fundamentally a doctrine about the multiple sources of value, then we can see that value conflict is important for the pluralist, not because of its prevalence, but because of its difficulty. Monism offers in principle an easy way with conflicts: as a rule, the purportedly single source of value will provide the means for commensurating the opposing commitments and for finding which of them makes the stronger claim. Pluralism harbors no such guarantees. I do not mean that conflicts between commitments that derive from different sources cannot be resolved. On the contrary. Sometimes we can find a solution to such conflicts, not by appealing to a common denominator of value, but rather by the exercise of judgment. For just this reason, however, the pluralist will recognize that discerning the correct solution (where one can indeed be found!) can be inherently difficult and open to controversy.

Beiner and I are in agreement about the importance of judgment.[4] The point on which I wish to insist is that judgment has an indispensable role within a pluralist perspective only because ultimately pluralism is a doctrine asserting that the sources of value are not one, but many. The fact that pluralism is indeed a *doctrine* has a significance for what divides Aristotelianism and liberalism that Beiner seems not to appreciate. But before coming to this point, I shall examine his effort to show that Aristotle, contrary to liberal polemic, was truly a pluralist.

Beiner's strategy is to loosen up the categories of Aristotelian ethics. Thus, he is concerned to separate the broad claim of book 1 of the *Nicomachean Ethics,* according to which our end is to unify our various strivings in a coherent vision of the good life, from the strict assertion of book 10 (chapters 7–8), according to which the contemplative life is superior to the practical life devoted to moral excellence.[5] Wishing to make Aristotle acceptable to contemporary sensibilities, he even suggests that Aristotle's assertion of the superiority of contemplation does not really mean what it seems to say. In reality, Beiner argues, Aristotle showed a "wonderful sensitivity to the complexity and multidimensionality of human ethical experience." He recognized that many different activities, some involving the exercise of moral virtue, others involving the contemplation of eternal truths, are equally valuable and sometimes conflicting. It is "grotesque," Beiner charges, to think of Aristotle as a monist.

Beiner gives a similarly latitudinarian interpretation of Aristotle's view (*Nicomachean Ethics* I.2) that ethics belongs to the domain of politics. According to him, it means no more than the idea that "full humanity presupposes a living awareness of politics." He seems to suggest that this Aristotelian principle is satisfied if we can name the president of the United States and keep abreast of current events.

On both of these points Beiner's interpretation of Aristotelian ethics seems to me less than convincing. The proposition that contemplation offers a higher form of happiness *(eudaimonia)* than action is not a statement that generations of readers have wrongly inferred from what Aristotle wrote in the second half of book 10. It is quite literally what Aristotle wrote there. Perfect happiness *(he teleia eudaimonia),* he wrote (1177a17–19), consists in contemplation *(theoretike),* and the life devoted to moral excellence achieves happiness only in a secondary sense *(deuteros)* (1178a9). It is true, as Beiner observes, that for Aristotle this perfect happiness is reserved for the gods (1177b26–27; 1178b21–22). But from this admission Aristotle did not draw the conclusion that the best human life consists in an even-handed mix of contemplation and action, as Beiner suggests. Instead, Aristotle urged that our aim should be, as far as possible, to become like gods, leaving behind the human sphere and putting on immortality *(athanatizein)* [1177b33; also 1178b23].

This aspiration is not confined to book 10. It is already present in effect in book 1, when Aristotle states that "the good for man is an activity of soul in accordance with virtue, or if there are more kinds of virtue than one, in accordance with the best and most perfect kind" (1098a16–18). The superiority of intellectual to moral virtue is a theme that runs throughout Aristotle's ethical writings. It is connected with his overall metaphysics, in which it is next to self-evident that there are many things in the world of greater value than the human affairs with which morality is concerned:

> It is extraordinary that anyone should regard political science or prudence *(phronesis)* as most important unless man is the highest being in the world. . . . There are other beings far more divine than man, the most evident examples being those bodies of which the heaven is composed. (*Nicomachean Ethics*, VI.7, 1141a20–22, a34–b2)

Beiner's view that "the priority assigned to the contemplative life is . . . subject to the comprehensive arbitration of phronesis," however attractive it may be to modern preconceptions, cannot count as a summary of Aristotelian doctrine.[6]

A clear sign, I might add, of the extent to which Beiner is prepared to cut down Aristotle's philosophy to the accepted terms of our own experience is the fact that he never asks just what Aristotle had in mind by contemplation or *theoria*. As a matter of fact, it was something very different from how we understand theory today. It did not mean theoretical inquiry, the discovery of truth. It meant going over what is already known, beholding it and appreciating it. Learning was no part of Aristotelian *theoria*, except as a precondition. I am not sure that we today can attach much sense to valuing this sort of activity. It has no role in modern science, which learns, not in order to contemplate, but in order to learn more. Perhaps the idea of *theoria* still resonates with certain kinds of religious experience.

In any case, the first part of Beiner's argument for Aristotle's "pluralism" does not succeed. Aristotle did not believe that there are many ways of life equally valuable. On the contrary, he held that the contemplative life is the supreme form of happiness. The moral life represented for him a lesser form of self-realization.

The precise nature of this subordination of moral to intellectual virtue is not quite clear in Aristotle's thought. His view may have been that the value of what the moral life aims to achieve lies in providing the *conditions* for contemplation. Or, as I am inclined to believe, it may have been that contemplation offers a more perfect realization of our nature. Either way, Aristotle turns out to be no pluralist. Different ways of life, he maintained, are to be ranked in accord with how closely they approximate to the one supreme form of existence, which is the divine life of contemplation.

Beiner's account of the connection between ethics and politics in Aristotle's thought is similarly inadequate. Aristotle did not wish simply to point out the importance of an informed citizenry, which takes an interest in politics. He embraced the much stronger claim that political life is the domain in which the moral virtues are best exercised. "The exercise of the practical virtues," he proclaimed in the *Nicomachean Ethics* (1177b6–7), "takes place in politics or in warfare." There are basically three kinds of lives, Aristotle argued: "the philosophical aspires to a concern with wisdom and contemplation, the political with fine actions,— actions that result from virtue—and the pleasure-loving with physical pleasures" (*Eudemian Ethics* 1215b1–5). Given his view that moral excellence is achieved through political participation, Aristotle appropriately assigned to the state the task, not simply of protecting individual persons and rights, but more grandly of fostering the good life (*Politics* III.9; also *Nicomachean Ethics* 1180a24–30).

Thus, Aristotle had no room for the pluralist idea that there are many different areas of social life in which the exercise of moral virtue can flourish. On this score, Aristotle's ethics is irrelevant to the conditions of modern life, except perhaps for those parts of its spent in imaginative nostalgia about earlier times. One of the great insights of modern times, beginning in the Reformation, has been an appreciation of the moral possibilities of ordinary life: moral excellence is not reserved for the hero or the saint, but is achievable even by the humblest of us, in the everyday areas of work and family.[7] Such unaristocratic thoughts form no part of Aristotle's ethical outlook. No one has put so well as Pufendorf what must seem in hindsight the disqualifying narrow-mindedness of Aristotle's ethics:

THE LIMITS OF ARISTOTELIAN ETHICS

[Aristotle's] *Ethics,* which deals with the principles of human action, apparently contains scarcely anything other than the duties
of a citizen in some Greek polis. Just as in his *Politics,* he seems
mainly to have had in view the practices of his own Greek states,
and to have put a special value on their liberty; which is a grave
defect in a study intended to serve the interests of the whole
human race.[8]

In sum, Beiner's Aristotle is too much like us to be much like
Aristotle himself. If, in fact, Beiner's portrait of Aristotle the
pluralist were correct, it would have little to teach us that we did
not already know. As it is, Aristotle's ethics does have much to
teach us, but largely because its outlook is so alien to any we
might accept today. We increase our self-understanding when we
reflect upon how we have become what we are, and, this means,
when we remember what we have had good reason to leave
behind.

Moral Disagreement and Liberal Politics

My deepest quarrel with Beiner's paper is not, however, over
matters of Aristotelian scholarship. It lies rather with his assumption that to bring out the pluralism in Aristotle's ethical outlook
is to dismantle the chief reason liberal thinkers may have for
being less than enthusiastic about Aristotelian ethics. No doubt,
the view that there are many valid forms of the good life, too
diverse in their commitments and purposes to admit of any ranking, has been used by many liberals (with a good deal more
justice than Beiner allows) to dismiss the claims of Aristotelian
ethics. Yet I do not believe that it is the decisive point at which
Aristotelian and liberal thought must part ways.

To see why, recall that pluralism, like monism, is itself an
affirmation about the nature of the good life: it asserts that the
forms of self-realization are at bottom not one, but many. Now
the enduring insight of liberal thought seems to me to lie at a
different, more reflective level. It consists in the recognition that
reasonable people tend to differ and disagree about the nature
of the good life, and in particular about the validity or the extent
of pluralism. Reasonableness, by which I mean thinking and
conversing in good faith and applying, as best one can, the gen-

eral capacities of reason that belong to every domain of inquiry, has ceased to seem a guarantee of unanimity. Liberal thinkers first focused on this fact in the realm of religion. But over the past four centuries its relevance has grown more general. It has become a salient feature of modern experience. It is here that the deepest departure from the Aristotelian perspective is located. On matters concerning the meaning of life, discussion among reasonable people has seemed to liberals to tend naturally not toward consensus, as Aristotle thought, but rather toward controversy. The more we talk about such things, the more we disagree—even with ourselves, as Montaigne observed ("De l'art de conférer," *Essais* III.8). Or as Thomas Paine wrote, "I do not believe that any two men, on what are called doctrinal points, think alike who think at all. It is only those who have not thought that appear to agree" (*The Rights of Man* II.5).[9] It is important to note that this outlook is not the same as scepticism. We may still believe we have sound reasons for certain views about what makes life worth living. So we may be entitled to claim that people who reject them are in error. The point is that, all the same, we would be foolish not to expect our views to meet with some disagreement in a calm and careful discussion.[10]

This natural tendency toward disagreement about matters of ultimate significance represents the central political problem for liberal thought—or, more exactly, for that current of liberal thought that should have the greatest claim on us today. Liberalism has maintained that we can find some way of living together, some form of political association, that avoids the rule of force. It has been the conviction that we can agree upon a core morality, while continuing to disagree about what makes life worth living. This outlook got its influential start in the natural law theory of Grotius, who seems to me a far better guide in these matters than Aristotle.[11]

A great many of Beiner's objections to my own formulation of liberalism arise from not recognizing that its aim is to be this sort of *minimal moral conception*. "Political neutrality," as the cardinal liberal principle, is in my view a moral conception, claiming that legitimate political principles are those that can be justified without any appeal to controversial views of the good life. Its own justification depends on moral premises, in particular on what I call the norms of rational dialogue and equal respect for persons. But at the same time it is meant to be a minimal conception, in the sense that it does not take sides in one of the central and enduring conflicts in our culture. Its justification is neutral between, on the one hand, individualist conceptions of the good life, which hold that forms of life can be valuable only if chosen from a standpoint of critical detachment, and which have often been invoked (since Kant and Mill) to defend liberal ideals, and on the other, the reaffirmation of the value of tradition and belonging, which Romantics from Herder and Hegel to MacIntyre and Sandel have often directed not just against individualist views, but by extension, against liberal principles as well. This neutrality is meant to be the advantage of such a minimal moral conception. Recognizing that the dispute between individualism and tradition is but one more instance of how the good life is an enduring object of dispute, "political liberalism" (as I would call it) seeks to lay out a minimal moral basis for liberalism that Romantic defenders of tradition and community, as well as individualists, can affirm.[12]

Thus, Beiner is wrong to say that the intention of my political liberalism is to foster "simply the negative goal of averting conflict and moral stalemate," to be "no longer a noble moral aspiration, a shared moral commitment . . . [but] instead . . . merely the exigency of mutual political accommodation," to affirm "no ordering principles that bind together and shape a liberal . . . political community." He mistakes the search for moral common ground for the abandonment of morality. Similarly, it is no real objection at all for him to reveal that my "political philosophy does contain a moral ranking, and must contain one. It ranks the virtue of tolerance . . . above other virtues, as all liberal political philosophies canot help doing." Of course it does, as the pivotal role of the moral norm of equal respect in my justification of liberal neutrality demonstrates. I should add that this norm, as I conceive it, demands equal respect for persons, and not for their views, as Beiner supposes when he quips, rhetorically, "should I respect a view of life that is servile, conformist, and unreflective?" The norm of equal respect holds that political principles—that is, principles to which compliance may be effected by force, if need be—must be justifiable to all who are to be subject to them, for otherwise persons would be being treated only as means (as objects of coercion) and not also as ends in themselves (as beings whose distinctive capacity of thinking and acting on the basis of reasons is engaged directly). My claim is that this moral commitment, along with a norm of rational dialogue, constitutes a core morality that individualists and Romantics can both affirm and that suffices to justify the liberal principle of political neutrality.

This version of liberalism need hardly be apologetic about the moral adequacy of existing liberal society, as Beiner charges. On the contrary, it strips away one of the chief props of contemporary individualism—namely, the assumption that individualism is essential to the viability of a liberal political order. To those who are convinced that individualism projects an impoverished view of life, political liberalism offers the means for a powerful argument against a leading contemporary prejudice. It shows that fundamental liberal principles are not at issue in this dispute, that they can continue to function as common ground. This is fortunate, since Beiner, like the antiliberals with whom he allies himself, has not even specified a political alternative, much less one that is discernibly better than the view that the state should not undertake to impose one controversial vision of the good life at the expense of others.[13]

Had Beiner seen that reasonable disagreement about the good life, not pluralism, is the central phenomenon for liberal theory, he would have given a fairer account of my own position. More importantly, he would have a more accurate view of what really divides liberal thought from Aristotelianism. He would not have wondered "why metaphysical economy should be considered [by liberals] the outstanding criterion of philosophical progress." Metaphysical ambition naturally sparks dispute, often about issues of deep conviction. Liberalism is the search for a minimal moral conception by which people can escape the rule of force and live together in political association, despite their enduring disagreements about the nature of the good life. This project is alien to Aristotelian ethics, which trusts that reasonable people tend naturally to agree about matters of ultimate significance. Aristotelian categories can be loosened up, as Beiner has done. They can be made amenable to contemporary sensibilities in various ways. They can be turned into near-platitudes. None-theless, the ideal of a common moral ground amidst profound and abiding disagreement remains nowhere to be found in Aris-totelian thought. As Beiner rightly says, the Aristotelian outlook is that "the central purpose of a society . . . is the cultivation of virtue." If the modern experience has turned on the recognition that the meaning of life is a natural object of disagreement, then the cultivation of virtue—if it means self-realization, and not just practicing the one virtue of mutual respect—cannot be our com-mon political bond, though it keeps its importance in other areas of social life. This is why Aristotle cannot be our guide.

NOTES

1. Beiner's claim goes back at least as far as Heidegger, *Brief über den Humanismus* (1947), pp. 179–80 in *Wegmarken* (Frankfurt: Kloster-mann, 1969).

2. For more on this sort of moral pluralism, see my *Patterns of Moral Complexity* (Cambridge: Cambridge University Press, 1987), pp. 131–53.

3. Cf. R. M. Hare, *Moral Thinking* (Oxford: Oxford University Press, 1981), pp. 25–49.

4. R. Beiner, *Political Judgment* (Chicago: University of Chicago Press, 1983), and my *Patterns of Moral Complexity*, pp. 1–21.

5. There have been others who in wishing to shunt aside Aristotle's intellectualism, have similarly sought, unsuccessfully I believe, to con-trast book 10 with the rest of the *Nicomachean Ethics*. See, for example, J. L. Ackrill, "Aristotle on *Eudaimonia*" (1974), in A. O. Rorty (ed.), *Essays on Aristotle's Ethics* (Berkeley and Los Angeles: University of Cali-fornia Press, 1980), pp. 15–33.

6. A fine précis of the connection between Aristotle's ethics and metaphysics can be found in J. Lear, *Aristotle: The Desire to Understand* (Cambridge: Cambridge University Press, 1988), pp. 318–20. See also Thomas Nagel, "Aristotle on *Eudaimonia*" in Rorty, op. cit., pp. 7–14.

7. For an excellent account of this development, see Charles Taylor, *Sources of the Self* (Cambridge: Harvard University Press, 1989), pp. 211–302.

8. Samuel Pufendorf, *Specimen controversiarum circa jus naturale ipsi nuper motarum* (Uppsala, 1678), p. 9.

9. Cf. Milan Kundera, *The Art of the Novel* (New York: Harper and Row, 1988), p. 158: "There is a fine Jewish proverb: Man thinks, God

laughs. Inspired by that adage, I like to imagine that François Rabelais heard God's laughter one day, and thus was born the idea of the first great European novel. It pleases me to think that the art of the novel came into the world as the echo of God's laughter. But why does God laugh at the sight of man thinking? Because man thinks and the truth escapes him. *Because the more men think, the more one man's thought diverges from another's.* And finally, because man is never what he thinks he is" (my emphasis).

10. I develop this view of liberalism further in "Political Liberalism," *Political Theory,* 18 August 1990.

11. See Grotius, *Prolegomena,* sections 39–40.

12. For more details, see "Political Liberalism."

13. I am also surprised that Beiner thinks it obvious that we have the particularistic duty of citizenship, as opposed to a general duty to support just regimes as best we can, which means usually that we focus our efforts on the country in which we live. On the difficulties in showing that there is a particularistic duty of citizenship, see A. John Simmons, *Moral Principles and Political Obligations* (Princeton: Princeton University Press, 1979).

9

THE LIBERAL VIRTUES

DAVID A. STRAUSS

Does it matter whether liberalism defends itself in the language of virtue, as opposed to the language of impartiality, rights, and equal respect? I will defend the following propositions, which amount to a qualified affirmative answer to that question. Liberalism presupposes a certain conception of the virtues—that is, a certain controversial view about what attributes are good in human beings. That is both an important and an attractive aspect of liberalism. But liberalism and the liberal virtues remain distinctive. The liberal virtues are not Aristotle's virtues, and importing a full Aristotelian vocabulary is not only unnecessary but incompatible with liberal premises.

A conception of virtue might have either a logical or a psychological relation to liberal theory. The logical claim is that such a conception is necessary to justify liberalism—that is, that we cannot justify liberalism unless we can establish that certain human traits are virtues. Alternatively, one might claim that liberalism, if implemented, will as a matter of fact encourage the development of certain traits; or that in practice, liberalism cannot be implemented unless people develop certain traits. Even if there are "liberal virtues" in this sense, there might still exist a justification of liberalism that will persuade someone who does not agree that those traits are virtues. One can accept liberalism without accept-

The Russell Baker Scholars' Fund at the University of Chicago Law School provided support for this project.

ing the excellence of all—or even any—of the human traits needed for its successful implementation.

My first claim is logical. There are two aspects of human nature that must be accepted as virtues if we are to have a coherent justification of liberalism. The reason for calling these characteristics virtues is that if they are not good characteristics for human beings to have, liberalism cannot be justified. These two virtues correspond, respectively, to the two capacities that Rawls identifies as foundations for his liberalism: the capacity for a sense of the right, and the capacity for a sense of the good.[1]

The first attribute is a respectful or tolerant attitude toward those with whom one disagrees, even on fundamental matters. Why must we accept such an attitude as virtuous if we are to accept liberalism? In brief, because any effort to justify liberalism as merely a modus vivendi will not succeed, and any effort to moralize the notion of the modus vivendi will require that we view a respectful and tolerant attitude as a virtue.

It is often suggested that the core liberal idea is a generalization of the regime of religious toleration that emerged in post-Reformation Europe.[2] Exhausted from religious wars, the contending factions settled on a regime of mutual toleration. But the modus vivendi justification is highly contingent. It works only if the contending factions are roughly equal in power. If one faction is able to dominate the others, the simple appeal to a modus vivendi cannot persuade the members of that faction to be tolerant. They can survive by dominating, as well as by tolerating, and presumably they would rather dominate. Since liberalism of course holds that toleration is required even when one faction could dominate others, the modus vivendi notion is an inadequate justification.

That is why, of course, liberal theorists moralize the notion of the modus vivendi. They claim not that toleration is actually the solution that will be chosen by people in the real world, but that toleration will be the "modus vivendi" chosen in ideal circumstances—behind the veil of ignorance, or in an ideal dialogue, or in a situation in which people demonstrate equal respect. But importing moral content into the idea of the modus vivendi raises the question of justification. The reasons for accepting an actual, real-world modus vivendi are clear enough.

But why should one accept the outcome of a nonreal, ideal process? What makes such a process an ideal to which we should aspire?

This is the point at which liberalism unavoidably invokes a conception of the virtues. We should take up the point of view of the ideal contracting party because if we do so, we display a good aspect of our nature. We side with our better selves. If we did not believe *that,* we would have no reason to adopt such a point of view. Imagine, for example, a person who holds the Nietzschean view that toleration is a sign of a weak and degraded character, and that true human excellence consists of seeking to impose one's views on others. It would surely be impossible to persuade such a person that the point of view of, for example, Rawls's original position, was worth adopting in deciding how to act. This shows, I believe, that one cannot justify liberalism without the premise that some form of tolerant or respectful attitude is a human virtue.

That first liberal virtue corresponds to the capacity for a sense of the right. The second liberal virtue corresponds to the capacity for a sense of the good. It is, roughly speaking, an openness to making choices about how one will live one's life. It might be thought of as a kind of moral courage, a willingness to face one's life without having its most important contours already determined.

Liberalism rejects a regime that seeks to assign people to stations, to limit the options open to them, and to shape their lives in a way that minimizes the choices they must make. It might be thought that this aspect of liberalism is just a corollary of toleration. Liberalism takes pluralism in society as a given (the argument would go); it assumes a substantial divergence among citizens' fundamental interests and commitments. Unless some people's central projects are to be suppressed, society must be structured in a way that leaves choices open. According to this view, the virtue of toleration and mutual respect does all the work; it is unnecessary to suppose that openness to choice is a separate liberal virtue.

The problem with this argument is that there is a great difference between a society that grudgingly accepts pluralism as unavoidable while trying to minimize the differences among people, and a society that considers it prima facie impermissible to limit people's options. One might take the view that to the extent fundamental differences exist among people, they must be tolerated; but that the entire educative apparatus of society (defining "educative" broadly) should be directed toward eliminating the differences and leaving as little as possible to individual choice.

That is neither an incoherent view nor, I think, a wholly unappealing one. Everyone needs to have his or her choices structured to some extent. Having (at the limit) every choice open all the time is a recipe for insanity. This is an important part of Burke's argument against subjecting traditional social institutions to rationalistic criticism; it is central to the conservatism of Durkheim and Comte; and I think an element of this way of thinking is important in Rousseau as well.

But this is not, of course, liberalism. Liberalism does not merely accept tolerance as a necessity forced upon it by uneliminable pluralism. Tolerance is the model, and liberalism values openness and choice generally. It would be antithetical to liberalism to say that society, through the various educative mechanisms open to it, must try to structure citizens' lives so that their need to make choices is reduced as far as possible, subject only to the minimal constraints of toleration.

How would one justify this aspect of liberalism to the person who said that having a wide range of choices open made him or her anomic and unhappy? One could not simply appeal to mutual respect and toleration, for the reasons I have given. One also could not say to such a person: liberalism leaves you free to find some private association that will confine your choices. It is true that liberalism does that, but the individual still must choose the particular association (after, of course, choosing whether to join such an association, instead of one that imposes less structure). Only society as a whole can really eliminate the need to make choices, if that is what a person desires.

Ultimately, therefore, liberals must say that the willingness to make fundamental choices about one's life is a capacity a person *should* have. That is, liberals must exalt that capacity as a virtue (specifically, as I said, a form of moral courage). Rhetoric celebrating this kind of courage is prominent among liberals.[3]

These are the liberal virtues: the capacity to be tolerant and respectful toward those with whom one disagrees; and the capacity to welcome, rather than fear or find unsettling, the availability of a wide range of choices about central issues in one's life. Liberalism cannot be justified unless one accepts these traits as virtues. To this extent, liberalism must speak the language of virtue; it must rely on an account of the virtues to justify its central tenets.

There is, however, nothing particularly Aristotelian about these virtues. They are different from, and possibly incompatible with, at least some of the virtues Aristotle celebrated. These are distinctively liberal virtues. In particular, by accepting this conception of virtue, liberals do not compromise their claim that society is a kind of community different from private associations. Private associations might easily reject these virtues (to the extent they are allowed to do so within an overall liberal regime). Certain religious orders, for example, reject (at least to that extent) both liberal virtues.

In fact, private associations can be seen as providing a kind of respite from the need to exercise the liberal virtues. Private associations enable us to be exclusionary toward those fellow citizens with whom we have fundamental disagreements. Also, private associations can provide a structure that permits us to escape the otherwise relentless demand to make choices. This conception of the liberal virtues therefore reinforces, and sharpens, the liberal idea that some Aristotelian accounts seem to threaten—the idea that society is a framework of accommodation among groups and individuals with fundamentally different projects.

One final question remains, and it concerns the psychological connection, if any, between liberalism and these virtues. Even if I am right that liberalism cannot be justified unless one accepts these attributes as virtues, should liberals celebrate this fact? Does it serve any interest, other than improved theoretical understanding, to emphasize the connection between liberalism and the virtues?

My answer is yes, for at least two reasons. First, liberalism requires sacrifices by the powerful. The rhetorical resources of liberalism may be less adequate to securing these sacrifices if liberal rhetoric does not include the language of the virtues. Modus vivendi arguments, as I said before, are least likely to appeal to the powerful. But even the rhetoric that goes beyond the modus vivendi may be deficient. Justifications for liberalism, for example, often treat toleration as a kind of necessary evil; pluralism is inescapable, so the only thing we can properly do is to put up with each other. Indeed, liberalism often paints the picture that our deepest loyalties are engaged only by private associations, and disengaged at the level of the state.

The language of the virtues allows liberalism to avoid these self-defeating rhetorical tendencies. If tolerance and respect are virtues, that is an affirmative reason for the powerful to comply with the liberal order: people who do so are siding with their better selves against their baser selves. They are not simply making a grudging but unavoidable accommodation. There is something about the liberal state that can engage you.

The second reason I can think of for liberals to resort explicitly to the language of virtue (there may be more) is of a different order. It has to do with the educative aspects of the state, which I alluded to before. Public schooling makes no sense without an account of the virtues: we have to be trying to teach *something*. But the educative aspects of the state include much more than the schools. There are a wide range of government programs, usually taking the form of subsidies to private persons and institutions, the objective of which is unquestionably educative. Even beyond that, a variety of laws, from welfare state measures to the criminal laws, serve in part an educative function.

Constitutional law in these areas is in conspicuous disarray. There is no agreed-upon approach to the most fundamental questions: what are the limits of the power of the public schools to shape students' minds? What are the limits of the power of the government to use expenditures (as opposed to so-called coercive measures) to shape public debate? What are the limits on the power of the government itself to speak through its officials in an effort to influence that debate? The reason for the disarray is clear enough: neutrality is the dominant theme in the constitutional law governing freedom of expression, and it is difficult to translate neutrality into these areas. What would a "neutral" education consist of?

It is possible that the first step out of the incoherence that characterizes this aspect of the practice of liberalism is to acknowledge the virtues that underlie liberalism, and to treat the educative apparatus of the state as a means of promoting those virtues. Probably this would be no more than a first step; it seems clear that the educative mission of the state, as we understand it, involves more than promoting the liberal virtues I have tried to define. But in any event, this is an important further reason for liberalism to acknowledge its implicit conception of the virtues: it provides some hope of progress in understanding and regulating this important aspect of the liberal state.

Liberalism, in sum, does depend on a conception of the virtues. Liberals should be happy to acknowlege that. But the virtues that liberalism presupposes are distinctive liberal virtues. Accepting them does not necessitate a move to, or an acceptance of, anything like a thoroughgoing Aristotelian outlook. On the contrary, acknowledging the distinctive liberal virtues does not disrupt the historic structure of liberal thought, and it may better equip liberalism to deal with the concrete challenges it faces.

NOTES

1. See, for example, John Rawls, "Kantian Constructivism in Moral Theory," *Journal of Philosophy* (1980), 515–72.

2. The suggestion is made, for example, by Charles Larmore, *Patterns of Moral Complexity* (New York: Cambridge University Press, 1987), pp. 74–76, 123–27.

3. The best example I know is the literature justifying freedom of expression, and in that literature the best example I know is the opinion written by Justice Brandeis in the case of *Whitney v. California*, 274 U.S. 357, 375–77 (1927). See Vincent Blasi, "The First Amendment and the Ideal of Civic Courage: The Brandeis Opinion in *Whitney v. California*," *William and Mary Law Review*, 29 (1988), 653.

10

CHARTING LIBERAL VIRTUES

STEPHEN MACEDO

1. INTRODUCTION

Communitarians charge that liberal regimes pay a high price for their central concern with diversity, individuality, impersonal law, and rights. What is lost, allegedly, is the possibility of a moral community, a common devotion to shared values, and citizen virtue, with the attendant risks of stability problems and legitimation crises.[1] Here, and in a larger work, I try to show that liberal theory can provide an attractive vision of a distinctively liberal community and liberal virtues while remaining true to its core political convictions: the centrality of freedom and the supremacy of liberal justice.[2] Liberals can reclaim a language that supposedly lies beyond the bounds of liberal politics, the language of virtue, citizenship, community, and human flourishing.

Liberal principles inform many of our political practices, and basic liberal values are affirmed by a large segment of the populace. Articulating the ideal state of affairs implicit in liberal theory and institutions is partly, then, an exercise in the critical interpretation of our own politics. Liberal ideals provide a vision of what we can and should stand for as a people.

There are many ways of living as a liberal. Submitting to

For kind and unflagging assistance on the project from which this chapter is drawn, the author's thanks go to Steven Lukes, Amy Gutmann, Walter F. Murphy, and the Institute for Humane Studies at George Mason University.

liberal justice and acting in conformity with the rules and regulations of the liberal state is, let us say, the proper extent of our
enforceable political duties. A common posture of outward conformity with liberal rights and rules is enough to describe a
situation of liberal coexistence, and is compatible with many attitudes, traits, and commitments: with mutual indifference or
even hostility overlaid by a common fear of reprisal or punishment for breaches of the liberal rules. Such attitudes might be
thought of as characterizing the "primitive moments" of liberalism, such as the period in which liberal tolerance emerged out of
religious strife and civil war.[3] Liberal possibilities are not, however, exhausted by liberalism's primitive moments.

To stress the priority of liberal justice and the liberal pedigree
of certain virtues, we can draw liberal ideals out of the idea of a
diverse polity composed of citizens who give their allegiance to
liberal justice as a public morality. That is, these citizens do not
simply act in outward conformity with liberal norms; they affirm
liberal justice as a supreme moral commitment—they recognize
and affirm the good reasons that justify and support liberal justice and are capable of lending support to liberal political institutions. Such a society would be composed of people who fully
exercise the first of what Rawls calls the two "moral powers": the
"capacity to understand, to apply, and to act from (and not only
in accordance with) the principles of justice."[4] This is the best
way of affirming liberal justice: a fully self-aware and critically
reflective way, it comports with the liberal commitment to public
justification and the constitutional citizen's engagement in the
critical interpretation of the basic principles of our fundamental
law. Liberal virtues are implicit in the practice of liberal justice,
public justification, and constitutional citizenship.

Tendencies and institutions often associated with modern liberalism may support liberal virtues: urbanization, industrialization, and open mass markets all serve to bring together large
numbers of people from disparate backgrounds and throw them
into a multiplicity of relations. As Voltaire observed,

> Enter the Exchange of London, that place more respectable than
> many a court; you will see there agents from all nations assem-
> bled for the utility of mankind. There the Jew, the Moham-
> medan, and the Christian deal with one another as if they were

of the same religion, and give the name of infidel only to those who go bankrupt.[5]

We should not, however, confuse the liberal character with *homo economicus* or assume that the pursuit of material gain is the overriding preoccupation of liberal citizens. Liberal citizens ought to subordinate their personal interests to public moral principles and actually do so much of the time. A more complete analysis would consider the ways that institutions related to liberalism, such as free markets, either support or subvert the liberal virtues, but here I must leave such questions aside.

At issue here are the character traits and virtues implicit in liberal justice. What can we say of a society whose citizens do not simply avoid what liberals consider injustice, but who understand liberal reasons and affirm the positive value of acting justly? What would citizens be like who do not simply respect one another's liberal rights however grudgingly, but who possess the understanding and the attitudes that make them enthusiastic proponents of liberal rights and eager supporters of liberal institutions and practices? What sort of character, in other words, would be associated with a liberal form of personal excellence and a flourishing liberal community?

Before describing the contours of liberal virtue and community, I want to consider several ideas, usually taken to be central to liberalism, that might seem to stand in the way of liberal virtues. Liberal society is often thought of as, at base, characterized by disagreement, or by neutrality, or by a sharp distinction between public and private spheres of life. Let us focus briefly on these three misconceptions in order to pry open adequate space for the liberal virtues.

2. Clearing the Decks: Pluralism, Neutrality, and the Public/Private Distinction

Liberals often regard "disagreement" or conflict as the basic fact of social life, taking their cues from Hobbes. Liberal toleration of individual liberty is a necessity, we are told, because people disagree about what is good in life: People disagree about their religious commitments and other goals and ideals. And from the purportedly basic fact of disagreement, liberal political imperatives are characterized in negative terms: avoiding injustice and tyranny, keeping rules of law purposeless or noninstrumental. Or liberals emphasize the fundamental importance of keeping government "neutral" or impartial between parties who disagree about what is good in life (as liberals like Dworkin, Ackerman, and Larmore have put it).[6] Or, sometimes, liberalism is taken to stand for nothing more definite than toleration and a "spirit of accommodation."

While the permanent fact of pluralism is the heart of the liberal political problem, conflict and disagreement are not the basic facts of liberal social life. It is, furthermore, wrong to think that liberal law is, can be, or even ought to be in any strong sense purposeless, noninstrumental, or neutral with regard to conceptions of the good life. Likewise, if liberalism stands for mere toleration or an indiscriminate spirit of accommodation, then it stands for everything, and it takes a stand for nothing.

These errors are related to the vulnerability of liberalism, as it is commonly understood, to the communitarian critique of liberalism. A political theory that appears to rest on the centrality of disagreement or conflict or self-interest, and that characterizes its basic political values in negative terms or in terms of neutrality or mere accommodation, has a kind of hard-headed quality to it—it modestly avoids reliance on contestable ideals. But to sap liberal politics of positive values in any of these ways is to misconceive what liberalism stands for, even in its minimal sense, and leads us to misunderstand what it means to be a liberal. When liberalism is underdescribed in these ways, a great gap looms between hard-headed, nonideal conceptions of liberalism, and positive ideals of virtue and community. When we underdescribe the authoritative public values of a liberal regime we also fail to see the extent to which liberalism shapes the lives of liberal citizens. Even in its limited forms liberalism cannot really be neutral among public values. It stands for the supreme worth of certain values: individual liberty and responsibility, tolerance of change and diversity, and respect for the rights of those who respect liberal values.[7]

A. Pluralism and Liberal Unity

Liberalism rules out certain conceptions of the good life altogether: any that entail the violation of liberal rights. And liberalism positively requires that everyone's scheme of values include certain features: respect for the equal rights of others, a willingness to persuade rather than coerce, and the subordination of personal plans, projects, and desires to impersonal rules of law. The coloring of liberal values splashes pervasively over the vast canvas of a pluralistic liberal society. Some things are excluded completely, and everything is limited and conditioned.

Besides a set of positive values, liberalism represents a set of political institutions: a system of legal rules establishing order and giving substance and specificity to the ideal of equal freedom, representative institutions, and courts of law to adjudicate disputes, test the reasonableness of government actions, and enforce constitutional limitations even against the people's representatives. All liberal governments provide certain public goods: at a bare minimum, the apparatus of national defense, and courts and police for justice (they are governments after all). Inducements to commercial activity, public schools, and poverty relief are almost always provided by liberal governments nowadays. These are not "neutral" goods, but nearly all liberals would agree that some range of these goods should be provided by a coercive state.

So liberals have positive political values and political institutions and practices designed to embody and sustain these values. What liberals often fail to recognize is that these values, institutions, and practices exert a pervasive effect on the lives and the character of liberal citizens. Because liberalism is not neutral (either in its direct or its indirect consequences), and because liberal citizens may and should affirm and act from liberal values, we can speak of a distinctive liberal "character."

And yet, one might object, decidedly nonliberal groups do survive within polities structured by liberal values, such as the small, but not insignificant, groups of American Nazis. But let us consider what is required of groups like the Nazis if they are to live peaceably in a liberal regime. They must, first of all, respect the rights of those they hate or else suffer at the hands of the law.

They must, that is, respect the property, political rights, and freedoms of Jewish Americans. They may, occasionally, march in Jewish communities, but they must get permits, keep order, and otherwise respect the peace and quiet of these neighborhoods. They can gather in uniforms, with broadsheets, slogans, music, and other paraphernalia, in legally rented private halls, as long as they don't make too much noise. Nazis must pay taxes to support the liberal institutions they detest, including public schools. The liberal polity requires that the Nazis be law-abiding Nazis, and that's not easy. They cannot be "gung-ho" Nazis; in fact they cannot really be Nazis at all, but can only play at it.

That a liberal society makes life hard on Nazis is not a matter for regret. But far less disagreeable and perhaps even admirable groups may find an open, pluralistic environment less than hospitable. Those who favor simple ways may be disoriented by the pace of change and movement. The devout are liable to object to the materialism and license of a liberal society. Among those prepared to go along with the liberal political settlement not all will readily embrace liberal virtues such as autonomy.[8]

B. The Mirage of Liberal Neutrality

It is, as I have already argued, impossible to deny that liberal practices and attitudes help determine which ways of life flourish and gain adherents. More sophisticated versions of the neutrality thesis do not, however, argue for neutrality of consequences. Liberal neutrality, Charles Larmore argues, "is not meant to be one of outcome, but rather one of procedure. That is, political neutrality consists in a constraint on what factors can be invoked to justify a political decision."[9] Sophisticated neutrality is neutrality in justification.

The sophisticated neutralist would carefully restrict the kinds of reasons that are admissible grounds for government action, requiring that "the state should not seek to promote any particular conception of the good life because of its presumed *intrinsic* superiority—that is, because it is supposedly a truer conception." The liberal state may restrict ideals of life only "for extrinsic reasons because, for example, they threaten the lives of others."[10]

Governmental neutrality expresses equal respect for moral persons who are defined by their reflective capacity for a conception of the good life and not by the particular conception they choose.

A neutral justification for neutrality can be found, Larmore claims, in "a universal norm of rational dialogue." When reasonable people disagree each should, out of concern with keeping the conversation going, "prescind from the beliefs the other rejects" and "retreat to neutral ground, with the hope either of resolving the dispute or of bypassing it."[11] What moves both sides is simply a wish to keep the conversation going until they can find grounds for agreement that neither could reasonably reject.

The consistent neutralist insists on neutral reasons "all the way down," as it were. But how neutral is reasonable conversation? Not very, as some people will find head bashing easier and more satisfying than reason giving. And so, Larmore's ideal of reasonable conversation purports to be "neutral only with regard to controversial conceptions," and not even "completely neutral in this regard either, [but] it is very nearly so, and certainly neutral enough for practical purposes."[12] Neutral enough for government work turns out to be not very neutral at all.

Sophisticated neutrality stands for mutual respect among people committed at base to values that are by no means neutral. Larmore would have us respect only those who are reasonable. Among those not to be respected are "fanatics and would-be martyrs" for whom "civil peace is not so important," racists, and all those who reject "the obligation of mutual respect."[13] The bounds and nature of neutral respect are defined by substantive criteria of reasonableness, criteria that are by no means neutral with respect to ideals of life. None of this is surprising since, as Larmore admits, "neutrality" is "too empty to generate any substantive political principles."[14]

The closer one gets, the faster the mirage of neutrality vanishes. Larmore finally advocates only what he calls "the spirit of neutrality," or "a higher neutrality; namely, that one should institute only the least abridgment of neutrality necessary for making a decision possible."[15] Larmore's neutrality, like any political neutrality, is selective, and selective neutrality is no neutrality at all.

The commitment to political neutrality rests on a vision of

social life in which citizens take seriously a public project of moral justification: where the banner of neutrality flies, citizens are committed to reasonable conversation about political morality with people who share their same basic interest. It seems to me right to think of this commitment to public justification as the moral core of liberalism, but wrong to think that this core is in any important sense morally neutral. Many are excluded from such a regime, and they are excluded because they have basic moral commitments at odds with those of this regime.

C. The Private Life of Liberal Values

The distinction between public and private spheres of life, like the allied beliefs in the fundamentality of disagreement and in neutrality, is apt to close off the possibility of liberal virtues. If liberal values are confined to a certain narrowly defined political sphere of our lives then it will be difficult to think about the ways in which those values shape our characters as a whole. Even so thoughtful a commentator as George Kateb describes a "mode of restriction . . . characteristic of constitutional democracy: absolute prohibition of governmental intervention in certain areas of life, such as religion, speech, press, and assembly."[16] Larmore, similarly, derides what he sees as a romantic "cult of wholeness" that seeks to overcome the public/private distinction, and he bemoans the fact that "liberal writers themselves have not always respected this separation of realms."[17]

The metaphor of distinct spheres of public and private life has a certain usefulness, but is also apt to be misleading. We must rethink it or else fall prey to serious confusions about the reach of public values in a liberal polity. The public/private distinction reflects the liberal conviction that people may rightly be coerced by the state only for certain limited reasons, and in pursuance of rules publicly promulgated according to certain procedures. This allows us to organize the conduct of our affairs so as to avoid, in general, unwanted public interventions or litigation. Nevertheless, it is wrong to think that the influence of public values on private life and personal character is neutral, or merely negative or external.

The family and home life may be the paradigm of a private

space, where intimate relations are shielded from the interference of outsiders, including the state. But this simple picture is misleading. Public norms do not simply shield but penetrate and shape the relations of persons, even in the sphere of family life. A husband cannot treat his wife and children however he wishes. Their relations, even their most intimate relations, are structured by public values. And so husbands have been sued by their wives for rape, and domestic violence is a matter of increasing concern.

Certain kinds of interventions in the most intimate sphere of family life are required by liberal norms, while others are prohibited. Until recently, many states made it a crime even for married couples to use contraceptives. This has now been ruled unconstitutional by a Supreme Court invoking a right to privacy shielding these intimate personal decisions from interference.[18] State bans on interracial marriages have also been struck down, and the right to view pornography in the privacy of the home is protected. The Court has, as we have seen, refused to extend these liberal rights by including homosexual relations among the personal decisions and intimate activities protected by the right to privacy. Liberal politics constitutes private relations in a certain way: requiring some things, prohibiting others, and permitting freedom of choice between adults.

For liberals, the *ends* of politics are properly limited but *pervasive* at the same time. Liberal politics is limited because its ends and purposes are limited; that is, there are a limited set of ends or reasons that justify public intervention in our lives. But liberal politics is pervasive because public reasons, liberal norms of respect for the rights of others, override competing commitments and claim authority in every sphere of our lives. The undoubted crime of raping one's spouse vividly illustrates the long reach of liberal norms and the fact that liberal politics, properly understood, has a private life.

Liberal politics does not insulate the private sphere from the public sphere; even in the absence of litigation, public values penetrate and partly constitute private relations. A closer relation exists between liberal justice and the good of liberal citizens than liberals and their critics often admit. Liberalism embodies a set of substantive moral values that should secure the highest allegiance of liberal citizens, values that override or preclude many commitments, require some, and condition all other goals and projects, positive values that penetrate and pervasively shape the lives and characters of liberal citizens. Liberal politics has a private life.

3. THE LIBERAL VIRTUES

Let us think about the attitudes and character traits connected with active support for liberal principles. In some cases these attitudes and traits are recognized more clearly by liberalism's critics than by liberals themselves, but the critics often misunderstand why they are necessary and sustainable. Liberal virtues do not need to be in place for us to say of a society that liberal justice is "in force" there, and neither the virtues nor the acts that would mark someone as possessing them are required by law. The liberal virtues will, nevertheless, distinguish a community flourishing in a distinctively liberal way from a community simply governed by liberal justice.

Let us begin with the idea of social pluralism. In the liberal community people disagree about goals, lifestyles, and religious beliefs. Such a community may, nevertheless, flourish in a liberal way and, if it does, it will have a discernible shape because liberal justice will be actively supported by all, irrespective of their particular commitments. Liberal justice exerts the positive requirement that every citizen's "good" include certain features, including a willingness to respect the equal freedom of others, to subordinate personal plans and commitments to impartial rules of law, and to persuade rather than coerce. Liberal justice could not be affirmed by a Protestant who believes he should fight to the death rather than live in peace with Catholics, and it could not be acknowledged as morally supreme by a citizen prepared to advance his interests through political means at the expense of the rights of others.

Liberal justice requires that we respect the rights of people with whom we disagree strongly over many particular values, allegiances, loyalties, and commitments. Differences of race, sex, religion, or ethnic background are all relegated to secondary, subpolitical importance by liberal justice. In their political relation, liberal citizens are members of what Popper has called the "abstract society."[19] Liberal citizens are called upon to respect not only members of their family, tribe or race, but humanity in general. All persons, as possessors of abstract, impersonal reflective capacities, share a decisive moral equality in the eyes of liberal justice.

To survey the world of human affairs from the point of view of liberal politics is to survey it from a moral perspective. In their political capacity, liberal citizens regard others as essentially like themselves, or like themselves in a decisive respect, despite a myriad of other differences that may have been decisive before the rise of liberal justice. Liberal politics represents an impersonal perspective that requires, in a sense, that we be capable of putting ourselves in the shoes of others, even those with whom we may disagree on nearly all of our substantive commitments.

The allegiance to liberal justice in a diverse society should encourage attitudes of tolerance and sympathy among people who disagree. Liberalism makes it possible, after all, for people with different religions and conceptions of the good to live together and peaceably interact. From a liberal political perspective we share a common moral nature and overriding interests in peace, freedom, security, and material prosperity. As we come to realize that those who live lives different from our own are nevertheless like us in important ways, we may come to sympathize not only with these persons but also with their projects and commitments, with choices different from our own, with careers and lifestyles not seriously considered before. To sympathize with a variety of projects and commitments is to internalize the value conflicts being played out in liberal society.

Liberal citizens who acquire the capacity to sympathize with widely divergent ways of life acquire a range of "live options" and an openness to change. Live options incite self-examination, self-criticism, and experimentation. Live options multiply with mobility and leisure, the diffusion of knowledge, the breakdown of gender-based stereotypes, the acceptance of divorce and remarriage, and with the acceptance of "off-beat" careers and different sexual orientations. The liberal ideal of character is one with "horizons" broad enough to sympathize with a variety of different ways of life.

The character that flourishes in a liberal, pluralistic social milieu will have broad sympathies. The liberal citizen, capable of reasoning and acting from an impersonal standpoint in a pluralistic social milieu will also have a less exclusive or unreflective commitment to anything in particular. That is, liberalism may temper or attentuate the devotion to one's own projects and allegiances by encouraging persons to regard their own ways as open to criticism, choice, and change, or simply as not shared by many people whom one is otherwise required to respect. If a liberal pluralistic society is also, as I have suggested, an experimental and dynamic society, then people may also be encouraged to regard their ways and ideals as contingent and vulnerable, as apt to become outmoded or trivial in an unpredictably changing world.

Social pluralism complements and supports the liberal capacity for reflective deliberation. The inner experience of value conflict is an imporant spur to reflection. It could also help brake what could otherwise be a fanatical adherence to a perfectly consistent and comprehensive set of values. The inner experience of value conflict encourages a degree of tentativeness in our commitment to any set of values, and this offers room for reflection, self-criticism, toleration, moderation, and an openness to reevaluation and change. As Joseph Cropsey puts it, "Men become dissatisfied with themselves when, and only if, what they are does not possess them exhaustively and to the exclusion of a power to scrutinize what they are."[20] The liberal personality thrives not on a harmonious inner life, but on both "internal" and "external" value plurality, and a consequent unease or dissatisfaction.

The internalization of diversity and conflict allows the reflective self to maintain some distance from any single end, or the values of any particular community with which we happen to identify. Each of our ends and the whole set of our ends can be seen as less than absolute, and not simply fixed or given. We cannot put aside all our ends and act from pure will or rationality. We can recognize, however, that we are not unreflectively, necessarily, or irrevocably tied to any particular form of life.

Contrary to what communitarians claim, the abstract, open view of the person, not detached from all commitments, but not inevitably, indissolubly, or unreflectively, identified with any, is fully situated, or at home, in a pluralistic social environment. Indeed, the liberal personality is more fully situated, more at home, and better equipped to thrive in a pluralistic society than the communitarian self, whose identity is inextricably linked with particular allegiances, commitments, and goals.

The open society and open-mindedness are alike characteristically liberal. "One who is riveted by fear of the unknown to one familiar life-form, or who has been so formed in suspicion and hate of outsiders that he can never put himself in their place" is, almost by definition, unreflective.[21] The liberal ideal excludes the bigot and the xenophobe. Toleration and broad-mindedness are liberal virtues by virtue of characterizing persons capable of thriving in a pluralistic, tolerant society and of giving supreme allegiance to liberal justice.

That broad sympathies and the acceptance of progress may lead to a certain attenuation in the more particular and local affections of preliberal societies is something communitarians seem reluctant to accept. Liberal justice itself requires a certain critical detachment from other, subordinate commitments, and the internalization of social pluralism leads to critical, experimental, open, autonomous attitudes. Those in whom liberal sensibilities are highly developed will be friendlier and more open to outsiders or strangers, but also less exclusively committed to neighborhoods, localities, and narrow allegiances. Constancy, fidelity, and dogged persistence may not be among the liberal virtues. Liberal affections will be broader but less intense or deep than preliberal ones, liberal allegiances more open to critical analysis, choice, and change.

Some severe critics of liberalism have noticed the relative unattractiveness of "preliberal" societies. As one such critic, commenting on the impact of British rule on life in "idealized" Indian villages, put it,

> sickening as it must be to human feelings to witness those myriads of industrious patriarchal and inoffensive social organizations disorganized and dissolved into their units . . . we must not forget that these idyllic village communities, inoffensive though they may appear, had always been the solid foundations of Oriental despotism,

that they restrained the human mind within the smallest possible compass, making it the unresisting tool of superstition, enslaving it beneath traditional rules, depriving it of all grandeur and historical energies.

Rather than "elevating men into the sovereign of circumstances," life in these closed, preliberal communities, Marx went on, perpetuated caste and slavery, "subjugated man to external circumstances and . . . transformed a self-developing social state into never changing natural destiny."[22]

Marx's comments prefigure Justice William O. Douglas's dissenting opinion in *Wisconsin v. Yoder*. Old Order Amish children must be consulted, argued Douglas, before the state allows their parents to keep them out of high school. An Amish child

> may want to be a pianist or an astronaut or an oceanographer. To do so he will have to break from Amish tradition. . . . If a parent keeps his child out of school beyond the grade school, then the child will be forever barred from entry into the new and amazing world of diversity that we have today. . . . If he is harnessed to the Amish way of life by those in authority over him and if his education is truncated, his entire life may be stunted and deformed.[23]

The Amish case and Justice Douglas's opinion raise some vexing problems for liberals. It is clear enough, I think, that liberal citizenship calls for what we might think of as *political* autonomy: a critical, questioning attitude toward official decisions, and self-critical participation in public debate. It also seems clear that liberal political practices and principles are bound to have important consequences for people's personal lives and their attitudes toward their own commitments: life in an open, diverse, tolerant liberal society would seem conducive to personal autonomy. So while liberal political autonomy does not entail personal autonomy, the two are closely connected. Without suggesting that the promotion of autonomy is a good liberal ground for government action, we may consider it among the liberal virtues.[24]

Striving for autonomy involves developing the self-conscious, self-critical, reflective capacities that allow one to formulate, evaluate, and revise ideals of life and character, to bring these evaluations to bear on actual choices and on the formulation of projects and commitments. To flourish as an autonomous person is actively to develop one's individuality. Autonomy implies the capacity to reflect critically and to act on the basis of these reflections. It implies the possession of what we might call "executive" virtues: initiative, independence, resolve, perseverance, diligence, and patience.

The achievement of autonomy is recognizable in the disposition, as Michael Oakeshott calls it, to experience the project of choosing in an ever-changing and uncertain world as an adventure rather than an ordeal.[25] The autonomous character is capable of affirming rather than bemoaning liberal modernity, with its many possible ways of life, the openness of all choices, and its protean ideal. The autonomous ideal contrasts sharply with Alasdair MacIntyre's depiction of the modern individual as a drifting, aimless, passive creature, with a stunted or merely instrumental form of reason, with no place in a settled social context, a mere passive locus of open possibilities with no grounds for choosing.[26]

We should not overemphasize what might in isolation be thought of as the "atomistic virtues." One who excels as a liberal is one who is not simply able to reflect upon, criticize, and shape his own character. Autonomy arises as one comes to understand the shared values and norms of a pluralistic and tolerant culture. There is no tension between being at home in a tradition or a set of social practices and the development of one's individuality. Autonomy is not a matter of discovering a deep, fixed core of individuality within the self; it is an actively critical and reflective way of comporting oneself within the complex matrix of a pluralistic culture and of making its resources one's own. Under the canopy of liberal political norms and attitudes, cultural and social resources are not threats to autonomy but opportunities for it.

Oakeshott explores with especial acuteness the notion that familiarity with the traditions and practices of one's society, an understanding of one's social inheritance, is not a contraint upon but really a condition of the development of individuality. To come to understand a social practice like a language or even a moral code is, for Oakeshott, to acquire a medium for the expression of one's individuality.[27] Of course, if law is to be liberty empowering, as Oakeshott envisions, then it must be liberal in character. If social practices and moral norms are to promote rather than constrain liberty, they must have certain substantive characteristics; they must embody attitudes of tolerance and openness to change rather than pressures to conformity.

Liberal citizens who act from and not only in accordance with liberal justice do not simply impose "side constraints" on self-chosen actions; rather, they seek to realize justice in their conduct as an independently valuable and regulative end. This overriding end will be shared by citizens who exhibit a liberal form of excellence. We must reject Sandel's suggestion that justice "speaks to that which distinguishes" persons whereas an independent conception of the good "connects" them to one another.[28] It is wrong to assume that only conceptions of the good can furnish persons with common ends capable of constituting people's character and binding them to one another. Justice furnishes liberal citizens with ends capable of imparting a deep and noble unity to liberal community.

The point of liberal politics is the realization of a common, substantive moral vision. Emile Durkheim described the social unity that liberal justice could provide:

> Doubtless if the dignity of the individual derived from his individual qualities, or from those particular characteristics which distinguish him from others, one might fear that he would become enclosed in a sort of moral egoism that would render all social cohesion impossible. But in reality he receives his dignity from a higher source, one which he shares with all men. . . . It is humanity that is sacred and worthy of respect. And this is not his exclusive possession. It is distributed among his fellows, and in consequence he cannot take it as a goal for his conduct without being obliged to go beyond himself and turn toward others. . . . Impersonal and anonymous, such an end soars above all particular consciences and can thus serve as a rallying point for them. . . . [I]ndividualism thus understood is not the glorification of the self, but of the individual in general. Its motive force is not egoism but sympathy for all that is human, a wider pity for all sufferings, for all human miseries, a more ardent desire to combat and alleviate them, a greater thirst for justice. Is this not the way to achieve a community of all men of good will?[29]

The rights of liberal citizen are grounded in public principles that justify and protect individuality in general. These principles are not based on self-love but on respect for diversity, plurality, and the dignity of beings with the capacity for considered and responsible choice. Liberal individualism properly understood is a moral commitment, depending upon a general and impartial perspective, not a self-centered one.

Some of the liberal virtues are now before us: broad sympathies, self-critical reflectiveness, willingness to experiment, to try and to accept new things, self-control and active, autonomous self-development, and an appreciation of inherited social ideals. The same virtues that contribute to individual flourishing in pluralistic liberal communities also contribute to the performance of liberal civic duties. The liberal virtues are both civic and personal virtues. The practice of liberal politics amplifies the liberal virtues. The rule of law teaches self-restraint, an appreciation for procedures and forms, and equality of respect.

By emphasizing the importance of a critical, questioning, challenging attitude toward official decisions, the practice of liberal politics helps develop reflective capacities, activity and independence of mind, and the autonomy of liberal citizens. Official acts, on the liberal constitutionalist's view, have no authority unless supported by the public moral principles that are objects of common interpretation.[30] The authority to interpret the law is leveled so that every citizen has a right to interpret for himself the public moral principles of the liberal order. The faithfulness of a liberal democratic order to its public morality depends ultimately on the seriousness with which citizens take their role as conscientious interpreters and reviewers of official acts.

Every liberal citizen must, to remain true to liberal justice, give highest allegiance not to his or her own particular plans and projects, but to liberal public reasons and principles. Liberalism does not "interiorize" the moral life, leaving politics and public life to the play of self-interest. Indeed, the liberal political space is pervaded by moral considerations. Not only the judicial process but politics more broadly should be, and often is, guided by the interpretation of liberal moral principles. Liberal citizens must, furthermore, engage in public argument if they wish to persuade others of the merits of their interpretations of public norms.

We can discern virtues connected fairly closely with active support for and participation in the core institutions of a liberal society. Different sets of virtues are especially required by office holders in each of the three branches of government, but citizens require these virtues as well. Citizens must be able to appreciate and assess the actions and perspectives of each of the three branches if they are to exercise competently their duty to engage in the oversight, criticism, and election of public officials. All three sets of virtues are required, furthermore, if citizens are to achieve the personal self-government required to flourish in a pluralistic social environment. They must be able to stand back from their own projects and judge them impartially, sympathize with and understand the projects of others, and decide, resolve, act, and persevere.

The judicial virtues are those that allow people to stand back from their personal commitments and projects and judge them from an impersonal point of view. Judicial impartiality makes one capable of respecting the rights of others and of acting justly, thus fulfilling the most basic duties of liberal citizens. Other judicial virtues would include attachment to principle, and a reluctance to bargain and compromise where basic rights are at stake. The judicial virtues are particularly requisite in a good judge, but all liberal citizens must, to some extent, cultivate these qualities if they are to treat as persons equally worthy of respect those who are not members of their particular religious or ethnic or other narrow community, or those whose interests come into conflict with their own.

The legislative virtues can be identified with the breadth of sympathies that may develop after we come to respect the rights of persons with whom we disagree and as we come to cooperate with others on matters of common concern. The legislative virtues would partake of a measure of judicial impartiality, but would focus on inclusive goods rather than specific cases, and would be geared toward compromise and accommodation. These virtues include the ability sympathetically to survey different ideals and the willingness to engage in dialogue with those with whom we disagree. The legislative virtues are characteristic, especially, of principled liberal legislators, but they will be possessed by all liberal citizens capable of electing fair-minded and impartial representatives, people with a lively sense of the public good, and people capable of realizing that democracy means not getting your way all of the time.

The executive virtues empower one, having judged and reflected, to resolve, act, and persevere rather than drift, dither, and crumple at the first sign of adversity, to perform rather than deliberate endlessly, to exercise independence of thought rather than be swayed by the prejudices and pressures to conformity exerted by others. The executive virtues are especially required by the executive officers of the liberal state, but they will also be required by liberal citizens if they are vigilantly to oversee and review official acts, to rally to the defense of the regime, and to act themselves to correct sustained injustices in the regime. Citizens who cultivate executive virtues will also take voluntary initiatives in association with others to undertake the many tasks not properly performed by the liberal state.

The virtues that make liberal self-government possible also help make possible the government of our personal lives. Following Plato we might say that the virtues that conduce to good government in the regime "without" have their analogues in the qualities that control and direct the regime "within."[31] Impartiality, reflectiveness, self-criticism, the articulation and defense of moral reasons, the celebration of diversity, the cultivation of broad sympathies, and decisiveness all conduce to liberal forms of public and private excellence. The liberal virtues are at once public and private, civic and personal.

Liberalism does not rely upon as strong a distinction between public and private morality as is often charged. "Political" values penetrate and shape the private lives of liberal citizens. Liberal institutions, values, and practices help constitute a political culture and not only a set of rights and rules and offices. Liberal law does not simply operate on liberal citizens from the outside, controlling their behavior only; it helps constitute the social setting in which people are educated and so helps constitute the habits and character of citizens. Our duty to respect the rights of others is as important in our personal as in our public lives, and since our personal dealings with others are bound to be more extensive, frequent, and earlier in life than our participation in

politics, the practice of justice in personal affairs is likely to be
the more important moral teacher.

Liberal citizens will not learn justice only, or even mainly, from
political participation as it is usually conceived of (voting, apprais-
ing candidates and political issues, campaigning, and so forth).
From early on and throughout their lives, liberal citizens learn
and apply public norms in their interaction with others. Children learn respect for rules and fair play from their parents and
from childhood games. They criticize, discuss, listen to others,
and take votes; they follow, debate, change, and help enforce
rules at home, in school, at work, and with their friends. They
gradually learn to restrain their impulses, to respect others as
equals, and to direct and apply their energies with diligence.
They learn to make judgments for themselves and hopefully
acquire a measure of individuality and autonomy. They should
learn the importance of taking initiatives. They learn something
about due process, and fairness, and respect for those who are
different. They develop judicial, legislative, and executive virtues. All of this takes place without political control, though it is
all importantly influenced by our political practices. It would be
wrong, therefore, to view participation in campaigns and elections as the sole or even primary fount of liberal virtue: private
life goes a long way in helping to prepare us for our public
duties.

4. Liberal Community

I have analyzed the liberal virtues, the qualities of a person who
excels in a peculiarly liberal way, and we can now discern a liberal
vision of the good community: a society whose members excel in
the liberal virtues and that, as a consequence, flourishes in a
distinctively liberal way. How might we characterize this flourishing liberal society? First, it would make room for individuality
and social pluralism. It would be tolerant, open, and dynamic,
and its members would be prone to experiment with different
lifestyles and commitments. It would probably pay for this diversity, tolerance, and experimentation with a degree of superficial-
ity, the consequence of a lack of depth or persistence in commitments. There might be a certain amount of feigned or affected

eccentricity, and with all the self-critical, self-shaping introspection, perhaps also a degree of self-absorption or even narcissism. Quiet obedience, deference, unquestioned devotion, and humility could not be counted among the liberal virtues.

Liberalism holds out the promise, or the threat, of making all the world like California. By encouraging tolerance or even sympathy for a wide array of lifestyles and eccentricities, liberalism creates a community in which it is possible to decide that next week I might quit my career in banking, leave my wife and children, and join a Buddhist cult. Life in a pluralistic liberal society is a smorgasbord confronting us with an exciting array of possibilities. Society is open to change and diversity: less of a stigma attaches to unconventional lifestyles and to changes in lifestyle. The combination of diversity and openness to change constitutes an incitement to self-examination and invitation to experiment.

If all the world became liberal, all the world would become the same in certain important respects. Individuality, constrained by liberal norms, would flourish everywhere, but the diversity of forms of political organization would be eliminated, the differences between forms of social life would be reduced, and every sphere of social life would bear the peculiar tint of liberal values. It would be a mistake to identify the spread of liberalism with the maximization of diversity or the liberation of unlimited experimentation. Liberal norms rule out many experiments in social organization, require common subscription to liberal rights, and encourage uniformity of tolerance, openness, and broadmindedness. If the spread of liberalism eliminates certain forms of diversity, it also extends the liberal community and liberal peace. In the history of the modern world, as Michael Doyle argues, no two liberal regimes have ever gone to war with one another.[32]

Certain things of value may be lost in, or absent from, the forms of the good life that flourish in open, diverse, critical, experimental, uncertain, and ever-changing liberal societies. Stronger forms of community, deeper, unquestioning, untroubled forms of allegiance (to family, church, clan, or class) might embody genuine forms of the good life lost to societies that flourish in a liberal way. A lifelong, unquestioned devotion to a simple life in a small homogeneous community will hardly be available to one whose attitudes have been shaped by liberal individualism, social pluralism, tolerance, and autonomy. Once a person recognizes the myriad possibilities of self-enactment that liberalism discloses, she forever regards her choices in a new light; in the very least what once may have been unquestioned components of a given identity or role become choices.

Everything chosen is one option among others; no "choices" have the certainty and security of an identity unreflectively taken as given. One cannot choose to be simple, or unworldly; by the time the issue arises it is too late. Once one's horizons are broadened to encompass a variety of possible ways of life, a range of "live options," no act of will can narrow the vistas again. You could not really choose to be Amish after working for a few years in a Wall Street brokerage firm.

Will liberals, faced with live options and prone to critical reflection, have only shallow commitments to causes, projects, and ideals? If the spread of liberal pluralism brings security and a promise of peace, it also confronts us with the loss of old certainties, of a secure future on a well-trodden path. An identity is no longer simply given; it must be achieved and it is always open to revision. Our standards of evaluation are never entirely fixed. Our potentialities and projects must be discerned, developed, and sustained in an uncertain and ever-changing world. What some people will experience as an adventure, others will find unbearably burdensome.

Liberal openness and critical thinking do not imply skepticism about the possibility of objective human goods or genuine moral values. Indeed, the possibility of making real progress would seem to be a presupposition of serious engagement in critical thought. Liberal openness and criticism do, however, imply doubt about our ability ever to identify the whole truth once and for all.

Liberals may well have the confidence appropriate to those who are committed to self-critical reason giving, in a world in which there are good reasons for being liberals, and many reasonable ways of living as a liberal. Autonomous liberal persons have the raw materials for making personal choices, but these choices will be less widely shared than basic political norms. And, as liberals have often argued, reflecting upon and actively exploring different conceptions of the good life itself helps constitute a good life. Liberalism defines a framework of freedom and peace and a stance of clear-mindedness from which to explore alternative conceptions of the good. And liberal ideals suggest a type of personality capable of finding in diversity and change conditions of human flourishing.

Some will find a world without more readily graspable absolutes and more accessible resting places for the soul to be full of despair and anxiety—or perhaps at times we all will find it so. But we should not make the mistake of holding liberalism responsible for all the problems of modernity (or, indeed, of the human condition), and we should not demand of liberalism more than it is reasonable to demand of any political system. Liberalism accommodates pluralism, it celebrates many forms of diversity, but it did not create the deep disagreements that underlie communal fragmentation. We should, moreover, avoid confusing the peculiarly intellectual anxieties of academics with more widespread sources of disaffection, which are likely to concern peace, economic security, and well-being. These are not goods that a liberal society neglects.

It is, in any case, difficult to see the plausibility or attractiveness of any deep alternatives to social pluralism and liberal openness to choice and change. In a pluralistic world, it certainly would not do to try to place attachments or projects that constitute our identities beyond the reach of critical reflection. Loyal Nazis may have been deeply constituted by their commitment to being "good Germans" but this hardly immunizes them from moral denunciation or provides for the stuff of good communities. A high degree of sincerity, authenticity, depth of commitment, or persistence does not and should not immunize a person or group from moral criticism and possible legal or even military intervention. Racial discrimination in the South was bound up with deep traditions, conventions, and expectations that constituted the identities of slaveowner and slave alike. But discrimination is not privileged by depth of commitment. Public justification is the work of articulable reasons, not of a plumb-bob testing of the depth of a commitment or a time-chart plotting of its persistence.

Unless a community consists of a homogeneous and totally isolated group of persons, all sharing the same constitutive attachments and never bothering anyone else, it should not do without reflective moral capacities. As it is, our world is increasingly a melange of ethnic, national, religious, and racial diversities. There are no extensive political territories in the world without minorities. Humanity is ill-served by tribalism in any of its forms. The fact that a liberal public morality, when institutionalized and practiced, helps people gain critical distance on their local attachments is one of its greatest achievements.

The political centrality of liberal critical reflection does not presuppose the existence of what Michael Sandel calls an "unencumbered" or "disembodied" self: an uncommitted locus of pure reflection buried deep beneath my particular commitments. Liberalism assumes that we can, and ought to, reflect on our particular commitments, which means standing at some distance from any commitment or allegiance. We must be able to imagine ourselves without the commitment being reflected upon if we are to test it by a public liberal standard of justice. But this does not mean that liberal citizens must, or even can, imagine themselves totally "unencumbered" by a personal identity. To say that we must be able to consider each of our commitments in turn (to my family, my church, my friends, my country, my university, and so on) does not assume that we can stand aside from all of our commitments all at once.

If liberal reflection does not empty the self of all attachments and disempower it, neither does it isolate individuals from their social context. Liberals seek a public rather than a self-centered point of view to give others their due, and to live up to our moral duties and our capacity for reasonableness and autonomy. Liberal reasonableness and reflection do not provide metaphysical ladders for persons seeking to climb out of this world. Rather, they define the proper aspirations of persons making their way in a pluralistic society mindful that others have lives of their own to live.

What drives the liberal project of critical reflection is the aspiration to act in a manner that can be publicly justified to ourselves and our reasonable fellow creatures. The point is not to purify or distill a wholly disembodied self or to leap for the perspective of the godhead. The point is to seek reasons that justify ourselves and our political arrangements here and now, to other persons whom we regard, and wish to treat, as reasonable and reasoning beings capable of sharing our reasons when they are good and of offering us better reasons when they are not. Our political project is not only to supply but to demand reasons of others, including public officials, and to accept good reasons from wherever they come—and all this because we wish to do the right thing and treat others reasonably. If communitarians have a better idea, it is not clear what it is.

5. Conclusion

Liberalism has often been portrayed as a thin and narrowly legalistic political program. It is more than that. Liberals have shared values, virtues, and a distinctive form of community, all of which can be advanced in the face of communitarian criticisms. Even if we limit ourselves to virtues forming a core around liberal justice, and ones fairly easy to discern in its penumbras, we see that liberalism has the resources to mount a positive response to its communitarian critics.

Liberals typically stress the fact that people disagree radically about the nature of the good life and that proper rules of law should not impose any particular conception of the good on society. But this simple picture is misleadingly incomplete. Liberalism acknowledges the primacy of certain social claims over individual claims, the primacy of a structure of rights and a system of proper law over individual desires, goals, and ends. When we add to shared liberal norms a capacity and willingness to participate in the public justification of liberal justice, then we approach the liberal ideal in which citizens share a public morality, recognize in each other a common moral personality, and acknowledge an overriding duty to respect that personality, and take a hand in preserving valuable political arrangements.

The liberal arrangements I have described are, of course, ideals that liberal practice often fails to achieve. Our practices and beliefs do, however, sometimes approach liberal ideals, as when the civil rights of blacks, women, homosexuals, or any minority are protected on grounds of justice—or whenever conscientious reasons are sought and offered for legislation. As education, mobility, and toleration for diversity and change increase, our private lives also often resemble the autonomous ideal. It should at least be clear that liberalism stands for ideals of character far nobler than MacIntyre's unhappy and purportedly liberal trio, "the Rich Aesthete . . . the Manager . . . and the Therapist."[33]

Thinkers as diverse as Friedrich Hayek, Irving Kristol, and Jurgen Habermas argue that the legitimacy and stability of liberal regimes is parasitic on the lingering presence of a precapitalist or preliberal ethic.[34] In light of the resurgence of liberal capitalism in the 1980s, and the sudden collapse of communism, the so-called liberal crisis of legitimacy now appears farfetched. Nevertheless, a certain dissatisfaction and unease probably comes with the liberal turf, and that is not obviously unhealthy. If pluralists are right that moral values are many and in conflict, if there are many reasonable ways of participating in human goods, if choice and change are compatible with a good life, then a certain amount of critical unease may be all to the good. Liberals are not typically overpowered by uncertainty or anxiety. Many attachments and choices remain fairly stable, and most people find many good things worth enjoying and striving for.

The direction of my inquiry points toward further questions: given the liberal virtues and forms of community life, does liberal society or government do enough to promote these ideals? Should it do more? Should it do anything? I cannot pursue these questions here, so I will offer only a caution and an observation. First the caution: liberals are not Spartans, a liberal society is first and foremost a free society, and liberals should not tolerate an oppressively educative state even when it purports to be educating for liberal ideals like autonomy. That said, liberals, even classical liberals, need not insist on totally disabling governments from education for citizenship. Adam Smith, whose classical liberal credentials are unimpeachable, advocated a variety of policies designed to use public education and militia training, and to shape religion, so as to ward off the potentially destructive consequences of the division of labor, and to promote minimal civic virtues.[35] Liberals rely on gentle educative measures, not indoctrination and not necessarily a policy of laissez-faire. Just how much liberal statecraft and policy ought to do to promote the liberal virtues is worthy of further study.

NOTES

1. The communitarians whom I mainly have in mind are Alasdair MacIntyre, *After Virtue* (Notre Dame: Notre Dame University Press, 1981), Michael Sandel, *Liberalism and the Limits of Justice* (Cambridge: Cambridge University Press, 1982), and Charles Taylor, especially the essays gathered in *Philosophy and the Human Sciences: Philosophical Papers, 2* (Cambridge: Cambridge University Press, 1985).

2. That larger work is *Liberal Virtues: Citizenship, Virtue, and Community in Liberal Constitutionalism* (Oxford: Oxford University Press, 1990).

3. On liberal "coexistence through mutual indifference," see Stephen Holmes, *Benjamin Constant and the Making of Modern Liberalism* (New Haven: Yale University Press, 1984), p. 245.

4. John Rawls, "Kantian Constructivism in Moral Theory," *Journal of Philosophy,* 77 (1980), pp. 515–72, p. 525.

5. Voltaire, "Lettres Philosophiques," in *Mélanges* (Paris: Pléiade, 1961), pp. 17–18, quoted in Holmes, *Constant,* pp. 253–54.

6. Ronald Dworkin, "Liberalism," in *A Matter of Principle* (Cambridge: Harvard University Press, 1985), pp. 181–204, p. 191; Bruce Ackerman, *Social Justice in the Liberal State* (New Haven: Yale University Press, 1980), p. 11; Charles Larmore, *Patterns of Moral Complexity* (Cambridge: Cambridge University Press, 1987), passim.

7. See Kant, *The Metaphysics of Morals,* Part 2: The Metaphysical Principles of Virtue, in *Kant's Ethical Philosophy,* trans. James W. Ellington, intro. Warner A. Wick (Indianapolis: Hackett, 1986); and Judith N. Shklar, *Ordinary Vices* (Cambridge: Harvard University Press, 1984), pp. 240–45.

8. The themes of the foregoing discussions are developed interestingly in William A. Galston, "Pluralism and Social Unity," *Ethics,* 99 (July 1989), pp. 711–26; see also Galston's important discussion in "Liberal Virtues," *American Political Science Review,* 82 (December 1988), pp. 1277–90.

9. Larmore, *Patterns,* p. 44.

10. Ibid., p. 43.

11. Ibid., p. 53.

12. Ibid., p. 55.

13. Ibid., p. 60.

14. Ibid., p. 67.

15. Ibid., p. 68.

16. George Kateb, "Remarks on the Procedures of Constitutional Democracy," in J. R. Pennock and J. W. Chapman, eds. *Nomos XX: Constitutionalism* (New York: New York University Press, 1979), pp. 215–37, p. 218.

17. Larmore, *Patterns*, pp. 42, 106.

18. Griswold v. Connecticut, 381 US 479 (1965); laws banning the distribution of contraceptives to unmarried couples were struck down in Eisenstadt v. Baird, 405 US 438 (1972).

19. Karl R. Popper, *The Open Society and Its Enemies, 1: The Spell of Plato* (London: Routledge and Kegan Paul, 1966), p. 173.

20. Joseph Cropsey, "U.S. as a Regime," in Cropsey, *Political Philosophy and the Issues of Politics* (Chicago: University of Chicago Press, 1977), pp. 1–13, p. 3.

21. Charles Taylor, "What's Wrong with Negative Liberty," in *Philosophical Papers, 2*, pp. 211–29, p. 204.

22. Karl Marx, "The British Rule in India," in *The Marx-Engels Reader*, 2d ed., Robert C. Tucker, ed. (New York: Norton, 1978), pp. 653–58, pp. 657–58.

23. 406 U.S. 205 (1972), at 244–6.

24. It may be that while liberal governments may encourage critically active liberal citizenship, they should avoid promoting personal autonomy (at least directly; they may not be able to avoid doing so as a side effect). People who fail to lead autonomous personal lives are, after all, still worthy of our respect: they are still liberal persons.

25. Michael Oakeshott, *On Human Conduct* (Oxford: Oxford University Press, 1975), pp. 236–39.

26. MacIntyre, *After Virtue*, pp. 30–34, and passim.

27. Oakeshott, op cit., pp. 78–80.

28. Sandel, *Limits,* p. 133.

29. Emile Durkheim, "Individualism and the Intellectuals," trans. and intro. by Steven Lukes, *Political Studies*, 17 (1969), pp. 14–30, pp. 23–24.

30. This point is developed in Macedo, *Liberal Virtues*, especially chapters 3 and 4.

31. Plato, *Republic*, see bks. 8 and 9.

32. See Michael Doyle, "Kant, Liberal Legacies, and Foreign Affairs," *Philosophy and Public Affairs*, 12 (1984), pp. 205–35 and 323–53.

33. MacIntyre, *After Virtue*, p. 29.

34. Friedrich Hayek, *The Constitution of Liberty* (London: Routledge, 1976), pp. 232–33; Irving Kristol, " 'When Virtue Loses All Her

Loveliness'—Some Reflections on Capitalism and 'the Free Society,' "
Public Interest, no. 21 (1976), pp. 3–15, p. 13; Jurgen Habermas, *Legiti-mation Crisis* (Boston: Beacon, 1975).

35. Adam Smith, *An Inquiry into the Nature and Causes of the Wealth of Nations,* R. H. Campbell, A. S. Skinner, and W.B. Todd, eds. (Oxford: Oxford University Press, 1979), volume 2, pp. 758–99 (bk. 5, ch. 1, part 3, articles 2 and 3).

4

JUDICIAL VIRTUE

11

JUSTICE HOLMES AND JUDICIAL VIRTUE

DAVID LUBAN

We number self-restraint among the human virtues. It is a platitude of our political culture that judicial self-restraint should likewise be numbered among the judicial virtues, alongside incorruptibility, disinterest, fairness, and wisdom. Should we accept this platitude? That question animates this chapter.

This formulation, however, puts the question badly. "Judicial self-restraint" in its most cogent usage designates not a personal virtue of judges but a structural relation between the judiciary and other branches of government.[1] What I shall call the *classical conception of judicial self-restraint* understands it as a policy regarding judicial review of the constitutionality of legislation, a policy according to which courts, and especially the United States Supreme Court, should adopt a cautious or "deferential" attitude toward voiding legislation on constitutional grounds.

Roughly put, this means upholding legislation even when the judge entertains doubts about its constitutionality, and thus deferring to the legislature's implicit judgment that the legislation is constitutional. This, in turn, has generally been taken to imply

I gratefully acknowledge support for this research from the John Simon Guggenheim Memorial Foundation and the Marton and Sophia Macht Foundation, and comments on an early draft by Richard Posner.

that the Court should uphold legislation unless it clearly bears no reasonable relation to a legitimate state purpose.

The classical conception was developed and elaborated by what might be called the main line of judicial self-restraint theorists: Harvard professor James Bradley Thayer, who proposed it in a celebrated 1893 article;[2] Justices Oliver Wendell Holmes, Louis Brandeis, and Felix Frankfurter; and Yale professor Alexander Bickel.[3] Holmes and Brandeis—personal friends before either was on the Court—were acquaintances of Thayer; Thayer had been Holmes's first legal employer and one of Brandeis's most esteemed professors. Frankfurter was a close friend of both justices, and Bickel was Frankfurter's law clerk. We are speaking, therefore, of something like an apostolic succession, or, in Old Testament imagery, a bloodline of patriarchs. The classical conception of judicial self-restraint emerged, therefore, from a kind of intellectual gemeinschaft almost unparalleled in the history of juridical ideas. Hence, we are not dealing with a broad consensus, but rather with a doctrine emerging from a surprisingly narrow base.

The classical conception—"Thayerism," we might also call it—holds that the Court should uphold legislation unless the justices deem it not merely unconstitutional but *clearly* unconstitutional. Thayerism, that is, amounts to what Bickel would later term the "rule of the clear mistake." It is important to add that the later exponents of judicial self-restraint grafted on additional elements, but these should be regarded as friendly amendments to the classical conception. For the moment, I characterize judicial self-restraint in classical terms alone simply to highlight the error of regarding it as a personal virtue of judges. A judge can defer to a legislature without exhibition or possessing a deferential character. Deference and judicial self-restraint on the classical conception are interpretive strategies, not traits of judicial character.

Nevertheless, even if asking whether judicial self-restraint is a judicial virtue commits a category mistake, the important question remains of what traits of character judges must possess to practice self-restraint. This is hardly an eccentric question. Indeed, it centrally occupied the theorists and judges who developed the classical conception. Is the virtue the "combination of a lawyer's rigor with a statesman's breadth of view" that Thayer extols in a pregnant and little-understood passage?[4] Is it prudence, Bickel's term for the political judgment by which the Court discerns that the country is unready to face a constitutional issue and hence in need of judicial temporizing?[5] Is it Holmes's skepticism, or Brandeis's sympathetic immersion in factual details, or the "judicial humility" of which Frankfurter speaks?[6] These are important and fascinating questions.

Whatever character traits make classical self-restraint possible count as judicial virtues only if judicial self-restraint is itself a worthwhile aim. The chief temptation to abandon judicial self-restraint arises from a judge's conviction that the legislature has done something bad for the nation and its constitution. The temptation is to play the white knight and save us from the wrongheadedness of our representatives. According to the classical conception, the judge must abstain from any such heroics; the judicial role outweighs what we may concede is an imperative of the patriot's conscience.

Self-restraint counts as a virtue only if fidelity to a tightly constrained judicial role is a virtue more important than adherence to the demands of conscience. Defenders of the classical conception argue that judicial deference to the judgment of majorities in close constitutional cases is essential to the operation of American constitutional democracy. Thus, in addition to an account of judicial virtue, defending the classical conception requires us to justify deference to legislative majorities even when their actions are clearly wrongheaded. What moral claim do foolish majorities exert?

I believe that each of the principal architects of the classical conception had answers to these questions; but their answers were by no means the same. In this chapter I discuss the answer offered by Justice Holmes.

THE PUZZLE OF SELF-RESTRAINT

The most frequently heard argument on behalf of judicial self-restraint takes off from what Bickel calls the "countermajoritarian difficulty": the anomaly, in a democratic system, of unelected judges nullifying acts of the people's elected representatives. No doubt judicial review is necessary to safeguard minority rights from the "tyranny of the majority." But beyond the clear protection of minorities judges must never second-guess the legislature, on pain of undercutting democracy.

This argument appears plausible on the surface, but on closer inspection it begins to unravel. To begin with, the fact that federal judges are unelected must be regarded as a red herring; the problem of judicial review would remain even if federal judges stood for periodic election. After all, supreme court justices are elected in several states, and it is hard to believe that these states experience no countermajoritarian difficulty. Indeed, if federal judges were elected, voters would confront the question of whether they ought, as good citizens, to hold judges' disagreeable constitutional decisions against them at the polls. Perhaps, after all, we have a civic duty to cast our votes for judges on different criteria than whether the judges work our will; perhaps we should favor judges who are willing to nullify acts of our passing fancy on constitutional grounds.

We see, of course, that this question simply raises the countermajoritarian difficulty all over again. Indeed, the same problem arises whenever a legislator decides to vote against legislation that a majority of her constituents supports because she believes it to be unconstitutional: this too is the countermajoritarian difficulty in action. The countermajoritarian difficulty has nothing essentially to do with the "anomaly" of a nonmajoritarian judiciary, and indeed nothing essentially to do with the judiciary at all. The difficulty inheres in the very nature of constitutionalism itself.[7] For constitutions by their very existence constrain the desires of majorities, and pure majoritarianism makes constitutions impossible.[8]

Indeed, nothing prevents us from turning Bickel's rhetoric on its head and observing that majority rule creates a "counterconstitutional difficulty." We might reinterpret the American constitution by noticing how few of its institutions were designed to be purely majoritarian. The president and vice-president are chosen by the electoral college, and until the seventeenth amendment was enacted in 1913 the Senate was nonmajoritarian. Neither the Cabinet nor executive agencies are majoritarian; and the major victory won by the federalists over the antifederalists, dividing

America into federated units of wide rather than narrow geographical scope to weaken local control, ensured that American representative democracy is removed as far as possible from direct democracy. Judicial review amounts to a buffering of majority rule, and fits in effortlessly with the many other buffering devices found in the Constitution's structure. Perhaps unbuffered majority rule, not judicial review, ought to be regarded as the anomalous institution, generating a counterconstitutional difficulty.

Obviously, this is a rather farfetched constitutional interpretation; I raise it merely to emphasize an objection to Bickel's way of stating the case that can be put less rhetorically: that in point of fact the Constitution is compounded of majoritarian and nonmajoritarian elements, and provides no hint that any of the institutions it creates are anomalies. Talk of the "countermajoritarian difficulty" merely begs the question at issue.

Nor do separation of powers considerations affect this conclusion. One often hears that Congress, not the courts, holds the power to legislate, and so courts should not be in the business of second-guessing Congress; critics denounce "government by judiciary" and "judicial legislation." But though Congress legislates, the executive issues orders and rulings, and the courts make decrees and interpret the laws. All three branches issue imperatives, and it settles nothing to characterize judicial interpretations and decrees as "legislation." This is merely an exercise in conclusory labeling.

Perhaps the point is rather that in close calls on the constitutionality of legislation separation of powers considerations demand that courts grant the benefit of the doubt to the legislature—the body, in Thayer's words, to which the "primary authority to interpret is given"[9]—rather than to themselves. That is part of Thayer's argument, and it seems quite plausible. "The judiciary may well reflect that if they had been regarded by the people as the chief protection against legislative violation of the constitution, they would not have been allowed merely . . . incidental and postponed control. They would have been let in . . . to a revision of the laws before they began to operate."[10]

Nevertheless, this argument also begs the question. The fact that the courts were granted a more limited power of review than they might have been implies nothing whatever about how they should exercise that limited power. Thayer's argument might equally be turned on its head: "the people's" choice to limit the reviewing role of courts to cases and controversies suggests that judges should refrain from second-guessing that choice by imposing further limitations on themselves with no popular mandate. Moreover, once we grant courts the power of judicial review, incidental and postponed though it may be— and no contemporary proponents of judicial self-restraint have gone on record against *Marbury v. Madison*—then the fact that legislatures legislate implies nothing about who should defer to whom. Legislatures legislate; courts interpret and review. These are equally fundamental powers of government, and as my earlier remarks about the tension between constitutionalism and majoritarianism indicated, both powers are essential to the total process of lawmaking under a constitution. This being the case, it makes no more intrinsic sense to require courts to defer to legislatures in constitutional questions than to require legislatures to defer to courts. From the point of view of the separation of powers legislators are constitutional amateurs, judges constitutional professionals. Now it may be that, as Thayer and others argue, we do well to entrust large tasks to the legislators, amateurs or not, to inculcate in them a sense of constitutional responsibility; but that argument actually pushes against the grain of the separation of powers.

Closely connected with Thayer's argument for deference is the commonly heard equation of judicial self-restraint with fidelity to law: judges are bound by the commands of the legislature and must keep faith with the law by putting aside their own personal scruples.

However, no statute has ever commanded that courts adopt the rule of the clear mistake, and if such a statute were adopted it would probably be deemed unconstitutional as a violation of the separation of powers. Thayer's argument for deference rests only on judicial tradition coupled with indirect and unsound inferences from constitutional history. Since Thayerism proposes judicial deference even in the absence of legal mandate, the classical conception of judicial self-restraint has nothing to do with the virtue of fidelity to law.

Since Thayerism requires the justices to defer to legislative judgments of constitutionality that they in fact disbelieve, a strict policy of fidelity to the law actually seems inconsistent with Thayerism. After all, a judge who wishes to keep faith with the constitution will not defer to what she regards as a constitutional error.

At this point we may turn from constitutional to more overtly normative considerations, such as Thayer's argument that we should not use the federal courts as a crutch enabling the rest of the country to legislate and agitate in happy oblivion to the Constitution, relying on the Court to pull our constitutional bacon out of the fire and bear the brunt of popular pique.[11] Periodically pollsters surveying the public rediscover the unhappy fact that most of our fellow citizens cheerfully advocate grotesque violations of our constitutional liberties.[12] If the courts rein themselves in, we would perhaps find ourselves more willing to think constitutionally in our political deliberations.

The supposition that legislative buck passing and popular indifference to liberty are greatly affected by marginal changes in federal court policy, and that deference in close constitutional cases is a marginal change, is quite fanciful. More importantly, deference to legislative majorities simply because they are majorities, whether or not they have seriously considered the subject they have legislated, and whether or not they accurately represent the views of their constituents, hardly seems like a policy calculated to instill political responsibility in the majoritarian branches.

Finally, proponents of judicial self-restraint may wish to argue that regardless of whether the constitution is majoritarian, and regardless of the effects of judicial self-restraint on the political branches of government, democracy requires deference to majority rule. To the extent that our constitution licenses antimajoritarian institutions it fails as a democratic charter. In that case, we ought to be better democrats than the framers and insist on strong majority rule.

Like the other arguments we are considering, however, this turns on a question-begging non sequitur. Democracy means self-rule; it need not mean majority rule. Genuine self-rule requires widespread political deliberation; voting as such requires none. To the extent that the political system responds to sheer numbers of votes—in Hirschman's terms, to voter exit rather than citizen voice—powerful and perverse incentives are generated for politicians to create easy escapes for the electorate from the tedious process of deliberation. Contemporary media politics contains many examples of this phenomenon.

I do not mean to say that majority rule is a bad idea; I mean only that democratic arguments do not show that it is a good idea. They beg the question by assuming that self-rule means majority rule. Unless majorities display the virtues of democracy, democrats need entertain no special love for majorities.

None of the objections I have been rehearsing offers a case *against* the classical conception of judicial self-restraint, or against majority rule, nor are they intended to. The point is rather to suggest that whatever arguments can be made on behalf of the classical conception must cut deeper than appeals to constitutional structure, the separation of powers, fidelity to law, or democratic ideals. At this point I wish to turn to Holmes, who offers what must surely stand as one of the most amazing arguments ever offered on behalf of the classical conception.

HOLMES

Holmes's views about Thayerism and judicial virtue flow from a unified and deep philosophical outlook. It is generally recognized that Holmes's broader views, for example his self-professed "skepticism," influenced his philosophy of judging, but my claim is somewhat stronger. I believe that Holmes was a more serious metaphysician and value theorist than is generally supposed, and that his approach to judicial self-restraint emerged from his theory of value.[13]

Judging from the frequent reflections on these matters in his letters and speeches, what Holmes called his "intimate and ultimate regions of thought"[14] concerned those most philosophical of questions: Does human life have meaning? Do human values possess any validity? Holmes was profoundly alive to the possibility that the answer to both questions is no; he once remarked, "We are all very near despair."[15] His interest was in spirit and even in details of doctrine and literary timbre very close to Nietzsche's problem: How, in a godless world filled up with senseless destruction, can one find meaning and avoid sinking into nihilism, "the radical repudiation of value, meaning, and desirability"?[16]

For Holmes as for Nietzsche atheism is a consequence of a scientific world outlook, and it signals the end not just of religion but of all anthropocentric comforts we may seek in the universe.[17] As Holmes puts it, "I don't believe in the infinite importance of man—I see no reason to believe that a shudder could go through the sky if the whole ant heap were kerosened."[18] Meditation on ultimate matters is a pronounced feature of Holmes's personality, as witness his catalogue of what he takes to be the basic elements of daily life: "victuals—procreation—rest and eternal terror."[19]

Holmes once wrote that "*good & universal* (or *general law*) are synonymous terms in the universe."[20] He does not mean that the universe has our interests at heart—far from it, as his remark about kerosening the ant heap makes clear. For Holmes, the "universal laws" governing human affairs are the Malthusian insight that procreation must outstrip the means of existence, and hence the evolutionary law that in the struggle for existence only the fittest will survive. Holmes's equation of "good" and "universal law" means that goodness from the point of view of the universe implies the savage destruction of living beings.[21]

Holmes does not solve the problem of meaning by insisting that the cosmos is in the least bit benign. Rather, he finds repose in the thought that humanity is *not* the measure or center of all things, that the universe utterly and finally transcends the human scale, including human understanding. Relief comes from the realization that the world, though savage, is unfathomably grand, that there are more things in heaven and earth than are dreamt of in your philosophy. This, he writes, "gives us our only but our adequate significance."[22]

Holmes sometimes refers to his "secret fountain of faith . . . the belief that I am in the universe, not it in me."[23] For Holmes, the source of meaning lies, paradoxically enough, in a thought not far removed from a kind of Cartesian doubt: the thought that from the point of view of the universe our strivings may signify something ironically or even ludicrously different from their meaning to us.

For Holmes, that the universe is indifferent to what we hold dear signifies that "one's own moral and aesthetic preferences" are "more or less arbitrary, although none the less dogmatic on that account. Do you like sugar in your coffee or don't you?"[24]

He often delivers himself of similarly nihilistic opinions about the intrinsic impossibility of reasoning validly to moral judgments rather than merely fighting over them. "I understand by human rights what a given crowd will fight for (successfully). . . . When men differ in taste as to the kind of world they want the only thing to do is to go to work killing."[25] "I used to say, when I was young, that truth was the majority vote of that nation that could lick all others."[26] "Deep-seated preferences can not be argued about . . . and therefore, when differences are sufficiently far reaching, we try to kill the other man rather than let him have his way."[27] "I don't see that . . . [reason] stands any differently from my preference of champagne to ditch water."[28]

Nevertheless, he contends, we may, as a matter of natural or evolutionary happenstance, be so constituted that we necessarily hold certain beliefs as to the intrinsic worth of many things. Those beliefs we hold, and perhaps must hold, most dear he calls "ideals," and it is ideals that we live for and—more importantly, as we shall see—kill and die for. Yet Holmes consistently maintains that ideals are fictions, though maybe necessary fictions. That we cannot help creating ideals he calls "the trick by which nature keeps us at our job."[29] Our ideals do not arise because they point toward objectively, or subjectively, valuable ends. On the contrary, ends are valuable only because they are the objects of ideals. As he remarks in a letter to Lady Castletown, "Nothing could be more enchanting than to see a man nearly killing himself for an end which derives its worth simply from his having affirmed it. You see the pure ideal in the concrete—Nonsensical and sublime."[30]

This last remark highlights an additional point about Holmes's notion of ideals that is exceptionally strange. Holmes believes that ideals are worthy only to the extent that they are "nonsensical and sublime," that is, unattainable. He speaks rapturously of "ideals the essence of which is that they never can be achieved,"[31] and decries as banausic ideals of making people healthier or more comfortable, seemingly because they turn us away from more dangerous and unattainable ends.

Why does Holmes hold this romantic and self-undermining conception of human ideals? Perhaps he fears that only if we pursue a goal that recedes as swiftly as we advance can nature work its trick of keeping us on the job; the chase is over once the donkey captures the carrot.[32] Or perhaps he thinks that only ideals "outreaching the flaming bounds of the possible"[33] are able to maintain the discrepancy between us and the transcendent grandeur of the universe in which he finds the solution to the problem of meaning. In any event, it proves to be an important point, a ruling delusion, in Holmes's theory of value that victory is to be won only through the passionate pursuit of self-defeat.

Why would pursuit of fictive, unattainable, and intrinsically worthless ideals itself be a source of value? Holmes, I believe, here incorporates an Emersonian idea that proved crucial to Nietzsche as well: the idea that the infusion of "vital force" can transfigure us and lift us out of the etiolated half-experience of daily life.[34] Affirmation, vitality, and joy as such amount to the overcoming of nihilism. Holmes expresses this vitalism eloquently in his Memorial Day address, when he speaks of "the great chorus of life and joy."[35] Or, more aphoristically: "Life is an end in itself, and the only question as to whether it is worth living is whether you have enough of it."[36]

It is against this philosophical background that Holmes's view of virtue, and specifically the virtue of doing one's duty, takes shape. He expresses the point in his "Soldier's Faith" address:

> I do not know the meaning of the universe. But in the midst of doubt, in the collapse of creeds, there is one thing I do not doubt, that no man who lives in the same world with most of us can doubt, and that is that the faith is true and adorable which leads a soldier to throw away his life in obedience to a blindly accepted duty, in a cause which he little understands, in a plan of campaign of which he has no notion, under tactics of which he does not see the use."[37]

It is a mistake to think that Holmes intends to restrict this conception of duty only to soldiers and soldiering. For the argument of this speech is that the soldier's faith is the sole viable faith for us all. Nor, I think, do I overread the tone of this speech if I suggest that Holmes finds the soldier's faith all the more admirable because he is ignorant of why he throws away his life. The hapless and duped draftee has in an important sense fought a better campaign and died a more meaningful death than the thoughtful citizen who enlists with open eyes and believes in the cause for which he lays down his life. Holmes's soldier's faith amounts almost to the proposition that a death is more meaningful the more meaningless it is.

This paradoxical and even frightening conception of duty makes sense only as a corollary of Holmes's general response to the problem of meaning. To affirm the greatness of the universe is to affirm our own finitude, and this we do by unswerving commitment to a calling that is in an ultimate sense arbitrary. "The rule of joy and the law of duty seem to me all one."[38] The virtue of dutifulness consists for Holmes in combining maximum intensity with arbitrarily focused narrowness. We must wreak ourselves on life, in his words, even in the face of our ironic appreciation that our ideals are unattainable and our actions are senselessly self-defeating and bitterly cruel.[39] Ours not to reason why, ours but to do or die. For Kant, the deontological commitment to duty arises as a consequence of "the moral law within." Holmes, for whom ideals are likewise "categorical imperatives,"[40] turns deontology into a desperate expedient against despair, by insisting on our duty in the face of full knowledge that no moral law is to be found. This is the central paradox in Holmes's conception of duty.

Now I can present the first of my theses about Holmes's philosophy of judging. For Holmes the virtue underlying judicial self-restraint is precisely the virtue of the soldier: the judge's temptation is to rectify legislative error, and for a judge to hold back is to defer to faulty commandments in the same way that the soldier Holmes glorifies obeys suicidal or ridiculous orders.[41] This Holmes conceives to be his duty. As he writes Laski about the Sherman Act,

> I hope and believe that I am not influenced by my opinion that it
> is a foolish law. I have little doubt that the country likes it and I

always say, as you know, that if my fellow citizens want to go to Hell I will help them. It's my job.[42]

This amazing remark turns us to the second question that a theory of judicial self-restraint must answer. Even granting Holmes's argument about why judicial virtue requires a judge to honor duty over the demands of conscience, we must still determine the contours of judicial duty. Judicial self-restraint asks judges to defer to majoritarian institutions; but why? What, exactly, accounts for the authority of majorities?

The question assumes urgency for Holmes, because he rejects a variety of easy answers. A judge so ready to speed his fellow citizens on their chosen path to Hell cannot believe that deference to majorities is in itself for the good of the country. Nor does Holmes believe, with Brandeis, the weaker thesis that social experimentation, even with its inevitable failures, is good for the country because the benefits outweigh the risks. As he writes to Brandeis, "Generally speaking, I agree with you in liking to see social experiments tried but I do so without enthusiasm because I believe it is merely shifting the pressure and that so long as we have free propagation Malthus is right in his general view."[43] Nor does Holmes believe that majorities exercise a moral claim on our loyalty. Criticizing utilitarianism, he asks rhetorically, "Why should the greatest number be preferred? Why not the greatest good of the most intelligent and most highly developed?"[44] Presumably Holmes would raise the same questions about majority rule.

No less an authority than Felix Frankfurter attributes Holmes's deference to majorities to "humility in passing judgment on the experience and beliefs expressed by those entrusted with the duty of legislating," so that Holmes "reached the democratic result by the philosophic route of scepticism."[45] Now it is true that Holmes once wrote Pollock, "I am so sceptical as to our knowledge about the goodness or badness of laws that I have no practical criticism except what the crowd wants."[46] Yet as Rogat rightly observes, Holmes holds to his social and economic views with no trace of either humility or scepticism.[47] Holmes's humility and skepticism emerged only on a philosophical plane: from the point of view of the universe I can't be sure "that my *can't helps* which I call . . .

truth are cosmic *can't helps*,"[48] but they are *can't helps* nonetheless, and Holmes does not doubt them for a moment on the plane of merely human disputation. The very next sentence of his letter to Pollock provides the dry antistrophe to his skepticism: "Personally I bet that the crowd if it knew more wouldn't want what it does— but that is immaterial."[49] So much as well for the possibility that Holmes attributed superior wisdom to the majority.

Nor does Holmes hold to the popular argument, based on considerations of institutional competence, that courts lack legis- latures' fact-finding capabilities. Holmes sees the matter the other way round: rather than founding the duty of deference on courts' supposed ignorance, Holmes makes it almost a point of pride to ignore facts—a point of pride because in his view it is the judge's duty. In the first opinion in which he articulated a theory of judicial self-restraint, his dissent in *Commonwealth v. Perry*,[50] Holmes plausibly explains the legislature's aim in enact- ing a statute that the Supreme Judicial Court was voiding, then comments,

> If their view was true, I cannot doubt that the Legislature had the right . . . , and I cannot pronounce the legislation void, as based on a false assumption, since I know nothing about the matter one way or another.[51]

The evident sarcasm of this remark prevents us from reading it at face value. Clearly, Holmes is not saying that a judge inevitably knows nothing about the matter one way or another. Rather, he is stressing that a judge's duty prevents him from relying on his own knowledge.

Brandeis disagrees with Holmes on this point: his Supreme Court opinions often present lengthy analyses of the economic and social realities underlying legislation.[52] As he writes, the reasonableness of state regulations "can ordinarily be deter- mined only by a consideration of the contemporary conditions, social, industrial and political, of the community to be affected thereby. Resort to such facts is necessary."[53] Holmes complains to Frankfurter that Brandeis "always desires to know all that can be known about a case whereas I am afraid that I wish to know as little as I can safely go on."[54] He complains that Brandeis adopted too much the attitude of an advocate of the state laws whose constitutionality he was upholding.[55] The difference is temperamental as well as principled. Holmes once wrote Frankfurter, "I have just received a typewritten report of the U.S. Coal Commission. Brandeis would be deep into it at once. I turn to Sainte-Beuve."[56]

Whether we agree with Holmes or with Brandeis, however, it is to Holmes's credit that he does not rely on the institutional competence argument that judges cannot find facts as well as legislatures can, for this is mistaken. Trial courts possess the power of subpoena and appellate courts may invite knowledgeable parties to submit amicus briefs; courts operate under less stringent time constraints than state legislatures; and courts work relatively free from the political pressures that inevitably lead legislatures to exclude controversial or powerless parties from presenting public testimony. In practice judges possess at least as much fact-finding ability as legislatures.

Neither does Holmes rest the policy of deference on the separation of powers. It is noteworthy that in Holmes's introduction to a reissue of Montesquieu's *Esprit des Lois,* he makes only one brief reference to the separation of powers, and that a dismissive remark that Montesquieu's "England of the threefold division of power . . . was a fiction invented by him."[57] Indeed, while Holmes writes Thayer that he "heartily agreed" with his essay on judicial review, which argues for the rule of the clear mistake on separation of powers grounds, he adds, "I am not entirely sure that you do not overvalue your formula as a matter of ultimate analysis" and stresses that as a principle of *state* constitutional law the real reason for judicial deference is that the legislature possesses "the power of Parliament—i.e., absolute power."[58]

It is in the emphasis on power that we at last come to what I take to be the heart of Holmes's allegiance to majoritarianism. The significance of majorities in Holmes's eyes is that they constitute the dominant force in the community, and Holmes attributes normative authority to the dominant force. He states his argument in two short essays. In each, he appears to offer an independent argument for deferring to dominant forces; but the appearance does not survive a closer reading, and I am prepared to conclude that Holmes attributes no significance to majorities, dominant forces, beyond dominance itself. One argument appears in his essay on Montesquieu:

> [T]he most perfect government is that which attains its ends with the least cost, so that the one which leads men in the way most according to their inclination is best. . . . What proximate test of excellence can be found except correspondence to the actual equilibrium of force in the community—that is, conformity to the wishes of the dominant power? Of course, such conformity may lead to destruction, and it is desirable that the dominant power should be wise. But wise or not, the proximate test of a good government is that the dominant power has its way.[59]

This argument has deceptive simplicity. Consider the first sentence. It begins with the seeming truism that the most perfect government attains its ends with the least cost, a proposition that we are inclined to accept without protest because it seems to advocate nothing more than the efficient pursuit of given ends. Who would prefer inefficient pursuit of given ends?

But Holmes infers from this a proposition about what ends government ought to adopt, namely those that can be pursued with least cost because they encounter the least opposition. This makes the argument into a non sequitur unless we read "the most perfect government attains its ends with the least cost" *not* as the proposition that government ought to choose the handiest means to given ends, but rather as the proposition that government ought to choose ends that correspond to the handiest available means.

But then it is no longer a truism that the most perfect government attains its ends with the least cost. Read as a constraint on the ends, rather than on the means, that government can rightfully adopt, Holmes's least-cost rule insists that ends be chosen to minimize possible opposition—to go with the flow. Far from providing an independent economic argument for taking "conformity to the wishes of the dominant power" as the "proximate test for a good government," the least-cost rule merely restates, hence presupposes, that test.

Holmes offers a somewhat different defense of "conformity to the wishes of the dominant power" in "The Gas-Stokers'

Strike." The heart of this brief essay is a methodological criticism of attempting to appraise legislation by asking whether it will promote the good "for society, considered as a whole." Holmes objects "that this presupposes an identity of interest between the different parts of a community which does not exist in the fact."[60] Oddly enough echoing Marx, Holmes rejects the very concept of a common good or aggregate public interest, and insists that the only sound criteria for assessing legislation are class relative:

> The objection to class legislation is not that it favors a class, but either that it fails to benefit the legislators, or that it is dangerous to them because a competing class has gained in power, or that it transcends the limits of self-preference which are imposed by sympathy.[61]

One must consequently adopt a class standpoint to assess legislation. Holmes concludes, as in the Montesquieu essay, "that legislation should . . . modify itself in accordance with the will of the de facto supreme power in the community":[62]

> The more powerful interests must be more or less reflected in legislation. . . . If the welfare of the living majority is paramount, it can only be on the ground that the majority have the power in their hands. The fact is that legislation . . . is necessarily made a means by which a body, having the power, puts burdens which are disagreeable to them on the shoulders of somebody else.[63]

Holmes argues, in brief, from the necessity of adopting *some* class standpoint to assess legislation to the necessity of adopting the dominant class's standpoint. Clearly, however, one could just as readily follow Marx and adopt the standpoint of the subordinate class, or for that matter any other class. Holmes's argument therefore presupposes the same normative supremacy of dominant social forces we find in his analysis based on the least-cost rule.

Ultimately, I think that Holmes's writings do not offer a clear explanation of his brute respect for force. His debunking of moral constraints on force, his vision of the limitations of reason, and his skepticism about the common good as well as the possibil-

ity of long-term consequentialist prediction—all help to explain
why the manifestation of force in law does not repel Holmes; but
why does it attract him?

My conjecture is that Holmes admires the manifestation of
force because he sees in it the vitality and joy that is our salvation
from despair. To put it another way, I connect Holmes's majoritarian commitment to the vitalism I mentioned earlier, his
belief that "the only question as to whether [life] is worth living is
whether you have enough of it." Nietzsche believes that the
world consists of will to power and nothing else. Holmes holds a
similar belief:

> I believe that we are in the universe, not it in us, that we are part
> of an unimaginable, which I will call a whole, in order to name it,
> that our personality is a cosmic ganglion, that just as when certain
> rays meet and cross there is white light at the meeting point, but
> the rays go on after the meeting as they did before, so, when
> certain other streams of energy cross, the meeting point can
> frame a syllogism or wag its tail.[64]

To affirm the cosmos, then, amounts to affirming the actuality of
this energy; hence Holmes's reverence for the dominant force.

On this reading, Holmes holds views similar to the conservative utopianism described by Karl Mannheim:

> The fact of the mere existence of a thing endows it with a higher
> value. . . . "There is something marvellous about experiencing
> something of which it may be said 'it is!' "[65]

Holmes puts it less breathlessly and in the negative: "I don't believe much in anything that is, but I believe a damned sight less in
anything that isn't."[66] Moreover, he values vitality, not existence,
and therefore transposes conservative utopianism from a static to
a dynamic key. But the conservative utopian's exaltation of the
actual over the merely possible, as holding the key to affirmation,
hence to redemption from futility, lies at the root of his reverence
for dominant social forces and so of majorities. To fly in the face
of the majority is to deny the actual and, in Nietzsche's words, to
"pass sentence on existence."[67] This Holmes was not prepared to
do.

What Do We Make of Holmes?

To fault Holmes's views is at once trivially easy and excruciatingly difficult. Taken in the large, we may find ourselves unable to accept his atheism, or his Emersonian mysticism, or his vitalism, or his irrationalism, or his virtually unargued insistence on the arbitrariness of morality. We may not share his preoccupation with the threat of meaninglessness, his "eternal terror" and his sense that "we are all very near despair." If we do share it we may fail to see how the solution can lie, as Holmes thinks it does, in celebrating the indifference of the universe to everything we hold dear. The cosmic indifference that Holmes seizes upon as the solution is, after all, very close to what most of us would take to be the problem.

Taken in the small, many of Holmes's views will surely provoke objections, particularly from analytic philosophers whose business is the careful assessment of arguments. Holmes's systematic blurring of the distinction between reasons and causes, his reduction of value judgments to naked preferences, his determinism, his bizarre view that ideals cannot be truly worthwhile if they are capable of being achieved, his insistence on pointless deontology, his conservative utopianism, and other aspects of his world view are all deeply problematic.

Nevertheless, it is a monumental and inspiring world view, and no useful purpose is served by carping at its margins or even, for that matter, sneering at its grand animating premises, with which we can all partly sympathize.

The doubts I wish to raise are of a different nature from direct disputation of the propositions Holmes advances. I wish to ask, first, whether Holmes's views can possibly form a satisfactory public justification of judicial self-restraint; second, whether they can form a psychologically stable self-conception of the judicial role; and third, whether the basic metaphors, entirely military, through which he understood social life and even existence as a whole can be accepted. To all three questions I think the answer is no.

The point of the first question is that classical judicial self-restraint is a public institution and not a private aspect of judicial deliberation. Public institutions require justifications that are publicly acceptable, not merely philosophically true. Kant claimed that it is a "transcendental formula of public law" that "all actions relating to the right of other human beings are unjust if their maxim cannot withstand publicity."[68] Though this "publicity principle" stands in need of justification that I cannot provide here, it seems plausible that a justification for an institution of public law that would excite widespread and principled condemnation if it were publicized has no place in a democracy.

Part of my motive for emphasizing the many similarities between Holmes and Nietzsche is to highlight what should be obvious: a more eccentric foundation for judicial self-restraint than Holmes's would be hard to find. A form of judicial review based on atheism and cosmic indifference to human aspiration, on the arbitrariness of value judgments, on the contemptibility of attempting to relieve human suffering through public policy, and on judicial "obedience to a blindly accepted duty" to speed one's fellow citizens on their self-elected path to Hell could not survive the test of publicity.

It is scarcely credible that we would accept as a job description of the federal judiciary "that if my fellow citizens want to go to Hell I will help them." Even Americans who back judicial self-restraint also expect the federal judiciary to perform acts of statesmanship, to hack through the Gordian knots of legislative stupidity and bureaucratic red tape.[69]

As government has become larger, more bureaucratized, and more administrative in the decades since the New Deal, the federal courts have taken on something of the role of the national complaints department, or, to shift metaphors, of the body politic's nervous system. When we cannot voice our grievances or obtain redress from politicians and bureaucrats, we go to federal court; when a public policy causes pain, we register that pain through the courts. Though we don't want government by judiciary—or at least we say we don't—we need and expect the federal courts to save government from its own infirmities, including legislatures with short time horizons, the well-known forms of democratic failure, the structural and political inabilities of national government to absorb information about past bad choices, and sheer official inertia. This is the point of a widely construed judicial role, "judicial activism," and it signals the gulf between our public expectations and Holmes's sardonic credo.

If Holmes's views cannot form a palatable public philosophy of judging, perhaps they can still constitute a judge's secret article of faith, as they did for Holmes himself.[70] Yet here too problems arise. On analogy to Kant's publicity principle, which asks whether a policy can stably be adopted without public deception, we can test a private world view by asking whether an agent can stably maintain it without self-deception. Holmes's outlook fails this test.

He writes, "I suspect that all my ultimates have the mark of the finite upon them, but as they are the best I know I give them practical respect, love, etc., but inwardly doubt whether they have any importance except for us."[71] But how do we tender practical respect if we are filled with doubts? The secret, according to Holmes, is to allow skeptical doubts only on "the Saturday half-holiday," when we "smile at the trick by which nature has kept us on the job."[72]

Yet talk of the "trick" that keeps us on the job makes it clear that self-deception lies at the heart of Holmes's "jobbism": to remain committed to the job, we must repress our knowledge of nature's trick. One corollary of Holmes's conception of ideals as the pursuit of "an end which derives its worth simply from his having affirmed it" is that the pursuit itself, not the end pursued, is the real source of value. That, of course, is why he calls framing ideals nature's *trick* rather than merely nature's way of keeping us on the job. If the pursuit itself is the real source of value, we must in our own conscious designs pursue something else. Pursuing a pursuit as such is meaningless, almost logically impossible, and thus a fully conscious realization that meaning comes from the pursuit rather than from the end pursued would itself undermine the very condition of meaningfulness by bringing us to a halt. Though Holmes never frames the argument in these terms, the point is closely related to the so-called paradox of hedonism, the fact that one sure way to fail in the pursuit of pleasure is to make pleasure as such the object of the pursuit. Pleasure can emerge only as the byproduct of other activities. In the end, then, Holmes offers a set of philosophical commitments that no judge can maintain without self-deception.

Finally, I wish to point to the most obviously troubling feature of Holmes's philosophy, and indeed his entire authorship: his insistence on understanding the world through military metaphors. The biographical reasons for this are clear: as virtually every writer on Holmes realizes, his Civil War experiences deeply colored his philosophy of life.[73] But whatever his reasons for viewing the world as a battle and all of us as soldiers, it should be clear that this leads to a deformation of our thinking about civilian and peacetime matters, including law. When Holmes writes "that all law means I will kill you if necessary to make you conform to my requirements,"[74] he fastens on the feature of law most like war, its physical enforcement, and uses it to obscure all other features, for example law as a peaceable alternative to violence.

Holmes's military way of thinking enters into every part of his argument for judicial self-restraint. It determines his "soldier's faith" conception of duty, but also his insistence on viewing electorial majorities as unanswerable military victors, and even his knightly conception of occupational virtue.

For our purposes, the most important misunderstanding fostered by Holmes's militarism is the last of these: his treatment of professional obligations as soldierly duties. The soldier's role is built around the exigencies of combat, chief among them being unquestioned obedience in dangerous situations. In the extremity of combat, the demands of discipline overwhelm concerns of conscience. But the same cannot be said of other occupations, including judging. Holmes's literary talents can almost persuade us that the life of the law is a perpetual struggle to the death, and thus that society exists in a permanent state of emergency in which common moral scruples must be set aside by judges who combine knightly honor with soldierly ruthlessness. But—we must say to him—things just aren't that bad.

NOTES

1. Part of the confusion arises because the term has come to possess multiple meanings, derived from the mostly polemical purposes into whose service it has been pressed. Especially in the decades since *Brown*

v. Board of Education, "judicial self-restraint" has become in popular parlance a kind of conservative code word used for the essentially base purpose of praising judges who are reluctant to interfere with the workings of white racial prejudice. The best discussion I have seen of the multiple *legitimate* meanings of the term is Richard Posner, *The Federal Courts: Crisis and Reform* (Cambridge: Harvard University Press, 1985), pp. 198–222. I attempt to sort out several meanings in "Judicial Activism vs. Judicial Restraint: A Closer Look at the Bork Nomination," *QQ: Report from the Center for Philosophy & Public Policy,* vol. 7, no. 4 (Fall 1987), 9–12.

Judge Posner also emphasizes the important distinction between judicial self-restraint and judicial personality: *The Federal Courts,* pp. 215–17.

2. James Bradley Thayer, "The Origin and Scope of the American Doctrine of Constitutional Law," *Harvard Law Review,* 7 (1893), 129–56. See Wallace Mendelson, "The Influence of James B. Thayer upon the Work of Holmes, Brandeis, and Frankfurter," *Vanderbilt Law Review,* 31 (1978), 71–87. Frankfurter once wrote to Hand, "When [Harlan] went off the other day I put a copy of J. B. Thayer's essay . . . into his hands, with the remark, 'Please read it, then reread it, and then read it again and then think about it long.' " Quoted in H. N. Hirsch, *The Enigma of Felix Frankfurter* (New York: Basic, 1981), p. 182.

3. See Bickel, *The Least Dangerous Branch: The Supreme Court at the Bar of Politics* (New Haven: Yale University Press, 1962), especially the discussion of Thayer at pp. 35–45.

4. Thayer, 138. Why "little understood?" Because here Thayer is arguing *against* a literalist and text-oriented mode of reading the Constitution, hence against the "strict constructionism" that modern exponents of judicial restraint hold dear.

5. *The Least Dangerous Branch,* p. 26. Here I follow Anthony Kronman's masterly exposition of Bickel's thought: "Alexander Bickel's Philosophy of Prudence," *Yale Law Journal,* 94 (1985), 1567–1616; the present point at 1586.

6. *West Virginia State Board of Education v. Barnette,* 319 U.S. 624, 667 (1943) (Frankfurter, J., dissenting).

7. I thank Robin West for this point. See the essays collected in Jon Elster and Rune Slagstad, eds., *Constitutionalism and Democracy* (Cambridge: Cambridge University Press, 1988), especially Elster's introduction and Stephen Holmes's "Precommitment and the Paradox of Democracy."

8. Efforts in Great Britain to create a written bill of rights on the American model raise theoretical objections related to this point. Even

if Parliament enacts such a bill, subsequent acts of Parliament inconsistent with its provisions would merely supersede those provisions rather than being constrained by them. Nothing could prevent this except a "self-sealing" provision voiding future attempts to supersede or repeal the bill, a self-sealing provision that many theorists believe to be impossible. The problem arises because Parliament is an unconstrained majoritarian institution.

9. Thayer, p. 136.

10. Ibid.

11. Paul Brest revives Thayer's concerns, arguing that overreliance on the courts weakens our constitutional democracy by making us worse citizens, in "Constitutional Citizenship," *Cleveland State Law Review,* 34 (1986), 1–23.

12. A 1989 Washington Post-ABC News Poll of 764 adults found 55 percent favoring mandatory drug tests for all Americans, 67 percent favoring drug test for all high school students, 67 percent favoring random stopping and searching of cars, 71 percent favoring bans on showing illegal drug use in movies, and 52 percent favoring warrantless searches of the homes of suspected drug dealers. Richard Morin, "Many in Poll Say Bush Plan Is Not Stringent Enough," *Washington Post* (September 8, 1989), pp. A1, A18.

13. Even Thomas Grey, who aims to vindicate Holmes's stature as a philosopher, in my view underrates his speculative abilities. Grey, "Holmes and Legal Pragmatism," *Stanford Law Review,* 41 (1989), 844–45.

14. Holmes to John Chipman Gray, February 19, 1915, quoted in Sheldon M. Novick, *Honorable Justice: The Life of Oliver Wendell Holmes* (Boston: Little, Brown, 1989), p. 314.

15. "Speech at a Dinner Given to Chief Justice Holmes," [hereafter: "Bar speech"], Oliver Wendell Holmes, *Collected Legal Papers* (New York: Smith, 1952), p. 248.

16. *The Will to Power,* sec. 1, p. 7. The suggestion that Holmes and Nietzsche inhabit roughly the same philosophical terrain has been made by Judge Richard Posner in *The Problems of Jurisprudence* (Cambridge: Harvard University Press, 1990), pp. 239–44. Posner focuses on Holmes's and Nietzsche's repudiation of subjectivity and the importance of our conscious thoughts; I suggest that the similarity encompasses their basic theory of value as well, and even their preoccupation with combat and bloodshed. Both Holmes and Nietzsche found in their wartime experiences—though Nietzsche, a military nurse, never saw combat—a metaphor for the universe at large, and both men affected military-style mustaches.

17. On Holmes's scientific outlook, see his letter to Cohen, February 5, 1919, in Felix Cohen, ed., "The Holmes-Cohen Correspondence," *Journal of the History of Ideas*, 9 (1948) [hereafter: "Holmes-Cohen"], 14.

18. Holmes to Laski, July 21, 1921, *Holmes-Laski Letters, 1916–1935* (Cambridge: Harvard University Press, 1953) [hereafter: *Holmes-Laski*], p. 351. Almost the identical remark appears in a letter from Holmes to Morris Cohen, May 27, 1917, "Holmes-Cohen," p. 9.

19. Letter to Frederick Pollock, August 21, 1919, in Mark DeWolfe Howe, ed., *Holmes-Pollock Letters: The Correspondence of Mr. Justice Holmes and Sir Frederick Pollock, 1874–1932*, vol. 2 (Cambridge: Harvard University Press, 1942) [hereafter: *Holmes-Pollock*], p. 22.

20. Mark DeWolfe Howe, ed., *Touched with Fire: Civil War Letters and Diary of Oliver Wendell Holmes, Jr., 1861–1864* (Cambridge: Harvard University Press, 1946), pp. 23–29.

21. "I believe that Malthus was right in his fundamental notion. . . . Every society is founded on the death of men." Holmes to Wu, July 21, 1925, in *Justice Holmes to Doctor Wu: An Intimate Correspondence, 1921–1932* (New York: Central Book Company, n.d.) [hereafter: *Holmes-Wu*], p. 31.

22. "Natural Law," *Collected Legal Papers*, p. 316.

23. Holmes to Baroness Moncheur, December 30, 1915, quoted in Novick, supra note 14, p. 319.

24. Holmes to Lady Pollock, September 6, 1902, *Holmes-Pollock Letters*, vol. 1, p. 105.

25. Holmes to Laski, December 3, 1917, in *Holmes-Laski*, pp. 115–16.

26. "Natural Law," *Collected Legal Papers*, p. 310.

27. Ibid., p. 312.

28. Holmes to Cohen, September 10, 1918, "Holmes-Cohen," p. 12.

29. Holmes to Wu, May 5, 1926, *Holmes-Wu*, pp. 35–36. This letter is one of the crucial documents for understanding Holmes's metaphysics and its connection with moral psychology and the theory of value. Clearly, his anthropomorphic way of speaking about nature is simply shorthand for a nonteleological evolutionary argument: human creatures possessing ideals are adaptively superior to human creatures who lack ideals, i.e., are more likely to reproduce their kind (perhaps because without ideals human beings sink into a kind of despondency that psychosomatically weakens them, or that makes them less attractive mates, or whatever).

30. Holmes to Lady Castletown, April 10, 1897, quoted in Novick, supra note 14, p. 216. Compare: "Man is born a predestined idealist, for he is born to act. To act is to affirm the worth of an end, and to

persist in affirming the worth of an end is to make an ideal." "The Class of '61," *The Occasional Speeches of Justice Oliver Wendell Holmes,* ed. Mark DeWolfe Howe (Cambridge: Harvard University Press, 1962) [hereafter: *Speeches*], p. 162.

31. "The Soldier's Faith," *Speeches,* p. 76 (emphasis added). Holmes's polemic in this speech against human comfort and the social reformers who take it as their aim, and the contrast he draws between comfort and the "soldier's faith" in violence and danger—and one should read the entire opening passage from which I have taken this extract—is cut from precisely the same cloth as the prologue to Nietzsche's *Zarathustra:*

"I say unto you: one must still have chaos in oneself to be able to give birth to a dancing star. . . . Alas, the time is coming when man will no longer give birth to a star. . . . Behold, I show you the *last man.* 'What is love? What is creation? What is longing? What is a star?' thus asks the last man, and he blinks. The earth has become small, and on it hops the last man, who makes everything small. . . . One still works, for work is a form of entertainment. But one is careful lest the entertainment be too harrowing. One no longer becomes poor or rich: both require too much exertion. . . . One has one's little pleasure for the night: but one has a regard for health. 'We have invented happiness,' say the last men, and they blink." (*Thus Spoke Zarathustra,* in *The Portable Nietzsche,* ed. and trans. Walter Kaufmann [Viking, 1954], pp. 129–30)

32. Holmes suggests this in his Northwestern University address, *Collected Legal Papers,* p. 276.

33. "The Soldier's Faith," p. 76.

34. Emerson, "Experience," in *Essays, First and Second Series* (New York: Dutton, 1906), pp. 242–45. "I can see nothing at last, in success or failure, than more or less of vital force supplied from the Eternal. . . . Our life seems not present, so much as prospective; not for the affairs on which it is wasted, but as a hint of this vast-flowing vigour."

35. "Memorial Day," *Speeches,* p. 16.

36. "Bar speech," *Collected Legal Papers,* p. 248. For similar sentiments, see also Holmes to Pollock, *Holmes-Pollock,* vol. 2, p. 22.

37. "The Soldier's Faith," *Speeches,* p. 73.

38. "Bar speech," *Collected Legal Papers,* p. 247.

39. The phrase appears in his famous appreciation of the legal profession: "I say . . . that a man may live greatly in the law as well as elsewhere; that there as well as elsewhere his thought may find its unity in an infinite perspective; that there as well as elsewhere he may wreak himself upon life, may drink the bitter cup of heroism, may wear his heart out after the unattainable." "The Profession of Law," in *Collected Legal Papers,* 30.

40. Northwestern University address, *Collected Legal Papers*, p. 274.

41. In his Memorial Day address Holmes describes a Civil War incident involving his friend Abbott in fighting at Fredericksburg. As Holmes puts it in a letter to his parents,

Macy says quietly "Mr Abbott you will take your first platoon forward" to wh. A. "1st Platoon forward—March" and walks quietly ahead—His 1st Platoon is knocked to pieces (He lost that day 30 out of 60—10 shot dead) instantly— "You'll have to put in the 2d says Col. H. "2d Platoon forward" and A. leads them into the storm with the same semi indifferent air that he has when drilling a Battn. (Holmes to his parents, March 18, 1863, quoted in *Touched with Fire*, p. 90)

42. Letter of March 4, 1920, *Holmes-Laski*, pp. 248–49.

43. Holmes to Brandeis, April 20, 1919, quoted in Philippa Strum, *Louis D. Brandeis: Justice for the People* (Cambridge: Harvard University Press, 1984), p. 310.

44. "The Gas-Stokers' Strike," *American Law Review*, 7 (1873), 583; reprinted in *Harvard Law Review*, 44 (1931), 796.

45. Frankfurter, "Holmes, Oliver Wendell," in *Dictionary of American Biography*, vol. 11 (New York: Scribner's, 1944), p. 423. See also Mendelson, "Mr. Justice Holmes—Humility, Skepticism, and Democracy," *Minnesota Law Review*, 36 (1952), 343: "Holmes brought to the Supreme Court . . . two striking qualities, scepticism and intellectual humility."

46. Letter of April 23, 1910, *Holmes-Pollock*, vol. 1, p. 163.

47. Rogat, "The Judge as Spectator," *University of Chicago Law Review*, 31 (1964), pp. 250–54.

48. *Holmes-Wu*, p. 14.

49. *Holmes-Pollock*, vol. 1, p. 163.

50. 155 Mass. 117, 123–25 (1891).

51. Ibid., pp. 124–25.

52. A famous example is his opinion in *New State Ice Company v. Liebmann*, 285 U.S. 262 (1932), with its fourteen-page survey of the social conditions that led the Oklahoma legislature to pass a law invalidated by the Court.

53. *Truax v. Corrigan*, 257 U.S. 312, 355–57 (1921) (Brandeis, J., dissenting).

54. Holmes to Frankfurter, December 3, 1925, quoted in Strum, *Louis D. Brandeis*, p. 311.

55. Holmes to Laski, January 13, 1918, *Holmes-Laski*, p. 127. For discussion of the differences between Holmes and Brandeis on this issue, see Rogat, "The Judge as Spectator," pp. 244–49; Robert A. Burt, *Two Jewish Justices: Outcasts in the Promised Land* (Berkeley: University of

California Press, 1988), pp. 20–24; and Strum, *Louis D. Brandeis,* pp. 309–14.

56. Quoted in Strum, p. 310. At one point Brandeis argues to Holmes "that if he really wants to 'improve his mind' (as he always speaks of it), the way to do it is not to read more philosophic books . . . but to get some sense of the world of fact. . . . I suggested the textile industry, and told him in vacation time he is near Lawrence and Lowell and he should go there and look about. He became much interested . . . but very unfortunately it was the time when Mrs. Holmes was very sick." Holmes's version of the incident, described in correspondence with Pollock, is this: "Brandeis the other day drove a harpoon into my midriff with reference to my summer occupations. He said 'you talk about improving your mind, you only exercise it on the subjects with which you are familiar. Why don't you . . . [t]ake up the textile industries in Massachusetts and after reading the reports sufficiently you can go to Lawrence and get a human notion of how it really is.' . . . I hate facts. I always say the chief end of man is to form general propositions— adding that no general proposition is worth a damn. . . . I have little doubt that it would be good for my immortal soul to plunge into them . . . but I shrink from the bore." Letter of May 26, 1919, *Holmes-Pollock,* vol. 2, p. 13.

57. "Montesquieu," in *Collected Legal Papers,* p. 263.

58. Holmes to Thayer, November 2, 1893, Holmes papers, Harvard Law School, Box 35, Folder 4. I quote Holmes's letter in its entirety, since as far as I know it has nowhere been published:

Dear Thayer

I have read your article and I think it admirable. Substantially I agree with it heartily and it makes explicit the point of view from which implicitly I have approached Constitutional questions upon which I have differed from some of the other judges. If were to make any criticism it would only be to express a doubt which you have articulated at the bottom of p. 144—I am not entirely sure that you do not overvalue your formula as a matter of ultimate analysis. Of the usefulness of insisting upon it at this time and of dispelling the illusion dealt with in the last sentence of the article I have no doubt. It is idle to rely upon Courts "to save a people from ruin"—And I think that an intelligent dissent by one of my brethren would make me hesitate long in pronouncing an act unconstitutional, because I believe in your formula.

There is another principle of *state* constitutional law not within the scope of your discussion which I always have supposed fundamental but which (between ourselves) I infer from the discussions I have had with my brethren does not command their assent—viz. that a state legislature has the power of Parliament, i.e. absolute power, except so far as expressly or by implication it is prohibited by the Constitution—that the question always is where do you find the prohibition—

not, where do you find the power—I think the contrary view dangerous and wrong. I should send the article to Brother Adams if I were you. He may have some suggestions.

The passage on the bottom of page 144 of Thayer's article to which Holmes alludes reads, "Will any one say, You are over-emphasizing this matter, and making too much turn upon the form of a phrase? No, I think not."

59. "Montesquieu," in *Collected Legal Papers*, pp. 257–58. Holmes is here praising Montesquieu's *Persian Letters;* the passage under discussion appears in Letter 80: "I have often asked myself what kind of government most conformed to reason. It has seemed to me that the most perfect is that which attains its goal with the least friction; thus that government is most perfect which leads men along paths most agreeable to their interests and inclinations" (George R. Healy, trans. [Indianapolis: Bobbs-Merrill, 1964], p. 136). But the subsequent analysis of this passage is pure Holmes: Montesquieu offers this proposition as the premise of an argument on behalf of mild government and moderate punishments, not on behalf of majoritarianism or democracy, a subject that in fact makes no appearance in the letter.

60. "The Gas-Stokers' Strike," p. 796.

61. Ibid. The third criterion transcends class relativity only in part, since it grounds limits on self-preference in the moral psychology of class-embedded individuals.

62. Ibid.

63. Ibid., p. 796.

64. Holmes to Wu, May 5, 1926, *Holmes-Wu,* pp. 35–36.

65. Karl Mannheim, *Ideology and Utopia,* trans. Louis Wirth and Edward Shils (New York: Harvest, 1936), p. 235.

66. Holmes to Wigmore, December 4, 1910, quoted in Grey, "Holmes and Legal Pragmatism," supra note 13, p. 812.

67. Nietzsche, *The Will to Power,* sec. 6, p. 10. "This is the *antinomy:* Insofar as we believe in morality we pass sentence on existence."

68. *Zum ewigen Frieden,* Prussian Academy edition, vol. 8, p. 381; in English in Hans Reiss, ed., *Kant's Political Writings* (Cambridge: Cambridge University Press, 1970), p. 126, and Lewis White Beck, ed., *On History* (Indianapolis: Bobbs-Merrill, 1963), p. 129.

69. See generally Richard Neely, *How Courts Govern America* (New Haven: Yale University Press, 1981).

70. Holmes added, in his letter to Wu concerning the cosmic ganglion, "This is private talk, not to be quoted to others, for one is shy and sensitive as to one's inner convictions, except in those queer moments

when one tells the world as poets and philosophers do." Holmes to Wu, May 5, 1926, *Holmes-Wu,* p. 36.

71. Ibid., pp. 35–36.

72. Ibid.

73. For a particularly ungenerous version of this argument, see Saul Touster, "Holmes's *Common Law:* A Centennial View," *American Scholar,* 51 (1982), pp. 521–31.

74. Holmes to Laski, September 7, 1916, *Holmes-Laski,* p. 16.

12

JUDICIAL VIRTUE AND DEMOCRATIC POLITICS

TERRY PINKARD

David Luban has given us the first part of what he projects to be a history and theory of judicial self-restraint. As he says, the idea is both relatively recent and can also be traced to a relatively definite beginning involving a definite set of people. The idea of judicial self-restraint is both a thesis about constitutional interpretation and a characterization of a certain type of virtue that judges are supposed to have. His strategy for dealing with the issue seems to be twofold: first, to examine the arguments that are generally given for the proposition: second, to examine its history and the arguments that were given for it. As matters turn out, judicial self-restraint fails on the first count. In following out his first strategy, Luban shows, I believe, that neither the thesis about constitutional interpretation nor the validity of claiming it as a judicial virtue follow from the standard arguments having to do with constitutional structure, with the duty of fidelity to law, nor with the arguments that appeal to democratic ideals per se. He then gives us the beginning of what will eventually be a historical argument concerning the apostles, or the patriarchs, of judicial self-restraint. If James Thayer is the founder, then the first apostle is Oliver Wendell Holmes.

What was Holmes's conception of judicial self-restraint? It amounts to a belief in the right of majorities to determine their fate, whatever they might determine. Holmes's quip about his duty to assist the majority in going to Hell should they choose to do so is one of his better-known aphorisms on this point. If to see the legislation in question as constitutional is reasonable, then it is constitutional. What gives majorities this right? It is not—like one of Mill's arguments against paternalism—that the majority, that is, the legislature, is always in a better position to know what is best for itself (that is, the majority) than, say, supposedly non-majoritarian institutions like the courts are. It was rather that dominance is a good in itself—this is Holmes's "vitalism." Suppressing the dominant forces is not good because in doing so, one is interfering with the general flow of life, indeed of the universe itself. Holmes was no Enlightenment figure holding that the providential order was working its way out for the best in human terms. Rather, he seemed to hold that putting oneself in consonance with this general flow of forces was just good in itself. David Luban is surely correct to hold that this would hardly satisfy conditions of publicity, much less give us a generally coherent account of judicial virtue.

But two questions must be asked. First, are there other arguments for judicial self-restraint that emerge in Holmesian corpus that do not depend on metaphysical musings? Holmes himself did not apparently bring many of his more metaphysical theses into public light and for good reason—maybe he had some idea of just how badly they would fail the publicity test! It is probably safe to say that Holmes's great reputation as one of the apostles of self-restraint does not rest on Holmes's reputation as a great metaphysician or as the author of the peculiar theodicy that Luban finds in his thought. So we must ask, what conceptual reasons have helped to make Holmes's and Thayer's notion of judicial self-restraint the influential idea that it has become?

Second, what is the relation between Holmes's legal realism, the belief that law is what judges say it is, and his doctrine of judicial self-restraint? After all, legal realism would seem to lead to exactly the opposite of a doctrine of self-restraint. For a full-blooded legal realist, self-restraint could just as well be the *vice* of the judiciary as it could be its virtue. His legal realism is also independent of his more metaphysical theses about getting in touch with the cosmic order.

What I wish to do here is to engage not in another apostolic history of the concept but in something more akin to what Hegel called "philosophical history." That is, I want to look at the emerging conceptions in terms of which Holmes located himself and try to understand what conceptual reasons could have motivated him to arrive at the positions he held. I do not argue that such and such actually caused any particular development. Rather, I want to look at the kind of dialectic that gets set up once certain basic ideas enter the scene and how the contingent events of history structure our specific understandings of these ideas and motivate us to hold certain options as actually open and others as closed. Holmes's conception of judicial self-restraint is best understood as a specific response to a deeper and a general problem about democratic liberalism that emerges in light of certain historical developments in American democratic liberalism and the kind of institution of judging that it has developed in its history. In the first part, I shall talk about the specific problems that emerged in Holmes's time concerning the image of the judge and how that generated its own set of conceptual issues. In the second part, I shall show how certain basic problems in democratic liberalism could be seen to have led Holmes to resolve these problems generated by the emerging image of the judge in the ways that he did.

JUDICIAL RESTRAINT AND AMERICAN LEGAL HISTORY

The idea itself of judicial restraint emerges in response to one of the oldest questions of American constitutional jurisprudence and political theory, that of the relation of democracy to republicanism. Granted that we have a democracy, in which self-rule had been proceduralized into majority rule, and that we have a "republic," in which we believe that certain rights are basic and more or less inviolable, two questions come to mind. First, how do we combine the two? Is the democratic republic a mixture or a compound? Is there a formula according to which each can serve as an essential component of some ordered whole? Or does liberalism pull us in one direction, democracy in another, and do we therefore just balance them as competing ideals as best we can? And second, of course, the question that our freshmen always ask us in ethics classes: who decides?

The answer to the question "who decides?" has been, judges decide. So the problem has been, on what basis should the judges decide? For the first century, the answer to this second question was phrased in terms of an ancient picture of judging that has been called the "oracular theory of judging."[1] On that view, judges do not "make" law; they only "find" law. They are the oracles through which law speaks. The judge does not and cannot change what the law is; he or she can only express what it is. Judges can be right or wrong as to what they say the law is, but they cannot change or create law by their decisions.

The oracular theory had been so thoroughly discredited in our own time that it may be hard for some to take it seriously. But it is important to see its force for those who held it. It is a view that supposes that our written law is only an attempt to capture what law really is in itself: an ideal ordering of human associations in terms of morally basic rules and principles. The origins of this modern form of this ideal of judging can probably be traced back to the triumph of the monk Hildebrand who on becoming Gregory VII established the supremacy of the papacy and with it the creation and supremacy of canon law.[2] Canon law claimed not merely to be the law of the dominant church but to be the *true* law. When it clashed with customary Germanic law, the customary law was supposed to give way to the true law. As Gregory's followers were fond of saying, when Christ came, He did not say "I am the custom," He said "I am the truth." Out of this came a view of temporal law, written law or law as proclaimed by judges, as legitimate only in expressing this higher law, although modernity and the Reformation quickly dispatched canon law's claims to being *the* expression of that higher law. The "higher law" in question might be only the principles of a civilization. But out of this came the modern oracular picture of judging.

Luminaries like John Marshall could appeal to this image of the judge in establishing judicial review. Marshall could legitimately see himself not as establishing merely a particular political position over other political positions but as enunciating what *the law* is. Against charges that he was imposing merely his own politics on the system, he could rely on the oracular picture of judges to distance himself from those charges.

On the oracular picture of judging, judicial self-restraint is unlikely to emerge either as a virtue or as a theory of interpretation. The virtues proper to a judge are impartiality and insightfulness. The lack of prejudice that a judge is supposed to exhibit is more akin to the same lack of prejudice that a scientist or philosopher is supposed to exhibit: the ability to look the truth coldly in the eye, unswayed by one's own predilections about what one would like the truth to be or even what is widely held. Just as we do not speak of philosophers needing self-restraint in order to avoid imposing their views on their theories, we do not need to speak of self-restraint on the part of judges in imposing their views on the matter in question. The important thing is not to let our prejudices interfere with the clarity of our vision and to have the courage to accept the truth, however uncomfortable it may be.

The problem with the oracular theory, even for those people who accepted the world view in terms of which that theory made sense, was that the decisions of John Marshall—unlike, say, those of Immanuel Kant—had definite and immediate political consequences. Marbury stood to lose or gain his commission depending on what Marshall held. Although the Marshalls of the world could reply that such were the consequences of the law, that they "found" it and did not "make" it, it remained nonetheless a suspicion that just *maybe* they were making more of it than they cared to admit. The suspicion that Marshall's formidable powers of reasoning effectively obscured what was really his imposition of his own views was expressed by Jefferson, who said. "When conversing with Marshall, I never admit anything. So sure as you admit any position to be good, no matter how remote from the conclusion he seeks to establish, you are gone."[3]

This suspicion about judges was bolstered in Holmes's time by what had developed as the unique character of the American judge. Early in the nineteenth century, Americans fused what had been two separate forms of English law: common law and equity. Equity originated in the English chancellor's office, where people could appeal to the conscience of the king when common law decisions were felt to be particularly onerous.[4] As the "keeper of the king's conscience," the Chancellor was empowered to dispense with or mitigate the results of unjust rules. At first, this was just a series of ad hoc decisions, but over a period of time the chancery became a court, and these rulings developed into a body of law called "equity," which ended up with its own system of rules and courts. One of the big differences between common law and equity was that the latter could compel only the payment of money, but could not compel performance, whereas equity, on the other hand, could compel performance, for example, through the development of the injunction, but could not compel the payment of money. In equity, the chancellor might order A to give B's property back, but he could not actually take A's property and transfer title to B; instead, he could take B and set him in jail until B came to the conclusion that giving the property to A was a better idea than he had originally been willing to grant.

In 1848, New York enacted the Field Code, which abolished the equity/common law distinction. By 1990, the Field Code was widely adopted around the country.[5] When the Americans fused common law and equity, they created a brand new type of creature, the American judge. Suddenly there appeared on the political scene a new figure of great power: a person who had the authority to decide what the law is; who could compel both performance and the payment of money; who could issue injunctions; and who could appeal to standards of justice or fairness, that is, equity, in making decisions on what one's legal duties were. This new judge's powers and latitude were greater than any judge's before. As the German jurist, Josef Esser, has remarked, the American judge came to be more like what Max Weber calls a charismatic figure than like the bureaucratic persona that still informs the continental civil law judge.[6] If he or she needs to, he or she may go outside the system of strict rules to produce just results. Something new and powerful was on the political scene, and that people began looking for a way to curb this power is no surprise. Given the new and broad powers of the new American judge, that people would begin to formulate ideas about the necessity of self-restraint on the part of such powerful individuals is not surprising. Although this new judge was at first only concerned with civil law, the model of judging that he or she embodied carried over into other areas, such as constitutional law.

The emergence of the new American judge was coupled with

the failed attempts in the late nineteenth century to adopt satisfactory political principles that would limit the power of constitutional judges. Natural law doctrines, or more charitably, the easy misuse of them, had led to, among other things, *Dred Scott,* to numerous decisions upholding freedom of contract to the disadvantage of the working class, and to the enshrining of the protection of property rights as part of the fabric of the universe. It was clear to many people that whatever their truth, natural law doctrines were not adequate *institutional* checks on judicial power. Something else had to be found.

One of the legacies of Holmes's public thought, leaving aside his eccentric fatalist, vitalist metaphysics, was the large role it played in helping to discredit the oracular view of judging in both civil and constitutional law. In his essay, "The Path of the Law,"[7] he expressed the idea that the oracular theory was just bunk resting on myth. Law was not some "brooding omnipresence in the sky", it was just what judges said. Holmes extended his earlier critiques of the new American judge in civil law to the image of the constitutional judge sitting on the Supreme Court. In his judicial practice on the Supreme Court, Holmes continually cast doubt on the idea that judges were oracles of anything. This begins to put Holmes's notion of self-restraint into its context. If there is no alternative to "making" the law, and if the people doing it have new powers, then perhaps calling for new institutional restraints and encouraging a little self-restraint on the part of judges is not a bad idea. Rather than just being insightful and impartial, judges should also be restrained in the use of their powers. For Holmes to extend this idea to constitutional adjudication was only natural. In all this, however, Holmes's eccentric metaphysics does not seem to play any necessary role in the line of reasoning, however much it may have played a role in Holmes's own mind.

Here it would be easy simply to point out how the various arguments that were given at the time simply did not arrange their premises in the right order. Where did people get the idea that electoral majorities would be any better than the new American judges? But that would miss part of the point. After all, what were the alternatives at that time?

The oracular theory of law coupled with the natural law doctrines popular in the nineteenth century led to what were seen by reformers as preposterous results. This was coupled with what was widely seen as the breakdown of consensual values in American society, a breakdown that led to many attempts at amelioration of the situation, including the passage of grossly racist immigration laws.

We can put this in a more general framework. The political issues arose precisely among problems of pluralism (no commonly accepted standards by which these new judges could decide); problems of "progress" (the industrialization of America with its growing urban proletariat) and problems of democratic participation, particularly by the growing masses. A guiding although often unspoken supposition of the American polity had been from the early days that it was a democracy *but* that an elite should rule, that the "masses" were not really fit for full participation. A long tradition of judging on the Supreme Court had seen the function of that judiciary as protecting basic rights, i.e., property rights, against the inevitable attempts by the "masses" to subvert them.

All of this is under attack when Thayer and Holmes come on the scene. Liberalism and progressivism are beginning to vie for political supremacy. Taken as ideal types, the progressives and the liberals could be seen to differ in something like the following way. The progressives were concerned with the social and political impediments that thwarted the workers from achieving the kind of substantive ideal of independence that they took American democracy to be about. In the parlance popular these days, we could say that the progressives built their vision around a conception of "the good." The liberals, on the other hand, were not so much interested in directly promoting a decent life for the workers but with insuring that they had a *fair* opportunity to voice their grievances and to promote their interests. We thus might say in contemporary parlance that the liberals were concerned with "the right."

Both the liberals and the progressives regarded themselves as not only on the right side of history; many of them also believed that the majority was with them, and it was only the obstructionist actions of the court that prevented their views from becoming policy. Both thought that a new professionalism on the part of judges, in keeping with the emerging professionalism of other guilds of society, would be appropriate to this task. But here the progressives and the liberals often parted company. As ideal types, the progressives were on the side of more mass participation in politics, whereas the liberals were more intent on creating a bureaucratic, administrative state. So Holmes had available to him an oracular picture of judging that had been overlaid with various bogus natural law doctrines; a growing liberal movement that wanted to professionalize the state and use state power administratively to generate general utility and fair opportunity; and a result-oriented progressivism that focused on creating lives of freedom and independence for the working population. Interestingly enough, Holmes chose none of these, even though he is often remembered as a champion of the liberals. To see why anyone would have thought that what Holmes did choose was superior to any of these is instructive.

JUDICIAL RESTRAINT: FROM LEGAL HISTORY TO POLITICAL THEORY

To get a better perspective of Holmes and his views, we need to look at the "progressive/liberal" debate in more general terms, since this clash is in a certain fashion still with us and is of much more than just historical interest. Indeed, the issues that Holmes confronted go to the roots of much contemporary political theory.

Let us distinguish between what is called in German jurisprudence the *Rechtsstaat,* the "*state based on law*" and what we call the "*rule of law.*" Although the term "*Rechtsstaat*" is often translated as the "rule of law," there are important differences between the two conceptions. The more literal translation of "*Rechtsstaat*" as "state of law" rather than "rule of law" helps to bring this out.[8] The idea of the *Rechtsstaat* is originally the idea of a state ruled by principles of natural law, that is, laws that are not made but are discovered. It came to be seen as a state based on a system of principles that protects rights of individuals or social classes, and it eventually evolved into a kind of positivist conception of a state governed by a set of laws issued by a sovereign. The model itself has its origins in the Gregorian assertions of the primacy of canon law as the "law of truth" against the more local customary laws. A *Rechtsstaat* is committed to legality in the sense of being committed to having all cases decided by "true" principles of law.

Kant's political philosophy embodies a kind of *Rechtsstaat*-oriented conception of the state. For Kant, the duties of the state consisted in enforcement of the duties of justice and not the duties of virtue, and the duties of justice could be determined by reason alone.[9] Notice that a *Rechtsstaat*, even a Kantian one, need not be a *democratic* state, but it may very well be a *liberal* state and a "republic." That a democratic state is in fact the best way to secure the protection of such liberties, especially property, is not an *a priori* truth. Many early liberals were no democrats, and apparently among early American liberals there was some genuine discomfort about whether democracy and liberal rights were compatible.[10] Many of the constitutional rulings in the nineteenth century seemed to correspond to the *Rechtsstaat* idea. The cases involving liberty of contract that effectively deprived workers of the right of enacting policy that would improve their lot are perhaps good illustrations of the idea.[11]

Political philosophers in particular can be tempted by the notion of the *Rechtsstaat* into seeing the Constitution as resting on a set of principles that themselves rest on some more basic principles, such as "a basic right to free choice," "neutrality," "equal concern and respect," and so on. These foundational principles put certain types of reasoning and decisions out of bounds. Consider, for example, the recent debate about liberal neutrality, that is, whether the liberal state may legitimately base its policies on principles that depend on judgments to the effect that some form of life is intrinsically better than another. Now, it only comes naturally to political philosophers to argue about whether, for example, a just state may or may not redistribute property or prohibit such and such form of private conduct; and if the Constitution is an embodiment of such principles, then it would seem to be at least partly up to political philosophers to determine what a just constitution will or will not permit and protect. Philosophers could only have been heartened when they first read Ronald Dworkin's articles on rules and principles in *Taking Rights Seriously*, particularly when they read the parts on how great questions of constitutional justice turn on whether certain propositions of moral philosophy are true, and these turn on whether, say, utilitarianism or Kantianism is the most defensible moral theory. The thought no doubt occurred to more than one philosopher that he or she knew the answer to that question about *which* moral theory was correct. Justice, after all, on the correct moral theory, requires, permits, or rules out the redistribution of property, and consequently the Constitution *must* therefore require, permit, or prohibit redistribution of property. The image of the *Rechtsstaat* goes nicely with the idea of putting moral philosophers in charge when it comes to questions of basic political principle. It also fits well with a particular version of the liberal state in which not democratic participation but a defense of basic rights (in the nineteenth and early twentieth century, usually property rights) becomes an unconditional imperative for the state. That the great heroes of the *Rechtsstaat* are academic thinkers formulating doctrine, not practitioners, is probably no accident. With its natural affinities with the oracular view of judging, the idea of the *Rechtsstaat* would have little appeal for a skeptic like Holmes.

The idea of the *rule of law* is another matter. This is the idea of types of decisions that affect people being reached through certain procedural means in which all the relevant voices to the dispute have a right to be heard. In fact, a good case can be made for saying that the rule of law both historically predates and conceptually lays the ground for democratic politics. Democratic politics extends to the *political* process the "rule of law model" of the *judicial* process: people are represented, and all voices are ideally heard in procedural fashion as mediated through their representatives.[12] Without this principle, the appropriateness of hearing of many different voices in a dispute, there could probably have been no development of modern democracy.[13] It is only when the procedural notion of the rule of law is united with *liberal* notions of limited government that we are on the road to liberal democracy.

The development of the two notions, the rule of law and the *Rechtsstaat,* illustrates the difference. Whereas the idea of the *Rechtsstaat* grew out of a certain type of philosophical theorizing about the state and its principles, the idea of the rule of law grew out of the *practice* of judicial interpretation of law and the establishment of precedent, with its more complex web of principles and rulings. The rule of law developed in a practical fashion, in which differing legal solutions to social problems competed for superiority against a backdrop of increasingly established precedent. It is also probably no accident that the great heroes in the tradition of the rule of law were not academic jurists or philosophers but judges.

Holmes comes on the scene as the battle was heating up between those who supported a more "*Rechtsstaat*" orientation and those who championed the ideal of the rule of law and democratic participation. Weighing into this was the new American judge with wide powers to compel performance and payment of money and to use broad principles of equity in doing so. On the one hand, the new American judge and the *Rechtsstaat* seemed to be made for each other, especially given the background of constitutional rulings in the latter half of the nineteenth century, in which basic principles, embodying the so-called immutable rights of property, were used to block legislation that was intended to benefit disenfranchised elements of the population. Although they disagreed with these nineteenth-century rulings, the liberals, taken as an ideal type, argued for a more *Rechtsstaat* conception of an elite possessing technical and administrative expertise deciding what is best for the masses. In some ways, these liberals replicated Hegel's arguments in his *Philosophy of Right* that the universal class was the class of civil servants.[14] Possessing technical expertise and having no axe to grind, they are best suited to implement in an *administrative* manner the principles and goals of the constitutionalist *Rechtsstaat*.[15]

For this emerging technocratic, state-oriented liberalism, the doctrine of self-restraint makes no sense. In its natural law form, the judge is simply declaring what the law is; his or her sagacity and insight are what is at issue, not his or her self-restraint. In its later legal realist form, the judge is simply doing what any administrator with expertise will do: using his or her knowledge to command what is best. Neither of these forms is particularly democratic. The so-called masses still get left out of the picture.

One more element of the picture needs to be mentioned. Prior to Holmes's and Brandeis's joining the bench, economic rights, captured in the liberty of contract cases, were often considered basic and inviolable, whereas free speech held a less exalted status, liable to be overridden or to be balanced against questions of social utility and order. By the time Holmes and Brandeis left the bench, the positions of the two types of rights had been reversed. In the post-Holmes/Brandeis era, the state more and more was held to have the right to interfere with economic rights to serve the public interest, while it was held less and less to have any legitimate basis to override rights to free speech. In the pre-Holmes era, our constitutional principles were in clear violation of Rawls's lexical ordering of the two principles of justice. As is well known, Rawls gives his first principle of liberty priority over his second principle of equality; on the Rawlsian view, one may not trade off any gain in equality of income and wealth for a diminution of the basic liberties. Thus in the Rawlsian picture, economic rights are not as sacrosanct as the rights embodied in the basic liberties. In the post-Holmes era, we began moving in what looks like a more distinctively Rawlsian direction.

Yet Holmes, who did so much to bring about this reversal, certainly never argued for it as a *philosophical* reversal. He certainly never approached anything even remotely resembling a Rawlsian conception of justice. He simply believed that the majority actually wished to put free speech ahead of economic rights, and as a self-restrained judge, it was his obligation to go along with this desire. However, an apparent anomaly in his reasoning on this matter is worth noting. In his rulings on free speech, Holmes eventually came to the following position: the legislative branches could legitimately suppress speech *only* if the speech was clearly subversive of majoritarian goals.[16] But if one believes in majoritarianism, as Holmes seemed to believe, then why must the majority be required to *demonstrate* that certain speech is clearly subversive of its goals? Why may it not just *believe* it to be subversive? Or more generally, why may it not just suppress such speech because it does not *like* it? Why *must* freedom of speech be freedom for the speech we hate? David Luban's reconstruction of Holmes's metaphysics gives us perhaps the missing explanation for this otherwise anomalous opinion. It lies in Holmes's vitalism: suppressing speech might harm the vital dominant forces in coming to some kind of expression.

This break from a purely majoritarian view in fact makes sense in terms of Holmes's basis for his majoritarian sentiments.

This missing element of Holmes's vitalism is crucial for understanding how his ideas on judicial self-restraint played themselves out in the public space of American legal discourse. Holmes provided a strong counterweight to any *Rechtsstaat* model of judging, however much the emerging liberal forces were attracted by his thought. Holmes's doctrine of judicial self-restraint, while sometimes reaching liberal results, seemed to shift the balance away from the imperatives of the emerging bureaucratic state in favor of a more participatory, democratic state. In his thought, democratic participation comes to full expression and firmly outweighs the older republican image.

Holmes's skepticism prevented him from accepting any of the emerging liberal technocratic theories. It also prevented him from thinking that judges ever discovered the law. "Discovering the law" is only a polite way of saying, "predicting the judge's behavior." Holmes's skepticism led him to the idea that there was nothing "out there" to stop him from making any law he pleased. The only restraint is his vitalist metaphysics and conception of value and his own virtue in recognizing that order in the universe. He should refrain from deciding against the majority because it would put him out of touch with the flowing, vital forces of dominance.

Why, however, would he then think that this was in any way a *legal* conception? The connection can be seen by tying Holmes's legal realism, his conception of deferring to majorities, and his extreme skepticism about progressivist schemes of social improvement with his conception of the rule of law. The rule of law for Holmes seems to be just going along with the flow of the vast evolutionary process of the universe, when by one's legal decision, one opens up the social process so that all the voices that make up part of that process come to be heard. On a Holmesian model, the superiority of the rule of law to something like the *Rechtsstaat* would lie in its procedural inclination to letting all the elements of the process express their part in the universal tumult, even if it also often entailed their eventually going under.

The doctrine of self-restraint emerges as one answer to problems of democratic liberalism. Democratic liberalism is not just liberalism plus democracy. It is a form of social and political life in which ideals of fairness and the integrity of the individual along with a doctrine of moral equality mesh into a constitutionalist political and social scheme; it is a type of understanding of personal, social, and political life.[17] As David Luban says, the countermajoritarian difficulties that supposedly animate the virtue of self-restraint arise from the nature of constitutionalism itself, since any constitution constrains majorities. The problem with the earlier nineteenth-century solutions in terms of natural law and the *Rechtsstaat* was that in constitutional matters they were too liberal in an old-fashioned sense and hardly democratic at all. From the cynical point of view of Holmes, these were judges who were imposing their own views on majorities under the pretense of just articulating the structure of that brooding omnipresence in the sky. Since, by Holmesian hypothesis, there were no such natural law principles to be found, nor any general and defensible progressivist conception of the good or liberal conception of the right to guide the professional elite of judging, it followed that these judges were violating the *rule of law* in the sense of a procedure that regulated the ongoing processual tumult on human life in which all sides are heard before some of them are swept under.

That is, the alternative pictures of judging available to Holmes were misguided natural law theories with their discredited oracular picture of judging, progressivist self-improvement doctrines that Holmes apparently thought either silly or false, liberal doctrines of professional expertise, and this conception of the rule of law, which Holmes interpreted, not without precedent, as a procedure enabling the hearing of the voices of all participating in the dispute. Holmes took that to be roughly equivalent to majoritarian politics. Holmes could therefore reasonably believe, and without necessarily relying on his vitalist metaphysics, that his only real option was the rule of law model. What his vitalist metaphysics gave him was his rather unprecedented conception of the rule of law being equivalent to letting the majority more or less work its will as it saw fit, provided only that the other nonmajoritarian voices were heard. Since Holmes's legal realism, according to which nothing in the law stopped him from ruling one way or another, entailed that he reject earlier doctrines of restraint as being found *in* the Constitution, *self*-restraint in the face of majoritarian wishes surely would have appeared to Holmes as the only rational alternative for a conception both of adjudication and of judicial virtue.

Holmes emerged as the hero of liberals because he seemed to shift the philosophical conceptions of freedom and economic rights in their direction, and his realist doctrines paved the way for the liberal realists of the thirties and forties. In particular, it paved the way for the early inclinations of realists to be deferential to the legislature during the New Deal, instead of striking down new legislation as unconstitutional. However, liberals should think twice about their lionization of Holmes. In the last analysis, Holmes was not really a partisan for the rule of law. Given his skepticism, he could not be, since on Holmes's view there was no *law* to be "a rule of," only the changing fancies of dominant forces.

Ultimately, the argument for Holmesian self-restraint is one that rests on two premises that I think we should reject. The first premise is the Holmes/legal realist belief that there really is nothing *but* the judge's own virtue to stop him or her from thwarting the wishes of the democracy, that all the arguments, institutional and philosophical, about democracy and liberalism are beside the point.

The second premise is that the notion of the rule of law is equivalent to the kind of pure majoritarianism that Holmes thought that it was. David Luban has exposed the kind of reasoning that actually led Holmes to this conclusion. But the conclusion should be rejected on other grounds as well. If nothing else, it would make a shambles out of constitutionalism, and there are really no other reasons, not the duty of fidelity, our constitutional structure, nor democratic ideals in general, to believe it.

I have argued in this kind of attenuated "philosophical history" that the Holmesian conception of judicial self-restraint makes partial sense as an attempt at an answer to questions that should still trouble us about the relation between our *liberal* republicanism and our *democratic* ideals. Faced with the ideals of the *Rechtsstaat* and the ideal of "progressivism," an ideal of the *rule of law* in which all voices are heard is not implausible. But

Holmes makes a mistake that is the mirror image of the mistake that sometimes appears in contemporary theories of "liberalism": emphasizing one element of the democratic liberal form of life to the detriment of the other. The democratic liberal republic is neither purely democratic nor purely liberal but is the union of these two ideals. It is a union that has a tension built into it, but it should not be conceived simply in terms of one of the elements that make it up, nor should one of the elements be seen simply as a function of the other.

The problem of judicial self-restraint remains, however, if one accepts that (1) we have created a new type of political power in the American judge, with his or her common law and equity powers, that has also influenced our conception of constitutionalist judging; (2) a theory of judging needs to be articulated that is consistent with democratic liberalism and its form of life; (3) excessive reliance on the *Rechtsstaat* model of judging, however initially attractive it may be to legal theorists, fails to capture the *democratic* element in politics as self-rule and rule of law; and (4) excessive reliance on the majoritarian impulse fails to capture the *liberal* element in the liberal politics of the rule of law. Even if we reject Holmes's solution, Holmes's problem remains with us.

Which conception of democratic liberalism in fact best answers these problems and integrates both elements of democratic liberalism is a story to be told at another time.[18]

NOTES

1. See G. Edward White, *The American Judicial Tradition: Profiles of America's Leading Judges* (Oxford: Oxford University Press, 1976), chapter 1.

2. See Harold J. Berman, *Law and Revolution* (Cambridge: Harvard University Press, 1983).

3. Quoted in G. Edward White, *Tort Law in America* (New York: Oxford University Press, 1980), p. 12.

4. See Lawrence Friedman, *A History of American Law* (New York: Simon and Schuster, 1973), pp. 21–23.

5. See Friedman, ibid., pp. 340–46.

6. Josef Esser, *Grundsatz und Norm in der richterlichen Fortbildung des Privatrechts*, 3d ed. (Tübingen: Mohr, 1974), p. 51.

7. Oliver Wendell Holmes, "The Path of the Law," *Harvard Law Review*, 10 (1897).

8. See Martin Kriele, *Einführung in die Staatslehre* (Reinbek bei Hamburg: Rowohlt Taschenbuch, 1975), sec. 27.

9. See Immanuel Kant, *Metaphysical Elements of Justice*, translated by John Ladd (Indianapolis: Bobbs-Merrill, 1965), p. 35.

10. See Rogers M. Smith, *Liberalism and American Constitutional Law* (Cambridge: Harvard University Press, 1985), pp. 18–60.

11. It should be clear that I am talking about a general conception of the state here. I hope it is obvious that I am not claiming that any American justice based his or her rulings on Kant, only that an idea of the state similar to Kant's idea informed some of the rulings.

12. As an example of this, Martin Kriele quotes the ancient German legalism, "Eenes Mannes Rede ist Keenes Mannes Rede, man muß sie hören alle beede"—roughly, "One man's speech is no man's speech, one must hear both sides." See Kriele, *Einführung in die Staatslehre*, p. 108.

13. See Kriele, ibid., p. 153.

14. See secs. 205, 303, *Hegel's Philosophy of Right*, translated by T. M. Knox (Oxford: Oxford University Press, 1952).

15. I discuss the relation of the rule of law to the model of the *Rechtsstaat* in Hegel's political philosophy in "Constitutionalism, Politics, and the Common Life," in H. T. Engelhardt, Jr. and Terry Pinkard (eds.), *Hegel and Transcendental Philosophy: Essays in Honor of Klaus Hartmann* (The Hague: Nijhoff, forthcoming).

16. This is attributed to Holmes by G. Edward White in *The American Judicial Tradition*. See pp. 157–60.

17. I have elsewhere argued for this view of democratic liberalism in Terry Pinkard, *Democratic Liberalism and Social Union* (Philadelphia: Temple University Press, 1987).

18. I have tried telling part of that story in *Democratic Liberalism and Social Union*.

13

JUSTICE WITHOUT VIRTUE

JUDITH N. SHKLAR

That two people can see the same topic as differently as David Luban and I do is extraordinary. The topic, *Judicial Virtue*, simply evokes quite different ideas in us. To be sure, he is well aware that the subject demands consideration of conflicts between various roles, and between conscience and public obligation. But he has chosen to dwell upon a small and overdiscussed corner, the range of choices that justices of the United States Supreme Court should have in deciding constitutional cases, and then rightly criticizes self-restraint as the relevant virtue, and especially Holmes's ill-conceived version of it, which he takes most seriously as a form of Nietzschean philosophizing. I cannot see why he does any of these things, given the topic in hand, because the Supreme Court is just too atypical to tell us much about judicial virtue.

I would also begin with role conflicts, which are usually stated in the form of Rousseau's famous remark that "a man may be a devout preacher, a brave soldier, a zealous patrician and a bad man." But the more interesting issue is, I think, whether a good man would fail at these estimable roles, and might regard them as degrading. We have, after all, known for some time that a good man and a good citizen are not identical. Can a good man, then, be a good judge in general and in America now especially? I cannot imagine why one would look at anyone other than state trial judges, of citizens. For while appeals courts and especially the U.S. Supreme Court do affect attitudes and opinions, they are scarcely alone in that function and they do so not as courts, but because of their peculiar job in the constitutional system, judicial review. But by all accounts the trial judges of the fifty states have far greater discretion and policy-making authority cumulatively and directly than appeals courts, which have only indirect and remote effects.

Moreover, none of the classical writers had anything like judicial review in mind when they discussed judicial virtue; rather, they were concerned with judicial agents like our trial judges, who in spite of the peculiarities of our system, are relatively normal judges. Let be begin with the philosophers, who certainly do not agree about the virtues of judges. To Plato it was clear that no rational person could be a judge in any conceivable historical city. All they do is perpetuate and legitimize a system in which aggression and greed are encouraged by offering services to those who collide with one another in their pursuit. Courts of law are circuses in which a hydra's head is cut off and immediately followed by a hundred new ones. A good man would never engage in so ridiculous and irrational an institution. Punitive measures in the kind of society envisaged in the *Laws* are essentially medicinal, designed to cure and unpollute the criminal.

The Aristotelian judge is a far more familiar figure. All he really needs is a firm grasp of syllogistic reasoning, and of the laws of his city. Only in cases of a conflict between law and equity does he have any choices and then he is to look to the spirit of the laws, since the letter is the problem. This is not difficult since as a good citizen he shares the political ethos of his city about how benefits and costs are to be distributed. He is only a lot more intelligent than most people because he can instantly recognize a defective syllogism, as he frequently must. This upbeat version is universally popular, especially when it is forgotten that it is an ideal model that defines justice in general. In any case, rationality is the virtue of a good judge, but he is only as good as the laws of his city permit him to be. A good man might not fit into every city.

While Aristotle offers us a complex enough set of ideas, they are simplicity itself when compared to St. Augustine's view of the judge's lot, which he called "lamentable." And so it is. This man who must condemn people to death, torture, and disgrace is never able to know the facts or the people involved properly. Original sin has warped his cognitive faculties also. But lest we become even more disorderly in our already appalling behavior, he is absolutely obliged to discipline us. Evidently it is not rationality or social knowledge that he needs, but profound humility. It is the same virtue we all need. There is no difference between the good man and the good judge. We all fail and in the same way. And in an odd way Nietzsche was quite close to the Augustinian view in the one passage he devoted to the virtue of judges, in his *On the Uses and Disadvantages of History for Life*. His point was to show that the virtue of judicial objectivity had nothing in common with the objectivity pursued by modern historians. In "inexorable disregard for himself, his eye is unclouded as he sees the scale rise and fall." Such a judge needs all the virtues, from magnanimity to justice, yet he is only "a poor human being" who must "at every moment atone for his humanity," even though he is set apart from the rest of us by the solitary height from which he must act. He is as such "the most *venerable* exemplar of the species man."[1] It is the tragedy of a human being forced to perform a superhuman task, and his virtue, though unattainable, is "justice," the rarest of all the virtues according to Nietzsche, and it is not a matter of knowledge, but of will, all of which is quite unlike Holmes's mindless soldier's faith. Nietzsche's good judge rises above the crowd who accost him incessantly. In his loneliness he creates himself.

Of course, a fourth model of good judging is Thomas Hobbes's. Now Hobbes, unlike Holmes, was a perfectly cheerful atheist. The sovereign, and he alone, makes laws and thus defines what is just. All that is required of judges is to enforce these rules in the manner prescribed by Aristotle, in fact, as mechanically and impersonally as possible, and there is no difficulty with that, Hobbes thought, except the vanity of the lawyers and judges of the common law courts. This is "slot machine justice," and it was touted by all those who thought that a just society depended on the supremacy of the legislature, especially a representative one, with a separation of powers, which Kant, in one of his less happy moments, described as a rational necessity, since it expressed a syllogism. We are in spite of many differences back with Aristotle, and the primacy of rationality as the obverse of the arbitrary. Not one of these basic models of judicial virtue mentions self-restraint as a significant trait. And common sense surely tells us that many roles demand far more in the way of self-control than judging, school teaching for instance. Nor do the models dwell much on the plight of the judge's conscience. Most people see the matter similarly.

The vices that judges are told not to indulge in derive from the Aristotelian/Hobbesian model. They should not be capricious, arbitrary, dilatory, inconsistent, or incomprehensible and must not favor friends, political cronies, the powerful, or the wealthy, and above all they must not be dishonest and accept bribes. Even with all this, their decisions may be rejected as pejoratively "political" if the outcome appears unacceptable, even to people who are not directly affected. This is no disaster. American citizens have always managed to live with a necessary contradiction: that judges are and should be impersonal oracles of the law, and that they are and must be political agents making policies and laws. It does put a strain on the notion of the virtuous judge, if not on the citizenry. Finally, even the most rigidly vice-abstaining judge may not be the best person, in spite of Nietzsche. Most of us might prize qualities of mind and heart other than these negative traits. Nevertheless, if judges abstain from the list of vices they are "good enough."

More interesting is whether the emphasis on rationality and prudence can survive the absence of a sovereign and the actual jungle and vagueness of our laws and legal institutions. To be sure, the discretionary authority of judges is far less now than that of the local judiciary of medieval England or of the newly settled West in nineteenth-century America. But public expectations have altered. And the traditional discretion of trial judges in many matters, especially in sentencing and in the need to act as a mediator in many civil cases, which continue to make them important policy makers, is now often disputed. Nevertheless, efforts to curtail their latitude by mandatory sentencing laws are notoriously ineffective, as the shambles of Nelson Rockefeller's tough drug law proved.

Until relatively lately the judge's job was quite manageable.

Trial judges relied heavily on what they took to be the prevailing ethics of their communities, and given that they were generally local citizens, elected by people who knew and respected them, they did quite well. However, in large cities, or in demographically and socially unstable states like California, trial judges must increasingly rely on their personal judgment, and it is at this point that character and even style may become glaring issues. What virtues do they need now? Hobbes is no use to them. There is no sovereign. That is the problem. Humility will not help them, though arrogance is no asset. A Nietzschean sense of tragic limitation is too vague. A Platonist might resign. Few if any will be as contemptuous of their fellow citizen as was Holmes, who in a passage to which David Luban refers wrote, "I am so skeptical as to our knowledge about the goodness or badness of laws that I have no practical criticism except what the crowd wants." Holmes's crude Hobbesian talk, puffed up with a far from skeptical social Darwinism, is certainly not serviceable. It certainly owes nothing to Nietzsche, of whom Holmes said that he did not take him "too seriously." Holmes's vulgarity was also all his own. No trial judge needs to resemble him, and one has no reason to believe that many do.

What then are the trial judges, who really do matter, to do? I think that in the end they may well have to be no better and no worse than any of our other policy makers. They are not without resources. They get more respect than state legislators and they get a lot of support from the attorneys who form part of the court system in which they work. Their virtue is to cooperate with them, within the limits of an adversarial system, and to come to what seem acceptable and fair decisions, all things considered, to lawyers as a group. Prudence rather than rationality is the guiding virtue, and it is not a matter of only following precedents and rules, but of local understandings. They also need a reputation for hard work and willingness to listen to all sides and to meet the standards of the rest of the bench and bar. Beyond that, good conduct demands that they use language intelligibly and be able to persuade the general public that is not directly involved in the cases in hand. Ultimately their virtue may just add up to being democratically patient and politically skilled enough to convince their fellow citizens that they are doing a fair and honest, though not a flawless job.

NOTES

1. Friedrich Nietzsche, *Untimely Meditations*, translated by R. J. Hollingdale (Cambridge: Cambridge University Press, 1983), pp. 88–89.

5

SOME SPECIAL VIRTUES

14

SOME VIRTUES OF RESIDENT ALIENAGE

ANNETTE C. BAIER

Cicero writes, "Peregrini autem atque incolae officium est nihil praeter suum negotium agere, nihil de alio anquirere minimeque esse in aliena re publica curiosum" (*De Officiis*, I, 125). The Loeb translation runs, "As for the foreigner or the resident alien, it is his duty to attend strictly to his own concerns, not to pry into other people's business, and under no condition to meddle in the politics of a country not his own." But resident aliens' own concerns can scarcely be taken to be the concerns of their own nation, for their very residence in a nation other than their own usually will, after a few years, disqualify them from properly knowledgeable participation in their own nation's affairs. Their right to cast an absentee vote will be better left unexercised, even if they keep in touch by mail with conditions in their homeland, for that will fall short of the sort of touch that comes by living there. The wearer knows where the shoe pinches. The resident knows where the country of residence pinches.

Is the resident alien, then, deprived of any opportunity for cultivating any political virtues? Is such status, therefore, to be discouraged, and morally deplored?[1] For after all we are political animals, and both for our own sake and for our fellows' sakes we surely ought to make some sort of minimal impact on the political order. As Pericles put it, we regard someone who takes no part in any political activity "not as minding his own business but as useless."[2] If we have settled for conditions of life in which we can neither rightly vote nor voice criticisms of the society in which we live, then we will have arranged for ourselves a lasting occasion of vice, of parasitism and moral sloth.

Many resident aliens, in many lands (Kuwait, for example), are where they are for work-related reasons. Are all of us to be condemned for choosing in live and work in a land where we do not choose to request citizenship? Or, if not outright condemned, are we condemned to a choice between political inaction and improper political action? Or is Cicero perhaps wrong about the duties of resident aliens? What *is* properly a resident's business?

Since resident aliens, unlike regular visitors, normally must, like any other resident, pay taxes in their country of residence, it is of course their business how those taxes are being spent, and whether they are getting the various sorts of security (from foreign attack, from crime, from crippling health costs) that the taxing power promises, as the "returns" that justify their "takings." "No taxation without representation" cannot be the resident alien's demand, but "no taxation without accountable spending on the security of all residents" surely can be. So one matter that clearly is the business of every resident, citizen or alien, is just how tax monies are being spent, just which promises are and are not being kept by elected representatives and executives. The record on this matter will surely be something that any sensible voluntary immigrant will investigate, prior to the decision to reside here, and it will remain an appropriate matter for vigilance, and, if necessary, voiced protests. It may be indeed that some immigrants' reason for residing here may be the expected taxation policy—I have known New Zealanders, with their eye on opportunities for acquiring wealth, who chose to reside here in the U.S. precisely because their native country's tax policy was found punitive to the would-be rich, while this nation held greater promise of being the home of tax-free profits, the land of the enterprisingly businesslike brave. (I have also known quite a few immigrants to New Zealand who chose it for its supposed security from the nuclear accidents that more industry-minded and less isolated countries were risking.)

It is fairly obvious that it will make some difference to the moral quality of a person's willingness to be a resident alien just what sort of society she chooses to reside in, for what reasons, and in what sort of society she chooses to retain (nonresident) citizenship, for what reasons. Should one choose one's country of residence for reasons of tax avoidance, or retain one's original citizenship from sheer inertia, one must expect some moral criticism from anyone who is aware of one's reasons for being and remaining a resident alien. Not very harsh criticism, for few are in a good position to criticize others for tax avoidance or for less than maximally active and enterprising use of opportunities for elective nationality. Sentimental attachment to the land of one's birth, even when it has great political faults, is a forgivable human weakness, and so is the willingness to move to where the grass grows greener. But we will perhaps wonder about the person who chooses to make a bigger buck in a land whose political regime is repugnant to her, or would be, should she let herself face that question. ("Ubi beni, ibi patria.") Those resident aliens who can tolerate their country of residence only as long as they can live in compounds of compatriots, safely protected from the conditions of normal life for the natives (unless, of course their duty to their own country requires of them such a "foreign tour of duty"), may get only limited sympathy when the host country fails in its duty to the aliens in its midst. If one chooses to live and earn, or live and make one's profits, in an oppressive or a grossly unjust society, one should not be too indignant if one there finds oneself the victim of oppression, or of injustice. One lies in the bed one has made for oneself, when one chooses residence alienation. The first duty of voluntary resident aliens is a duty to themselves, to be choosy about where they reside.

Faced with the requirement to "renounce all foreign allegiance" in order to be granted United States citizenship, those residents who have ties of allegiance to their native land that they are unwilling to renounce must, however reluctantly, put up with noncitizen permanent residence, if they wish to continue working here. Their reasons for doing so may be perfectly proper ones, a combination of affection for the home soil with appreciation for both the political and the work climate here. They need not be thought, by their choice, to have morally disqualified themselves for responsible political opinion. It would seem a waste to adopt Cicero's rule, and so put a moral muzzle on them (us). It is even possible that resident aliens, by the very fact that they are aliens, may have a distinctive contribution to make to the political conversation. At any rate, they will have the same basis for some comparative evaluation of this society as that possessed by naturalized citizens, and by native sons and daughters who have resided long enough in other countries to have an insider's basis for comparative judgments. One needs to have had at least two pairs of shoes in order to compare pinches. Of course patriots will always believe that things are best done here, even if they have only second-hand knowledge of how they are done elsewhere, but a wider first-hand knowledge helps, and one who becomes a resident alien in adulthood must have some such knowledge. Commentary on United States affairs by some well-informed European observers and visitors, such as de Tocqueville, has been valued precisely for its "foreign" detachment. Resident foreigners will normally be a little more committed, a little less detached than visitors, but they do satisfy a minimal "range of experience" requirement for impartial evaluation, and their bias will be less than, or at any rate different from, that of native-born citizens. Their opinions can usefully supplement those of citizens in the debate over national policy, both internal and external.

Socrates in *The Apology* described his patriotic citizen role in Athens as that of gadfly. A gadfly must be both outside the animal it keeps from stupor and yet close to it, indeed parasitic on it, or on its like. It is as if Socrates opted for a kind of citizen resident alienation—not "internal emigration," but precisely its inverse, voluntarily staying put because of the virtues of the place, yet being detached enough from its values and policies to identify oneself as an outsider, to just the extent that the gadfly is outside the horse, and has a life distinguishable from the horse's life. The critical role Socrates saw himself as playing, of course, was notoriously underappreciated by his criticized fellow citizens, so that analogy may not hold much consoling power for uneasy resident aliens, unsure how long their welcome holds, and suspecting that they are more easily tolerated if seen but not heard. (One must be seen. Being visibly here often and long enough is a condition of retention to one's permission to keep resident alien status. Too many too long return trips to one's homeland, or anywhere else, can, appropriately enough, disqualify one from resident status.) Socrates was not "alien" in the sense of being or being able to be at home somewhere else, at least not in his own judgment. For him it was Athens or nothing. Still, the role he chose to try to play in Athens was one that required a viewpoint a bit like that which comes naturally to a resident alien, who sees alternative possibilities—who, having already made a self-conscious decision about what political community to live in, is at least a little practiced in the activity of comparing and judging communities, from a resident's point of view.

Not all resident aliens, indeed most likely only a tiny minority, will play, or aspire to play, a gadfly role. This is just as well, since a plague of gadflies would be as bad as none. And it is dubious, in any case, if the role of gadfly should be a specialized one played all the time by a few, rather than a role that most of us play some of the time. If those citizens who are innocent of foreign residence are to be able to play it well, they will need the help of some sort of aliens or ex-aliens—de Tocquevilles, Kissingers, or less celebrated people who like them really know how pinched or comfortable life is or was in some different, literally "un-American" society. We all need to know and learn from aliens and ex-aliens. The most easily available aliens are those who reside in our communities.

Criticism of one's country of residence, when that is not one's country of citizenship, has to be done more tactfully than a citizen's criticism need be, since a guest owes some duty of courtesy to her host. This is the grain of truth in Cicero's claim. The perhaps forced cultivation of tact is itself the cultivation of a political virtue, as long as the tact is not tantamount to servility or timidity. A tactfully made criticism need not be one lacking force and impact, and the courteous guest is not necessarily a reticent one. Niklas Luhmann has underlined the fact that tact leaves open options that bluntness or rudeness would have closed, for both parties. It leaves troubled relations salvageable, it allows for a graceful ending of relations that are no longer mutually valuable, and it allows invitations to be refused without insult or loss of face to the rejected party, so that new invitations are not unduly discouraged.[3] There may be times when foreclosing one's own and the other party's options is precisely what one judges to be called for by the situation, but these will be rare occasions in any country where it was sensible to emigrate in the first place, unless it has undergone a dramatic change for the worse in the interim. In that case the resident alien may not much mind if her outspoken criticism or protest (the sort that is an affront to the host country) brings risk of deportation. In normal conditions when the state of the nation in which one resides is found to be only normally imperfect, and improvable without resort to extreme measures (illegal ones or very offensive ones), forthrightness can normally be combined with some degree of tact.

Are there any conditions in which it would be proper for a resident alien to resort to violent opposition to the authorities in her host country? Are they different conditions from those that would justify a citizen from such "appeal to heaven"? There are surely some violations of human rights, crimes against humanity (torture by authorities, police brutality, terrorism by officials), that we believe should be protested by bystanders as well as victims, regardless of whether the witnesses are citizens of the oppressive and barbaric regime. Whereas citizens may justifiably resort to violent opposition if blocked from taking peaceful constitutional steps to end what they reasonably perceive to be some unconstitutional denial of right, or unconstitutional exercise of power or neglect of responsibility, the resident alien will be justified in resorting to violence only to protect universal human rights, not to protect peculiarly American rights. The Constitution of the United States guarantees its citizens some rights that are not normally taken to be universal human rights. These include not just rights to particular forms of political participation, but rights such as that guaranteed in the second amendment, to bear arms. This right was understandably salient at this nation's birth from a revolutionary war, but it would scarcely be the proper business of a resident alien, especially one from a country not recognizing any such right, to leap into action to protect it from any threatened infringements, and certainly not to resort to force to help to defend it. (Should its defenders "appeal to heaven" in order to protect it, it would be the better part of resident alien wisdom to try to keep well out of the fray.) But if there are, when there are, violations of recognized human rights—if for example there is torture, or police brutality—then surely anyone, citizen or not, should protest. If some protest against apparent police brutality (such as the protests taking place in Los Angeles as I write) should degenerate into violent protest when the police use violence against the protesters, then should any resident alien be among the attacked protesters, she surely would be in the right in resisting such force with force. Her citizenship would be of no more relevance to the propriety of her form of protest than was the citizenship of the person who filmed and reported the police brutality that sparked the protests. There surely are many possible wrongs that residents should protest, be they resident aliens or resident citizens. Torture and cruelty are the clearest cases, but child neglect, slavery, gross humiliation, false assurances, or other false pretenses on vital matters are equally clear wrongs, regardless of the citizenship of victim, perpetrator, witness, or protester. When the Chinese authorities used deadly force against student demonstrators in Tiananmen Square, and executed the survivors after brutal and humiliating "trials," de we think that any foreign residents who tried to come to their aid by resisting the Chinese authorities by force would thereby have shown ingratitude to their host country? It might have been improper ingratitude had they been politically active in helping organize the demonstrations (which are not antibrutality demonstrations), but surely it would be only common human decency to have an urge to intervene to help the victims of the brutality (however uncommon the courage it would take actually to intervene). What is sauce for the foreign goose is sauce also for the domestic gander. Any nation, for all its resident aliens can be sure, might revert to barbarism in its conduct at official levels, and if it does, protest will be a dangerous duty, rather than the sin of ingratitude for past hospitality. One hopes that the frequency of such official barbarism will not be great in a nation with a bill of rights and checks on the performance of officials, but absolute assurance on such matters is not to be had. The virtues of both citizens and resident aliens have, alas, always to include courage.

The resident alien necessarily has to have acquired some modicum, if not of courage at least of foolhardiness, since her security will never be great. A change of government policy could wreck her retirement plans, wipe out her social security equity, or deny her any pension payments if she decides to reside elsewhere. We resident aliens necessarily learn to live with more insecurity as regards our future options and assets than do out fellow residents who are citizens. No one has security against inflation, mounting health costs, breaches of promise to working people (or at any rate disappointment of their encouraged expectations) by authorities in the face of mounting national debt or shifts in the proportion of the population paying into and drawing out of social security funds, but in addition to these shared insecurities, resident aliens have extra sources of insecurity, since they are unprotected in a way citizens are not against suddenly announced changes in their recognized rights to benefits. It is not inappropriate that, in these matters, resident aliens should be second-class residents, that they should be the first to have their interests sacrificed and the last to be provided with any right of appeal or insurance against sudden losses due to changes of regulation. After all, if one is not represented, one must lose something. The practice in living with uncertainty about the future that this gives a resident alien, while it is not itself practice in any virtue, might be seen as a good training ground for certain Stoic virtues that Cicero would have welcomed—fortitude, resilience, adaptability. Adaptability or flexibility is, however, a somewhat dangerous virtue, since the person who can, without undue personal distress, up tent and move elsewhere, change her plans from, say, retirement in the Seychelles Islands to retirement in Florida (to retain her benefits) is unlikely to have any great loyalty to either place of residence. And while the ability to accept with composure an income that is only a small fraction of what one had been led to expect may be fine personal virtue, it is less clear if it is a political virtue. Diogenes was not notable for his public service or his patriotism.

A resident alien, of course, cannot in any case show "patriotism" to her country of residence, given the patriarchal requirements of that concept. Only *one* country can be one's fatherland, and that must be one's country of citizenship. Even countries that prefer "motherland" to "fatherland" still mostly balk at the idea that *two* countries, let alone three or more, might be a person's parent countries. Although the metaphor of one's country as one's superparent is hallowed, and well-nigh universal, that superparent is rarely allowed to be a coparent. One-sex procreation is the rule, in parenting of subjects by states. Joint citizenship, and with it the notion of a country as a *coparent* of a resident subject, is yet to be worked out as a real possibility for many people. We do not think that children must necessarily be traitors to their mothers in order to retain loyalty to their fathers, even after divorce, yet with citizenship, that rule of a patriarchal religion that "no man can serve two masters" still holds sway. Were multiple citizenship and multiple residence to become real options, then the status of resident alien, with its undoubted disadvantages, would be much less frequently occupied, and the virtues of resident alienation could be absorbed in those of plural citizenship and multiple residence. But these are utopian thoughts, and one thing that resident alien status pretty effectively guards a person against is the vice of utopian thinking.

A resident alien who retains some (what we might call) matriotism, as well as an appreciation of her place of residence, is likely to consider herself some sort of cosmopolitan, or aspiring cosmopolitan, an adherent of what David Hume called "the party of humankind." Recently there have been criticisms of the sort of universalism that such aspirations seem to entail. Michael Walzer, in *Interpretation and Social Criticism*,[4] and Richard Rorty, in *Contingency, Irony, and Solidarity*,[5] have contrasted solidarity with one's "own" community (which might of course become that by adoption, as well as by birth to the motherland) with universalist cosmopolitan loyalties, when those are supposed to be based on a recognition of some common human essence that we all share, despite our manifest cultural differences. Rorty, discussing the slogan, "We have obligations to human beings simply as such," writes, "If one reads that slogan the right way, one will give 'we' as concrete and historically specific a sense as possible. It will mean something like 'we twentieth century liberals,' or 'we heirs to the historical contingencies which have created more and more cosmopolitan, more and more democratic political institutions'. If one reads it the wrong way, one will think of our "common humanity," our 'natural human rights.' "[6]

It is, for Rorty, a historical contingency that *our* political institutions—that is, those of citizens and some other residents of the U.S.—tolerate or encourage some cosmopolitan tendencies. And so I suppose it is, for what aspect of our condition is not a historical contingency? It is a historical or prehistorical contingency that Homo sapiens occurred at all, or survived once it did turn up, and a historical contingency that Britain lost her American colonies, and that fascism did not defeat its "liberal" and "democratic" allies in World War II. Someone like David Hume, who advocated the point of view of humanity,[7] was not an heir to democratic and liberal institutions, but a rebel against authoritarian and repressive ones. Of course Hume had, both in Scotland and in France, plenty of "enlightened" friends who shared his cosmopolitan sympathies, but it was not just solidarity with his home culture that bequeathed him those wider sympathies. It was travel, reading, learning foreign languages, and residing abroad. Nietzsche, who preaches "not love of neighbour, but love of the farthest," was also no heir to democratic traditions.

Rorty believes that our "common human nature" is enough to enable us to recognize suffering in another person, however alien, so that those of us who regard cruelty as the worst vice will cultivate sensitivity to the sufferings of all persons, not just those in our own group. "The right way to take the slogan 'We have obligations to human beings simply as such' is as a means of reminding us to keep trying to expand our sense of 'us' as far as we can . . . the family in the next cave, than the tribe across the river, then of the tribal confederation beyond the mountains, then of the unbelievers beyond the seas (and perhaps last of all, of the menials who, all this time have been doing our dirty work.)"[8] This metaphor of the widening circle (which then comes back to its center and repeats its movement to gather up the forgotten of the earth) is not one that a menial, or a frequent traveler, will adopt, even when she agrees that cruelty should always be protested, whoever inflicts it and whomever it is inflicted upon. That metaphor is apt only for one whom others have served, and who has kept one home base (a male stay-at-home?).[9] For the nomad, for the itinerant grape picker, for the refugee, for the resident alien, there will be shifting centers. One may go beyond the mountains, one may become an unbeliever, and then one's generosity of sympathy may be tested by one's willingness to include one's unforgotten ex-compatriots in one's concern. My fellow citizen, Keith Sinclair, in his poem "Memorial to a Missionary," writes of New Zealand's first resident missionary, the Englishman Thomas Kendall, who, "Instructed to speak of God with emphasis / On sin and its consequence, to cannibals," had his earnest efforts to understand the alien souls in his charge crowned by his own conversion to their ways, "And reached for a vision past his mother-land / Converted by heathen he had come to save." The poem ends with a lament that, having "gone native," as so many do when they visit the South Seas, "He could not turn to teach his countrymen, / And lost, (our sorrow), lost our birthright forever."[10]

Someone like Kendall, before he had learned the Maori language, would also have come to appreciate, better than Rorty seems to, just how far, beyond cries and groans, our common human (and to some extent animal) body language can extend. One can express and recognize a lot more than pain without benefit of a shared "natural language" (and wrongs against humanity are not restricted to cruelty. Humiliation and slavery are such wrongs, even if no physical torture is involved in them). Our most natural language is that of expressive gesture. Every conquered people knows how to surrender, to express abasement, to bend the knee, and to beg. The body language of domination and humiliation, as well as of love and hate, amusement and perplexity, is as shared as that of pleasure and pain. One need not play down the enormous importance of shared words (shared funeral orations, shared poetry) for full mutual understanding, in order to do justice to the reassuringly common currency of the shoulder shrug, the eyebrow flash, the begging hand, the handshake, the bearhug (even if the kiss turns out to be more local in its currency—and, like Kendall, some of us have to learn expressive nose rubbing).

Alexander Nehamas, writing about Rorty's defense of ethnocentrism, puts the cosmopolitan's case with eloquence that has the ring of truth: "One can be Greek born, American educated, a Spanish citizen, . . . a late twentieth century male, a reluctant bourgeois, and much more besides. We can be, and we are, foreign to ourselves. Everything we are and in respect of which we change has, in different degrees, effects on the nature of the groups to which we belong; and changes in these groups, in turn, affect the nature of the individual who consists of their interrelations."[11] Brian Barry, defending universalism against Michael Walzer's criticisms of it,[12] writes with equally convincing eloquence; "Walzer may be right in saying that criticism of a society is more likely to be taken to heart by its members if it comes from someone who manifestly identifies with the society. But efficacy among the members of the society is not the only criterion of good criticism. It may be that members of a society are systematically blinded by their belief system to grave defects in their practices, and that an outsider is better placed to illuminate the darkness."[13] He cites the American South's complacency about the institution of slavery as a case in point. "Outsiders" such as Amnesty International can discern what needs changing, and sometimes can even get it changed.

I take it, then, that the case for cosmopolitan aspirations, and for the value of the cosmopolitan's criticisms, is not difficult to defend against these contemporary doubters. If to aspire to be cosmopolitan is to have a worthy aspiration, then there must be some value in knowledge of the willingness to participate in a variety of different national communities, cultures, and "forms of life." This is not to be equated with being a perpetual tourist, gaping at everything and participating in nothing, and there are doubtless severe real-world constraints on how many cultures a person can become tolerably at home in. For those, like me, who find if difficult to learn a new language, cosmopolitan ambitions must remain very modest. (But the flip side of this is the enormous satisfaction that is gained when one does at last succeed in gaining fluency in the language of a country where one has been spending some time.)[14] If we value peace, if we believe that international friendship makes it less fragile, if we believe that we must *know* our friends to be their friends and that friends stay in touch, then it must be our goal to cultivate cosmopolitan virtues. A special attachment to the home soil, or to the soil to which one has transplanted oneself, can coexist with an active interest in life elsewhere, and a wish to know a bit about it from the inside. We need not become cultural nomads in order to become cosmopolitans, but it is likely that we may wish to have more than one "homeland" or place of residence, successively or simultaneously.

It is in times of war that it can become difficult or impossible for cosmopolitans actively to retain all their loyalties, and that the need to choose can arise. In such times the natives may reasonably entertain suspicions about even the "friendly enemy aliens,"[15] resident or nonresident, who live in their midst. Military service is the one duty, as distinct from right,[16] from which resident aliens are excepted, and it is the continuing perceived possibility of war that can make multiple citizenship appear a foolish notion, an invitation to fifth columnists, subversion, and treachery. The resident alien is not just exempt from military service, but is blocked from occupation in any "sensitive" government job, even in peace time. As long as we live in a climate of war, then such supercautious exclusion of all aliens from the heart, brain, and nerve centers of the nation will be seen as only prudent, as will the demand that any new citizen renounce all foreign allegiance. But as we begin to move to a climate of peace, where intractable conflicts of perceived national interest give way to perceived common interests, maybe it need not be utopian to hope for some relaxation of these measures.

On the whole we need not fear that anyone operating as a spy for a foreign power will choose resident alien status in the land of her espionage activities, since the extra vigilance that makes her subject to will not make for very good cover. Better far to become a citizen! (On my return from a cultural exchange visit to the USSR in 1986, I was subjected to careful questioning by immigration officials because I was a resident alien whose New Zealand passport allows me travel to Cuba. I was delayed by questioning to check that I had not swung by Cuba on my way back from the USSR, and to find out if I had ever visited Cuba. My fellow delegates who were citizens sailed through U.S. immigration with no such checks.) Only a rather foolish, or an extraordinarily confident spy would arrange for herself conditions of extra official inspection. As for dual citizenship, that too would seem a bad choice for the would-be spy, whose best cover is the appearance either of undivided allegiance or of the absence of any particular political opinions.[17]

I have tried to sketch the case that can be made for the virtues special to the form of life of those whose country of residence is not the country of which they are citizens (or, where applicable, not the only country of which they are citizens). The virtues that I have claimed can be, and often are, cultivated in this form of life are, firstly, "alienation" itself, if this is taken to mean critical distance, the ability to see the merits of other countries and cultures as well as of the one where one lives; secondly, the tact that has to be cultivated in order to exercise this informed critical evaluation from the position of a "guest" in the nation whose ways are evaluated; thirdly, a certain degree of fortitude necessarily induced by living with uncertainty about one's rights as resident alien; and, fourthly, a will to peace and some degree of international friendship, a reluctance to tolerate enmity between one's different "homelands." These virtues are relatively easily acquired by those who are, by their own choice, resident aliens. They may compensate, a little, for the perhaps more evident temptations that the resident alien is subject to, temptations to political sloth and to the vice of parasitism, of taking the liberties and private empowerments that a free society like this one offers all its residents, without making any contributions in kind. Such vices will be discouraged to the extent that there is recognition and welcome for the virtues for which resident alienation provides a good home ground. That exemplary cosmopolitan, David Hume, who traveled widely in Europe and left his homeland (the recently formed and still imperfectly unified Great Britain) to reside for two lengthy periods in France (on the second of them in the service of his country), announced that his preferred citizenship was in "the world." He also saw himself as belonging to "the Republic of Letters," a republic that included ancient civilizations as well as modern ones, and in whose various languages and literature he was at home to an extent that is both exemplary and daunting. When he first visited Mantua, he wrote to his brother that he had "Kiss'd the Earth that produc'd Virgil."[18] (One can kiss more soils than the home soil, as the Pope frequently demonstrates to us.) Hume's own attachment to "The Republic of Letters" made him keener on volunteer "citizenship" in those parts of the world where a flourishing literary culture was to be found than in less literary cultures. But by his own account in his essays and *History of England*, the links between progress in the fine arts and in the mechanical arts are close, and acquaintance with foreign achievements is found beneficial for both. So the would-be world citizen could as well be one who has an informed interest in foreign weaving, printing, or shipbuilding techniques as one who knows foreign literary works. "The same age which produces great philosophers and politicians, renowned generals and poets, usually abounds with skilfull weavers and ship-carpenters."[19] In his *History of England* Hume carefully records the improvements to life in Britain that came from various voluntary and involuntary cultural imports—from the Roman and Norman conquerors came skills in building, from the rediscovered *Pandects* of Justinian in Italy came jurisprudential skills, as from Germany came the equally world-altering skill of printing. (Hume praises the Earl of Rivers for his patronage of Caxton, for importing this liberating revolution into Britain.) As well as Roman road and wall builders, Norman castle builders, and German printers, there were Flemish weavers and Jewish bankers, all contributing to the gradual civilizing of once-barbaric Britain, and Hume gives them all their due. "Can we expect, that a government will be well modelled by a people, who know not how to make a spinning wheel, or to employ a loom to advantage?"[20] Hume's recent fate is to have been accused of ingratitude and apostasy, and called "subversive" within his home culture.[21] This is a fate that would-be cosmopolitans who dream of being "citizens of the world" always risk, especially from eulogists of the virtue of patriotism.[22] Like Hume, they usually learn to risk it fairly cheerfully. But as more and more people share the cosmopolitan's values (which need not be purely intellectual values), the fear of the foreign that usually fuels such charges of disloyalty and subversion can be expected to die down. It takes first-hand knowledge of some other nations' literatures, and of the cultures that fostered them, in order for us to begin to consider that nothing human may be alien to us. And to Terence's boast ("Homo sum: humani nihil a me alienum puto")[23] we need to add a complementary more modest confession, that even the most familiar human things tend to become a little alien, as we see them in a wider context. Aliena sum: alieni nihil a me alienum puto.[24]

NOTES

1. This is no idle question for one like me, whose green card is a subject of comment by immigration officials for its antiquarian interest. There is veiled or sometimes open censure in their comments, and the unspoken demand, "Join us or leave us," is not hard to hear. Or is it only my own unease that voices it? But my unease would be no less were I to renounce my citizenship in the land of my birth, in order to be a fuller participant in the land of my chosen residence. I am proud to remain a citizen of the first country to extend suffrage to women, and grateful to a country that gave me, free of cost, an excellent education to the university level and a scholarship to study at Oxford for a higher degree, all without any strings attached. There was no moral pressure to return. I did gladly return when a suitable job was available—who would not choose to live in such an enlightened country, where equality of opportunity is not just a slogan? But I also eventually chose to move away, to alien soils, and eventually to this soil, where the academic grass, or at least the philosophical grass, grows greener and thicker than it possibly could in my native land, whose population is not much larger than that of the medium-sized city in which I now live and work.

2. Thucydides, ii 40 2, quoted and translated by T. H. Irwin in his review of I. F. Stone, *The Trial of Socrates*, "Socrates and Athenian Democracy," *Philosophy and Public Affairs*, 18 (1989), 198.

3. Niklas Luhmann, *Trust and Power: Two Works* (New York: Wiley, 1979), p. 84.

4. Michael Walzer, *Interpretation and Social Criticism* (Cambridge: Harvard University Press, 1987).

5. Richard Rorty, *Contingency, Irony, and Solidarity* (Cambridge: Cambridge University Press, 1989).

6. Rorty, op. cit., p. 196.

7. David Hume, *An Enquiry concerning the Principles of Morals*, ed. L. A. Selby-Bigge and P. H. Nidditch (Oxford: Clarendon, 1975), pp. 272–75.

8. Ibid.

9. Rorty writes that the ironist will tell people "that the language they speak is up for grabs by her and her kind" (op. cit., p. 89). I therefore feel encouraged to have a bit of a grab at his language.

10. *The Penguin Book of New Zealand Verse*, ed. Allen Curnow (London: Woking, 1960), pp. 261–65, passim.

11. Alexander Nehamas, "A Touch of the Poet," *Raritan*, 10, 1 (Summer 1990), 114.

12. Walzer takes John Rawls to be a universalist opponent, while Rorty invokes him as an ally on his side of the issue.

13. Brian Barry, "Social Criticism and Political Philosophy," *Philosophy and Public Affairs*, 19 (Fall 1990), 367.

14. I speak with a little knowledge of linguistic and other barriers to making one's home in new places. As a person who grew up in a tiny egalitarian ex-colonial country, New Zealand (where two languages, Maori and English, are spoken, and where the Maori citizens are beginning to resent their assimilation, partly through intermarriage, into the dominant European culture, and are making efforts to recover and preserve their preconquest Polynesian culture), I felt very much at a social loss in race-conscious and class-conscious Oxford and England, where I went for postgraduate study, and equally an outsider in my first job in Aberdeen, in less class-conscious but very nationalistic Scotland, where the local accents and dialects can present communication barriers even to those with officially the same native language. I more or less fitted in, later in Australia (whose culture is more different from that of New Zealand than often appreciated by "foreigners"), and then in the United States. My summers were spent regularly in Austria, where I was at first an inarticulate and gaping tourist, astonished at and entranced by the novel folkways, and later became a tolerably acculturated and tolerantly accepted member of my husband's extended family there, speaking ungrammatical but fairly fluent German. So I have some experience of linguistic and other obstacles to settling in.

15. This was the category to which Jewish refugees from Austria and Germany were assigned by Britain during World War II.

16. This will not be true in countries like Australia, where voting is a duty, not just a right.

17. I am grateful to Nicholas Rescher for raising the question of whether resident alien status might not be chosen by the would-be underground lobbyist for foreign interests, or by the spy.

18. *The Letters of David Hume*, ed. J. Y. T. Greig (Oxford: Clarendon, 1932), vol. 1, p. 132.

19. David Hume, *Essays, Moral, Political, and Literary*, ed. Eugene Miller (Indianapolis: Liberty Classics, 1985), p. 270.

20. Hume, *Essays*, op. cit., p. 273.

21. Alasdair MacIntyre, *Whose Justice, Which Rationality?* (Notre Dame, IN: Notre Dame University Press, 1988), ch. 15. See also my review article, "MacIntyre on Hume," in *Philosophy and Phenomenological Research*, 51 (March 1991), 159–64.

22. Alasdair MacIntyre, "Is Patriotism a Virtue?" *Lindley Lecture* (University of Kansas Press, 1984). For a response to MacIntyre see Stephen

Nathanson, "In Defense of Moderate Patriotism," *Ethics,* 99 (1989), 535–52.

23. Terence, "Heauton Timorumenos," 1, 1.

24. I am grateful to my fellow cosmopolitans Kurt Baier, Alexander Nehamas, and Nicholas Rescher for discussion of the topics raised in this chapter.

15

VIRTUE AND OPPRESSION

JOAN C. WILLIAMS

Columbus, Ohio, June 27—John Karras, 28 years old, was in a card shop the other day as the radio . . . [reported] on the dead and missing in the floods that had just flashed through southeastern Ohio. The cashier, a man a bit younger than Mr. Karras, looked up at the radio and said, "I wish they'd stop talking about it. I'm sick of hearing about it." Mr. Karras, a doctoral student in education at Ohio State, recalled this incident to illustrate what he sees as a "pervasive" attitude among members of his generation toward the larger world: the typical young person doesn't want to hear about it "unless it's knocking on my door."[1]

Scholars became obsessed with virtue in the eighties because there was so little of it. Polls suggest that Americans, particularly young Americans, find needs they don't experience first-hand profoundly uninteresting.[2] The 1970s motto that "all we need is love" was replaced in the 1980s with Madonna's "I am a material girl" and Gordon Gekko's adage that "greed is good." Reagan opined that the homeless slept in the streets by choice; a top official stated that the hungry chose soup kitchens "because they were free." While Reagan ordered over two hundred thousand

Special thanks for comments on prior drafts from Gregory S. Alexander, James X. Dempsey; James T. Kloppenberg, Joseph William Singer, the Boston University Law School Faculty Workshop, and the members of the Conference on Law and Pragmatism, Charlottesville, Virginia, November 8–9, 1990. Thanks to Catherine Stavrakis, George Thomas, and Arzoo Osanloo for research assistance.

dollars of table china, his administration gave massive tax relief
to the rich and said that ketchup was a suitable vegetable for the
poor. By the end of the decade, the top 1 percent of Americans
saw their after-tax income grow by 87 percent, while families just
above the median saw their after-tax income grow by only 3
percent.[3]

Substantial numbers on both the Right and the Left agree that
something is amiss, something linked with selfishness and materialism. Cultural conservatives decry a lack of values and focus on
the "breakdown of the family," drugs, pornography, and abortion. Progressives focus on conspicuous consumption, rising in-
fant mortality rates, homelessness, and other symbols and realities of our insensitivity to the human cost of income redistribution
in favor of the wealthy. But both sides are deeply troubled by
America's loss of commitment to values other than self-interest,
and both agree on the need for a vision of the public good.

In the sphere of practical politics, then, both progressives
and cultural conservatives are in revolt against the celebration
of self-interest as the engine of the greater good. This revolt is
echoed by a diverse group of intellectuals. A key figure is Alasdair MacIntyre, who articulates the somewhat counterintuitive
project I pursue here: to link virtue with a nonfoundationlist
approach.[4]

One can readily see how liberalism fits with nonfoundationalism: if no "common good" exists because of the incommensurability of people's projects of self-creation, society's goal should
be to facilitate the broadest possible range of personal projects.
How to combine the common good with nonfoundationalism is
considerably less obvious. Charles Taylor has argued that the
apparent contradiction between nonfoundationalism and a commitment to the common good stems from "atomist-infected notions" that personal projects and identity are inherently individualistic. Taylor follows William James and John Dewey in
arguing that a rejection of the individualist epistemology of
Descartes and Hume leads not only to a social theory of knowledge but also to a revision of liberalism's picture of society as
composed of atomistic individuals.[5]

In Taylor's view (and my own), nonfoundationalism has
strong, if ultimately elective, affinities with a rejection of atomistic

individualism. This is not to say that nonfoundationalism is inconsistent with every strand of the complex liberal tradition. Instead, the task at hand is to mobilize liberalism and other elements in our heritage to challenge the particular strain of liberalism I will call self-interest ideology: the notion that society is best served if its citizens each pursue their own self-interest.[6]

I will argue that "virtue" in American political discourse often serves as the repository for uneasiness with self-interestedness. The challenge is to recover and rehabilitate our native languages of virtue. This approach differs markedly from that of political theorists whose goal is to enumerate a list of character traits desirable for the flourishing of liberalism.[7] Instead, it carries on two themes of American pragmatism. One links nonfoundationalist epistemology with a critique of atomistic individualism, a linkage that dates back to pragmatists such as James and Dewey. Another pragmatist theme is the commitment to mine "precious values embedded in social traditions" in order to "clarify [our] ideas as to the social and moral strifes of [our] own day." To quote John Dewey in full,

> When it is acknowledged that under disguise of dealing with ultimate reality, philosophy has been occupied with the precious values embedded in social traditions, . . . it will be seen that the task of future philosophy is to clarify men's ideas as to the social and moral strifes of their own day.[8]

A pragmatist pursuit of virtue entails not the discovery of preexisting truths, but the practice of cultural criticism. To pursue virtue we need detailed knowledge of the rhetorics by which Americans have exhorted themselves to virtuous pursuit of values other than self-interest.[9] This project will not look like traditional political theory. It will be closer to intellectual history, but with an important difference. In a much more open way than is admitted by historiographical norms, pragmatists' historical accounts will be framed with an eye towards deploying these rhetorics as moral and political weapons. In the words of contemporary pragmatist Cornel West, philosophy becomes "a cultural battle to transform popular morality."[10]

The pragmatist denial of a "God's Eye point of view" suggests that differing perspectives are inevitable—and inescapable—on matters of crucial social importance. The key task is to understand the logic behind others' perspectives well enough to persuade those with whom you disagree. If the goal is to spark a challenge to self-interest, one starts with a heavy burden of implausibility because of the central role of atomistic individualism in Western political economy and epistemology. Moreover, the obvious place to turn—to socialist language of mutual interdependence—offers a sure route to political marginalization. Instead, one must turn to alternative rhetorics that hold the promise of making the critique seem familiar and commonsensical.[11]

To do so, we must reaccess the native languages in which Americans have pursued values other than self-interest. One such discourse is the language of republicanism. The resurgence of interest in republicanism in the past decade is rarely linked with the equally striking resurgence of interest in the canons of traditional femininity as a language of social critique. Yet both these movements, as well as the much more tentative revival of interest in religion, are best understood as part of a sustained interdisciplinary effort to revive the rhetorics in which Americans have urged virtue as an antidote to excessive focus on self-interest.

In section 1, I explore the rhetorics of virtue. Section 2 argues that the contemporary scholars of virtue often ignore the extent to which our traditional languages link virtue with oppression. To illustrate this connection, and to illustrate a pragmatic approach to redesigning rhetorics that persuade, I end by examining the contemporary abortion debate.

1. Virtue

In 1981 Alasdair MacIntyre set out to resuscitate virtue as a key category of social thought. His interest in virtue stems from his critique of liberalism. MacIntyre's analysis of "emotivism" targets the liberal assumption that "the social world [is] nothing but a meeting place for individual wills, each with its own set of attitudes and preferences and who understand [the] world solely as an arena for the achievement of their own satisfaction." He traces this world view through literature, philosophy, psychology, and political theory. Underlying all these fields is a

> deep cultural agreement . . . that there are only two alternative modes of social life open to us, one in which the free and arbitrary choices of individuals are sovereign and one in which the bureaucracy is sovereign. . . . Given this deep cultural agreement, it is unsurprising that the politics of modern societies oscillate between a freedom which is nothing but a lack of regulation of individual behavior and forms of collectivist control designed only to limit the anarchy of self-interest.[12]

MacIntyre contributes to a growing literature on the influence of the liberal notion that society will prosper best if its members pursue their own self-interest. MacIntyre disapproves of this conception of social life, and proposes virtue as a language in which to challenge it.[13]

Although MacIntyre's work was influential in reintroducing virtue as a category of social thought, his discussion has serious limitations from a pragmatic perspective. He fails, first, to follow through on his nonfoundationalist premise that ethical values do not reflect truths abstracted from time and place. Richard Bernstein has argued convincingly that MacIntyre is unsuccessful in trying to synthesize "the type of metaphysical understanding of human nature characteristic of Greek philosophic thought with the type of historicism, or historicity, which only makes sense in a modern post-Hegelian setting." What ultimately gives way is historicism. MacIntyre ultimately advocates a single "best" version of our twenty-five-hundred-year tradition with little sense that shifts in sociology since the Greeks make his chosen path unsuitable for late twentieth-century America. Notable is that the tradition of virtue he advocates has always relied on exclusion—of barbarians, slaves, and women. In fact, as Bernstein shows, MacIntyre melds elements of Aristotelianism with Enlightenment values (notably equality), despite his excoriation of the Enlightenment project as a failure.[14]

Not only is MacIntyre's attempt to go back to the future inconsistent with his nonfoundationalist premises; the Augustinian Christianity he advocates has severe limitations from a pragmatic perspective. Though it clearly has proved transformative for MacIntyre, it has limited potential to move the American public. The authors of the best-seller *Habits of the Heart* adopt MacIntyre's project and adapt it with an ear more attuned to the structure of American persuadability. The social scientists and philosophers who wrote *Habits* follow MacIntyre in arguing that Americans are alienated from their languages of virtue, but they focus on two traditions with profound resonance in American culture: republicanism and Protestant evangelicalism.[15]

Habits popularizes historians' rediscovery of the republican tradition, as well as the conclusion that the apparent "liberal consensus" masks a more complex and contradictory tradition. The republicanism they recover is, of course, just one more version of MacIntyre's Aristotelianism: it may well be impossible to talk about the common good in European culture without speaking some dialect of Aristotelianism. But if the goal is to persuade to virtuous action, it matters which version we choose. The *Habits* authors intuit republicanism's power to formulate Americans' yearning for social solidarity in a way resonant of obvious truths.[16]

The republican revival has proved the single most influential rhetoric of virtue among contemporary American academics. A key figure is J. G. A. Pocock, who in 1975 challenged the century-old truism that the liberal individualism of John Locke had dominated American political thinking from the founding fathers on. He argued that eighteenth-century American politics was dominated by a tradition of civic humanism that set up "a dialectic of virtue and commerce."[17] This formulation of the republican tradition sets up self-interest as the opposite of the virtuous citizen's selfless pursuit of the common good. Some later scholars followed Pocock's lead, siphoning off self-interest ideology from the complex strands of the liberal tradition, and offering up republicanism as an antidote. Morton Horwitz, with his usual penchant for a clear and vivid story line, has been particularly open in claiming that American political discourse has been dominated by a clash between liberalism and republicanism. As critics have noted, this scheme involves considerable oversimplification of each tradition to make it fit a simple "virtue versus self-interest" model.

This neorepublican formulation urges a return to the wisdom not of the fathers of the church, but of the fathers of the American republic. Given the central role of the wisdom of the founders in American political mythology, this argument offers a powerful revision of MacIntyre's "back to the future" story line.[18]

Religion offers a second native American language of virtue. Historians, particularly historians of religion, have long recognized that religion has played a key role in American politics. *Habits* points out, and historian James Kloppenberg confirms, the key role of religion in preserving what Kloppenberg calls "the virtues of liberalism." By this Kloppenberg means that liberals, including Locke himself, have often turned to religion to constrain self-interested behavior within the confines of virtue as defined, in part, by the religious tradition.[19]

Studies of religion's role in political speech have been few and far between, in sharp contrast to the explosion of writing on republicanism. Moreover, the studies of religion have not found the wide academic audience that studies of republicanism have enjoyed. Even in the realm of intellectual history, a commitment to the study of religion as a key language of political discourse remains something to be defended and explained. Historian Henry May argues that to talk about religion in an academic context involves some well-entrenched taboos. He notes that the predominant view in American academia is that religion is "dependent on a series of dogmas and legends that no serious intellectual could entertain."[20]

Some history is in order to help explain the origins of this taboo. Until the Gilded Age, higher education in America took place largely in seminaries or in universities dominated by religious missions. An important key step in establishing the modern university system was to secularize, often through adherence to a model of science, topics that formerly had been dealt with in a religious framework. Uneasiness about religion remains integral to the institutional structure of American universities, which came increasingly to distinguish themselves and their mission from the small denominational colleges that continued to adhere to the older model of higher education. This background helps explain the slow pace at which scholars have reclaimed religion as a potentially powerful force in political life.[21]

Nonetheless, religion remains a powerful influence. Approximately 40 percent of Americans attend religious services once a week or more, a much higher percentage than in Canada or

Western Europe; religious membership is roughly 60 percent of
the population. Three-fourths of American women identify religious faith as the most important influence in their lives. The
potential power of religion is dramatized by the impact of funda-
mentalism in recent American politics.[22]

The approach to religion I propose is nonfoundationalist in
that it does not rest on assumptions about the existence of God,
nor on arguments that religious principles embody truth. My
point is rather that religion has such potential power that no one
committed to MacIntyre's project should ignore it.

Habits begins this task by exploring how Americans use Protestant evangelicalism to articulate their rejection of self-interest in
favor of a Christian ethic based on mutual caring and responsibility. Kloppenberg continues it by showing that religion played a
central role in reining in self-interest in the thought of early
liberals. Kloppenberg also has examined how religion influenced the Progressive era's reformation of the liberal tradition to
stress an expanded commitment to social responsibility.[23]

If relatively few nonlegal theorists have turned to the American religious tradition as an antidote to self-interest, even fewer
legal commentators have done so. Republicanism swept the law
in the 1980s, but legal scholars who have turned to religion have
been few and far between. Elizabeth Mensch and Alan Freeman
are most explicit about their desire to resuscitate religion as a
language of virtue. After a long and thoughtful essay rejecting
republicanism as a language of critique, Mensch and Freeman
offer religion as an alternative idiom in which to "tap . . . a
deeply felt anxiety about the problem of moral emptiness in a
polity dedicated to nothing more than the careful management
of interest-group acquisitiveness. People almost sense," they conclude, "a need for a jeremiad."[24]

Mensch and Freeman, who played central roles in the critical
legal studies movement, view their turn to religion as a logical
next step. Many critical race theorists would agree. Anthony
Cook argues that critical legal scholars' critique of liberal society
has limitations as a basis for reconstructing a just social order,
and proposes the reconstructive theology of Dr. Martin Luther
King, Jr., as an alternative. He stresses both its powerful cultural
resonance and its potentially transformative messages about indi-

vidual dignity, community, and economic rights.[25] Mensch, Freeman, and Cook all draw on the work of earlier legal scholars,
notably Milner Ball and Michael Perry, who look to religion for a
language of human flourishing. Perry's goal is to use religious
language to challenge central truths of liberalism.[26]

The ideology of domesticity, the final major rhetoric of virtue,
has a literature as developed as that of republicanism, combined
with a status more marginalized than that of religion. Outside of
women's history, domesticity remains largely unrecognized as an
integral and continuing force in American political discourse.
Nancy Cott's groundbreaking study of domesticity as an important political ideology was published only two years after the
publication of *The Machiavellian Moment*, yet when *Habits* discussed the traditions Americans use to articulate their reservations about self-interest almost a decade later, its authors discussed religion and republicanism but ignored the large literature
on domesticity. Kloppenberg's influential article followed the
same pattern shortly afterwards. The republican revival followed
a similar pattern: it focused on a public, traditionally masculine
language to the exclusion of the traditionally feminine language
of domesticity. Because the importance of domestic ideology as a
major critique of self-interest evidently remains difficult for
many to see, I discuss it at some length below.[27]

Cott's 1977 study *The Bonds of Womanhood* argued that the
ideology of domesticity, which crystallized between 1780 and
1835, allocated self-interest to men and selflessness to women.
While "real" men went out and made money in the rough-and-
tumble world of nineteenth-century capitalism, their pursuit of
self-interest was balanced by women's selflessness, for "real"
women stayed home, far away from, in the words of one Victorian lady, "that bank note world." Women's role was to provide
the "haven in a heartless world" that could serve as a refuge
from the growing alienation of wage labor and the growing com-
mercialization and bureaucratization of the outside world. Men
sallied forth to pursue their self-interest, but they returned to
"Home Sweet Home" to escape the ruthlessness and alienation
of what was perceived as an increasingly hostile world. Domesticity, Cott argued, functioned as a critique of the alienation of
wage labor, as an internal critique of capitalism, a "*cri de coeur*

against modern work relations," or, as I have called it, a Marxism you can take home to mother.[28]

Domesticity since its invention has coexisted with the liberal celebration of self-interest as a formal societal acknowledgement that self-interest has its limitations. At first domesticity's rebuke was limited to the point that self-interest was unsuitable as a model for behavior within the family. Gradually, however, women activists in the nineteenth century used domestic ideology to confront the primacy of self-interest in the public sphere. Historians have detailed how nineteenth-century female reformers transformed the notion that women's selfless moral purity *unsuited* them for public life into a claim that women's elevated moral stature made their influence *indispensable* in the public arena. By the Progressive era, female reformers had become forceful advocates of governmental regulation of foodstuffs and sanitary conditions, on the grounds that this political activity was called for by their duties as mothers to protect their children's health. In addition, Jane Addams supported governmental help for the needy with the assertion that her activism was a form of "enlarged housekeeping."[29]

Contemporary feminists began their romance with domesticity at virtually the same time other scholars were attracted to republicanism. Just as neorepublicans were attracted by civic humanism's potential challenge to the primacy of self-interest, feminists were attracted to domesticity by its internal critique of self-interest ideology.[30]

The most influential contemporary proponent of domesticity is Carol Gilligan. While Gilligan and other relational feminists reject the Victorian view that women are naturally submissive, pious, and passionless, they accept the Victorian dichotomy between men pursuing self-interest and women rejecting it. One of Gilligan's informants described the moral person as "one who helps others; goodness is service, meeting one's obligations and responsibilities to others, if possible without sacrificing oneself." Her subjects often refer to the influence of their mothers: "endlessly giving"; "selfless"; "her mother's example of hard work, patience, and self-sacrifice . . ."[31]

Gilligan's association of selflessness with femininity tracks the Victorian association of femininity with virtue. This association emerges most strongly in passages where she celebrates the different voice as fundamentally better than the mainstream alternative. Gilligan notes that women, as they mature, shift from selfishness to responsibility, in a "move toward social participation." At one point, Gilligan decries the male concept of the separate self as an "adolescent ideal." Men's conception of justice she refers to as "blinded"; she points to men's "willingness to sacrifice people to truth." Conventional femininity, she concludes, quoting Jean Baker Miller, promises "more advanced, more affiliative ways of living."[32]

Gilligan adopts from domesticity not only the association of women with selflessness and virtue; she adopts as well domesticity's traditional association of men with liberal imagery of self-interest, rights, and autonomy. Gilligan contrasts women's morality with a "morality of rights and noninterference" that celebrates "separation, autonomy, individuation and natural rights" and equates maturity "with personal autonomy." This is the imagery of the liberal tradition, although what self-interest ideology celebrates as the legitimate pursuit of self-interest Gilligan discounts as merely selfish. "You go about one-fourth for others and three-fourths for yourself", says Jake, Gilligan's paradigm male.[33]

Gilligan's followers, like their nineteenth-century predecessors, mobilize the language of conventional femininity to undermine the legitimacy of self-interest as the reigning principle of public life. From Jean Baker Miller's hopes that the canons of femininity can offer "more advanced, affiliative ways of living" to Carrie Menkle-Meadow's hopes that women's voice can transform "all the institutions in which we live," Gilligan's adherents seek to galvanize the virtues of domesticity to transform a public arena they see as dominated by self-interest, bureaucracy, and adversary models. They turn to domesticity to accomplish a project similar to that of the new republicans: to energize a native language of virtue that offers alternatives to society as we know it.[34]

The revivals of republicanism, religion, and domesticity write virtue back into the American political tradition. This new virtue scholarship intersects with a reinterpretation of liberalism that stresses that self-interest ideology is only one strand of liberal thought. Three publications in the past five years have explored "the virtues of liberalism." All three syntheses openly contest the conflation of liberalism with self-interestedness.[35]

The rediscovery of republicanism, religion, and domesticity as languages of social critique shows "the precious values embedded in [our] social traditions." If it is "the task of future philosophy to clarify [our] ideas as to the social and moral strifes of [our] own day," a close assessment of these traditions is necessary to assess their potential for deployment as "moral and political weapons." In the following sections I argue that, when mobilizing our native languages of virtue, we must be wary of the ways they combine virtue with oppression.[36]

2. Oppression

That virtue and oppression are linked is a key insight of feminist theory. An example is Catharine MacKinnon's analysis of the eroticizing of dominance and submission. She explores ways in which our sexuality, a key expression of hope and aspiration in modern life, involves eroticization of inequalities of power. At times MacKinnon seems to assume that the ties between eroticism, dominance, and submission mean that all sexuality is bad sexuality. Her analysis is more convincing if we use her analysis to see how our most positive expressions of human aspiration are intertwined with oppression of self and others. The truly threatening thing is not that sexuality is all bad, but that gender ties elements of our sexuality to dynamics that oppress us.[37]

Our most precious cultural expressions of human aspiration mix virtue with oppression. Many of the virtue scholars discussed in section 1 tend to overlook this. They have been so focused on the potential of republicanism, religion, and domesticity to undermine self-interest ideology that thay overlook the ways their chosen rhetorics link challenges to self-interest with dynamics oppressive both to out-groups and to society at large.

Republicanism provides a ready example. The revivalists' fascination with republicanism as a language of the common good ignores central elements of historical republicanism. The republican tradition predated not only the liberal abandonment of virtue in favor of self-interest as the engine of the good; it also predated the liberal insistence on the equality of all men (and, as of the twentieth century, of women as well). As scholars explored the ties between republican virtue and elitism, patriarchy, and militarism, many neorepublicans became less sure that historical republicanism offered a tradition they could embrace without reservation.[38]

Social theorists nonetheless could not resist republicanism as a language in which to criticize the primacy of self-interest. The flowering of neorepublicanism in law reviews, for example, post-dated historians' studies of republicanism's amalgam of virtue and oppression. Republicanism's virtues have proven particularly irresistible in constitutional law, where Pocock's "back to the future" story line is institutionalized in the doctrine of original intent.[39]

The most sophisticated contemporary commentators acknowledge republicanism's mixture of virtue and oppression. Instead of trying to track a Manichean struggle between liberalism and republicanism, they pay close attention to the ways Americans have united liberal with republican rhetoric, often adding elements from religion and elsewhere. As Linda Kerber points out, neorepublicans want some combination of liberal and republican principles: "participation without exclusion, virtue without elitism . . . , a large state *with* participatory democracy; a neutral state *with* substantive visions of the public good; minority rights *with* majority rule." Dorothy Ross traces many such unions in her magisterial work on the history of American social science. James Kloppenberg notes how early liberals mixed liberalism, republicanism, and religion, and how Progressives later created different compounds. Among law professors, Cass Sunstein advocates a meld of republicanism and liberalism; Frank Michelman acknowledges that his use of republicanism is selective.[40]

The challenge is not to go back to an unsullied past, but "to manipulate the tensions within [our] own epoch in order to produce the beginnings of the next epoch." For this we need to assess the pitfalls as well as the potential of the rhetorics that persuade. The experience of the neorepublicans provides several lessons. It shows, first, that the goal is not to go back to the future. Instead, the challenge is to use republican rhetoric and the other "voices to which we have been trained to listen" to exhort Americans to challenge the primacy of self-interest, while avoiding oppressive elements in our traditional languages of virtue. The *Habits* authors show how our contemporaries use the idiom of republicanism to work towards the common goal of preserving the dignity of each individual. Yet we should not confuse the usefulness of republican rhetoric with the desire to regain a republican past. Instead, republicanism's potential lies in its promise of shifting the focus of contemporary liberalism from Hobbes to Kant.[41]

The other major traditional rhetorics of virtue also tie virtue to oppression. Religion's reactionary potential, which has been amply revisited in the 1980s, is well recognized. Yet political theorists should not shy away from religion on the grounds that it has been in reactionary and oppressive ways, for the same can be said of republicanism and every other rhetoric of virtue. The challenge is to work what we have to get where we want to go.

Like the neorepublicans, the contemporary advocates of domesticity have shown little awareness of its reactionary potential. For example, the contemporary rehabilitation of domesticity as "women's voice" has been used to justify women's continued relegation to low-paying "women's work."[42] This explicit use of contemporary feminism to perpetuate the marginalization of women is part of a much larger pattern. The following section analyzes the contemporary abortion debate to examine how domesticity's allocation of virtue to women serves both to marginalize women and to justify self-interest for men. Simultaneously, this final section begins the task of deconstructing and reconstructing one native language of virtue to dissolve its complex compound of virtue and oppression.

3. THE ABORTION DEBATE

Current "pro-choice" rhetoric uses the language of liberalism to defend women's access to abortion. "Abortion—upon demand and without apology" read a recent placard in Washington, D.C. Women should be free to choose abortion because pregnancy violates their autonomy and their freedom to control their own lives. Freedom, autonomy, choice: underlying this language is the image of autonomous actors creating the greatest good by pursuing their own self-interest.[43]

This imagery has played into the hands of "pro-life" forces. To understand how requires a grasp of the ways domesticity links virtue with the marginalization of women. This understanding must start with a reassessment of liberalism using gender as a category of analysis.[44]

The contemporary version of self-interest ideology rests on the assumption that women are included among liberalism's autonomous and self-interested actors. In fact they are not. Or, to be more precise, women are included, but mothers are not. Americans no longer believe that a woman's career should be subservient to the needs of her husband, but they do believe that a mother's career should be subservient to her children's needs. A mother who follows her plans for self-development to the detriment of her children is not only a bad mother, but a morally defective adult. The same is not true of men. A striking example is from an interview with Secretary of State James A. Baker III, who worked his normal workaholic schedule after his wife died in 1970. As he readily admitted, his children went adrift; one got deeply involved in drugs and ultimately attempted suicide. Baker's conclusion was that they needed a mother. If the idea that he should subsume his career to his children's needs crossed his mind, it clearly did not hold his attention for long.[45]

While Baker's case may be extreme, it illustrates the immunity fathers generally expect and receive from the time and emotional demands children place on their parents. Mothers do not receive the same immunity. This is the sense in which self-interest ideology is gendered: it mandates selflessness for mothers, while others feel entitled to the freedom to pursue their own plans for self-development in, or outside of, the world of work. Contemporary self-interest ideology, properly understood, mandates selflessness for mothers, and self-interest for others. This is a central dynamic in the current abortion debate.

a. "Pro-Life" Mothers: Selflessness in a Selfish World

"Pro-life" advocates are the modern-day moral mothers, who use the language of domesticity to challenge the premise that society is better off if adults act as autonomous actors pursuing their own self-interest. In the words of one "pro-life" activist,

I think we've accepted abortion because we're a very materialistic society and there is less time for caring. To me, it's all related. Housewives don't mean much because we do all the caring and the mothering kinds of things which are not as important as a nice house or a new car.[46]

In a recent study, Faye Ginsberg documents similar sentiments again and again. She finds "pro-life" mothers stating "an embedded critique" that involves "the challenge of nurturance to the values of materialism and competitive individualism that they see as negative social forces." Then women Ginsberg interviewed see their "pro-life" stance as part of a system of values that chooses nurturance over "success," defined as the successful pursuit of self-interest. "Let's not repeat the mistakes the men have been making," says one activist. The man's world of self-interest is belittled as selfish and materialistic, in contrast to the maternal world of unconditional nurturance. "Pro-life" advocates are vague and often ambivalent about whether the pursuit of self-interest is acceptable for men, but they are united by the theme that it is unacceptable for mothers and destructive for the society at large. Linda Gordon aptly summarized their feelings:

[Right to lifers] fear a completely individualized society with all services based on cash nexus relationships, without the influence of nurturing women counteracting the completely egoistic principles of the economy, and without any forms in which children can learn about lasting human commitments to other people.[47]

National polls suggest that many Americans agree with the "pro-life" subtext that responsible mothering involves a selflessness that entails setting aside one's own plans for self-development to the extent that those plans conflict with the needs of one's children. This analysis helps to illuminate some of the "inconsistent" answers the American public gives in polls on abortion. While nearly 70 percent of respondents are "pro-choice" if the question is framed in libertarian rhetoric, if Americans are asked *when* abortion should be legal, many fewer are willing to support abortion for the reasons most women abort. Only 34 percent support access to abortion if the decision is based on a women's desire to pursue career opportunities. The reasons for this low number are obvious: the question itself sends many cues that project the image of an affluent career woman aborting to preserve her next promotion. This image, of course, greatly distorts the facts about why women work and why they abort. But the low percentage of Americans who support access to abortion in this situation suggests that the American public sees abortion as involving women who choose money or, God forbid, self-development, in favor of giving selfless care to tender babes. The abortion issue enables us as a society to blame on women the results of our choice to empower the pursuit of money and power, and disempower caregiving. Why, after all, do mothers have to be "selfless"? Because their commitment to caregiving entails a "choice" that results in decreased life chances for independence and responsibility in the adult world.[48]

When the choice is between caregiving and "mere" career development, the specter of selfish women looms most threatening. But the depth of American uneasiness about our cultural trade-off between money and humane values emerges most dramatically if we examine the polls a little further. Forty-four percent of Americans think abortion should be illegal if sought by teenagers to enable them to finish school. But then, that, too, can be conceptualized as a trade-off between caregiving and self-development if one conveniently ignores that what is often involved is not that extra-fancy job that more schooling could bring, but the grinding poverty that disproportionately characterizes teenage mothers.[49]

The most dramatic response is to a question concerning access to abortion for mothers who dont't want to bear another child because the family is low income and cannot afford more children. Only 49 percent of Americans support access to abortion in this context. Why? Perhaps there lurks the image of an upwardly mobile mother choosing yet one more pair of expensive Nikes over the sanctity of human life: the ubiquitous theme of short-sighted and materialistic women.[50]

Fueled by the hidden assumption that virtue is the province of women, "pro-life" advocates and their supporters blame the selfishness and materialism of contemporary American society on women who refuse to follow the prescribed route of "selflessness."

b. *Virtue and Subservience*

The connection "pro-lifers" see between access to abortion and
self-interested materialism is best explained by reexamining the
historical process by which the civic virtue of republican (male)
citizens was reallocated to women. Republican virtue was the public, civic, manly virtue required for citizenship in a virile state.
With the rise of liberalism, virtue was shorn of its public role,
redefined as private, and relocated in the bourgeois family. Here
is the dark underside of the nineteenth-century reform movements dominated by women. A whole range of civic concerns such
as regulation of business and concern for the poor were marginalized by allocating them to the presumptively private and
indisputably feminine realm of women. True, women were successful in using the language of femininity to bring such activities
back into the public sphere, to a degree. Yet such activities were
marginalized through their association with femininity.[51]

An example is industrial medicine, the study of diseases produced by industrial exposure to toxics. In the United States it
was the only medical field (or any field, for that matter) that
Harvard hired a woman to teach. Alice Hamilton, a reformer
associated with Hull House, was the preeminent American practi-
tioner. In the early twentieth century Hamilton complained that
while industrial medicine in Europe engaged the best intellects
in the profession, American physicians dismissed the subject as
"tainted with Socialism or with feminine sentimentality for the
poor."[52]

One way liberalism tamed the republican virtues was by femi-
nizing them, thereby leaving self-interest as the ideological norm
in the economic and political spheres traditionally allocated to
men. We see this in the "pro-life" narratives, which often assume
that it is up to women to counter the primacy of self-interest in
the public sphere by choosing nurturance at home. Gone is the
sense, so prized by republican revivalists, that civic virtue is an
ideal of *public* life that presents a challenge to the primacy of self-
interest in the *public* sphere.

This history highlights two drawbacks of domesticity as a language of critique. First, by associating its attack on self-interest
with femininity, domesticity actually bolsters the legitimacy of

self-interest as the reigning principle of civic life. Second, its association of women with virtue serves to complicate the issue of equality for women. If equality means equal access to a life based on self-interest, equality for women threatens to plummet the entire social order into a harsh, uncaring world of selfish, materialistic adults and neglected children. Thus women who reject selflessness and claim the freedom to choose self-interest are perceived as threatening the very survival of values other than self-interest. This is a central fear underlying the abortion debate.[53]

c. Rhetorics that Persuade

Domesticity's allocation of selflessness to women needs to be confronted much more directly than has yet been done. The core argument is that women should have equal autonomy and access to the conventional roads of self-development, while men should have equal responsibility for meeting the needs of children even if that interferes with their pursuit of self-development. This confrontation is best launched in the context of the work/family conflict. Why should men's work lives be supported by a flow of domestic services from women, while women do not enjoy anything approaching the same level of services from their partners? Why should men's pursuit of self-development be parasitic on women's selflessness? Why should children's needs be pitted against the work aspirations of their mothers but not their fathers?[54]

In the work/family context, the liberal rhetoric of equality has the potential to undermine the norms of selflessness for mothers and self-interest for others. But to fight this battle in the abortion context is a losing proposition. For there we lose the focus on equal access to self-development for men and women. Instead, the question is framed as, what is more important, this child's life or this woman's vaulting ambition? Insisting on equal access to self-development in the abortion context results in pregnant, vulnerable women being blamed for the selfish materialism of American society.

Instead, "pro-choice" advocates need to reassure "pro-life" forces that they, too, share their opponents' uneasiness over society's materialism and its canonization of self-interest. The most effective approach may well be to fight domesticity with domesticity. Consider, for example, the slogan "Abortion: sometimes it's the loving choice." It could be linked with stories of women who have had abortions for the good of existing children, or to prepare for a motherhood they can handle instead of a motherhood that overwhelms both them and their children into dead-end lives.

The goal is less to convince the "pro-life" activists than to reach others who might be persuaded to support access to abortion if they can be persuaded that abortion is, in some contexts, a moral choice. The current "pro-choice" rhetoric cedes the moral high ground to "pro-lifers." This strikes me as a source of political vulnerability. "Pro-choice" forces need to provide a picture of abortion that connects the abortion decision with the exercise of virtue under pressure. This is particularly crucial for younger women, whose idealism may well preclude abortion unless they can be convinced that it can be, in some situations, the only responsible decision. But more than that, all women need to be able to think of their reproductive choices as loving, responsible decisions. Not all women are upset by abortions, but many are. They need the image of abortion as a loving choice to help them forgive themselves and the friends who turn to them in need. After all, 30 percent of all pregnancies in American end in abortion.[55] Not only have many American women had abortions; many who haven't have helped a friend through the experience.

"Pro-choice" forces have made a few steps in this direction, but they have been unsteady ones. Shortly before the *Webster* decision, a moving Op-ed piece described a mother whose husband left her pregnant; the only way she could support her child was with a job that would be precluded if she carried the second pregnancy to term. So she aborted . . . and we find out she is Mary Travers, of Peter, Paul, and Mary fame.[56]

Good beginning; bad end. This story is well designed to confirm "pro-life" fears of women aborting in favor of vaulting ambition. The subtext of "pro-choice" stories needs to be that "pro-choice" forces share with "pro-life" advocates a reverence for human life. That's why, in some cases, they respect the decision to abort.

Ultimately, the abortion controversy may hold the potential to convert domesticity's critique into a frontal assault on the primacy of self-interest in the public sphere. Tentative, preliminary efforts suggest the possibility that "pro-choice" and "pro-life" forces could forge an alliance to challenge the conditions that increase the need for abortions in our society, notably the lack of high-quality publicly supported health care, the lack of high-quality publicly supported child care, and the lack of income support to parents with dependents. The United States could not effectively address the conditions that make abortions so common without abandoning self-interest ideology in favor of policies premised on more communal notions of what is in the interest of society as a whole.[57]

Could the abortion debate destabilize self-interest ideology to this extent? Perhaps not, but at least we can decouple virtue from oppression to the extent of disentangling domesticity's visions of nurturance and selflessness from an insistence on the continued marginalization of women.[58]

NOTES

1. Michael Oreskes, "Today's Youth Cares Less for Worries of the World," *New York Times,* June 28, 1990, p. A1 (late edition).

2. Ibid. (poll of young Americans).

3. Lennon/McCartney, "All We Need Is Love," *Magical Mystery Tour* (New York: Capitol Records, 1967) (first quotation); Peter Brown/Robert Rans, "Material Girl," *Like a Virgin* (New York: Warner Brothers, 1984) (second quotation); *Wall Street* (Twentieth Century Fox, 1987) (Gordon Gekko quote); Sydney H. Schanberg, "New York: Overcrowded by Choice," *New York Times,* June 19, 1984, p. A27 (homeless by choice); Robert Pear, "Counting the Hungry—A Contentious Census," *New York Times,* Nov. 15, 1987, Sect. 4, page 5 (week in review) (free soup); Marjorie Hunter, "$209,508 China Purchase Is Defended by President," *New York Times,* Oct. 2, 1981, p. A27 (elegant china); Margaret Engel, "Social Workers Told to Dispel Myths about Welfare Recipients," *Washington Post,* Dec, 4, 1982, p. B4 (ketchup); Thomas Byrne Edsall with Mary D. Edsall, "Race," *Atlantic Monthly* 267 (May 1991), 53, 70 (1980s income redistribution).

4. Alasdair MacIntyre, *After Virtue* (Notre Dame, Ind.: University of

Notre Dame Press, 1981, reprinted 1984). "Foundationalism" is defined in Richard Rorty, *Philosophy and the Mirror of Nature* (Princeton, N.J.: Princeton University Press, 1979), pp. 155–64, 315–56.

5. See Charles Taylor, "Cross-Purposes: The Liberal-Communitarian Debate," in Nancy L. Rosenblum, ed., *Liberalism and the Moral Life* (Cambridge, Mass.: Harvard University Press, 1989), p. 160, 181 (quote), and Charles Taylor, "Overcoming Epistemology," in Kenneth Baynes, James Bohman, and Thomas McCarthy, eds., *After Philosophy: End or Transformation?* (Cambridge, Mass.: MIT Press, 1987), p. 464. The interpretation of the early pragmatists is from James T. Kloppenberg, *Uncertain Victory* (New York: Oxford University Press, 1986), pp. 95–107, and Daniel T. Rodgers, "Of Shepherds and Interlopers," *Intellectual History Newsletter* 9 (April 1987), 49 (book review of *Uncertain Victory*).

6. For a recent study of the complexity of the liberal tradition, see James T. Kloppenberg, "The Virtues of Liberalism: Christianity, Republicanism, and Ethics in Early American Political Discourse," *Journal of American History* 74 (1987), 9.

7. See, e.g., William A. Galston, "Liberal Virtues," *American Political Science Review* 82 (December 1988), 1277.

8. John Dewey, *Reconstruction in Philosophy* (New York: Henry Holt, 1920), p. 26. I have left the gendered "men's" without a "sic" to signal shifts in norms since the 1920s. My interpretation of the early pragmatists relies on Kloppenberg, *Uncertain Victory*, pp. 95–107, and Rodgers, op. cit.

9. For an analysis of philosophy as cultural criticism, see Cornel West, *The American Evasion of Philosophy* (Madison: University of Wisconsin Press, 1989), p. 230–35.

10. See West, op. cit., 230 (philosophy as a "cultural battle"), 210 ("moral and political weapons"). For a discussion of historiographical norms, see Peter Novick, *That Noble Dream: The "Objectivity Question" and the American Historical Profession* (New York: Cambridge University Press, 1988).

11. Hilary Putnam, *Reason, Truth, and History* (New York: Cambridge University Press, 1981, reprinted 1989), p. 49 ("God's Eye point of View"). For the linkage of atomistic individualism and political economy, see Thomas C. Heller, Morton Sosna, and David E. Wellbery, eds., *Reconstructing Individualism: Autonomy, Individuality, and the Self in Western Thought* (Stanford, Cal.: Stanford University Press, 1986), especially pp. 1–14. For the linkage between epistemology and atomistic individualism, see the essays of Charles Taylor cited above. Much of critical legal scholarship is dedicated to showing the central role of atomistic individu-

alism in American law. See, for example, Peter Gabel and Jay M. Fein-man, "Contract Law as Ideology," in David Kairys, ed., *The Politics of Law: A Progressive Critique,* revised ed. (New York: Pantheon, 1990), pp. 373–86.

12. MacIntyre, op. cit, 25 (first quote), 35 (second quote).

13. For an insightful analysis that hightlights the central role of self-interest ideology in MacIntyre's work, see Martha Nussbaum, "Recoil-ing from Reason," *New York Review of Books,* Dec. 7, 1989, p. 36 (review of MacIntyre's *Whose Justice? Which Rationality?*).

14. MacIntyre, op. cit., 23. Richard Bernstein, "Nietzsche or Aris-totle? Reflections on Alasdair MacIntyre's *After Virtue,*" *Soundings* 67 (Spring 1984), 6, 23 (quote), 24 (MacIntyre adopts Enlightenment proj-ect). MacIntyre forgets—though Bernstein does not—that the Greek tradition of virtue excluded not only non-Greeks, barbarians, and slaves but also women. Id. at 25. For MacIntyre's argument that the Enlighten-ment project is a failure, see MacIntyre, op. cit., 51–78.

15. MacIntyre provides an extended defense of Augustinian Chris-tianity in Alasdair MacIntyre, *Whose Justice? Which Rationality?* (Notre Dame, Ind.: University of Notre Dame Press, 1988). Robert N. Bellah, Richard Madsen, William M. Sullivan, Ann Swidler, and Steven M. Tipton, *Habits of the Heart* (New York: Harper & Row, 1985), pp. 28–31, 50, 303.

16. Bellah, et al., op. cit., 214, 251, 285.

17. J. G. A. Pocock, *The Machiavellian Moment* (Princeton, N.J.: Prince-ton University Press, 1975). The literature on republicanism is enor-mous. My interpretation of Pocock draws heavily on Isaac Kramnick, "Republican Revisionism Revisited," *American Historical Review* 87 (June 1982), 629. The phrase quoted is from page 632. Other key figures in the republican revival include Bernard Bailyn, Gordon Wood, and Joyce Appleby. See Bernard Bailyn, *The Ideological Origins of the Ameri-can Revolution* (Cambridge, Mass.: Harvard University Press, 1967); Gordon Wood, *The Creation of the American Republic, 1776–1787* (New York: Norton, 1969); Joyce Appleby, "Republicanism in Old and New Contexts," *William and Mary Quarterly* 43 (1968), 20. I do not attempt to provide a comprehensive review of the literature on republicanism. Informative recent reviews included Linda K. Kerber, "The Republi-can Ideology of the Revolutionary Generation," *American Quarterly* 37 (Fall 1985), 474; Isaac Kramnick, "The 'Great National Discussion': The Discourse of Politics in 1787," *William and Mary Quarterly* 45 (1988), 3; Lance Banning, "Quid Transit? Paradigms and Process in the Transformation of Republic Ideas," *Reviews in American History* 17 (1989), 199.

18. For an explication of the complexity of the liberal tradition, see Dorothy Ross, "Liberalism," in Jack P. Greene (ed.), *Encyclopedia of American Political History* (New York: Scribner's, 1984). Kloppenberg has lucidly challenged the conflation of liberalism with self-interest ideology. Kloppenberg, "Virtues." The Horwitz article referred to is in *William & Mary Law Review* 29 (Fall 1987), 57. Horwitz's critics (whose essays are printed in the same volume) include Hendrik Hartog, "Imposing Constitutional Traditions," G. Edward White, "The Studied Ambiguity of Horwitz's Legal History," and Mark Tushnet, "The Concept of a Tradition in Constitutional Historiography." See also other articles in the symposium of which Horwitz's paper is the centerpiece, *William & Mary Law Review* 29 (1987).

19. Kloppenberg, "Virtues." See also John Dunn, *The Political Thought of John Locke* (New York: Cambridge University Press, 1969).

20. A recent collection that takes stock of existing historical knowledge is Mark A. Noll, *Religion and American Politics* (New York: Oxford University Press, 1990). For recent laments over religion's marginalized role, see Henry F. May, "Religion and American Intellectual History, 1945–85: Reflections on an Uneasy Relationship," in Michael J. Lacey, *Religion and Twentieth-Century American Intellectual Life* (New York: Cambridge University Press and Woodrow Wilson International Center for Scholars, 1991), p. 12 (quote); John F. Wilson, Robert T. Hardy, Stanley N. Katz, and Albert J. Rabotean, "Foreword" to Robert Wuthnow, *The Restructuring of American Religion* (Princeton, N.J.: Princeton University Press, 1988), p. ix.

21. Ross, op. cit., 35–36, 49, 54, 56, 63 n. 18; Van A. Harvey, "On Intellectual Marginality of American Theology," in Lacey, op. cit.

22. The first two statistics are from Bellah, et al., op. cit. 219; the third is from Elizabeth Mensch and Alan Freeman, "The Politics of Virtue: Animals, Theology, and Abortion," *Georgia Law Review* 24 (1991), 923, 935 (statistic).

23. Bellah, et al., op. cit., 219–49. Richard Wightman Fox, "The Religious Revival in American Intellectual History," *Intellectual History Newsletter* 10 (April 1988), 12 (*Habits'* Protestant evangelicalism). See also John Diggins, *The Lost Soul of American Politics* (Chicago: University of Chicago Press, 1986), especially 334–46, which argues that Calvinism is the lost soul that can save America from its current ills. Kloppenberg, "Virtues," 12–15; Kloppenberg, *Uncertain Victory*, 277–97. Dorothy Ross's study also documents the persistent influence of religion as a language in which to challenge self-interest. Ross, op. cit., 103–4, 116, 139, 162, 232, 412. The social gospel movement is of particular interest because it reworked Christian ethics to emphasize

the theme that individual self-realization involves an expanded commitment to social responsibility (not the mere pursuit of self-interest). See
William McGuire King, "An Enthusiasm for Humanity: The Social
Emphasis in Religion and Its Accommodation—Protestant Theology,"
in Lacey, op. cit., p. 49.

24. Elizabeth Mensch and Alan Freeman, "A Republican Agenda
for Hobbesian America?," *Florida Law Review* 41 (1989), 581, 621
(quote).

25. Anthony E. Cook, "Beyond Critical Legal Studies: The Reconstructive Theology of Dr. Martin Luther King, Jr.," *Harvard Law Review*
103 (1990), 985.

26. Milner S. Ball, *Lying Down Together: Law, Metaphor, and Theology*
(Madison: University of Wisconsin Press, 1985), p. xiv; Michael J. Perry,
Morality, Politics, and Law (New York: Oxford University Press, 1988),
pp. 180–84; Michael J. Perry, "Comment on the Limits of Rationality
and the Place of Religious Conviction: Protecting Animals and the Environment," *William and Mary Law Review* 27 (1986), 1067. See also symposium issue on Michael Perry's book in *Tulane Law Review* 63 (1989),
1283.

27. Nancy F. Cott, *The Bonds of Womanhood* (New Haven, Conn.: Yale
University Press, 1977), pp. 63–74; Bellah, et al. op. cit.; Kloppenberg,
"Virtues."

28. Cott, op. cit., 67–71; Joan Williams, "Domesticity as the Dangerous Supplement to Liberalism," *Jornal of Women's History* 2 (Winter
1991), 69.

29. For a recent review of the literature linking nineteenth-century
women, reform, and the ideology of domesticity, see Faye D. Ginsberg,
Contested Lives (Berkeley: University of California Press, 1989), pp. 227–
47. Ginsberg discusses Addams on p. 209. For a recent reassessment of
the literature on women's sphere, see Linda K. Kerber, "Separate
Spheres, Female Worlds, Women's Place: The Rhetoric of Women's
History," *Journal of American History* 75 (June 1988), 9.

30. For a more extended discussion, see Joan Williams, "Deconstructing Gender," *Michigan Law Review* 87 (1989), 810–13, 819–22.

31. For more extended discussions of the relationship between
Gilligan's "different voice" and domesticity, see Williams, "Dangerous
Supplement," 70–76; Williams, "Deconstructing Gender," 806–13. Quo-
tations are from Carol Gilligan, *In a Different Voice* (Cambridge, Mass.:
Harvard University Press, 1982), pp. 66–67 (first quotation), p. 54 (sec-
ond), p. 136 (third), p. 93 (fourth). See also Nel Noddings, *Caring*
(Berkeley: University of California Press, 1984), pp. 1–3. The descrip-
tions of men and women provided by domestic ideology were, and still

334 *Joan C. Williams*

are, part of a system of race and class privilege. See Christine Stansell, *City of Women: Sex and Class in New York 1789–1960* (New York: Knopf, 1986). The relation of African-American and working-class women to the images of "true" womanhood is complex, and has not yet fully been explored. See Stansell, op. cit.; James Oliver Horton, "Freedom's Yoke: Gender Conventions among Antebellum Free Blacks," *Freedom Studies* 12 (1986), 51; Susan Levine, "Class and Gender: Herbert Gutman and the Women of 'Shoe City'," *Labor History* 29 (1988), 344. On the problem of universalizing the experience of white, upper-class women, see Elizabeth V. Spelman, *Inessential Women: Problems of Exclusion in Feminist Thought* (Boston: Beacon, 1988).

32. Gilligan, op. cit., 79, 98, 100, 104, 49.

33. Ibid., 22, 23, 17, 35.

34. Jean Baker Miller, *Toward a New Psychology of Women* (Boston: Beacon, 1976), quoted in Gilligan, op. cit., 49. Kathy E. Ferguson, *The Feminist Case against Bureaucracy* (Philadelphia: Temple University Press, 1984). The second quote is from Carrie Menkel-Meadow, perhaps the leading follower of Gilligan in the law. See Carrie Menkel-Meadow, "Feminist Discourse, Moral Values, and the Law—A Conversation," *Buffalo Law Review* 34 (1985), 11, 57, and "Portia in a Different Voice: Speculations on a Woman's Lawyering Process," *Berkeley Women's Law Journal* 1 (1985), 39. See also Rand Jack and Dana Crowley Jack, *Moral Vision and Professional Decisions* (New York: Cambridge University Press, 1989).

35. Kloppenberg, "Virtues".; Galston op. cit. (see note 7); Stephen Macedo, *Liberal Virtues* (New York: Oxford University Press, 1991).

36. Dewey, op. cit. (see note 8), 26 (first quotation); id. (second); West, op. cit. (see note 9), 210 (third.)

37. Frances Olsen has highlighted the strategic goals that may motivate MacKinnon's tendency to submerge the existence of nonoppressive sexuality. Frances Olsen, "Feminist Theory in Grand Style," *Columbia Law Review* 89 (1989), 1147, 1176.

38. Examples are Kerber, "Republican Ideology" (see note 17), 483–84, 486–87; Hanna Fenichel Pitkin, *Fortune Is a Woman: Gender and Politics in the Thought of Niccolo Machiavelli* (Berkeley: University of California Press, 1984); Hartog, op. cit. (see note 18); 81–82; Gregory Alexander, "Fragmented Survival: Republicanism as Rhetoric," *CLS: Newsletter of the Conference on Critical Legal Studies*, November 1989, p. 76. Legal scholars who carefully distance themselves from historical republicanism include Frank Michelman, "Law's Republic," and Cass Sunstein, "Beyond the Republican Revival," both in *Yale Law Journal* 90 (1988), 1453 (Michelman), 1539 (Sunstein).

39. Influential work in the neorepublican tradition includes Michelman, op. cit.; Frank Michelman, "The Supreme Court 1985 Term—Foreword: Traces of Self-Government," *Harvard Law Review* 100 (1986), 4; Sunstein, op. cit.; Geoffrey Stone, Louis Seidman, Cass Sunstein, and Mark Tushnet, *Constitutional Law* (Boston: Little, Brown, 1986), pp. 5–13. For a critical appraisal of the revival, see Richard H. Fallon, Jr., "What Is Republicanism and Is It Worth Reviving?," *Harvard Law Review* 102 (1989), 1695.

40. Linda K. Kerber, "Making Republicanism Useful," *Yale Law Journal* 97 (1988), 1663, 1672; Dorothy Ross, *The Origins of American Social Science* (New York: Oxford University Press, 1991); Kloppenberg, "Virtues" and *Uncertain Victory*. See also Tushnet, op. cit., 95–98; Michelman, op. cit; Sunstein, op. cit.

41. Richard Rorty, *Contingency, Irony, and Solidarity* (Cambridge: Cambridge University Press, 1989), p. 50 (first quotation); Kerber, "Making Republicanism Useful", 1672 (second); Bellah, et al., op. cit., 216.

42. For discussions of how "women's voice" was used to justify relegating women to lower-paying jobs, see discussions of Equal Employment Opportunity Commission v. Sears, Roebuck & Co., 628 F. Supp. 1264 (N.D. Ill. 1986), affirmed 839 F. 2d 302 (7th Cir. 1988), in Williams, "Deconstructing Gender" (see note 30), pp. 813–21; Vicki Schultz, "Telling Stories about Women and Work: Judicial Interpretations of Sex Segregation in the Workplace in Title VII Cases Raising the Lack of Interest Argument," *Harvard Law Review* 103 (1990), 1749, 1796, 1803–5; Lucinda Finley, "Choice and Freedom: Elusive Issues in the Search for Gender Justice," *Yale Law Journal* 96 (1987), 914, 937–40; Joan W. Scott, "Deconstructing Equality-Versus-Difference; or, The Uses of Poststructuralist Theory for Feminism," *Feminist Studies* 14 (1988), 33, 38–47.

43. For other feminist critiques of "pro-choice" rhetoric, see Ruth Colker, "Feminism, Theology, and Abortion; Toward Love, Compassion, and Wisdom," *California Law Review* 77 (1989): 1011; Colker, "Feminist Litigation: An Oxymoron? A Study of the Briefs filed in William L. Webster v. Reproductive Health Services." *Harvard Womens' Law Journal* 13 (1990): 137; Mensch and Freeman, "Politics of Virtue" (see note 22); Catharine MacKinnon, "Privacy v. Equality: Beyond Roe v. Wade," *Feminism Unmodified: Discourses on Life and Law* (Cambridge, Mass.: Harvard University Press, 1987, p. 93.

44. Joan W. Scott, "Gender as a Category of Historical Analysis," *American Historical Review* 91 (December 1986), 1053.

45. For a more extended development of this argument, see Joan Williams, "Gender Wars: Selfless Women in the Republic of Choice," *New York University Law Review* (forthcoming). For background on Baker,

see Marjorie Williams, "He Doesn't Waste a Lot of Time on Guilt," *Washington Post Magazine*, Jan. 29, 1989, p. A20.

46. Ginsberg, op. cit. (see note 29), 185. See also Kristin Luker, *Abortion and the Politics of Motherhood* (Berkeley: University of California Press, 1984).

47. Ginsberg, op. cit. (see note 29), 195 (first and second quotation), 188 (third), 196 (Linda Gordon quotation).

48. R. W. Apple, Jr., "Limits on Abortion Seem Less Likely," *New York Times,* Sept, 29, 1989, Sect. 1, p. 1. An earlier poll reported that 56 percent of respondents said that abortion should be illegal in these circumstances. E. J. Dionne, Jr., "Poll Finds Ambivalence on Abortion Persists in U.S.," *New York Times,* Aug. 3, 1989, p. A18.

49. Dionne, op. cit., A18.

50. Apple, op. cit., A13.

51. For a fascinating discussion of republican virtue as male, see Pitkin, op. cit. (see note 38). For an influential discussion of an intermediate step between domesticity and republican virtue, see Linda Kerber, *Women of the Republic* (New York: Norton, 1986). The links between virtue and gender are explored in depth in Ruth H. Bloch, "The Gendered Meanings of Virtue in Revolutionary America," *Signs: Journal of Women in Culture and Society* 3 (1987), 37.

52. Barbara Sicherman, *Alice Hamilton* (Cambridge, Mass.: Harvard University Press, 1984), pp. 4, 169.

53. I have suggested that domesticity played a role in chasing the "virtues" out of liberalism, leaving self-interest unchecked by the late nineteenth century. Williams, "Dangerous Supplement" (see note 28), 77–79. For an insightful discussion of the cultural meanings of equality for women, see Donald G. Mathews and Jane Sherron De Hart, *Sex, Gender, and the Politics of the ERA* (New York: Oxford University Press, 1990), pp. 152–80.

54. Williams, "Gender Wars" (see note 45).

55. Joyce Price, "30 percent of Pregnancies Terminated Yearly," *Washington Times,* Aug. 10, 1990, p. A5.

56. Mary Travers, "My Abortion, Then and Now," *New York Times,* Aug. 10, 1980, p. A23.

57. One nonsocietal condition that makes continued access to abortion so crucial is that pregnancy can be and childbirth is painful and physically taxing. For an enumeration of the physical burdens of pregnancy, see Donald Regan, "Rewriting *Roe v. Wade,*" *Michigan Law Review* 77 (1979), 1569, 1579–83. In my view, even a society that eliminated the economic burdens of childrearing would not have the right

to force unwanted pregnancy on women because of the physical hardships involved.

58. Ginsberg, op. cit. (see note 29), 222–26; National Abortion Rights Action League Foundation Advertisement, "America: Our Goal Should Be to Make Abortion Less Necessary—Not More Dangerous, Not More Difficult," *New York Times,* July 7, 1991, p. E12.

16

LIBERAL PHILANTHROPY

JONATHAN RILEY

"But sometimes Virtue starves, while Vice is fed."
What then? Is the reward of Virtue bread?
. . . .
Know then this truth (enough for Man to know)
"Virtue alone is happiness below."
Alexander Pope, An Essay on Man

I. Introduction

William Galston has recently reminded us that the liberal polity—
state and society—is conceived by many as if it could be comprised entirely of institutions that are nothing more than prudent
contrivances for channeling self-interest.[1] Political liberty, for example, is conceived in terms of fundamental constitutional laws
that, by means of frequent and regular elections, hold ambitious
rulers accountable to voters; and that, by dividing authority
among rulers in such a way as to pit ambition against ambition,

I am grateful to Joyce Appleby, John Chapman, and Bill Galston for helpful
comments and encouragement. Earlier versions of this chapter were presented
at the Second Annual Symposium of the Center on Philanthropy, Indiana
University-Purdue University at Indianapolis, June 7–9, 1989, on the general
theme of "The Responsibilities of Wealth"; and at a Murphy Institute conference, Tulane University, March 9–11, 1990, on the general theme of "The Culture of the Market." Responsibility for the views expressed is mine alone.

discourage government corruption and violation of legal and customary rights of the individual. Economic liberty is defined in terms of capitalist market institutions that, by means of frequent and voluntary exchanges, hold ambitious producers accountable to consumers; and that, by dividing economic power among property owners, including government, in such a way as to pit ambition against ambition, promote efficient resource allocation and growth of wealth. Those liberal political and economic institutions may seem not to depend for their successful operation on any conception of individual virtue. But Galston defends a modest claim that, to some extent, "the viability of liberal society depends on its ability to engender a virtuous citizenry."[2] More specifically, "the operation of liberal institutions is affected in important ways by the character of citizens (and leaders) and . . . at some point the attenuation of individual virtue will create pathologies with which liberal [institutional] contrivances, however technically perfect their design, simply cannot cope."[3]

In Galston's view, numerous "instrumental virtues" are essential to the operation and perservation of the liberal polity, namely, tolerance, the work ethic, respect for the rights of others, and so on. He also suggests that different strands of "the liberal tradition" unite around "a common core" conception of "intrinsic virtue." Lockean, Kantian, and Millian liberalisms, for all their differences, share "a vision of individuals who in some manner take responsibility for their own lives . . . , [of] excellence [linked] to a kind of activity . . . , [and of] the dignity of every individual and . . . the practice of mutual self-respect."[4] But Galston never denies that "there is a tension at the heart of liberalism" in the sense that "the liberal state must by definition by broadly tolerant, yet it cannot be wholly indifferent to the character of its citizens."[5] Moreover, he implies that this tension is irremediable: liberal ideas of intrinsic individual excellence are not fully consistent with the instrumental virtues required to sustain the liberal polity. "Indeed, it would not be farfetched to interpret some of the deepest tensions within liberal polities as a clash between means and ends, that is, between requirements of liberal citizenship and aspirations toward liberal excellence."[6]

Without necessarily accepting Galston's value-pluralist outlook, according to which we must recognize certain irremediable tensions or conflicts among plural liberal virtues, I think he is correct to emphasize that liberal theory and practice are neither bereft, of, nor hostile to, all conceptions of individual virtue.[7] Indeed, in the absence of virtue, to understand how socially beneficial institutions can be established or maintained becomes difficult.[8] In this regard, I propose to focus attention on an oft-neglected liberal institution, distinct in principle from both constitutional government and the market economy, that morally constrains the operation of the latter two sorts of institutions. This third kind of liberal institution is philanthropy or charity, the practice of giving aid voluntarily to others when they may reasonably expect our help under prevailing norms and customs. Galston himself speaks of "the humanitarian disposition" to help others as an instrumental liberal virtue. In his view, "every contemporary liberal theory" presupposes individuals who, among other things, "value their earthly existence," and "the worth of existence implies [among other things] . . . an endorsement of the humanitarian disposition to act affirmatively to preserve the existence of others, at least when this can be done without excessive cost to ourselves."[9]

In my view, a theory of philanthropy is no less essential than a theory of justice to liberalism. After all, one of the most accepted connotations of that ambiguous term "liberal" is "free in bestowing; bountiful, generous, open-hearted."[10] Indeed, unless generosity and beneficence can be integrated with justice and rights, no adequate liberal theory of community seems possible.[11] Unfortunately, modern liberals and their critics tend to be so preoccupied with theories of justice that the distinctive liberal tradition of voluntary giving seems in danger of fading from sight. Even as acute and sympathetic a critic as Michael Walzer, for example, reduces liberal artifice in the context of a particular society entirely to the interpretation and protection of separate spheres of justice, each of which is governed by its own distinct principles of fair distribution.[12] The relevant principles are implicit, he says, in the "social meanings" of different goods such as money, political power, and ecclesiastical office. In other words, criteria of distributive justice are internal to, and may be inferred directly from, the given society's common institutions and practices, its shared beliefs and customs, relating to the various goods. In his view, liberalism is best understood as an argument against interference with the "internal logics" of those basic institutions and practices:

> We can say that a (modern, complex and differentiated) society enjoys both freedom and equality when success in one institutional setting isn't convertible into success in another, that is, when the separations hold, when political power doesn't shape the church or religious zeal the state, and so on. . . . The play of internal logic can only be repressed by tyrannical force, crossing the lines, breaking through the walls established by the art of separation. Liberalism is best understood as an argument against that sort of repression. . . . Distributive justice [conceived in terms of freedom and equality] is (largely) a matter of getting the lines right.[13]

Because this sort of reduction of liberalism to considerations of justice is so common in the literature, though rarely carried out so elegantly, and because I propose to argue that liberalism traditionally involves more than a theory of justice, it is convenient to review briefly how Walzer interprets the art of separation in its traditional liberal form.

According to Walzer, liberals traditionally have built walls to separate individuals from one another, to render each person "free within his or her circle of rights. . . . Liberal society, ideally, is simply a collection of these circles, held together by all the tangential connections and actual overlappings that their solitary inhabitants voluntarily establish."[14] Ideal liberal institutions are based merely on contracts or other "willful agreements" among right holders, "valuable because of the agreement they embody but at the same time subject to schism, withdrawal, cancellation, and divorce."[15] Moreover, liberals have focused their attention on protecting the individual from political tyranny but have paid insufficient attention to other forms of tyranny: "The liberal achievement has been to protect a number of important institutions and practices from political power, to limit the reach of government. . . . Limited government is the great success of the art of separation, but that very success opens the way for what political scientists call *private* government, and it is with the critique of private government that the leftist complaint against liberalism properly begins."[16]

As is well known, Walzer proposes to improve upon traditional liberal artifice thus interpreted. First, he rejects as "literally unattainable" the putative liberal goal that governments, markets, churches, schools, and families should be grounded solely on the mutual consent of their individual participants. He insists that institutions have "particular histories" or "internal logics," reflected in particular patterns of rules and customs that are not simply constructed de novo by the current participants. His "socialized" art of separation recognizes that individual agreement is always situated within and constrained by these rules and customs. Thus: "We do not separate individuals; we separate institutions, practices, relationships of different sorts. The lines we draw encircle churches and schools and markets and families, not you and me. We aim, or we should aim, not at the freedom of the solitary individual but at what can best be called institutional integrity. . . . Men and women are free when they live within autonomous institutions."[17]

Second, Walzer advocates extending liberal artifice to protect the integrity of basic institutions from all forms of tyranny, not merely *political* tyranny. He seems especially troubled by "the ways in which wealth . . . takes on tyrannical forms."[18] To protect the internal logics of basic practices from market tyranny, he says we need "to enlist liberal artfulness in the service of socialism."[19] In his view, "the walls that wall in the market . . . will never be effective until private governments are socialized . . . , that is, turned over to their participants."[20] Once we design and protect suitable forms of industrial democracy that, on the one hand, prevent wealth from breaking outside the market realm to upset the integrity of nonmarket practices and, on the other, also make "room for the entrepreneur and the new company," "we can glimpse a consistent liberalism—that is, one that passes over into democratic socialism." This version of democratic socialism "does not require the abolition of the market . . . but rather the confinement of the market to its proper space."[21]

A serious ambiguity in Walzer's approach is, however, already apparent. Protection of the integrity of actual market practices is a conservative goal that involves insulating existing beliefs and customs relating to the fair distribution of wealth. But Socialist reforms are hardly compatible with that conservative goal in a capitalist society whose members more or less share a belief that wealth should be distributed in accord with conventions of private property. More generally, a deep tension exists between protection of the internal logic of any actual institution, and reform of that institution. To avoid mindless conservatism, it seems that Walzer must propose some general theory to identify the internal logic of any institution independently of the observed conduct of participants. Then the fact that people are observed not to conform to that internal logic may be cited as evidence of cultural distortion in terms of the theory, and used to justify reform of the actual practice. For example, as Ronald Dworkin suggests, Walzer might recognize "a hidden and mystical premise . . . that there are only a limited number of spheres of justice whose essential principles have been established in advance and must therefore remain the same for all societies."[22] Given fixed, preordained spheres of this Platonic sort, he could investigate the fit between them and actual practices, "and then insist that [the latter] be reformed so as to be entirely like those of the [ideal] sphere they most resemble."[23]

But Walzer explicitly rejects Dworkin's suggestion as "contrary to the method and intention" of his approach. He is not concerned, he says, to construct or discover abstract principles of justice whose foundation is divorced from prevailing practices. Instead, "Social goods and distributive spheres have first to be found through a process of empirical investigation, and then they have to be understood through a process of interpretation. They have the forms they take in a particular society: there are no preordained forms."[24] Now, it may be true that Walzer need not commit himself to any a priori theory of what an entirely undistorted culture would look like.[25] An empirical account of actual practices, and a contextualist theory of interpretation telling us how to infer shared norms of justice *from* those very practices, will suffice. On that basis, a critic could explain and evaluate existing practices, including the ways in which they are distorted

in terms of shared cultural norms. But, as several commentators
have noted, Walzer's own theory of interpretation does not tell us
how to adjudicate among the competing and conflicting principles of fair distribution that can be associated with any given
good.[26] Indeed, Dworkin's original objection was that *shared* principles of justice cannot be inferred merely from actual practices
whose meaning and appeal is essentially contested by different
groups within society.

Rather than subscribe to any theory of fixed and preordained
spheres of justice, however, Walzer might claim that basic institutions and their internal logics can be identified and assessed only
through democratic procedures, in other words, only after suitable debate and decision by some qualified body of citizens. In
that case, spheres of justice are artifacts that emerge and evolve a
posteriori, solely on the basis of popular beliefs and customs. Any
criteria for evaluating actual practices are temporary emanations
from the democratic process, and are ultimately reducible to the
evolving social meaning of democracy itself. Now, there is much to
suggest that Walzer has something like this in mind.[27] He seems to
say, for example, that institutions are autonomous if governed by
their respective participants: "A free state . . . is . . . a state that is
in the hands of its citizens generally—just as a free church is in the
hands of believers, a free university in the hands of scholars, a free
firm in the hands of workers and managers."[28] Moreover, this
self-government for members of some fundamental plurality of
institutions emanates from, and ultimately is contingent upon,
the democratic state:

> The state . . . always has a special influence, for it is the agent of
> separation and the defender, as it were, of the social map. It is not
> so much a night watchman protecting individuals from coercion
> and physical assault as it is the builder and guardian of the walls,
> protecting churches, universities, families, and so on from tyranni-
> cal interference. . . . What goes on in this or that institutional
> setting? And what is the internal logic of what goes on? These
> questions have to be debated, first in particular institutional set-
> tings and then in the general setting of the state. . . . But what if
> some political majority misunderstands or overrides the auton-
> omy of this or that institutional setting? That is the unavoidable
> risk of democracy.[29]

The meaning of democracy here remains ambiguous, however, because placing an institution in the hands of its members is such a loose criterion. Indeed, unless democratic procedures are specified independently of existing practices, democracy seems to become but another name for the whole set of prevailing beliefs and customs, shared or otherwise, and however inegalitarian. To avoid that unhelpful result, self-government might be defined, in the context of any institution, as internal majority rule by some qualified membership after broad discussion and debate encouraged by certain liberal devices that effectively divide the power to lead among different hands.[30] The resulting vision of democracy is reminiscent of Robert Dahl's social ideal, in which the political demos grants autonomy, within limits, to some indefinite plurality of self-governing institutions.[31] But any such Dahl-like vision constitutes an abstract democratic theory of justice, of the same general sort that Walzer apparently wishes to reject because it transcends a particular society's practices.

Walzer's theory that criteria for the just distribution of any good are implicit in a particular society's actual practices relating to that good must, it seems fair to conclude, be modified. More specifically, we must recognize that actual practices, even when they do not vary significantly across groups in the society, admit of competing interpretations, both descriptive and normative; and that the critic's preferred interpretations must be justified by reference to criteria that are inevitably controversial. It remains possible, of course, that liberal artifice might yet be justified on the basis of some general normative theory. But, whether or not some such foundational argument is available to rescue liberalism, it is important to keep in mind that liberals traditionally do not conceive their art as Walzer says they do. The point deserves emphasis because his arguments are revealing of widely shared beliefs about the nature of liberalism. Many commentators seem to believe that liberalism is traditionally committed to some sort of presocial self (usually Kantian in flavor), for example, despite the absence of any such metaphysical claim in the dominant strands of Anglo-American liberalism that may be traced from Locke through Madison and Mill to modern writers such as Friedrich Hayek.[32] From that Anglo-American perspective, Walzer misconstrues liberal artifice in at least two ways.

First, liberals traditionally have not been concerned to protect isolated individuals. Second, liberals have not focused their skills solely on justifying and protecting spheres of *justice*.

On the first point, liberals traditionally have not assigned rights as a way of separating individuals in the strong metaphysical sense of disencumbering each from all social ties except mutual agreements. Rights have been assigned to secure for individuals an opportunity to fulfill their own purposes within a general framework of known laws and customs, none of which need depend on unanimous consent. When speaking of recognized property rights in a society, for example, liberals necessarily refer to the rules of property within the society, that is, to its laws and customs that define what things may be owned, who may own them, the terms and conditions under which exclusive control may be held, how such titles may be transferred to others, and so on. More generally, when speaking of any legal rights, liberals must refer to laws that define, assign, and sanction the rights and their corresponding duties. Similarly, when speaking of any moral or customary rights not afforded legal protection, liberals must refer to spontaneous practices that define, assign, and enforce, not by legal penalties but merely by penalties of opinion, the rights and their corresponding duties. The point is that any liberal society's impartial rights assignments are by definition situated within a particular web of rules, traditionally termed its rules of justice. Individuals who follow those general rules are thereby empowered to exercise certain rights and are compelled, under threat of some form of punishment, to satisfy corresponding duties. Individuals who break those rules are forewarned to expect some form of organized intervention against their socially impermissible actions. This view of rights within settings is thoroughly familiar to liberalism, although perhaps it has been obscured by recent neo-Kantian doctrines.

Given that society's laws and customs of justice underlie what Friedrich Hayek calls "protected spheres" of individual freedom, Walzer's approach is novel only to the extent that he advocates different sorts of rules and rights assignments than those traditionally applauded by liberals. As already noted, he prescribes both political democracy and market socialism, and may share

Dahl's vision of equal rights for relevant members to participate in the internal government of some plurality of basic institutions. Traditional liberals, on the contrary, advocate other sorts of rights such as property rights and rights to be left alone in intimate matters such as religious belief and sexual lifestyle. In any case, the difference in not that Walzer wants to protect institutional integrity whereas liberals wish to protect isolated individuals. The difference is that he apparently wishes to reform traditional liberal rights assignments, in other words, to alter the rules defining a rightful distribution of individual power both within and among basic institutions such as market and state. To evaluate alternative rights assignments, however, we would require a normative test or standard, as well as a general theory to justify the test.[33]

Turning to the second way in which Walzer misconstrues liberalism, liberals traditionally do not carve all of social life into so many spheres of justice. Instead, some realms of life are held to be properly beyond justice, that is, participants in those realms should not be assigned rights either by law or by custom. Consider the familiar ethical distinction between rules of justice and rules of charity, for example. In the sphere of charity, where aid would be desirable but is strictly speaking not a matter of immediate life or death for any individual recipient, givers are held to have a moral duty to provide help to others in situations where help may be reasonably be expected under prevailing customs. But the duty is termed "imperfect" because recipients are thought to have no corresponding rights to the help, either in law or custom. "No one has a moral right to our generosity or beneficence," as J. S. Mill puts it, "because we are not morally bound to practice those virtues towards any given individual. . . . [T]hough [charity] is obligatory, the particular occasions of performing it are left to our choice [under prevailing customs]."[34] This implies, among other things, that the liberal state should not enact laws compelling people to redistribute the fruits of their labor and saving to ablebodied persons who are merely unwilling to work or save. It is true that the liberal practice of voluntary giving is made possible by the state's protection of property rights, that is, the sphere of philanthropy flourishes *within* the sphere of justice. But that does not alter the fact that charity and justice are distinct spheres governed by different kinds of rules, one of which has nothing to do with rights. Moreover, the moral conventions that constitute the voluntary practice of charity are ties of liberal community that emerge independently of state coercion. Indeed, these sorts of community norms may tend to atrophy to the extent the state— democratic or otherwise—seeks to enforce charitable obligations by means of legal penalties.[35] Similar remarks may be made with respect to conventions of trust underlying market exchange. Spheres of voluntary exchange and of charity may grow only in the interstices of the sphere of justice, but they constitute crucial realms of traditional liberal life where *both the individual and the community* are supposed to be left alone by the state.

If my claims are accepted, then liberal artifice is not concerned exclusively with separate spheres of justice governed by their own rules and rights assignments. It is also concerned with spheres beyond the realm of justice, for example, separate sphere of charity and competition governed respectively by distinctive kinds of rules that do not assign rights to participants in those spheres.[36] Moreover, this more complex art of separation must be justified on the basis of a credible normative theory. Criteria are required to assess and adjudicate among alternative sets of rules or, more generally, alternative sets of shared dispositions.[37] The development of a credible liberal art is, of course, beyond the scope of this paper.[38] My more limited purposes are to clarify the traditional liberal sphere of philanthropy, and to indicate what sorts of reforms are needed to rehabilitate that sphere in a modern society such as the United States.

Moral conventions of philanthropy may be interpreted as liberal institutional contrivances designed to encourage, under threat of public humiliation or stigma but not of legal coercion, positive assistance for the projects of other members of the community. Rendering assistance requires the agent to divert scarce resources, the means of attaining his own immediate ends, to other people, and in that sense may be said to display moral virtue. This may or may not be reducible to long-term or enlightened self-interest but, in any case, it is indispensable for successful operation of the liberal polity.[39] On the one hand, voluntary giving in accord with customary expectations reduces the inequality of wealth that is otherwise associated with the unbridled pursuit of self-interest under capitalism. On the other hand, giving also restrains the scope of government, by funding community spirit without its involvement.

Some will insist that philanthropy is not a *liberal* institution but instead is a legacy of preliberal religious and moral traditions to which liberalism is at best indifferent and probably hostile.[40] But, even if we admit, as Galston does, that liberal individual excellence sits uneasily with loyalty to traditional values, to insist that individuality and tradition are entirely incompatible, with no possibility of a middle ground, is surely going too far. Of course, to go so far is easy enough, as the literature readily attests. If individuals are conceived as "radically unsituated" atoms motivated solely by their own notions of immediate gain, for example, then liberal excellence cannot be reconciled with traditional values. Or if tradition is equated with blind, unquestioning acceptance of custom or of some other authority external to the individual, then enlightened individuals, situated in a given social context but capable of imagining or remembering alternatives to existing rules and customs, cannot be integrated into traditional cultures. But merely to state these extremes is to reveal their absurdity. A liberal individual, capable of imagining an ideal community and of remembering moral and religious traditions that are imbued with some communitarian ideal, not necessarily earthly, *can* reflect upon those traditions and deliberately choose to guide his conduct in accord with certain prevailing conventions of philanthropy.[41] This person must be motivated, at least occasionally, by something other than immediate gain, in particular, a desire to help others, even strangers, when help is reasonably expected.[42] But we are entitled to assume that some such motivation is not completely foreign to liberal individuals, despite the caricatures of liberalism so frequently painted by its friends and foes alike. In short, no logical barrier arises to prevent due recognition by liberals of cultural traditions, religious or otherwise, encouraging philanthropy.[43]

It would be surprising, of course, if philanthropic practices under capitalism had not evolved from earlier religious practices. W. K. Jordan and David Owen have traced the modern evolution of English philanthropy, for example, lending considerable support to a Weber-like hypothesis that would locate the calculating spirit of liberal philanthropy in the Protestant ethic.[44] Nevertheless, whatever we make of the argument that aspirations to do good for others are rooted in certain religious traditions, it remains convenient to distinguish liberal from nonliberal philanthropy. At the risk of oversimplification, nonliberal philanthropy rests on personal devotion to some authority, for example, the will of god or the opinion of a majority. The right motivation, the wish to help others, is sufficient for charity and moral virtue on this view. No attempt rationally to assess the consequences of one's giving is necessary. Beneficence is reduced to benevolence. Charity is simply a matter of being disposed to help, without question, in accord with certain social and religious customs. Doing good becomes equivalent to *wishing* to do as authority dictates, nothing more.

Liberal philanthropy, in contrast, holds that the wish to help others may be necessary but is certainly not sufficient for authentic charity and moral virtue. Doing good also requires a warranted belief that the effects of one's giving will be beneficial to the community. Rational assessment of the consequences of the gift is necessary, particularly of its effects on the characters of the recipients. Unwise gifts that actually do more harm than good by encouraging idleness and undue dependence, for example, are *not* philanthropic even though well-intentioned. In Benjamin Franklin's words, "Liberality is not giving much but giving wisely."[45] Thus, liberal moral virtue demands not merely a benevolent disposition but also an intellectual capacity to discern the probable consequences of giving, with a view to evaluating and perhaps modifying actual charitable practices. In short, actual practices may be unfit as means, and should be open to reform through free discussion, education, and persuasion.

The two kinds of philanthropy conceive moral virtue in the recipient differently as well. Nonliberal philanthropy equates virtue in the recipient with the right feelings of gratitude or loyalty toward authority, whether represented by the giver, by god, or by the community at large. Liberal philanthropy is more concerned with the recipient's desire to transform himself into a giver by becoming self-reliant through his own efforts. Because moral virtue is manifested in giving, not in receiving, the recipient displays virtue by reciprocating his gift, not necessarily to the original giver (who may, after all, be wealthy) but to others in the community. Such reciprocity can lead the numbers of gifts to multiply, and encourage community goodwill to flourish accordingly.

My main theme is that liberal philanthropy so understood is an indispensable ingredient of any adequate form of liberalism.[46] Moreover, its role in the preservation and operation of the American polity is not sufficiently appreciated and deserves clarification. Daniel Boorstin pursues this line of thought, for example, by pointing to at least three peculiar aspects of the American philanthropic spirit: its concern for the character of the recipient, not that of the giver; its focus on solving problems in this life, not on saving souls for the next; and its preoccupation with uplifting the community, not palliating the conscience. Those peculiarities may be taken to illustrate an idealistic kind of individualism that underpins the traditional American notion of community:

> A wise act of philanthropy would sooner or later benefit the giver along with all other members of the community. . . . Just as the value of a charitable gift tended to be judged less by the motive of the giver than by the social effect of the gift, so the suitability of a recipient was judged less by his emotional response—his gratitude or his personal loyalty to a benefactor—than by his own potential contribution to the community.[47]

More generally, Merle Curti suggests that "philanthropy has both reflected and helped create an American middle way between a type of capitalism characteristic of the old world, in which owners surrender little of what they have unless forced to do so, on the one hand, and socialism on the other."[48] Put in other words, liberal philanthropy affirms a distinctive conception of moral virtue that suitably constrains both capitalism and democratic government for the good of the community.[49]

Nevertheless, liberal philanthropy with its "middle way" between crude materialistic individualism and coercive state socialism continues to face major challenges from both the Left and Right in the United States.[50] Those challenges are in large part tied up with the idiosyncratic development of American federalism, in particular, the changing role of the national government.[51] Many critics see philanthropy as merely a temporary handmaiden

for the late-emerging national welfare state, whereas some putative defenders seem to assume that more unrestrained capitalism
will automatically generate sufficient philanthropy to replace any
federal cutbacks in social programs. In any case, the boundaries
among capitalism, philanthropy, and democratic government
have become increasingly blurred, raising serious doubts that philanthropy is really all that distinctive an activity anyway.[52]

To begin to clarify the importance of a particular kind of
philanthropy for the liberal polity in theory and for the American polity in practice, I propose to reconsider Andrew Carnegie's so-called gospel of wealth.[53] Whatever we may think of
Carnegie the man, there is little doubt that this gospel influenced
significantly the shape not only of his own life but also that of
American capitalism.[54]

II. CARNEGIE'S GOSPEL OF WEALTH

"The fundamental idea" of the gospel of wealth is that "surplus
wealth should be considered as a sacred trust to be administered
by those into whose hands it falls, during their lives, for the good
of the community."[55] By surplus wealth, Carnegie appears to
mean wealth that legitimately accrues to an individual as a result
of his property rights but which is beyond the needs of his family
and not otherwise invested in real plant and equipment. Family
needs are to be determined according to tacit community standards: "There must be different standards for different communities."[56] Essentially, the rule is to avoid offending middle-class
customs through ostentatious living: "Whatever makes one conspicuous offends the canon."[57] Capital goods are exempt from
redistribution because wealth in this form is not available for
personal use. Such wealth is already engaged in "beneficent wonders," that is, "enterprises which give employment and develop
the resources of the world" Surplus wealth, by contrast, apparently consists of idle assets like cash, stocks, and bonds that people hoard beyond their needs in banks and elsewhere, "adding
the interest . . . to the principal, and [perhaps] dying with their
treasures 'laid up,' which should have been used as they accrued
during the life of the individual for public ends, as the gospel of
wealth requires."[58]

Although the notion of surplus wealth remains a bit unclear, Carnegie's gospel suggests two main ethical principles for guiding the practice of philanthropy under capitalism. First, wealthy individuals have a moral obligation to distribute their surplus wealth for beneficial public purposes such as the provision of higher education. That obligation to the community apparently supersedes legal property rights, despite Carnegie's view that "upon the sacredness of property civilization itself depends—the right of the laborer to his hundred dollars in the savings-bank, and equally the legal right of the millionaire to his millions."[59] Second, the wealthy are also obligated to administer the distribution of wealth themselves during their own lifetime. That responsibility cannot be discharged through bequests. And it is positively at odds with any claim that governments, democratic or otherwise, should be solely responsible for the provision of public goods.[60] Instead, it requires any individual blessed with unusual riches to become an unusual kind of leader in his community, that is, a leader whose activities are not necessarily approved by government officials. The wealthy person has a duty to sponsor projects that *he* has reason to believe will actually benefit his fellows: "the surplus which accrues from time to time in the hands of a man should be administered by him in his own lifetime for that purpose which is seen by him, as trustee, to be best for the good of the people. To leave at death what he cannot take away, and place upon others the burden to the work which it was his own duty to perform, is to do nothing worthy. This requires no sacrifice, nor any sense of duty to his fellows."[61] Active participation by the wealthy in community affairs distinguishes the liberal kind of philanthropy exemplified by Carnegie's own life.[62]

Nevertheless, Carnegie's two ethical principles raise a host of difficulties. The key concern here is to find a coherent liberal justification of the principles. Both capitalists and constitutional democrats may be expected for different reasons to entertain serious doubts. For example, isn't the first principle simply at odds with property rights? Don't the wealthy have a right to pass on their property to their descendants? Even if this conflict can be cleared up, isn't the second principle at odds with democracy? Why does morality apparently prescribe active giving by the wealthy themselves rather than simply government redistribution through progressive taxation? Shouldn't the rich feel free to leave the administration of charity entirely to democratic officials? Why is it wrong, as opposed to merely inefficient, for government alone to oversee the provision of public goods? And what should be done if the wealthy refuse even when encouraged to give actively during their lifetimes? These sorts of questions must be answered persuasively to justify philanthropy along the lines proposed by Carnegie.

To examine how Carnegie himself seems to have answered them is instructive. For convenience, my analysis is organized around each of his two principles in turn.

A. The First Principle

According to the first principle, property owners are morally obligated to give to the community some of the property to which they are legally entitled. That seems to imply no great respect on Carnegie's part for the law of private property. Yet he explictly defends the capitalist system, including its "intense Individualism" and "great inequality," as the engine of "our wonderful material development, which brings improved conditions in its train." In his view, even if socialism is a "nobler ideal" in theory, "it is not practicable in our day or in our age" because "it necessitates the changing of human nature itself—a work of eons, even if it were good to change it, which we cannot know."[63] Given human nature as we know it, he suggests, some form of capitalism is best for the foreseeable future. Most people simply will not work efficiently unless they are assigned rights to the fruits of their own labor and saving. Carnegie rejects any attempt to overturn the institution of private property until human nature has evolved sufficiently to realize "Swedenborg's idea of heaven, where . . . the angels derive their happiness, not from laboring for self, but for each other." Instead of indulging in such revolutionary folly, he says,

> Our duty is with what is practicable now—with the next step possible in our own day and generation. . . . We might as well urge the destruction of the highest existing type of man because he

failed to reach our ideal as to favor the destruction of Individualism, Private Property, the Law of Accumulation of Wealth, and
the Law of Competition; for these are the highest result of human
experience, the soil in which society, so far, has produced the best
fruit.[64]

Despite his admiration of capitalism, however, Carnegie acknowledges that the existing economic arrangements are far
from perfect: "often there is friction between the employer and
the employed, between capital and labor, between rich and
poor."[65] Indeed, he concedes that capitalism in its present form is
perhaps even unjust. Although capitalism is "the best and most
valuable" economic system "that humanity has yet accomplished"
and remains "essential to the future progress of the race," the
present laws and customs of private property are not beyond criticism and should be reformed if that would promote "the best
interests" of the community.[66] This interpretation of Carnegie's
philosophy of life is compatible with his well-known objections to
contemporary property arrangements, in particular, the laws of
inheritance. Moreover, it may help to clarify his *capitalist* rationale
for urging the wealthy to distribute surplus wealth to which they
and their families are entitled under the law. Society's legal definition of private property may be morally unattractive as it stands
even if capitalism in some revised form should be defended.

To illustrate the point, a striking implication of Carnegie's
first principle deserves emphasis: private property should be
reformed to limit sharply any individual's right to inherit wealth.
According to Carnegie, "surplus wealth . . . left to the families of
the decedents . . . is the most injudicious" of the three possible
modes of disposition he identifies (the other two modes are bequests and lifetime gifts for public purposes).[67] Indeed, "a great
obstacle to the adoption of the gospel of wealth" is "the desire,
futile as vain, to found or maintain hereditary families."[68] With
rare exceptions, he claims, enormous legacies are inspired by
"the vanity of the parents, rather than a wise regard for the good
of the children." In his view, it is indisputable that a large legacy,
and, by implication, a large lifetime gift to an individual, "generally deadens the talents and energies" of the recipient, to his own
detriment as well as that of the community.[69] Harmful in-

tergenerational transmission of surplus wealth ought to be discouraged, he thinks, by a graduated inheritance tax rising to a ceiling of "at least" 50 percent of the rich man's estate at his death.[70]

Carnegie's opposition to legacies beyond modest limits is so strong that it leads him into public disagreement with William Gladstone. Gladstone favors the hereditary transmission of wealth and rank through entails of lands and of businesses.[71] His view seems to be that wealth is made responsible if it is attached visibly to one's customary social station. He recalls that "when the principal form of property was the possession of land," for example, "wealth and station . . . were seen to be placed in proximity, at every point, with the discharge of duty; and as the neglect of this duty in the public eye, they were in a partial yet real way responsible." But when property mainly consists of assets like capital equipment, stocks and bonds, ownership becomes less visible and there is danger of "what may be called irresponsible wealth: wealth little watched and checked by opinion, little brought into immediate contact with duty."[72] To counteract that danger, he recommends that industrial enterprises as well as landholdings should be identified with particular families whose pride and ambition are thus visibly linked to public duty: "I rejoice to see it among our merchants, bankers, publishers: I wish it were commoner among our great manufacturing capitalists."[73]

So-called irresponsible wealth is not quite what Carnegie means by surplus wealth. Irresponsible wealth apparently includes real capital stock free of entails, for example, but capital goods are not surplus wealth. Indeed, Carnegie dismisses Gladstone's aristocratic vision of society as fatal to both economic efficiency and "republican simplicity." The managerial talents essential to a successful capitalist economy are not something that can be transmitted through a particular family: "The transmission of wealth and rank, without regard to merit or qualifications, may pass from one peer to another . . . without serious injury, since the duties are a matter of routine, seldom involving the welfare or means of others; but the management of business, never."[74] Moreover, the honor and civic virtue essential to a successful constitutional democracy are linked "almost without exception" to a "lineage of honest poverty—of laborious, wage-receiving parents, leading lives of virtuous privation, sacrificing comforts that their sons might be kept at school—lineage from the cottage of poverty, not the palace of hereditary rank and position."[75] In short, capitalism and democracy both work well, he thinks, only if individuals willing to work have a more or less equal opportunity to compete for managerial and political posts. Hereditary transmission of wealth and rank is incompatible with equal opportunity, and so with the "best interests" of the community.

Like Gladstone, Carnegie believes that the good of the community depends upon the high intellectual and moral capacities of its leading members. But unlike Gladstone, he argues that those high capacities can be developed and maintained *only* through sustained exercise.[76] For Carnegie, nobility is not the birthright of an hereditary elite. Instead, noble capacities and dispositions must be acquired through hard work and competition. This might almost be called the axiom of liberal community. Moreover, it follows that enormous bequests tend to harm recipients by encouraging sloth: "poverty and struggle are advantageous" for improving character. Large gifts to individuals further harm the community by tempting recipients to hoard or conspicuously consume their surplus rather than investing it for the benefit of their fellows.[77]

B. The Second Principle

According to the second principle, the wealthy are morally obligated to distribute their surplus wealth during their lifetimes in ways that will actually benefit the community. But to do genuine good and not mischief, Carnegie believes, wealthy people must systematically study, with the help of experts, if necessary, the likely consequences of alternative gifts, including the likely effects on the recipients' characters. Serious complications are apparently caused for philanthropists by the fact that whereas a gift per se may provide immediate benefits, the consequences of relying on these gifts may be of far more harm to able-bodied recipients. A calculating "scientific philanthropy" is essential to avoid "the evil produced by indiscriminate giving."[78]

Indeed, Carnegie's view is that indiscriminate gifts are "one of the serious obstacles to the improvement of our race."[79] He evidently agrees with Josephine Shaw Lowell's statement that such giving tends to impair the characters of its recipients: "Almsgiving and dolegiving [two forms of poor relief that do not discriminate between able-bodied and disabled recipients] are hurtful to those who receive them because they lead men to remit their own exertions and depend on others, upon whom they have no real claim, for the necessaries of life."[80] Indiscriminate giving is false charity based not on any rational expectation of beneficent consequences but rather on thoughtless benevolence, blind pity, or perhaps on a selfish desire to avoid persistent requests: "[H]owever benevolent may be the motive, if the action be not beneficent, there is no charity. Almsgiving and dolegiving are hurtful—therefore they are not charitable."[81] By contrast, true charity is giving calculated to stimulate self-help and self-improvement: "There is really no true charity except that which will help others to help themselves, and place within the reach of the aspiring the means to climb."[82] To be truly philanthropic, the wealthy have a duty to the community *not* to give indiscriminately:

> Neither the individual nor the race is improved by almsgiving. . . . [T]he only true reformer . . . is as careful and as anxious not to aid the unworthy, and, perhaps, even more so, for in almsgiving more injury is probably done by rewarding vice than by relieving virtue.[83]

The discrimination required for true charity appears to have been an important factor underlying Carnegie's rejection of bequests for public purposes as a desirable mode of distributing surplus wealth: "The cases are not few in which the real object sought by the testator is not attained. . . . It is well to remember that it requires the exercise of not less ability than that which acquires it, to use wealth so as to be really beneficial to the community."[84] In short, the wealthy have a duty to make sure, as far as possible, that their surplus wealth is not used indiscriminately. At the same time, of course, testators who leave vast sums to be administered by others "may fairly be thought men who would not have left it at all had they been able to take it with them."[85]

Carnegie's gospel recommends lifetime gifts carefully designed permanently to uplift the community by promoting the self-improvement of its members: "[T]he millionaire [should] take care that the purposes for which he [gives his surplus wealth] . . . shall not have a degrading, pauperizing, tendency upon its recipients, but that his trust shall be so administered as to stimulate the best and most aspiring poor of the community to further efforts for their own improvement."[86] "What we must seek . . . for surplus wealth, if we are to work genuine good, are uses which give nothing for nothing, which require cooperation, self-help, and which, by no possibility, can tend to sap the spirit of manly independence, which is the only sure foundation upon which the steady improvement of our race can be built."[87] The best uses of wealth, he makes clear, are gifts to build universities, free libraries, hospitals, scientific laboratories, museums, halls, parks, and the like. Those gifts provide opportunities for people to improve themselves "in body and mind."[88] Conspicuously absent are gifts of cash or goods in kind to the needy poor.

Yet Carnegie certainly does not deny society's obligation to guarantee the necessities of life to all: "Common humanity impels us . . . to see, through our poor laws, that none die of starvation, and to provide comfortable shelter, clothing, and instruction."[89] Moreover, "our assistance . . . should *never* be withheld in times of accident, illness, or other exceptional cause."[90] His point is that each person should have a legal right to those things, conditional, where possible, "upon work performed." The policy of "indoor relief" that both he and Lowell favor seems harsh by contemporary standards. But that government has a duty to enact suitable laws guaranteeing to all some basic standard of subsistence is not questioned.[91] By implication, general taxpayers, not wealthy philanthropists, have the responsibility to provide necessities like poor relief.[92]

The implied devision of responsibilities between government and philanthropy correlates nicely to the ethical distinction between justice and charity, whereby citizens are held to have equal moral rights in matters of justice but no moral rights in matters of charity. Carnegie and Lowell, like many of their contemporaries, apparently take that classical distinction for granted, with the implication that liberal philanthropy must not be expected to do the work of a just government. In their view, provision of poor relief by the wealthy should only be contemplated in the event of government's failure to respect the equal rights of citizens to basic subsistence. Government failure of that sort warrants strong protest, of course, and liberal philanthropists have both a moral obligation and an incentive to lead the protest. Even if this explains why a wealthy philanthropist like Carnegie is reluctant to engage in public relief, however, it does not tell us why government itself should refrain from taking over true philanthropy by suitably taxing away Carnegie's surplus. After all, the gospel of wealth admits that the rich are merely administrators on behalf of the community. Why not rely exclusively on public administrators more or less subject to popular control?

One answer comes from Lowell: charity is defined as voluntary giving, in which case "all official and public relief is . . . outside the pale of charity, since it lacks the voluntary element."[93] But to that answer a radical democrat may well reply: do away with charity altogether as you define it, then, and legally force the taxpayer to finance all the universities, museums, parks, and the like that elected representatives decide are justified. Without further argument, a fair reply is that political leaders alone should be responsible for promoting the good of the community.

A more substantial answer is pluralist, that wealthy philanthropists should be permitted to compete with government to provide a greater variety of public goods than might otherwise be the case. As J. S. Mill puts it, "The truth needs reasserting, and needs it every day more and more, that what the improvement of mankind and of all of their works most imperatively demands is variety, not uniformity."[94] But even to that answer the radical democrat may fairly respond: anything philanthropy can do, government can and perhaps should do too. In other words, government's role in the provision of public goods is unlimited in principle, even if wealthy philanthropists should also be granted a subsidiary role. By implication, nothing is distinctive about philanthropy, and its proper scope is entirely at the discretion of political leaders.

But Carnegie apparently relies largely on a third answer that also seems to be decisive for his contemporaries like Lowell and Mill: A liberal government cannot discriminate justifiably among worthy and unworthy recipients as required for true charity. The problem is *not* that government officials are necessarily less competent or more corrupt than wealthy philanthropists or foundation administrators. Indeed, we have little reason to expect either government officials or private philanthropists to be paragons of virtue in the absence of suitable legal checks on their conduct. Rather, the problem is that liberal justice requires government to "act by general rule," that is, according to laws and policies that do not discriminate between citizens merely on the basis on their character. By contrast, liberal philanthropy requires discrimination precisely on that basis, and is not extended to able-bodied individuals or communities known to be unwilling to help themselves. In short, the *means* essential to liberal justice are incompatible with those intrinsic to liberal philanthropy. Just political leaders will tend to do more real harm than good through indiscriminate giving if they attempt to usurp the role of independent philanthropists. As Mill summarizes, "The state . . . cannot undertake to discriminate between the deserving and the undeserving indigent. . . . Private charity can make these distinctions."[95]

In this light, government and philanthropy have distinct purposes. If government tries to discriminate as true charity requires, then it acts unjustly, contrary to the rule of law. But if goverment gives indiscriminately all sorts of public goods, then it simply encourages degrading dependence on the state, the very reverse of beneficence, because working taxpayers may choose to become idle without losing the goods. This policy tends to hinder, in other words, the possibility of liberal community.[96] It follows that a liberal government is justly limited to the provision of only those public goods that all citizens, and all communities, within its jurisdiction may reasonably be said to need, as evidenced by general willingness to finance through tax revenues. Liberal philanthropy, on the other hand, is properly a distinct activity whose chief purpose is to provide what are considered luxury public goods that permit citizens to explore tastes beyond their customary needs. At any given point in time, a wealthy philanthropist or private foundation may properly give one community but not another a free library, for example, if working members of the first but not the second show they are serious about self-improvement by agreeing to contribute matching

funds, through user fees or local taxes, for operating and maintenance costs.[97] But a liberal government cannot properly provide
public goods to one community and then turn around and deny
that those same goods are needed elsewhere. If general tax dollars are used to build a free library for one community, then
government must acknowledge that every community in its jurisdiction has an equal claim, even if some will not agree to maintain and support their libraries. The latter may well press their
claims to get something for nothing; construction jobs are jobs
after all. Yet deteriorating buildings with meager collections that
pass for "libraries" are unlikely to do much good.

Notice that philanthropy itself may cause the government-
philanthropic division of function to evolve in practice, by altering social customs. What was once thought a luxury may come to
be considered a need, if large numbers acquire a taste for it. If
most acquire a taste for reading or for advanced studies so that it
becomes customary to consider possession of the abilities in question a necessity, then philanthropy may safely share their cultivation with government. In that case, most every taxpayer under
the government's jurisdiction now considers libraries and universities necessary for all, and will pay for his own use of those
goods. Such taxpayers are simply workers of high moral and
intellectual capacity who agree to help themselves by way of
government. Moreover, the changing partnership between government and philanthropy need not in principle ever involve
indiscriminate giving. Indeed, gifts to able adults who refuse to
help themselves, whether provided by government, by individual citizens, or by private corporations, simply tend to destroy
the community by encouraging habitual dependence on the labor and savings of others.

Even if we accept all this, however, the question remains: what
should be done if the wealthy simply refuse to give during their
lifetimes? Carnegie does mention estate tax rates of at least 50
percent to discourage the "vain and futile desire" to establish a
dynasty. But his main emphasis seems to be on a suitable evolution of the opinions and customs of the wealthy themselves: the
rich who care about their reputations, he thinks, will increasingly
adopt the gospel of wealth to avoid dying "disgraced."[98] That
this sort of development has not occurred is pretty clear. Instead,

the ethos of Veblen's leisure class seem to have been democratized. Before taking up this important question, however, I want to comment briefly on possible sources of Carnegie's liberal ethic of philanthropy.

III. Continuity with British Liberal Values

One important intellectual source of Carnegie's thinking is, of course, the gospel of Christ, with the caveat that Carnegie's own religious faith is not restricted to any official creed.[99] A second important source is American individualism, particularly the writings of Emerson. Indeed, Carnegie may have deliberately cast his gospel as a solution to what Emerson sees as "the problem of civilization," that is, "how to give all access to the masterpieces of art and nature."[100] But the source I wish to underscore is classical British liberalism, epitomized for Carnegie by the works of Herbert Spencer and J. S. Mill. Gladstone himself points to the influence of liberalism on Carnegie's character: "There is no hardier liberalism in this island than that which has flourished in Dundee."[101]

Carnegie openly acknowledges that the works of Spencer and Darwin "were revelations to me . . . ; what the law of gravitation did for matter, the law of evolution did for mind."[102] But that should not be taken to imply his acceptance in detail of Spencer's political economy. For example, Spencer adamantly defends complete freedom of bequest as essential to human evolution, contrary to Carnegie's philosophy of life.[103] Recall that Carnegie also has the highest praise for Gladstone, despite his defense of inheritance.

Carnegie also praises Mill's works, and even acknowledges himself to be a "thorough disciple" on the tariff question.[104] But how closely the gospel of wealth mirrors Mill's own ideas is not sufficiently appreciated. A brief comparison is in order.[105] Like Carnegie, Mill rejects socialist revolution in favor of gradual reform of the capitalist system for the foreseeable future.[106] He also argues that unlimited inheritance is no part of capitalism at its best, primarily because recipients do not deserve to get money for which they have not worked or saved.[107] He implies as well that capitalists have no moral right to excess profits, but instead are properly viewed as trustees of that wealth on behalf of the community.[108] And he claims that citizens have equal basic rights to at most some customary level of living; that government has a duty to provide that basic minimum to all; and that individual philanthropists can and should give in ways that promote self-help, recognizing that indiscriminate giving tends to degrade recipients by encouraging habits of dependence.[109]

Clearly, the gist of Carnegie's message is already present in the writings of Mill, probably the most influential liberal thinker of the century. My intention is not to depreciate Carnegie's originality, however, but to emphasize that his philanthropic manifesto is best understood in terms of liberal values. By implication, American philanthropy represents at least in part the flowering of an Anglo-American liberal tradition. Mill himself remarked on this as early as 1869:

> [P]rivate persons' . . . liberty of making themselves useful in their own way, without requiring the consent of any public authority, has mainly contributed to make England the free country she is; and . . . is covering America with the very institutions which her state of society most needs, and was least likely in any other manner to get—institutions for the careful cultivation of the higher studies.[110]

More generally, this Carnegie-Mill perspective encourages us to keep in mind an ideal liberal polity or "middle way" in which capitalism, philanthropy, and limited democratic government coexist in harmony. Carnegie, for example, asks us to imagine "a reign of harmony, another ideal, differing, indeed, from that of the Communist in requiring only the further evolution of existing conditions, not the overthrow of our civilization."[111] And, as I have argued at length elsewhere, Mill similarly envisions an ideal polity as the ultimate goal of liberal artifice.[112] Figure 16. 1 hints at the main spheres of that ideal polity. The different spheres, their governing principles, and their general justification require further clarification. But I leave these matters open for now. The figure also avoids the troublesome terms "public" and "private" because of their many conflicting connotations.[113]

Carnegie for most of his life seems more optimistic than Mill about attaining such a liberal democratic ideal. "This day already

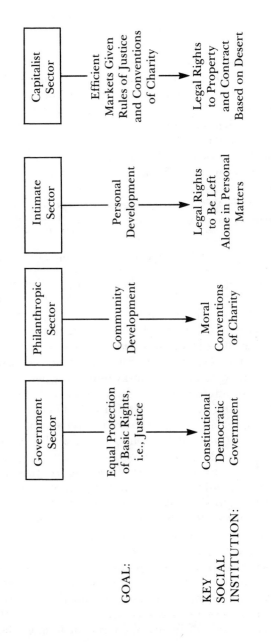

FIGURE 16.1
An Ideal Liberal Polity

	Government Sector	Philanthropic Sector	Intimate Sector	Capitalist Sector
GOAL:	Equal Protection of Basic Rights, i.e., Justice	Community Development	Personal Development	Efficient Markets Given Rules of Justice and Conventions of Charity
KEY SOCIAL INSTITUTION:	Constitutional Democratic Government	Moral Conventions of Charity	Legal Rights to Be Left Alone in Personal Matters	Legal Rights to Property and Contract Based on Desert

dawns" is not a statement we could expect to find in the latter's writings, given his fears that a despotism of ignorant mass opinion and custom would lead to stagnation and decline in Britain.[114] Of course, Carnegie's greater optimism was itself shattered by World War I. But before the war, he seems to have insisted upon a peculiar Spencerian brand of evolutionism. He apparently had faith that human evolution manifests the will of a Supreme Creator whose name "matters not." Evolution is the Creator's way of unfolding the perfection of mankind.[115] That sort of a priori belief is precisely what Mill could never accept about Spencer's philosophy, even though both he and Spencer agreed that this epistemological divergence was greatly outweighed by their practical agreement on liberal doctrine.[116]

IV. Current American Practice

If something like Carnegie's brand of philanthropy is essential to the flourishing of a liberal polity, then the attitudes and conduct of wealthy Americans are for the most part lamentable from a liberal perspective.[117] Available data suggest that although individuals are now giving more in total than ever, the wealthy pay little heed to Carnegie's second principle. For example, "top wealthholders tend to give away only a tiny percentage of wealth during their lifetimes," typically less than half of 1 percent of net wealth for the year prior to death.[118] They tend to wait until death to give: "In the aggregate, [their] charitable bequests represent over 20 times the amount of charitable contributions in a single year."[119] Moreover, largely as a result of legislative changes in which the Tax Reform Act of 1969 figures prominently, fewer and fewer wealthy donors seem to be prepared to create private foundations to administer their holdings during their lifetimes. Instead, "since 1970 there has been a decrease in the formation of charitable corporations and an increase in the number of testamentary trusts."[120] Some evidence exists that tax attorneys are encouraging this pattern of large bequests and small lifetime gifts, as well as a shift away from private foundations to public charities, including community foundations.[121] And, unfortunately, the 1986 Tax Reform Act is likely to exacerbate matters by discouraging all forms of charity, including volunteering.[122]

The distinctive liberal kind of philanthropy associated with Carnegie's gospel is under siege, and is perhaps even in some danger of withering away.[123]

Despite the current situation, however, some wealthy Americans still cling to something like Carnegie's philanthropic manifesto. According to Teresa Odendahl's analysis of recent interviews with over 135 millionaries, some rich families continue actively to dispose of their surplus through private foundations and view conspicuous consumption with distaste. These people seem to support what Odendahl calls an "ideology," that is, the sort of liberal "middle way" presented in figure 16.1, in which capitalism, philanthropy, and constitutional democracy all have key roles to play. Moreover, family tradition is apparently an important factor underlying attitudes and conduct, with some families exercising leadership in particular communities for generations. Unfortunately, these particular cultural traditions may become increasingly difficult to preserve in a modern mass society.[124]

In my view, they ought to be preserved and fostered. Deserving and undeserving recipients still need to be distinguished today, and liberal philanthropy is as crucial as it ever was for encouraging deserving individuals and communities to strive for something better than is customary. A fine illustration of liberal philanthropy in modern circumstances is provided by Eugene Lang's well-known promise, in 1981, to finance a college education for any member of a sixth-grade class at East Harlem's Public School 121 who earned a high school diploma.[125] The gift was not an indiscriminate handout to everyone in the class. Instead, it went only to deserving recipients, those who showed they were serious about self-development by doing school work. Dropouts who refused to help themselves got nothing. Of the original class of sixty-one, at least forty-five graduated from high school and thirty-six went on to college, an impressive result in light of the area's apparent 60 percent high school dropout rate. Moreover Lang himself went on to start the "I Have a Dream" Foundation, comprised of like-minded sponsors (not all of whom are wealthy) who have offered similar help to some nine thousand low-income students in forty cities. This philanthropy, like all liberal philanthropy, rewards self-help and is denied to able adults who choose to remain dependent on the work and saving of others.

Government agencies could, of course, be created to replace Lang's foundation, extending the concept to communities all across the country. But, although government funding for higher education is certainly a laudable goal, it cannot be expected in a democracy until most taxpayers believe that a college education is a necessity of life. More importantly, given that higher education is felt by most to be a need, the general taxpayer cannot be presumed to consent to finance that need for some people rather than others, including himself, perhaps, and his children. Instead, a college education must be seen as a basic right of all citizens or, at least, of all duty qualified to enter college. In short, government cannot justifiably underwrite a college education for qualified low-income but not for qualified high-income applicants, or for some qualified racial and ethnic minorities but not for others. To do so would be to substitute arbitrary discretion for equality under the law.

When most taxpayers believe that higher education is a luxury rather than a need, however, so that a college education is not underwritten for anyone by a just government, this leaves the self-starting poor at a serious disadvantage to the rich, to the detriment of the community at large. Independent philanthropy can mitigate this problem by supporting low-income students who wish to help themselves. At the same time, such philanthropy may facilitate a far more active role for democratic government in supporting the higher education of all citizens, by altering common beliefs and expectations.

V. CONCLUSION: LIBERAL POSSIBILITIES

What should be done to foster and preserve the liberal spirit of philanthropy that I think is essential to America's "middle way"? How might *liberal* charitable practices be developed to promote an ideal liberal polity? Certain legal reforms are important for this purpose. But even more important is public education, including learning by doing good for the community, under the leadership of the churches and the school system, in particular universities. Indeed, unless appropriate dispositions are inculcated in young people, popular support for the requisite legal reforms cannot reasonably be expected. Any liberal polity relies in part on virtuous traits in its citizenry, including a disposition to help others conjoined with intelligence to discern the probable consequences of one's conduct.[126]

Carnegie's gospel of wealth suggests various legal changes that should be considered seriously by Americans seeking to foster an atmosphere in which liberal habits of philanthropy and community service might breathe.[127] Ironically, given the Carnegie-Mill penchant for gradual social change, the legal reforms in question have now almost a radical air about them. In any case, reforms such as the following are essential for promoting a liberal American polity:

- sharply progressive taxation of all gifts and bequests to able-bodied individuals beyond some moderate ceiling (for example, the cost of a higher education and/or of an average home), so that large holdings of surplus wealth will tend to be dispersed among many recipients to avoid taxation (such dispersion is not really encouraged under the current policies involving a maximum 50 percent tax rate on gifts and estates valued at $2.5 million and over with special exemptions for trusts);
- sharply progressive taxation of luxury expenditures, to discourage ostentatious living;
- equal tax treatment for private foundations and public charities, as opposed to the current bias established by the 1969 Tax Reform Act against the former;
- a requirement that for-profit corporations should establish independent "pass-through" foundations (that is, legal entities under independent management) for any disbursement of corporate profits for philanthropic purposes; the establishment, management, and specific disbursements of the independent foundation should be subject to approval by a majority of the founding corporation's shareholders at an open public meeting (so that shareholders' democracy would be exposed to local community views when funding philanthropic projects in that community);
- unlimited charitable deductions from taxable income for itemizers, including shareholders of for-profit corporations who agree to disburse their dividends through an independent

foundation for community purposes; as well as restoration of a minimum charitable deduction for nonitemizers;

- a substantial increase (say, doubling) of the required annual payout rate (currently 5 percent of investment assets) for private foundations, as a means of underscoring the goal of philanthropy as opposed to perpetual growth of foundation assets;
- perhaps even a constitutional amendment to permit suitable public recognition of extraordinary philanthropy during one's lifetime, for example, a ceremonial Order of Benefactors of the U.S. with terms and conditions of membership to be fixed in Article 1, section 9, no formal political privileges attaching to membership.

These kinds of reforms would go a long way toward reviving liberal philanthropy in America, although we cannot be optimistic about the prospects for their implementation. Even if implemented, they would not force any individual to give for philanthropic purposes during his lifetime. Still, suitable laws can strongly discourage adverse attitudes such as exclusive love of family and taste for ostentation. People who persist in acting on the basis of these attitudes will have to pay dearly through the tax system, thereby reducing, at least in principle, the general tax burden for the rest of us.

Nevertheless, a package of legal changes, "however technically perfect," cannot by itself engender liberal philanthropy and community. Clearly, laws alone cannot generate the disposition to help others or the intellectual discrimination required for liberal moral virtue. Only a suitable liberal education can hope to do this. Church and school officials must take the lead in evoking in young people a liberal character, including a disposition to help the community and an intellectual capacity to assess the likely outcomes of various types of aid. Universities could facilitate this by undertaking curriculum reforms that engage more faculty and students in community service, including volunteer work for local libraries, museums, and environmental groups as well as for various organizations designed to support disadvantaged minorities. After all is said and done, of course, some individuals might still never be motivated by anything stronger than their own immediate material interest. Perhaps there will always be what Gladstone calls "that class of men, amongst all the most miserable, for whom the word 'surplus' can never exist."[128] But liberalism is characteristically optimistic that men and women are capable of much better, that the class of misers can be rendered insignificant by suitable laws and moral conventions. A passion to hoard is not so strong in many people that it can withstand public contempt of an educated community.[129]

Moral and political advocacy is required to prevent further decline of philanthropic activity, the one feature of modern American life that is both individualistic and communitarian. That tradition of giving is crucial to the flourishing of both the individual and the community, and is deservedly cherished. After all, as Mill so eloquently says, "Among the works of man, which human life is rightly employed in perfecting and beautifying, the first in importance surely is man himself."[130] Isn't that what the love of men is really all about?

NOTES

1. "Liberal Virtues," *American Political Science Review* 82 (1988): 1277–90.

2. Ibid., p. 1279.

3. Ibid.

4. Ibid., p. 1287.

5. Ibid., p. 1279.

6. Ibid., p. 1288.

7. Galston rejects what he calls the "Millian strategy" according to which, "in a liberal order, the same virtues are both ends and means: the good citizen and the good human being are identical" (1280). Against Mill thus interpreted, he suggests that the liberal "good man" is not the same as the liberal "good citizen" (1287). Intrinsic liberal individual excellence, whether conceived in terms of Lockean rational self-direction, Kantian moral autonomy, or Millian individuality, may be incompatible with instrumental liberal virtues such as law-abidingness and tolerance, for example. Consistently with this, Galston sees an opposition between civic and philosophic education in the sense that rational inquiry may tend to erode the civic principles on which any liberal society is founded. William Galston, "Civic Education in the Liberal State," in *Liberalism and the Moral Life,* ed N. L. Rosenblum (Cambridge: Harvard University

Press, 1989), pp. 89–101. For insights into the central role of individual virtue in Mill's liberalism, see Bernard Semmel, *John Stuart Mill and the Pursuit of Virtue* (New Haven and London: Yale University Press, 1984). In my view, Semmel does not emphasize sufficiently Mill's claims that virtue is compatible with true happiness and that our feeling of moral freedom is compatible with determinism, although not with fatalism. For a defense of the Millian strategy, see J. Riley, *Liberal Utilitarianism* (Cambridge: Cambridge University Press, 1988); and "Individuality, Custom, and Progress," in *Utilitas* 3 (1991): 217–44.

8. Nobody seriously pretends that socially optimal rules and customs will evolve spontaneously in every situation on the basis of voluntary interactions among individuals who are interested solely in their own immediate goals. In situations such as the Prisoner's Dilemma, for example, invisible-hand explanations of the emergence of reciprocity work only under certain special conditions. See, for example, Robert Axelrod, *The Evolution of Cooperation* (New York: Basic, 1984); Viktor Vanberg, "Spontaneous Market Order and Social Rules: A Critical Examination of F. A. Hayek's Theory of Cultural Evolution," *Economics and Philosophy* 2 (1986): 75–100; Robert Sugden, *The Economics of Rights, Cooperation, and Welfare* (Oxford: Blackwell, 1986); Michael Taylor, *The Possibility of Cooperation* (Cambridge: Cambridge University Press, 1987); and Ken Binmore, "Evolution and Utilitarianism," *Constitutional Political Economy* 1 (1990): 1–26.

9. "Liberal Virtues," p. 1285. Galston argues that contemporary liberalism presupposes what he calls a "triadic theory of the human good," more specifically, "individuals who value their earthly existence, who give positive weight to the achievement of their purposes, and who are prepared to accept rationality as a constraint on social action and principle" (ibid.). For development of the argument in the context of Rawlsian liberalism, See Galston, "Defending Liberalism," *American Political Science Review* 76 (1982): 621–29. It remains a bit unclear how Galston's triadic "liberal theory of the noninstrumental good" relates to what he calls the common liberal "vision" of intrinsic individual excellence, or to his claim that the latter vision may clash irreconcilably with liberal instrumental virtues. In a personal communication dated June 5, 1990, he agrees that "I have provided no characterization of the relation between the noninstrumental goods and the intrinsic virtues. But the former is surely not just another name for the latter. There may well be (I haven't worked this out yet) two independent kinds of intrinsic value lurking in liberal theory."

10. *The Compact Edition of the Oxford English Dictionary* (Oxford: Oxford University Press, 1971), Vol. 1, p. 1612.

11. We might speak of the need for an Aristotelian liberalism that recognizes both justice (*dike*) and philanthropy (*philia*) as essential interests of the community (*koinonia*).

12. For Walzer's argument, see his "Philosophy and Democracy," *Political Theory* 9 (1981): 379–99; *Spheres of Justice: A Defence of Pluralism and Equality* (New York: Basic, 1983); "Liberalism and the Art of Separation," *Political Theory* 12 (1984): 315–31; *Interpretation and Social Criticism* (Cambridge: Harvard University Press, 1987); *The Company of Critics: Social Criticism and Political Commitment in the Twentieth Century* (New York: Basic, 1988); and "The Communitarian Critique of Liberalism," *Political Theory* 18 (1990): 6–23.

13. "Liberalism and the Art of Separation," pp. 319, 321, 323.

14. Ibid., pp. 323–24.

15. Ibid., p. 324.

16. Ibid., p. 321.

17. Ibid., pp. 325–26.

18. Ibid., p. 321.

19. Ibid., p. 318.

20. Ibid., p. 322.

21. Ibid., p. 323.

22. Ronald Dworkin, "To Each His Own," *New York Review of Books* 30 (April 14, 1983), p. 6.

23. Ronald Dworkin and Michael Walzer, "Spheres of Justice: An Exchange," *New York Review of Books* 30 (July 21, 1983), p. 45.

24. Walzer, "Spheres of Justice: An Exchange," p. 44.

25. On this point, see Ian Shapiro, *Political Criticism* (Berkeley: University of California Press, 1990), pp. 55–82.

26. See, for example, Brian Barry, "Intimations of Justice," *Columbia Law Review* 84 (1984): 806–15; and Shapiro, op. cit., pp. 82–88, 229–30.

27. For cogent discussion of Walzer's fundamental commitment to democracy, see William Galston, "Community, Democracy, Philosophy," *Political Theory* 17 (1989): 119–30.

28. "Liberalism and the Art of Separation," p. 327.

29. Ibid., pp. 327–28.

30. Equal rights to participate in the internal governance of an institution do not preclude the relevant membership from deciding to delegate and divide authority among various leaders, as when citizens elect legislators and other representatives who may themselves be authorized to appoint still more representatives (judges and administrators, for example), or when workers elect managers who may then appoint other specialists to serve a Socialist enterprise.

31. See, for example, Robert Dahl, *A Preface to Economic Democracy*

374 *Jonathan Riley*

(Berkeley: University of California Press, 1985); and *Democracy and Its Critics* (New Haven: Yale University Press, 1989). Ian Shapiro proposes to modify Walzer's approach in the direction of a Dahl-like theory of democratic justice. See, for example, Ian Shapiro, *Political Criticism*, pp. 231–98; and Shapiro, "Three Fallacies Concerning Majorities, Minorities, and Democratic Politics," in John W. Chapman and Alan Wertheimer, eds., *Majorities and Minorities: NOMOS XXXII* (New York: New York University Press, 1990), pp. 79–125.

32. I do not mean to imply that these traditional liberals make no controversial metaphysical claims. They do, of varying sorts. But the claim that there is a presocial self is not one of them. Locke's state of nature, for example, is simply a state of society prior to the establishment of government: individuals in that state are evidently situated in the midst of social norms and conventions (whose origins, divine or otherwise, do not affect the point), even though positive legal sanctions are not in place, It is worth remarking that the idea of natural law seems to have evolved insensibly from the Roman notion of a *jus gentium*, or portion of positive law found by the praetors to be common to all communities within the empire. The universality of these laws was attributed to a higher origin than human design; and, through the ages, the rules were gradually extended to include merely moral or merely customary rules that had obtained general acceptance in virtually all Western societies. For discussion, see J. S. Mill, "Austin on Jurisprudence" [1863], in *Collected Works of John Stuart Mill*, ed. J. Robson (London: Routledge & Kegan Paul; Toronto: University of Toronto Press, 1984), 21:182–88; and references cited therein to John Austin and Henry Maine.

33. Walzer's theory of justice may deliberately incorporate a fundamental tension between the value of democratic procedure and the goods internal to basic social practices. If so, it is not clear how he could justify choosing one rights assignment over another. For example, the value of democracy may call for equal rights for members of economic enterprises to participate in their internal governance; but property rights may be positively valued by existing market practices. If the value of democracy is incommensurable with the values internal to basic institutions, then no principled way to choose between them is possible. If, on the other hand, the value of democracy trumps the internal values of actual social practices, then we seem no longer to have a value-pluralist theory.

34. J. S. Mill, "Utilitarianism" [1861], in *Collected Works*, ed. J. Robson, 10:247.

35. On the general point, see Michael Taylor, *Community, Anarchy, and Liberty* (Cambridge: Cambridge University Press, 1982).

36. Thus, for example, liberal rules of charity obligate givers to provide help when they can, but do not assign corresponding rights to individual recipients. Liberal rules of laissez-faire within some limited economic sphere do not even assign moral obligations to market competitors with respect to terms of exchange, so that competitors are left free to negotiate contracts and other agreements that will be enforced by the state. Because rules of charity and of laissez-faire do not assign moral rights, the liberal state should not enforce these sorts of rules by means of legal penalties. It is also worth remarking that John Stuart Mill saw liberal artifice extending to the definition and protection of an intimate sphere of justice governed by no rules or customs, other than a rule that there are no rules. In his view, liberals should recognize and enforce a general limit on the legitimate authority of all laws and customs, by assigning rights to consenting adults to do as they like with respect to certain intimate matters. Such rights would be assigned by a rule or principle of liberty that in effect leaves the government of intimate matters entirely to individual spontaneity, the desires and choices of the moment. See Mill, "On Liberty" [1859], in *Collected Works*, ed. J. Robson, 18:213–310; J. Riley, "Rights to Liberty in Purely Private Matters, Parts I & II," *Economics and Philosophy* 5/6 (1989–90): 121–66, 27–64; and *Liberty in Private Matters: Mill's Classic Doctrine*, forthcoming.

37. In my view, dispositions or habits are formed by repeated acts on the basis of identifiable motives, and comprise an individual's character. To the extent that dispositions are shared by members of a group, we may speak of a common character manifest in the practices of the group. Shared dispositions are broader than common rules of behavior in the sense that rules can never be fully articulated to cover all possible situations. In exceptional circumstances, a person's dispositions may limit his possible actions, and his fellows may know this, even though no known rules apply. Nevertheless, shared dispositions underlie the recognized laws and customs of the group. Assessment of alternative rules and dispositions requires a general normative theory. For various approaches to these issues, see Peter A. French, Theodore E. Uehling, Jr., and Howard K. Wettstein, eds., *Ethical Theory: Character and Virtue: Midwest Studies in Philosophy 13* (Notre Dame: University of Notre Dame Press, 1988).

38. For an attempt to defend a credible utilitarian version of liberalism based on an interpretation of J. S. Mill's philosophy, see J. Riley, *Liberal Utilitarianism*.

39. Benevolence, or a wish to help others, may conflict with the desire for immediate material gain yet at the same time may promote self-interest in some enlightened or longer-term sense by encouraging

reciprocity. Galston resists this point and asserts that instrumental liberal virtues "are not reducible to self-interest, even self-interest 'rightly understood' " ("Liberal Virtues," 1281). The basis of his assertion remains unclear, however. On the key norm of reciprocity, see, in addition to the references cited above at note 9, Robert Payton, *Major Challenges to Philanthropy* (Washington: Independent Sector, 1984), pp. 35ff; Lawrence C. Becker, *Reciprocity* (Chicago: University of Chicago Press, 1986); and K. J. Gergen, et al., "Obligation, Donor Resources, and Reactions to Aid in Three Cultures," *Journal of Personality and Social Psychology* 31 (1975): 390–400.

40. For discussion of the idea that liberalism attacks the preliberal cultural traditions on which its success depends, see, for example, Joseph A. Schumpeter, *Capitalism, Socialism, and Democracy*, 3d. ed. (New York: Harper & Row, 1956); Daniel Bell, *The Cultural Contradictions of Capitalism* (New York: Basic, 1976); Irving Kristol, *Two Cheers for Capitalism* (New York: Basic, 1978); Kristol, "The Adversary Culture of Intellectuals," *Encounter* 53 (1979): 5–14; Alasdair MacIntyre, *After Virtue* (Notre Dame: University of Notre Dame Press, 1981); Robert Heilbroner, *The Nature and Logic of Capitalism* (New York: Basic, 1985); and Michael Walzer, "The Communitarian Critique of Liberalism," *Political Theory* 18 (1990): 6–23.

41. Walzer has recently admitted that "contemporary liberals are not committed to a presocial self, but only to a self capable of reflecting critically on the values that have governed in socialization" ("Communitarian Critics of Liberalism," 21). Contemporary liberals should not be distinguished from traditional ones on this score. Any individual who can remember or imagine alternatives to the status quo, and who can reason about the best means to his goals, is capable of the required critical reflection. Indeed, in a pluralistic society where practices vary significantly across religious and ethnic minorities, the person may not even require much memory or imagination because he can observe actual alternatives to the customs of his group or class.

42. It should be noted that supererogatory assistance, or help beyond what is reasonably expected under existing conventions, may be morally praiseworthy. But, by definition, no one has a moral duty to offer such help under existing customs relating to charity.

43. On the more general point that "intimations of community" exist within liberal values, see Will Kymlicka, "Liberalism and Communitarianism," *Canadian Journal of Philosophy* 18 (1988): 181–204; and *Liberalism, Community, and Culture* (New York: Oxford University Press, 1989).

44. W. K. Jordan, *Philanthropy in England, 1480–1660* (London: Allen & Unwin, 1959); and David Owen, *English Philanthropy, 1660–1960*

Cambridge: Harvard University Press, 1964). In Weber's famous view, originally published in 1904–1905, the capitalist disposition to accumulate wealth yet forego ostentatious consumption has its roots in the Protestant duty to succeed in a worldly "calling" to promote the glory of god. Under Calvinism, fulfilment of that duty became a sign of one's election by god to salvation. In short, the Calvinist must have faith in his election; and must carefully calculate how to do good in this world as a sign of his faith. As Jordan explains, "The Protestant clergy, being Calvinist, could not argue that good works were necessary to grace, but they did hold with a most persuasive and sustained vehemence that good works were an authentic and a necessary fruit of grace categorically demanded of His saints by God. . . . The Calvinist not only said but he believed that we are but stewards of wealth for which we are accountable to God" (op. cit., 152). Thus, economic individuality emerges rather paradoxically from blind obedience to religious authority. For Weber's argument, see Max Weber, *The Protestant Ethic and the Spirit of Capitalism,* trans. Talcott Parsons, 2d ed. (London: Allen & Unwin, 1976). For the continuing debate over Weber's claims, see David Little, *Religion, Order, and Law* (New York: Harper & Row, 1969); and the introduction by Anthony Giddens to the Parsons translation cited earlier. For relevant discussion in the context of J. S. Mill's thought, see Thomas Haskell, "Persons as Uncaused Causes: John Stuart Mill, the Spirit of Capitalism, and the 'Invention' of Formalism," paper presented at a conference on "The Culture of the Market," Murphy Institute of Political Economy, Tulane University, March 9–11, 1990 (conference proceedings are to be published by Cambridge University Press). Although he does not necessarily accept Weber's perspective, Haskell argues that the rise of capitalism during the period 1750–1850 is associated with an expansion of the individual's causal horizon, and that this heightened sense of agency brought with it a new "humanitarian sensibility" and awareness of one's moral responsibilities. By implication, moral conventions (including those of philanthropy) have altered significantly under capitalism. See Haskell, "Capitalism and the Origins of the Humanitarian Sensibility, Parts I & II," *American Historical Review* 90 (1985): 339–61, 547–66; and subsequent forum involving Haskell, David Brion Davis, and John Ashworth, *American Historical Review* 92 (1987): 797–878.

45. "Poor Richard's Almanac Improved, 1748," in *Benjamin Franklin: Writings,* ed. J. A. Leo Lemay (New York: Library of America, 1987), p. 1247.

46. It should be emphasized that the distinction between liberal and nonliberal philanthropy does not correspond to the distinction between

Christian (or, more generally, religious) and secular charity. The first
distinction is essentially one between calculating beneficence and blind
pity or benevolence; the second distinction hinges on the agent's motivation for doing good. A Calvinist may carefully calculate how she can
best help her community, for example, because she is motivated to find
signs of her own election and to promote god's glory in this world.
Thus, she practices liberal philanthropy while believing with Alexander
Pope that "virtue's prize" is "what nothing earthly gives, or can destroy,
the soul's calm sun-shine, and the heart-felt joy." *An Essay on Man*
[1733–34], ed. M. Mack (London and New Haven: Methuen and Yale
University Press, 1950), p. 143; Epistle IV, lines 167–69. Or, to take
another example, a pagan may thoughtlessly divert his wealth to waste-
ful community projects because he habitually conforms to prevailing
majority opinion in that community. Thus, he practices nonliberal philanthropy for purely secular reasons.

47. "From Charity to Philanthropy" [1962], in Daniel Boorstin, *Hidden History* (New York: Harper & Row, 1987), pp. 205–6. Unlike Boorstin, I do not distinguish between the terms "charity" and "philanthropy" for present purposes. According to what I am calling the liberal
view, either term means beneficence or doing good for other people,
and excludes unwise gifts that (although inspired by love or pity) actually do net harm. Thus, liberal philanthropy is restricted to beneficence
whatever the agent's motivation, whereas nonliberal philanthropy affirms benevolence as both necessary and sufficient for doing good,
whatever the consequences.

48. American Philanthropy and the National Character," *American
Quarterly* 10 (1958): 436.

49. See also Michael Novak, *The Spirit of Democratic Capitalism* (New
York: Simon & Schuster/ American Enterprise Institute, 1982), esp. pp.
143–55, 333–60. He speaks of "the communitarian individual" who
understands that "the highest good of the political economy of democratic capitalism is to be suffused by *caritas*" (357; emphasis in original).
Such an individual is, in other words, able to recognize that "the love of
friends for one another is . . . the way by which humans *participate* in the
life of God"; and is motivated to guide his conduct accordingly (355;
emphasis in original). On one interpretation, Novak is painting a religious gloss on an ideal liberal polity: "Caritas is at one and the same time
an ideal of individual autonomy . . . and an ideal of community" (358).

50. For an introduction to the modern debate, see Payton, *Major
Challenges to Philanthropy;* and Virginia A. Hodgkinson, et al., *The Future
of the Nonprofit Sector: Challenges, Changes, and Policy Considerations* (San
Francisco: Jossey-Bass, 1989).

51. See, for example, Barry Karl, "Philanthropy, Policy Planning, and the Bureaucratization of the Democratic Ideal," *Daedalus* 105 (Fall 1976): 129–49; Karl and Stanley Katz, "The American Private Philanthropic Foundation and the Public Sphere, 1890–1930," *Minerva* 19 (1981): 236–70; and Karl and Katz, "Foundations and Ruling Class Elites," *Daedalus* 116 (Winter 1987): 1–40.

52. Lester Salamon calls for a new theory of government-nonprofit partnership in his "Partners in Public Service: The Scope and Theory of Government-Nonprofit Relations," in W. Powell, ed., *The Nonprofit Sector: A Research Handbook* (New Haven and London: Yale University Press, 1987), pp. 99–117. See also Jon Van Til, *Mapping the Third Sector: Voluntarism in a Changing Social Economy* (New York: Foundation Center, 1988); and Virginia A. Hodgkinson, et al., op. cit.

53. "The Gospel of Wealth" [1889], in E. C. Kirkland, ed., *The Gospel of Wealth and Other Timely Essays* [1990] (Cambridge: Harvard University Press, 1965), pp. 14–49.

54. As Robert Heilbroner remarks; "[I]t is not enough to conclude that Carnegie was in fact a smaller man than he conceived himself. For this judgment overlooks one immense and irrefutable fact. He did, in the end, abide by his self-imposed duty. He did give nearly all of his gigantic fortune away. . . . Carnegie is something of America writ large. . . . In his curious triumph, we see what we hope is our own steadfast core of integrity." "Carnegie and Rockefeller," in Byron Dobell, ed., *A Sense of History: The Best Writing from the Pages of American Heritage* (Boston: Houghton Mifflin, 1985), pp. 442–43. On the more general point, see also Karl, "The Moral Basis of Capitalist Philanthropy," in *Spring Research Forum Working Papers: Philanthropy, Voluntary Action, and the Public Good* (Washington: Independent Sector, 1986), pp. 103–18; and Robert Nisbet, "America as Utopia," *Reason* 18 (March 1987): 35–40.

55. Carnegie, "The Advantages of Poverty" [1891], in Kirkland, op. cit., p. 55.

56. "Gospel of Wealth," p. 25.

57. "Gospel of Wealth," p. 26.

58. "Advantages of Poverty," p. 72.

59. "Gospel of Wealth," p. 18.

60. Public goods are goods like free libraries, public parks, or even limited-access research laboratories that cannot be efficiently provided through the market because users who refuse to pay a full price (so-called free riders) cannot or should not be excluded from using the goods once produced. Government may thus decide to legally coerce everyone to finance the goods through taxes. Alternatively, individuals or groups may decide to voluntarily pay a disproportionate part (per-

haps all) of the costs of the goods, because of motivations other than immediate material self-interest, for example, benevolence.

61. "Gospel of Wealth," p. 48.

62. See Carnegie, *Autobiography* [1920], ed. J. Van Dyke (Boston: Northeastern University Press, 1986).

63. "Gospel of Wealth," p. 14–19.

64. "Gospel of Wealth," pp. 18–19. See also "Advantages of Poverty," pp. 75–76.

65. "Gospel of Wealth," p. 16.

66. "Gospel of Wealth," p. 19.

67. "Gospel of Wealth," pp. 19–20.

68. "Advantages of Poverty," p. 59.

69. "Advantages of Poverty," p. 56.

70. "Gospel of Wealth," p. 22. At the same time, Carnegie remarks that "it is difficult to set bounds to the share in a rich man's estate which should go at his death to the public through the agency of the State."

71. "Mr Carnegie's 'Gospel of Wealth': A Review and a Recommendation" [1890], in B. J. Hendrick, ed., *Miscellaneous Writings of Andrew Carnegie* (Garden City: Doubleday, Doran, 1933), Vol. 2, pp. 136–39.

72. Ibid., p. 129.

73. Ibid., p. 138.

74. "Advantages of Poverty," pp. 57–58.

75. "Advantages of Poverty," pp. 62–63.

76. It should be noted that, inheritance aside, Gladstone is essentially in sympathy with Carnegie's gospel. Relying on his memory of what he calls the "Universal Beneficent Society," he suggests that the wealthy should form a voluntary beneficent association, binding themselves in honor to donate some fixed annual proportion of their incomes ("fixed, that is to say, by themselves") for philanthropic purposes. See Gladstone, "Mr. Carnegie's 'Gospel of Wealth' " pp. 149–56. Reverend Hughes corrects Gladstone's faulty recollection of the British and Foreign Systematic Beneficence Society, a Christian association established in 1860 "to promote the principle and practice amongst all professing Christians" of giving away at least one-tenth of one's weekly income "for God and the poor." See "Irresponsible Wealth III," in Hendrick, op. cit., pp. 198–202. The tithe is salient, of course, in both Christian and Jewish religious traditions.

77. It is worth emphasizing that Carnegie sees the growth of a so-called leisure class as incompatible with American capitalism and democracy. As described by Thorstein Veblen and depicted in the novels of Henry James and Edith Wharton, the leisure class is an idle elite

whose conspicuous consumption is supported largely by inherited wealth and motivated for the most part by a concern to emulate European aristocracy.

78. "Advantages of Poverty," p. 69. See also John D. Rockefeller. "The Difficult Art of Giving" [1908–1909], in *Random Reminiscences of Men and Events* (Tarrytown, N.Y.: Sleepy Hollow Press & Rockefeller Archive Center, 1984), pp. 90–106.

79. "Gospel of Wealth," p. 26.

80. Lowell, *Public Relief and Private Charity* [1884] (New York: Arno, 1971), p. 90. In her preface, Lowell describes her work as a "restatement of the principles upon which the modern methods of charity are based."

81. Ibid., p. 89.

82. Carnegie, "Advantages of Poverty," p. 68.

83. "Gospel of Wealth," p. 27. See also pp. 31–32.; "Advantages of Poverty," pp. 67–69; and, more generally, Edward N. Saveth, "Patrician Philanthropy in America: The Late Nineteenth and Early Twentieth Centuries," *Social Service Review* 54 (1980): 76–91.

84. "Gospel of Wealth," p. 21.

85. Ibid.

86. "Gospel of Wealth," p. 31.

87. Carnegie, "The Best Uses of Wealth" [1895], in Hendrick, op. cit., p. 210.

88. "Gospel of Wealth," p. 28.

89. "Advantages of Poverty," p. 68.

90. "Best Uses," p. 208.

91. According to the "indoor relief" policy, poor relief to able-bodied people unwilling to help themselves should be administered "indoors," that is, in state workhouses where the "unfortunates" should be made to do some form of work for their basic subsistence. Those in the workhouse would thus be separated from the rest of society and should forfeit various rights enjoyed by other citizens, including the franchise and the right to procreate. Disabled people would not be subject to this sort of stigma, of course, because they are by definition unable as opposed to unwilling to work. They should be supported by both government and philanthropy outside the workhouse. For an interesting argument that ambiguities in the term "disabled" opened the door to expansion of the welfare state, see Deborah Stone, *The Disabled State* (Philadelphia: Temple University Press, 1985).

92. Bernard Shaw also insists on this point in his inimitable style. See "Socialism for Millionaires," *Contemporary Review* 69 (1896): 204–17.

93. *Public Relief and Private Charity* p. 89.

94. "Endowments" [1869], in *Collected Works,* ed. J. Robson, 5:617. See also "On Liberty," pp. 260–75.

95. *Principles of Political Economy* [1848], in *Collected Works,* ed. J. Robson, 3:962.

96. For further development of the general theme, see Michael Taylor, *Community, Anarchy, and Liberty.*

97. Such was Carnegie's practice. See "The Gospel of Wealth," pp. 36–40.

98. "Gospel of Wealth," pp. 28–30.

99. Carnegie, "A Confession of Religious Faith," in Hendrick, op. cit., pp. 291–319. On the religious tradition of philanthropy in America, see also Virginia Bernhard, "Cotton Mather and the Doing of Good: A Puritan Gospel of Wealth," *New England Quarterly* 49 (1976): 225–41.

100. *The Conduct of Life* [1860], chapter 3 ("Wealth"), in J. Porte, ed., *Emerson: Essays and Lectures* (New York: Library of America, 1983), p. 995. Emerson also says, "They should own who can administer; not they who hoard and conceal . . . but they whose work carves out work for more, opens a path for all. For he is the rich man in whom the people are rich." See also "Gifts" [1844], in Porte, op. cit., pp. 535–38.

101. "Mr. Carnegie's 'Gospel of Wealth'," p. 127. Carnegie was born in Dunfermline, "a radical town" in the vicinity of Dundee, Scotland.

102. "Confession of Religious Faith," p. 297.

103. *The Principles of Ethics* [1892–1893], ed. T. Machan (Indianapolis: Liberty Classics, 1978), Vol. 2, pp. 135–42. As Edward Kirkland suggests, Carnegie may have had a pretty casual understanding of Spencer's law of evolution. See Kirkland, *The Gospel of Wealth and Other Timely Essays,* p. 81, n.2.

104. Carnegie, "Imperial Federation" [1891], in Kirkland, *The Gospel of Wealth and Other Timely Essays,* pp. 216–17.

105. For a more complete discussion of Mill's view of capitalism, see J. Riley, "Justice under Capitalism," in J. Chapman and J. R. Pennock, eds., *Markets and Justice: Nomos XXXI* (New York: New York University Press, 1989), pp. 122–62.

106. *Principles of Political Economy,* 3:765–96; and "Chapters on Socialism," in *Collected Works,* ed. J. Robson, 5:727–53.

107. *Principles of Political Economy,* 2:218–26.

108. Principles of Political Economy, 2:207–8, 215–17, 226–32.

109. *Principles of Political Economy* 3:960–62, 968–70; and "Endowments," pp. 613–29.

110. "Endowments," pp. 616–17.

111. "Gospel of Wealth," p. 23. See also p. 28.

112. See J. Riley, *Liberal Utilitarianism*.

113. See, for example, Michael Novak, "An Essay on 'Public' and 'Private'," in Robert Payton, et al., *Philanthropy: Four Views* (New Brunswick: Transaction, 1988), pp. 11–25. I have discussed the public-private distinction at length elsewhere, See J. Riley, "Rights to Liberty in Purely Private Matters, Parts I & II."

114. On this aspect of Mill's thought (reminiscent in many ways of earlier Country Whig pessimism), see J. W. Burrow, *Whigs and Liberals: Continuity and Changes in English Political Thought* (Oxford: Clarendon, 1988), pp. 77–124.

115. "Confession of Religious Faith." In some respects, Michael Novak's views are now reminiscent of this Spencer-Carnegie metaphysical perspective. See *The Spirit of Democratic Capitalism*.

116. Whereas Spencer supposes the individual is endowed genetically with some basic perceptions and norms that reflect the accumulated experience of the race, Mill suggests the individual has no such innate practical knowledge. Rather, for Mill, practical knowledge can be acquired by any person only after her mental capacities are called into action by her *own* experience of the actual world. Spencer's view implies that some basic moral concepts are known intuitively to us prior to our experience: we simply cannot conceive at least some things other than as we do because of those a priori ideas. Moreover, if evolution is taken to mean progress ordained by some superhuman Creator, then our inherited ideas and beliefs will necessarily improve as evolution proceeds. Mill denies all this. Even so, he and Spencer arrive at a large number of the same practical conclusions anyway, hence their general sympathy for one another's work. For the relevant debate between them, see, for example, Mill, *System of Logic* [1843], in *Collected Works*, ed. J. Robson, 7:262–79; Mill, *An Examination of Hamilton's Philosophy* [1865], in *Collected Works*, 9:143–45; Mill's letter to Spencer of August 12, 1865, reprinted in *Collected Works*, 16:1089–91; Spencer, "Mill versus Hamilton: The Test of Truth" [1865], in *Essays: Moral, Political, and Aesthetic* (New York: Appleton, 1883), pp. 383–413; and Spencer, "Replies to Criticisms" [1881], in his *Principles of Ethics* [1897], ed. T. Machan (Indianapolis: Liberty Classics, 1978), 2:483–504.

117. I do not mean to imply that charitable attitudes and conduct of the wealthy have been any better in the past.

118. Eugene Steuerle, "Charitable Giving Patterns of the Wealthy," in Teresa Odendahl, ed., *America's Wealthy and the Future of Foundations* (New York: Foundation Center, 1987), p. 207. The results are based on a sample of matched estate and income tax returns filed during the

mid-1970s. Steuerle indicates that annual gifts do not appear to be unusual for the year prior to death.

119. Ibid.

120. Elizabeth Boris, "Creation and Growth: A Survey of Private Foundations," In Odendahl, op. cit., p. 73. Not only are the numbers of new foundations declining; so is the relative financial importance of foundations in the economy. See Ralph Nelson, "An Economic History of Large Foundations," in Odendahl, op. cit., pp. 127–77.

121. Francie Ostrower, "The Role of Advisors to the Wealthy," in Odendahl, op. cit., pp. 247–65.

122. For some preliminary evidence, see Charles T. Clotfelter, *The Impact of Tax Reform on Charitable Giving: A 1989 Perspective,* Working Paper 26 (Durham: Duke University Center for the Study of Philanthropy and Volunteering, 1990).

123. See Brian O'Connell, "Private Philanthropy and the Preservation of a Free and Democratic Society," in Robert Payton, et al., *Philanthropy: Four Views,* pp. 27–38.

124. Odendahl, "Wealthy Donors and Their Charitable Attitudes," in Odendahl, op. cit., pp. 223–46. Odendahl herself has recently criticized what she views as the elitist ideology associated with private philanthropy in the United States. She apparently rejects the appeal of what I am calling the liberal approach, and favors instead a more democratic philanthropy in which minority groups (including the poor) have more control over the sorts of projects funded by wealthy philanthropists. Rather than "uplift the community" by funding elitist institutions such as universities and museums, philanthropy should concentrate on poor relief and on supporting the activities of disadvantaged minorities. Although her call for a redirection of private giving is understandable in light of the shameful recent cuts in federal social programs, she simply ignores the traditional liberal perspective on philanthropy and takes for granted that minority groups have a moral right to use other people's wealth for purposes rejected by the latter. See Odendahl, *Charity Begins at Home: Generosity and Self-Interest among the Philanthropic Elite* (New York: Basic, 1990).

125. My account of Lang's activities is based on Dennis Kelly, "Benefactor Still Nurtures Young Adults" and "Dream Maker Does the Right Thing for Students," *USA Today* (September 4, 1990), pp. 1D–2D, 4D.

126. Evidently, a liberal commitment to the rule of law does not imply toleration for uncharitable ways of life nor indifference towards unkind traits of character. The rule of law implies only that rules should be impartial or neutral in the sense of being indifferent to personal identity per se. But that is compatible with those same rules being biased

in favor of individual moral virtue, including giving to others in some circumstances, because virtue is something that can generally be acquired by individuals, whoever they happen to be, through their own efforts.

127. For an introduction to the relevant legislation as it exists now, see, for example, Edward Jay Beckwith and Jana DeSirgh, "Tax Law and Private Foundations," in Odendahl, ed., *America's Wealthy and the Future of Foundations,* pp. 267–93; Charles Clotfelter, "The Impact of Tax Reform"; Clotfelter, *Federal Tax Policy and Charitable Giving* (Chicago: University of Chicago Press, 1985); and John Simon, "The Tax Treatment of Nonprofit Organizations: A Review of Federal and State Policies," in Powell, *The Nonprofit Sector,* pp. 67–98.

128. "Mr. Carnegie's 'Gospel of Wealth'," p. 135.

129. Galston distinguishes without choosing among three approaches to "engendering liberal virtues": (1) an "optimistic" approach that assumes everyday life in a modern polity like America in sufficient to "shape us in the manner required for the operation of liberal institutions"; (2) a "neutral" approach that supplements everyday life with deliberate and cooperative efforts by "authoritative institutions such as families, schools, churches, the legal system, political leaders and the media" to foster liberal virtues; and (3) a "pessimistic" approach that requires new values and institutions to counteract "powerful strands of contemporary liberal culture tend[ing] to undermine liberal virtues" ("Liberal Virtues," 1288). He calls for "systematic, theory-guided empirical research" to help us sort through these approaches (ibid.). See also Galston, "Civic Education in the Liberal State." I lean toward the "pessimistic" end of Galston's scale, although I am more inclined to say that new laws and institutions are required to counteract *illiberal* strands of contemporary culture tending to undermine liberal values. In other words, I do not necessarily subscribe to a value-pluralist outlook that sees fundamental tensions among liberal values leading to the erosion of liberalism. I am inclined instead to affirm the possibility of an ideal liberal community involving a certain harmony among basic liberal virtues. For further discussion of the features of what I call a "liberal character" in the context of Mill's thought, see J. Riley, *Liberal Utilitarianism,* especially part 2.

130. "On Liberty," p. 263.

VIRTUE: A BRIEF BIBLIOGRAPHY

WILLIAM A. GALSTON

Anscombe, G. E. M. "Modern Moral Philosophy." In *Ethics, Religion, and Politics*. Minneapolis: University of Minnesota Press, 1981.

Becker, Lawrence. *Reciprocity*. London: Routledge, 1986.

Budziszewski, J. *The Resurrection of Nature: Political Theory and the Human Character*. Ithaca: Cornell University Press, 1986.

Casey, John. *Pagan Virtues*. Oxford: Oxford University Press, 1990.

Foot, Philippa. *Virtues and Vices*. Berkeley: University of California Press, 1978.

Frankfurt, Harry. "The Importance of What We Care About." *Synthese* 53 (1982): 257–72.

French, Peter A., Theodore E. Uehling, Jr., and Howard K. Wettstein (eds.). *Midwest Studies in Philosophy*. Vol. 13, *Ethical Theory: Character and Virtue*. Notre Dame: University of Notre Dame Press, 1988.

Galston, William A. *Liberal Purposes: Goods, Virtues, and Diversity in the Liberal State*. Cambridge: Cambridge University Press, 1991.

Geach, Peter. *The Virtues*. Cambridge: Cambridge University Press, 1977.

Gilligan, Carol. *In a Different Voice*. Cambridge, Mass.: Harvard University Press, 1982.

Hirshman, Linda R. (ed.). "Symposium on Classical Philosophy and the American Constitutional Order." *Chicago-Kent Law Review* 66, 1 (1990): 1–242.

Kloppenberg, James T. "The Virtues of Liberalism: Christianity, Republicanism, and Ethics in Early American Political Discourse." *Journal of American History* 74 (1987): 9–33.

Kruschwitz, Robert B., and Robert C. Roberts (eds.). *The Virtues*. Belmont Cal.: Wadsworth, 1987. [This volume concludes with a comprehensive and well-organized bibliography on virtue ethics and the virtues as interpreted by contemporary philosophers.]

Macedo, Stephen. *Liberal Virtues.* Oxford: Clarendon, 1990.

MacIntyre, Alasdair. *After Virtue.* Notre Dame: University of Notre Dame Press, 1981.

Noddings, Nel. *Caring: A Feminine Approach to Ethics and Moral Education.* Berkeley: University of California Press, 1984.

Nussbaum, Martha. *The Fragility of Goodness.* Cambridge: Cambridge University Press, 1986.

———. "Non-Relative Virtues." In French, et al., *Midwest Studies in Philosophy.* Vol. 13.

Pence, Gregory E. "Recent Work on Virtues." *American Philosophical Quarterly* 21 (1984): 281–96.

Pincoffs, Edmund L. *Quandaries and Virtues.* Lawrence: University Press of Kansas, 1986.

Pocock, J. G. A. *The Machiavellian Moment.* Princeton: Princeton University Press, 1975.

———. "Virtues, Rights, and Manners: A Model for Historians of Political Thought." *Political Theory* 9, 3 (August 1981): 353–68.

Rorty, Amelie O. (ed.). *Essays on Aristotle's Ethics.* Berkeley: University of California Press, 1980.

Sandel, Michael. *Liberalism and the Limits of Justice.* Cambridge: Cambridge University Press, 1982.

Seung, T. K. (ed.), "The Nature of Virtue Ethics: its Political Relevance; A Conference Honoring Edmund L. Pincoffs." *Social Theory and Practice* 17,2 (Summer 1991): 137–344.

Sherman, Nancy. *The Fabric of Character.* Oxford: Oxford University Press, 1989.

Shklar, Judith. *Ordinary Vices.* Cambridge Mass.: Belknap, 1984.

Slote, Michael. *Goods and Virtues.* Ithaca: Cornell University Press, 1983.

Stocker, Michael. "The Schizophrenia of Modern Ethical Theories." *Journal of Philosophy* 73 (1976): 453–66.

"Symposium: The Republican Civic Tradition." *Yale Law Journal* 97, 8 (July 1988): 1493–1723.

Taylor, Charles. *Philosophy and the Human Sciences: Philosophical Papers, 2.* Cambridge: Cambridge University Press, 1985.

Taylor, Richard. *Ethics, Faith, and Reason.* Englewood Cliffs, N.J.: Prentice-Hall, 1985.

Wallace, James D. *Virtues and Vices.* Ithaca: Cornell University Press, 1978.

Williams, Bernard. "Persons, Character, and Morality." In Amelie O. Rorty (ed.), *The Identities of Persons*. Berkeley: University of California Press, 1980.

———. *Ethics and the Limits of Philosophy*. Cambridge Mass.: Harvard University Press, 1985.

INDEX